Laura
S0-HXF-195

SAS® Procedures Guide for Personal Computers, Version 6 Edition

SAS Institute Inc.
Box 8000
Cary, North Carolina 27511-8000

Laura Punnett

Marian Saffer edited the *SAS® Procedures Guide for Personal Computers, Version 6 Edition*. Writers who contributed to this manual were **Larry Crum**, **Gretel Easter**, **Robert Hastings**, **Brenda C. Kalt**, **J. Robin Keller**, **Regina Luginbuhl**, **Carol Myrick**, and **Holly S. Whittle**.

Copyeditors who provided editorial support were **Betty Fried** and **Judith K. Whatley**. Proofreaders were **Ellen Fussell**, **James K. Hart**, and **Frances A. Kienzle**. Manuals composition coders were **Gail C. Freeman**, **Amy G. Power**, and **Blanche Weatherspoon**. **Barbara D. Johnson**, **Toni P. Sherrill**, and **June F. Zglinski** provided administrative support.

Graphic Arts provided the text composition and production under the direction of **Carol M. Thompson**. Programming support was provided by **Craig R. Sampson** and **Pamela A. Troutman**. Compositors were **Arlene B. Drezek** and **Sarah M. Richardson**. Artists were **Lisa N. Clements** and **Michael J. Pezzoni**.

The correct bibliographic citation for this manual is as follows: SAS Institute Inc. *SAS® Procedures Guide for Personal Computers, Version 6 Edition*. Cary, NC: SAS Institute Inc., 1985. 373 pp.

SAS® Procedures Guide for Personal Computers, Version 6 Edition

Copyright © 1985 by SAS Institute Inc., Cary, NC, USA.
ISBN 0-917382-79-X

All rights reserved. Printed in the United States of America. No part of this publication may be reproduced, stored in a retrieval system, or transmitted, in any form or by any means, electronic, mechanical, photocopying, or otherwise, without the prior written permission of the publisher, SAS Institute Inc.

86 85 4 3 2 1

Base SAS® software, the foundation of the SAS System, provides data retrieval and management, programming, statistical, and reporting capabilities. Also in the SAS System are SAS/GRAPH,® SAS/FSP,® SAS/ETS,® SAS/IMS-DL/I,® SAS/OR,™ SAS/AF,™ SAS/IML,™ SAS/REPLAY-CICS,™ and SAS/STAT™ software. These products and SYSTEM 2000® Data Base Management System, including the Multi-User,™ QueX,™ Screen Writer,™ CREATE,™ and CICS interface products, are available from SAS Institute Inc., a private company devoted to the support and further development of the software and related services. *SAS Communications,® SAS Training,® SAS Views,®* and SASware Ballot® are published by SAS Institute Inc.

SAS, SAS/FSP, SAS/GRAPH, SAS/ETS, SAS/IMS-DL/I, SYSTEM 2000, *SAS Communications*, *SAS Views*, *SAS Training*, and SASware Ballot are registered trademarks of SAS Institute Inc., Cary, NC, USA. SAS/OR, SAS/AF, SAS/IML, SAS/REPLAY-CICS, QueX, SAS/STAT, Multi-User, Screen Writer, and CREATE are trademarks of SAS Institute Inc.

dBASE II is a registered trademark of Ashton-Tate, Inc. dBASE III and Ashton-Tate are trademarks of Ashton-Tate, Inc. Lotus and 1-2-3 are trademarks of Lotus Development Corporation. VisiCalc is a trademark of VisiCorp, Inc.

Contents

Illustrations

Figures

Tables

Credits

The implementation of the PC version of the SAS System was led by John P. Sall and Robert L. Cross under the guidance of President James H. Goodnight.

The staff credits for the supervisor, DATA step, full-screen interface, display manager, and communications features are contained in the companion "Language" volume. Similarly, credits for support areas such as development support, testing and quality assurance are listed in the "Language" volume. Credits for other SAS System software are listed in the user's guides for those products.

The procedures were implemented primarily by the Applications Group, but with many contributions from the Core Group, Portable Systems Division, and, in the case of mainframe communications, the Graphics Division.

Program development includes design, programming, debugging, support, and preliminary documentation. Most Version 6 procedures were converted from Version 5 procedures (in PL/I), but in several cases were written from scratch, and in many cases were greatly enhanced. Listed below for each procedure are, first, the developer currently supporting each procedure, and then earlier developers. (Developers no longer with SAS Institute are listed in the Acknowledgments section.) Consult the corresponding section in the SAS/STAT guide for additional contributors.

APPEND	Stephen M. Beatrous
CALENDAR	Jack J. Rouse, G. Kenneth Howell
CHART	Mark V. Schaffer, Katherine Ng, James H. Goodnight
COMPARE	Mark R. Little
CONTENTS	Stephen M. Beatrous
COPY	Stephen M. Beatrous
CORR	Yang C. Yuan, David M. DeLong
DATASETS	Stephen M. Beatrous,
DBF	Rebecca A. Perry
DIF	Rebecca A. Perry
DOWNLOAD	W. Craige Hales
FORMAT	Richard D. Langston
FORMS	Thomas E. Disque
FREQ	William M. Stanish
MEANS	Katherine Ng
PLOT	Brian T. Schellenberger, James H. Goodnight
PRINT	Brian T. Schellenberger, Darylene C. Colbert, Warren S. Sarle
RANK	Brian T. Schellenberger
SORT	Katherine Ng
STANDARD	Brian T. Schellenberger
SUMMARY	Katherine Ng
TABULATE	Katherine Ng, Jack J. Rouse, Alan R. Eaton, G. Kenneth Howell

TIMEPLOT	Jane E. Pierce, Richard D. Langston
TRANSPOSE	Brian T. Schellenberger, Warren S. Sarle
UPLOAD	W. Craige Hales
UNIVARIATE	Yang C. Yuan, David M. DeLong

The following staff members made special contributions in the form of leadership and support for other procedure developers: Richard D. Langston, Philip C. Spector, G. Kenneth Howell, Warren S. Sarle, Jeffrey A. Polzin, Jack J. Rouse, Leigh A. Ihnen, Thomas E. Disque, Karen L. Hoffman, and Terri L. Betancourt. The statistical staff was led by David M. DeLong.

Acknowledgments

SAS Institute Inc. is unusually fortunate to have had many people make significant and continuing contributions to its development.

First among them are the chairpersons and other active members of the SAS Users Group International (SUGI). Julian Horwich, now of Arnar-Stone Laboratories, set up the first regional meetings at Abbott Laboratories in North Chicago in 1975, and organized and chaired the first international SUGI meeting in Lake Buena Vista, Florida, in 1976. Dr. Ronald W. Helms of the University of North Carolina at Chapel Hill chaired the second annual conference, held in New Orleans in 1977; Kenneth Offord of the Mayo Clinic was program chairman.

The 1978 SUGI conference in Las Vegas was co-chaired by Dr. Rodney Strand and Dr. Michael Farrell of Oak Ridge National Laboratories. Dr. Ramon C. Littell of the University of Florida and Dr. William Wilson of the University of North Florida co-chaired the 1979 SUGI meeting in Clearwater, Florida. The 1980 SUGI conference in San Antonio, Texas, was chaired by Rudolf J. Freund of Texas A&M University. Kenneth L. Koonce of Louisiana State University chaired the 1981 SUGI conference held in Lake Buena Vista, Florida. The 1982 conference held in San Francisco, California, was chaired by Helene Cavior of the Bureau of Prisons. In 1983 SUGI was in New Orleans with J. Philip Miller of Washington University School of Medicine as chairman. Hollywood Beach, Florida was the site of the 1984 SUGI conference chaired by Sally Carson of the Rand Corporation. Rodney Strand, Science Applications, Inc., and Mike Farrell of ORNL co-chaired SUGI in Reno, Nevada in 1985.

The University Statisticians of the Southern Experiment Stations have made numerous contributions over the years. We are especially indebted to:

Wilbert P. Byrd	Clemson University
Richard Cooper	USDA
R.J. Freund	Texas A & M University
Charles Gates	Texas A & M University
Don Henderson	ORI
David Hurst	University of Alabama at Birmingham
Kenneth Koonce	Louisiana State University
Clyde Y. Kramer (deceased)	Virginia Polytechnic Institute, University of Kentucky, and Upjohn Laboratories
Robert D. Morrison	Oklahoma State University
Richard M. Patterson	Auburn University
William L. Sanders	University of Tennessee
Glenn Ware	University of Georgia
T.J. Whatley	University of Tennessee

We are deeply grateful to our good neighbor, the Department of Statistics at North Carolina State University, and especially to these staff members:

David D. Mason	Chairman (retired)
Jolayne Service	(now at the University of California, Irvine)
Sandra Donaghy	
Carroll Perkins	(now with Westinghouse)
Francis J. Verlinden	
Evelyn Wilson.	

We also wish to express our sincere gratitude to the following people who have contributed in many different ways to the success of the SAS System. See other manuals for other contributors.

Ray Barnes	Upjohn Pharmaceutical Co.
Mark Bercov	Gulf Canada
William Blair	Consultant
Dick Blocker	Washington University
George Chao	Arnar-Stone Laboratories
Daniel Chilko	University of West Virginia
Ray Danner	National Institute of Health
Paul Fingerman	Boeing Computer Services
Terry Flynn	Tymshare
Michael Foxworth	University of South Carolina
Harold Gugel	General Motors Corporation
Donald Guthrie	University of California at Los Angeles
James Guthrie	Ameritrust
Frank Harrell	Duke University
Loren Harrell	Consultant, Business Information Technology Inc.
Jim Harrington	Monsanto Research
Walter Harvey	Ohio State University
Ronald Helms	University of North Carolina at Chapel Hill
Harold Huddleston	Data Collection & Analysis, Inc., Falls Church, Virginia
Emilio A. Icaza	Louisiana State University
Ruth Ingram	Proctor & Gamble
William Kennedy	Iowa State University
Melvin Klassen	University of Victoria
John Klinkner	American Republic Insurance Company
Steve Kuekes	Consultant
Jon Mauney	Consultant
H.W. (Barry) Merrill	Merrill Consultants
J. Philip Miller	Washington University
Mario Morino	Morino Associates Inc.
Curt Mosso	University of California at Santa Barbara
Richard Nelson	Clemson University
Robert Parks	Washington University
Virginia Patterson	University of Tennessee

Jim Penny	Academic Computer Center University of North Carolina at Greensboro
Pete Rikard	Virginia Commonwealth University
John Ruth	University of Toronto
Robert Schechter	Scott Paper Company
Roger Smith	USDA
Robert Teichman	ICI Americas Inc.
John Toebes	Consultant
Jim Walker	Morino Associates Inc.
Charles Whitman	Consultant

The Version 6 project especially acknowledges the contribution of Lattice Inc., who developed the C compiler used for the PC, and Apollo Computer, which supplied us with our main development machines.

Two of the founders of SAS Institute Inc. deserve special mention.

The present SAS documentation can be traced to the work of Jane T. Helwig, now at Seasoned Systems Inc., Chapel Hill, N.C., who gathered and wrote much of the material on which this manual is based.

Finally, SAS Institute and all SAS users owe a debt of gratitude to Anthony J. Barr, Barr Systems, now of Gainesville, Florida. His work on the SAS supervisor and compiler, as well as the procedures that he wrote, help make the SAS System the useful tool it is today.

The final responsibility for the SAS System lies with SAS Institute alone. We hope that you will always let us know your feelings about the system and its documentation. It is through such communications that the progress of SAS software has been accomplished.

The Staff of SAS Institute Inc.

Preface

The *SAS Procedures Guide for Personal Computers* is one of a set of three manuals documenting base SAS software on microcomputers. The other books in the set are *SAS Introductory Guide for Personal Computers* and *SAS Language Guide for Personal Computers*.

This manual, *SAS Procedures Guide for Personal Computers*, contains descriptions of all procedures in the Version 6 base SAS software. There are four categories of procedures:

- elementary statistics
- reporting
- scoring
- utilities.

Whether you are a new or experienced SAS user, we encourage you to read the *SAS Introductory Guide for Personal Computers* as you begin to use SAS software on your PC. Then, depending on your application, you can quickly advance to the SAS language and this book. After you have become familiar with the syntax of the SAS language, you may want to use fill-in-the-blank menu screens as a shortcut to writing some of your SAS programs. See the *SAS Introductory Guide for Personal Computers* for details.

What is the SAS System?

The SAS System is a software system for data analysis. The goal of SAS Institute is to provide data analysts one system to meet all their computing needs. When your computing needs are met, you are free to concentrate on results rather than on the mechanics of getting them. Instead of learning programming languages, several statistical packages, and utility programs, you only need to learn the SAS System.

To the all-purpose base SAS software, you can add tools for graphics, forecasting, data entry, and interfaces to other data bases to provide one total system. The SAS System runs in batch and interactively under OS, TSO, CMS, DOS/VSE, SSX, and ICCF on IBM 370/30xx/43xx and compatible machines; on Digital Equipment Corporation's VAX™ 8600 and 11/7xx series under VMS™ ; on Data General Corporation's ECLIPSE® MV series under AOS/VS; on Prime Computer, Inc.'s Prime 50 series under PRIMOS® ; on the IBM PC AT/370 and XT/370 under VM/PC; and on the IBM PC XT and PC AT under PC DOS. To use any software product in the SAS System, you first need base SAS software. The PL/I Optimizing Transient Library is required for mainframe and VM/PC IBM systems. SYSTEM 2000 DBMS supports IBM 370/30xx/43xx and compatible machines under OS, TSO, CMS, DOS/VS(E), and CICS; the Sperry Series 1100 under OS 1100; and the Control Data 6000 and Cyber series under NOS and NOS/BE. Note: not all products are available for all operating systems.

Base SAS software provides tools for:

- information storage and retrieval
- data modification and programming
- report writing
- statistical analysis
- file handling.

Information storage and retrieval The SAS System reads data values in virtually any form and then organizes the values into a SAS data set. The data can be combined with other SAS data sets using the file-handling operations described below. The data can be analyzed statistically and can be used to produce reports. SAS data sets are automatically self-documenting since they contain both the data values and their descriptions. The special structure of a SAS data library minimizes maintenance.

Data modification and programming A complete set of SAS statements and functions is available for modifying data. Some program statements perform standard operations such as creating new variables, accumulating totals, and checking for errors; others are powerful programming tools such as DO/END and IF-THEN/ELSE statements. The data-handling features are so valuable that base SAS software is used by many as a data base management system.

Report writing Just as base SAS software reads data in almost any form, it can write data in almost any form. In addition to the preformatted reports that SAS procedures produce, SAS software users can design and produce printed reports in any form, including output files on disk.

Statistical analysis The statistical analysis procedures in the SAS System are among the finest available. They range from simple descriptive statistics to complex multivariate techniques. Their designs are based on our belief that you should never need to tell the SAS System anything it can figure out by itself. Statistical integrity is thus accompanied by ease of use.

File handling Combining values and observations from several data sets is often necessary for data analysis. SAS software has tools for editing, subsetting, concatenating, merging, and updating data sets. Multiple input files can be processed simultaneously, and several reports can be produced in one pass of the data.

Other SAS System Products

With base SAS software, you can integrate other SAS software products to provide one total system. Among the other products scheduled to become available on personal computers are:

- SAS/STAT software—a wide range of statistical applications for data analysis and estimation
- SAS/IML software—multi-level, interactive programming language whose data elements are matrices
- SAS/FSP software—interactive, menu-driven facilities for data entry, editing, retrieval of SAS files, and letter-writing
- SAS/AF software—a full-screen, interactive applications facility
- SAS/GRAPH software—device-intelligent color graphics for business and research applications
- SAS/OR software—decision support tools for operations research and project management
- SAS/ETS software—expanded tools for business analysis, forecasting, and financial planning.

SAS Institute Documentation

Using this manual Chapters 1 through 4 of this book introduce you to the four groups of procedures in the base product (elementary statistics, reporting, scoring, and utilities). The introductory chapter for each group briefly describes the procedures available for that category and what they do.

In the remaining chapters you will find the procedure descriptions, which are arranged alphabetically. Each procedure description is self-contained; you need to be familiar with only the most basic features of the SAS System and SAS terminology to use most procedures. The statements and syntax necessary to run each procedure are presented in a uniform format throughout the manual. You can duplicate the examples by using the same statements and data to run a SAS job. The examples are also useful as models for writing your own programs.

Each procedure description is divided into the following major parts:

ABSTRACT: a short paragraph describing what the procedure does.

INTRODUCTION: introductory and background material, including definitions and occasional introductory examples.

SPECIFICATIONS: reference section for the syntax of the language for the procedure.

DETAILS: expanded descriptions of features, internal operations, output, treatment of missing values, computational methods, required computational resources, and usage notes.

EXAMPLES: examples using the procedure, including data, SAS statements, and printed outputs. You can reproduce these examples by copying the statements and data and running the job.

REFERENCES: a selected bibliography.

New features in Version 6 base SAS procedures The Version 6 base SAS software procedures consist of a subset of the Version 5 procedures and four new procedures. Many of the procedures available in the Version 5 have new features. See the appendix of this book for a summary of the changes to Version 5 procedures, and synopses of the new procedures in Version 6.

SAS release? To find out which release of SAS software you are using, run any SAS job and look at the release number in the notes at the beginning of the SAS log. This user's guide documents Version 6 base SAS software.

Other SAS Institute manuals and technical reports Below is a list of other manuals that document Version 6 SAS System software:

SAS Introductory Guide for Personal Computers, Version 6 Edition
SAS Language Guide for Personal Computers, Version 6 Edition

The SAS Technical Report Series documents work in progress and covers a variety of applications areas. Some of the features described in these reports are still in experimental form and are not yet available as SAS procedures.

Write to SAS Institute for a current publications catalog, which describes the manuals as well as technical reports and lists their prices.

SAS Services to Users

Technical support SAS Institute supports users through the Technical Support Department. If you have a problem running a SAS job, you should contact your site's SAS Software Consultant. If the problem cannot be resolved locally, your local support personnel should call the Institute's Technical Support Department at (919) 467-8000 on weekdays between 9:00 a.m. and 5:00 p.m. Eastern Standard Time. A brochure describing the services provided by the Technical Support Department is available from SAS Institute.

Training SAS Institute sponsors a comprehensive training program, including programs of study for novice data processors, statisticians, applications programmers, systems programmers, and local support personnel. *SAS Training*, a semiannual training publication, describes the total training program and each course currently being offered by SAS Institute.

News magazine *SAS Communications* is the quarterly news magazine of SAS Institute. Each issue contains ideas for more effective use of the SAS System, information about research and development underway at SAS Institute, the current training schedule, new publications, and news of the SAS Users Group International (SUGI).

To receive a copy of *SAS Communications* regularly, send your name and complete address to:

SAS Institute Mailing List
SAS Institute Inc.
Box 8000
Cary, NC 27511-8000

Sample library The base SAS software installation diskettes contain a directory of sample SAS applications illustrating features of SAS procedures and creative SAS programming techniques that can help you gain an in-depth knowledge of SAS capabilities. Check with your SAS Software Consultant to find out how to access the sample library.

SUGI

The SAS Users Group International (SUGI) is a nonprofit association of professionals who are interested in how others are using the SAS System. Although SAS Institute provides administrative support, SUGI is independent from the Institute. Membership is open to all users at SAS sites, and there is no membership fee.

Annual conferences are structured to allow many avenues of discussion. Users present invited and contributed papers on various topics, for example:

- computer performance evaluation and systems software
- econometrics and time series
- graphics
- information systems
- interactive techniques
- statistics
- tutorials in SAS System software.

Proceedings of the annual conferences are distributed free to SUGI registrants. Extra copies may be purchased from SAS Institute.

SASware Ballot SAS users provide valuable input toward the direction of future SAS development by ranking their priorities on the annual SASware Ballot. The top vote-getters are announced at the SUGI conference. Complete results of the SASware Ballot are also printed in the *SUGI Proceedings*.

User-written procedures Under many operating systems, (not yet including PC DOS), SAS users have written their own SAS procedures for a wide variety of specialized applications. SAS Institute will notify your SAS Software Consultant when this facility is available for microcomputers.

Licensing the SAS System

The SAS System is licensed to customers in the Western Hemisphere from the Institute's headquarters in Cary, NC. To serve the needs of our international customers, the Institute maintains subsidiaries in the United Kingdom, New Zealand, Australia, Singapore, Germany, and France. In addition, agents in other countries are licensed distributors for the SAS System. For a complete list of offices, write or call:

SAS Institute Inc.
SAS Circle
Box 8000
Cary, NC 27511-8000
(919) 467-8000

Chapter 1

SAS® Elementary Statistics Procedures

Introduction

The following SAS procedures compute univariate or bivariate statistics, such as means, sums, standard deviations, and correlations:

UNIVARIATE computes univariate statistics, including quantiles, and draws distributional plots.

SUMMARY and MEANS	compute elementary univariate statistics within groups of observations. The groups are defined by variables in a CLASS statement. The statistics can be printed or output to a SAS data set.
TABULATE	prints complex tables of elementary statistics.
CORR	for quantitative variables.

Other procedures that compute elementary statistics include

CHART	draws bar, block, pie, and star charts of counts, means, or sums.
FREQ	computes frequency distributions for categorical variables and does multi-way crosstabulations.

Comparison of Procedures

Table 1.1 indicates the statistics available from each procedure and summarizes some other important features.

Table 1.1 SAS Elementary Statistics Procedures and Their Features

Statistic	MEANS	UNIVARIATE	SUMMARY	TABULATE	CORR
number of missing values	x	x	x	x	
number of nonmissing values	x	x	x	x	x
sum of weights	x	x	x	x	x
mean	x	x	x	x	x
sum	x	x	x	x	x
minimum	x	x	x	x	x
maximum	x	x	x	x	x
range	x	x	x	x	
uncorrected sum of squares	x	x	x	x	x
corrected sum of squares	x	x	x	x	x
variance	x	x	x	x	x
standard deviation	x	x	x	x	x
standard error	x	x	x	x	

Continued on next page

Table 1.1 *Continued*

Statistic	MEANS	UNIVARIATE	SUMMARY	TABULATE	CORR
coefficient of variation	x	x	x	x	
skewness		x			
kurtosis		x			
Student's *t*	x	x	x	x	
prob>*t*	x	x	x	x	
median		x			
quartiles		x			
mode		x			
Pearson correlation					x
Other Features					
printed output	yes	yes	yes	yes	yes
output to a SAS data set	yes	yes	yes	no	yes
CLASS statement	yes	no	yes	yes	no
BY statement	yes	yes	yes	yes	yes

Efficiency

Quantiles, including the median, require time proportional to *n*log(*n*) for large sample sizes, so PROC UNIVARIATE may require more time than other elementary statistical procedures. UNIVARIATE also requires more storage because the data are held in core.

If you need to compute statistics for each of several groups of observations, you can use any of the above procedures with a BY statement to specify the groups. However, BY-group processing requires sorting the data set, which can be expensive for large data sets. SUMMARY, MEANS and TABULATE can produce statistics across a classification without sorting. PROC SUMMARY and PROC MEANS can create output data sets, while PROC TABULATE prints tables of statistics in hierarchical crosstabulations but produces no output data set.

Keywords and Formulas

A standardized set of keywords is used to refer to the univariate statistics in SAS procedures. These keywords are used in SAS statements to request statistics for printing or storing in an output data set.

The following notations are used where summation is over all nonmissing values:

x_i	the *i*th nonmissing observation on the variable
w_i	the weight associated with x_i if a WEIGHT statement is specified, otherwise 1
n	the number of nonmissing observations
$\bar{x}$	$= \Sigma w_i x_i / \Sigma w_i$
d	$= n$ if the option VARDEF=N is specified, $= n - 1$ if VARDEF=DF, $= \Sigma w_i$ if VARDEF=WEIGHT or WGT, $= \Sigma w_i - 1$ if VARDEF=WDF
s^2	$= \Sigma w_i (x_i - \bar{x})^2 / d$
z_i	$= (x_i - \bar{x})/s$ standardized variables.

The formulas and standard keywords for each statistic are given below. In some formulas a keyword is used to designate the corresponding statistic.

N	number of nonmissing observations
NMISS	number of missing observations
MIN	minimum value
MAX	maximum value
RANGE	MAX-MIN, the range
SUM	$\Sigma w_i x_i$, the weighted sum
SUMWGT	Σw_i, the sum of weights
MEAN	$\bar{x}$, the arithmetic mean
USS	$\Sigma w_i x_i^2$, the uncorrected sum of squares
CSS	$\Sigma w_i (x_i - \bar{x})^2$, the sum of squares corrected for the mean
VAR	s^2, the variance
STD	s, the standard deviation
STDERR	$s/\sqrt{n}$, the standard error of the mean
CV	$100\, s/\bar{x}$, the percent coefficient of variation
SKEWNESS	$\Sigma z_i^3 \times n/(n-1)(n-2)$, measures sidedness
KURTOSIS	$\Sigma z_i^4 \times n(n+1)/(n-1)(n-2)(n-3) - 3(n-1)^2/(n-2)(n-3)$, measures heaviness of tails
T	$t = \bar{x}\sqrt{n}/s$, Student's t for H_0: population mean=0
PRT	the two-tailed p value for Student's t with $n-1$ degrees of freedom, the probability under the null hypothesis of obtaining an absolute value of t greater than the t value observed in this sample
MEDIAN	the middle value when the x_i are arranged in order of value and n is odd; the mean of the two middle values when n is even.
QUARTILE	the values such that one quarter of the x_i are larger and one quarter of the x_i are smaller
MODE	the most frequent value of x_i .

Data Requirements for Univariate Statistics

Statistics are reported as missing if they cannot be computed. N and NMISS do not require any nonmissing observations. SUM, MEAN, MAX, MIN, RANGE, USS, and CSS require only one nonmissing observation. The requirements for other statistics are as follows:

- VAR, STD, STDERR, CV, T, and PRT require at least 2 observations
- SKEWNESS requires at least 3 observations
- KURTOSIS requires at least 4 observations
- SKEWNESS, KURTOSIS, T, and PRT require STD>0
- SKEWNESS and KURTOSIS are not computed if a WEIGHT statement is used
- CV requires MEAN 0.

Background

This section provides a brief introduction to some of the statistical concepts necessary for interpreting the output of SAS procedures for elementary statistics. For a more thorough discussion, consult an introductory statistics textbook such as Moore (1979), Ott (1977), or Snedecor and Cochran (1967).

Populations and Parameters

Usually, there is a clearly defined set of elements in which you are interested. This set of elements is called the *universe*, and a set of values associated with these elements is called a *population* of values. The statistical term *population* has nothing to do with people per se. A statistical population is a collection of values, not a collection of people. For example, we may have as the universe all of the students at a particular school and may have two populations of interest: one of height values and one of weight values. Or the universe could be the set of all widgets manufactured by a particular company, while the population of values could be the length of time each widget is used before failing.

A population of values can be described in terms of its *cumulative distribution function*, which gives the proportion of the population less than each possible value. A discrete population can also be described by a *probability function* giving the proportion of the population equal to each possible value. A continuous population can often be described by a *density function*, which is the derivative (see a calculus book) of the cumulative distribution function. A density function can be approximated by a histogram giving the proportion of the population lying within each of a series of intervals of values, such as produced by the CHART procedure. A probability density function is like a histogram with an infinite number of infinitely small intervals.

In technical literature, when the term *distribution* is used without qualification, it generally refers to the cumulative distribution function. In informal writing, *distribution* sometimes means the density function instead. Often the word *distribution* is used simply to refer to an abstract population of values rather than some concrete population. Thus the statistical literature refers to many types of abstract distributions, such as normal distributions, exponential distributions, Cauchy distributions, and so on. When a phrase such as *normal distribution* is used, it frequently does not matter whether the cumulative distribution function or the density function is intended.

It may be expedient to describe a population in terms of a few measures that summarize interesting features of the distribution. Such a measure, computed from the population values, is called a *parameter*. Many different parameters can be defined to measure different aspects of a distribution.

The most commonly used parameter is the (arithmetic) *mean*. If the population contains a finite number of values, the population mean is computed as the sum of all the values in the population divided by the number of elements in the population. For an infinite population, the concept of the mean is similar but requires more complicated mathematics.

We write $E(x)$ to denote the mean of a population of values symbolized by x, such as height, where E stands for *expected value*. We can also consider expected values of derived functions of the original values. For example, if x represents height, then $E(x^2)$ is the expected value of height squared, that is, the mean value of the population obtained by squaring every value in the population of heights.

Samples and Statistics

It is often impossible to measure all of the values in a population. A collection of measured values is called a *sample*. A mathematical function of a sample of values is called a *statistic*. A statistic is to a sample as a parameter is to a population. It is customary to denote statistics by Roman letters and parameters by Greek letters. For example, the population mean is often written as μ, whereas the sample mean is written as $\bar{x}$. The branch of mathematics called *statistics* is largely concerned with the study of the behavior of sample statistics.

Samples can be selected in a variety of ways. Most SAS procedures assume that the data constitute a *simple random sample*, which means that the sample was selected in such a way that all possible samples were equally likely to be selected.

Statistics from a sample can be used to make inferences, or reasonable guesses, about the parameters of a population. For example, if you take a random sample of thirty students from the high school, the mean height for those thirty students is a reasonable guess, or *estimate*, of the mean height of all the students in the high school. Other statistics, such as the standard error, can provide information about how good an estimate is likely to be.

For any population parameter, there are many statistics that can be used to estimate it. Often, however, there is one particular statistic that is customarily used to estimate a given parameter. For example, the sample mean is the usual estimator of the population mean. In the case of the mean, the formulas for the parameter and statistic are the same. In other cases, the formula for a parameter may be different from that of the most commonly used estimator. It should not be assumed that the most commonly used estimator is the best estimator in all applications.

Measures of Location

Measures of location include the mean, the mode, and the median. These measures can generally be thought of as describing the center of a distribution. In the definitions below, notice that if the entire sample is changed by adding a fixed amount to each observation, then these measures of location are shifted by the same fixed amount.

Mean As discussed above, the population mean $\mu = E(x)$ is usually estimated by the sample mean:

$$\bar{x} = \Sigma x_i / n \quad .$$

Median The population median is the central value, lying above and below half of the population values. The sample median is the middle value when the data are arranged in ascending or descending order. For an even number of observations, the midpoint between the two middle values is usually reported as the median.

Mode The mode is the value at which the density of the population is at a maximum. Some densities have more than one local maximum (peak) and are said to be multimodal. The sample mode is the value that occurs most often in the sample. If there is a tie for most-often-occurring sample value, UNIVARIATE reports the lowest such value. If the population is continuous, then all sample values occur once and the sample mode has little use.

Quantiles

Quantiles, including percentiles, quartiles, and the median, are useful for a detailed study of a distribution. For a set of measurements arranged in order of magnitude, the *p*th percentile is the value that has *p*% of the measurements below it and (100−*p*)% above it. The median is the 50th percentile. Since it may not be possible to divide your data so that you get exactly the desired percentile, a more precise definition is used (see the UNIVARIATE procedure).

The upper quartile of a distribution is the value below which 75% of the measurements fall (the 75th percentile). Twenty-five percent of the measurements fall below the lower quartile value. Selected percentiles and quartiles are calculated by the UNIVARIATE procedure. The RANK procedure can be used to calculate any desired quantiles.

Example: Quantiles and Measures of Location

The data in the following example are artificially generated by a call to a pseudo-random-number function. The UNIVARIATE procedure computes a variety of quantiles and measures of location, and outputs the values to a SAS data set. A DATA step then uses the SYMPUT routine to assign the values of the statistics to macro variables. The macro variables are used in the macro %FORMGEN to produce value labels for PROC FORMAT. The resulting format is used with PROC CHART to display the values of the statistics on a histogram.

The program below produces **Output 1.1**.

```
TITLE 'EXAMPLE OF QUANTILES AND MEASURES OF LOCATION';
DATA RANDOM;
   DROP N;
   DO N=1 TO 1000;
      X=FLOOR(EXP(RANNOR(314159)*.8+1.8));
      OUTPUT;
      END;

PROC UNIVARIATE;
   VAR X;
   OUTPUT OUT=LOCATION MEAN=MEAN MODE=MODE MEDIAN=MEDIAN
         Q1=Q1 Q3=Q3 P5=P5 P10=P10 P90=P90 P95=P95 MAX=MAX;
PROC PRINT;

DATA _NULL_;
   SET LOCATION;
   CALL SYMPUT('MEAN',ROUND(MEAN,1));
   CALL SYMPUT('MODE',MODE);
   CALL SYMPUT('MEDIAN',ROUND(MEDIAN,1));
   CALL SYMPUT('Q1',ROUND(Q1,1));
```

```
      CALL SYMPUT('Q3',ROUND(Q3,1));
      CALL SYMPUT('P5',ROUND(P5,1));
      CALL SYMPUT('P10',ROUND(P10,1));
      CALL SYMPUT('P90',ROUND(P90,1));
      CALL SYMPUT('P95',ROUND(P95,1));
      CALL SYMPUT('MAX',MIN(50,MAX));
   RUN;

   %MACRO FORMGEN;
      %DO I=1 %TO &MAX;
         %LET VALUE=&I;
         %IF &I=&P5     %THEN %LET VALUE=&VALUE  P5;
         %IF &I=&P10    %THEN %LET VALUE=&VALUE  P10;
         %IF &I=&Q1     %THEN %LET VALUE=&VALUE  Q1;
         %IF &I=&MODE   %THEN %LET VALUE=&VALUE  MODE;
         %IF &I=&MEDIAN %THEN %LET VALUE=&VALUE  MEDIAN;
         %IF &I=&MEAN   %THEN %LET VALUE=&VALUE  MEAN;
         %IF &I=&Q3     %THEN %LET VALUE=&VALUE  Q3;
         %IF &I=&P90    %THEN %LET VALUE=&VALUE  P90;
         %IF &I=&P95    %THEN %LET VALUE=&VALUE  P95;
         %IF &I=&MAX    %THEN %LET VALUE=>=&VALUE;
         &I="&VALUE"
         %END;
      %MEND;

   PROC FORMAT PRINT;
      VALUE STAT %FORMGEN;
   PROC CHART DATA=RANDOM;
      VBAR X/MIDPOINTS=1 TO &MAX BY 1;
      FORMAT X STAT.;
      FOOTNOTE  'P5  =  5TH PERCENTILE';
      FOOTNOTE2 'P10 = 10TH PERCENTILE';
      FOOTNOTE3 'P90 = 90TH PERCENTILE';
      FOOTNOTE4 'P95 = 95TH PERCENTILE';
      FOOTNOTE5 'Q1  =  1ST QUARTILE  ';
      FOOTNOTE6 'Q3  =  3RD QUARTILE  ';

   RUN;
```

Output 1.1 Example of Quantiles and Measures of Location

```
                           EXAMPLE OF QUANTILES AND MEASURES OF LOCATION                                1

                                              UNIVARIATE

VARIABLE=X

              MOMENTS                                     QUANTILES(DEF=5)                          EXTREMES

N               1000  SUM WGTS        1000       100% MAX        62      99%      37.5        LOWEST  HIGHEST
MEAN           7.605  SUM             7605        75% Q3          9      95%      21.5             0       44
STD DEV     7.381698  VARIANCE    54.48946        50% MED         5      90%        16             0       44
SKEWNESS    2.730385  KURTOSIS    11.18706        25% Q1          3      10%         2             0       57
USS           112271  CSS         54434.97         0% MIN         0       5%         1             0       61
CV          97.06375  STD MEAN    .2334298                                1%         0             0       62
T:MEAN=0    32.57939  PROB>|T|       .0001       RANGE           62
SGN RANK    244777.5  PROB>|S|       .0001       Q3-Q1            6
NUM ¬= 0         989                             MODE             3
```

```
                           EXAMPLE OF QUANTILES AND MEASURES OF LOCATION                                2

                 OBS     MEAN    MAX    P5    P10    Q1    MEDIAN    Q3    P90    P95    MODE

                   1    7.605     62     1      2     3         5     9     16   21.5       3
```

```
                           EXAMPLE OF QUANTILES AND MEASURES OF LOCATION                                3

                                       FREQUENCY BAR CHART

FREQUENCY

120 +     *
    |     *
    |     * *
    |   * * *
 90 + * * * * *
    | * * * * *
    | * * * * * * *
    | * * * * * * *
 60 + * * * * * * *
    | * * * * * * * * *
    | * * * * * * * * *
    | * * * * * * * * *
 30 + * * * * * * * * * * * *
    | * * * * * * * * * * * *       *
    | * * * * * * * * * * * * * * * *   *
    | * * * * * * * * * * * * * * * * * * * * * * *     *   *
    ----------------------------------------------------------------------------------------------------
      1 2 3 4 5 6 7 8 9 1 1 1 1 1 1 1 1 1 1 2 2 2 2 2 2 2 2 2 2 3 3 3 3 3 3 3 3 3 3 4 4 4 4 4 4 4 4 4 4 >
                        0 1 2 3 4 5 6 7 8 9 0 1 2 3 4 5 6 7 8 9 0 1 2 3 4 5 6 7 8 9 0 1 2 3 4 5 6 7 8 9 =
                                                                                                        5
      P P Q   M     M Q                                                                                 0
      5 1 1   E     E 3             P           P
        0     D     A               9           9
              I     N               0           5
          M   A
          O   N
          D
          E

                                           X MIDPOINT

                                      P5  =  5TH PERCENTILE
                                      P10 = 10TH PERCENTILE
                                      P90 = 90TH PERCENTILE
                                      P95 = 95TH PERCENTILE
                                      Q1  =  1ST QUARTILE
                                      Q3  =  3RD QUARTILE
```

Measures of Variability

Another group of statistics important for studying the distribution of a population measures the *variability*, or spread, of values. In the definitions given below, notice that if the entire sample is changed by the addition of a fixed amount to each observation, then the values of these statistics are unchanged. The values of these statistics are changed, however, if each observation in the sample is multiplied by a constant.

Range The sample range is the difference between the largest and smallest values in the sample. For many populations, at least in statistical theory, the range is infinite, so the sample range may not tell you much about the population. The sample range tends to increase as the sample size increases. If all sample values are multiplied by a constant, the sample range is multiplied by the same constant.

Interquartile range The interquartile range is the difference between the upper and lower quartiles. If all sample values are multiplied by a constant, the sample interquartile range is multiplied by the same constant.

Variance The population variance, usually denoted by σ^2 when it is clear what population is being considered, is the expected value of the squared difference of the values from the population mean:

$$\sigma^2 = E(x-\mu)^2 \quad .$$

The sample variance, denoted s^2, is usually computed as

$$s^2 = \Sigma\ (x_i-\bar{x})^2\ /\ (n-1) \quad .$$

The difference between a value and the mean is called a *deviation from the mean*. Thus the variance is the mean of the squared deviation. When all the values lie close to the mean, the variance is small but never less than zero. When values are more scattered, the variance is larger. If all sample values are multiplied by a constant, the sample variance is multiplied by the square of the constant.

Sometimes values other than $n-1$ are used in the denominator. The VARDEF option controls what divisor is used.

Standard deviation The standard deviation is the square root of the variance, or root-mean-square deviation from the mean, in either population or sample. The usual symbols are σ for the population and s for a sample. The standard deviation is expressed in the same units as the observations, rather than in squared units. If all sample values are multiplied by a constant, the sample standard deviation is multiplied by the same constant.

Coefficient of Variation

The coefficient of variation is a unitless measure of relative variability. It is defined as the ratio of the standard deviation to the mean expressed as a percentage. The coefficient of variation is meaningful only if the variable is measured on a ratio scale. If all sample values are multiplied by a constant, the sample coefficient of variation remains unchanged.

Measures of Shape

Skewness The variance is a measure of the overall size of the deviations from the mean. Since the formula for the variance squares the deviations, both positive and negative deviations contribute to the variance in the same way. In many distributions, positive deviations may tend to be larger in magnitude than negative deviations, or vice versa. *Skewness* is a measure of the tendency of the deviations to be larger in one direction than in the other. For example, the data in the last example are skewed to the right.

Population skewness is defined as

$$E(x-\mu)^3/\sigma^3 \ .$$

Since the deviations are cubed, rather than squared, the signs of the deviations are maintained. Cubing the deviations also emphasizes the effects of large deviations. The formula includes a divisor of σ^3 to remove the effect of scale, so multiplying all values by a constant does not change the skewness. Skewness can thus be interpreted as a tendency for one tail of the population to be heavier than the other.

SAS calculates the sample skewness as

$$n/(n-1)(n-2) \ \ \Sigma_{i=1}^{n}(x_i-\bar{x})^3/s^3 \ .$$

Skewness can be positive or negative and is unbounded.

Kurtosis The heaviness of the tails of a population affects the behavior of many statistics. Hence it is useful to have a measure of tail heaviness. One such measure is *kurtosis*. The population kurtosis is usually defined as

$$E(x-\mu)^4/\sigma^4 \ - \ 3 \quad ,$$

although some statisticians omit the subtraction of 3. Since the deviations are raised to the fourth power, positive and negative deviations make the same contribution, while large deviations are strongly emphasized. Because of the divisor σ^4, multiplying each value by a constant has no effect on kurtosis.

Population kurtosis must lie between -2 and positive infinity, inclusive. If m_3 represents population skewness and m_4 represents population kurtosis, then

$$m_4 >= {m_3}^2 - 2$$

SAS uses the formula below to calculate sample kurtosis:

$$n(n+1)/(n-1)(n-2)(n-3) \ \Sigma_{i=1}^{n}(x_i-\bar{x})^4/s^4 - \ 3(n-1)(n-1)/(n-2)(n-3).$$

There is a myth in the statistical literature that kurtosis measures the *peakedness* of a density. This myth stubbornly persists despite repeated debunking (Kaplansky 1945; Ali 1974; Johnson, Tietjen, and Beckman 1980).

Sample skewness and kurtosis are rather unreliable estimators of the corresponding parameters in small samples. Trust them only if you have a very large sample. However, large values of skewness or kurtosis may merit attention even in small samples because such values indicate that statistical methods based on normality assumptions (see below) may be inappropriate.

The Normal Distribution

One especially important family of theoretical distributions is the *normal* or *Gaussian* distribution. A normal distribution is a smooth symmetric function often referred to as "bell-shaped." Its skewness and kurtosis are both zero. A normal distribution can be completely specified by only two parameters: the mean and standard deviation. Approximately 68% of the values in a normal population are within one standard deviation of the population mean; approximately 95% of the values are within two standard deviations of the mean; and about 99.7% are within three standard deviations. Use of the term *normal* to describe this particular kind of distribution does not imply that other kinds of distributions are necessarily abnormal or pathological.

Many statistical methods are designed under the assumption that the population being sampled is normally distributed. Nevertheless, most real-life populations do not have normal distributions. Before using any statistical method based on normality assumptions, you should consult the statistical literature to find out how sensitive the method is to non-normality and, if necessary, check your sample for evidence of non-normality.

Example: Normal Distribution

The following data are sampled from a normal distribution with mean 50 and standard deviation 10. This example generates **Output 1.2.**

```
TITLE 'SAMPLE OF 2000 OBSERVATIONS FROM A NORMAL DISTRIBUTION';
TITLE2 'WITH MEAN=50 AND STANDARD DEVIATION=10';
DATA NORMAL;
   DROP N;
   DO N=1 TO 2000;
      X=10*RANNOR(53124)+50;
      OUTPUT;
      END;

PROC UNIVARIATE NORMAL;
   VAR X;

PROC FORMAT PRINT;
   PICTURE MSD
      20='20.0 MEAN-3*STD' (NOEDIT)
      30='30.0 MEAN-2*STD' (NOEDIT)
      40='40.0 MEAN-STD  ' (NOEDIT)
      50='50.0 MEAN      ' (NOEDIT)
      60='60.0 MEAN+STD  ' (NOEDIT)
      70='70.0 MEAN+2*STD' (NOEDIT)
      80='80.0 MEAN+3*STD' (NOEDIT)
   OTHER='00.0';

PROC CHART;
   VBAR X/MIDPOINTS=20 TO 80 BY 2;
   FORMAT X MSD.;
```

Output 1.2 Sample from a Normal Distribution

```
                 SAMPLE OF 2000 OBSERVATIONS FROM A NORMAL DISTRIBUTION                      1
                         WITH MEAN=50 AND STANDARD DEVIATION=10

                                       UNIVARIATE
VARIABLE=X

               MOMENTS                                 QUANTILES(DEF=5)                           EXTREMES

 N              2000  SUM WGTS        2000        100% MAX  87.48835       99%    73.06189        LOWEST  HIGHEST
 MEAN       49.96062  SUM         99921.25         75% Q3   56.54204       95%    66.30259      17.02475 78.69852
 STD DEV    10.03666  VARIANCE    100.7346         50% MED  50.06123       90%    62.70629      21.18527 79.36738
 SKEWNESS   -.001408  KURTOSIS    .0184036         25% Q1   43.18642       10%    37.01378      21.44239 81.95677
 USS         5193497  CSS         201368.5          0% MIN  17.02475        5%    33.39005      21.58781 83.30135
 CV         20.08915  STD MEAN    .2244266                                  1%    27.16487      21.76644 87.48835
 T:MEAN=0   222.6145  PROB>|T|       .0001        RANGE      70.4636
 SGN RANK    1000500  PROB>|S|       .0001        Q3-Q1     13.35562
 NUM ¬= 0       2000                              MODE      17.02476
 W:NORMAL    .989254  PROB<W          .738
```

```
                 SAMPLE OF 2000 OBSERVATIONS FROM A NORMAL DISTRIBUTION                      2
                         WITH MEAN=50 AND STANDARD DEVIATION=10

                                   FREQUENCY BAR CHART
```

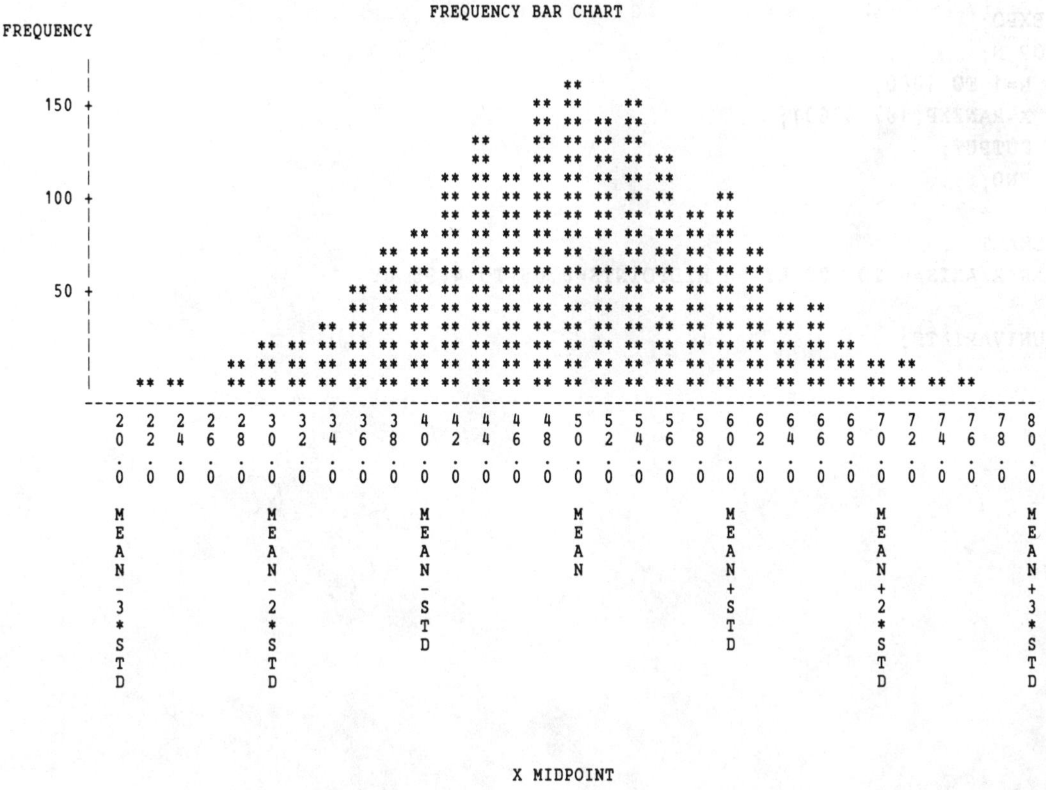

Sampling Distribution of the Mean

If you repeatedly draw samples of size *n* from a population and compute the mean of each sample, then the sample means themselves have a distribution. Consider a new population consisting of the means of all the samples that could possibly be drawn from the original population. The distribution of this new population is called a *sampling distribution*.

It can be proven mathematically that if the original population has mean μ and standard deviation σ, then the sampling distribution of the mean also has mean μ, but its standard deviation is $\sigma/\sqrt{n}$. The standard deviation of the sampling distribution of the mean is called the *standard error of the mean*. The standard error of the mean provides an indication of the accuracy of a sample mean as an estimator of the population mean.

If the original population has a normal distribution, then the sampling distribution of the mean is also normal. If the original distribution is not normal but does not have excessively long tails, then the sampling distribution of the mean can be approximated by a normal distribution for large sample sizes.

Example: Sampling Distributions

The following DATA step creates a sample of 1000 observations from an exponential distribution generated by the RANEXP function. The theoretical population mean is 1.00, while the sample mean is 1.01, to two decimal places. The population standard deviation is 1.00, the sample standard deviation 1.04.

This is an example of a non-normal distribution. The population skewness is 2.00, which is close to the sample skewness of 1.97. The population kurtosis is 6.00, but the sample kurtosis is only 4.80. This example generates **Output 1.3**.

```
TITLE 'SAMPLE OF 1000 OBSERVATIONS FROM AN EXPONENTIAL DISTRIBUTION';
DATA EXPO;
   DROP N;
   DO N=1 TO 1000;
      X=RANEXP(18746363);
      OUTPUT;
      END;

PROC CHART;
   VBAR X/AXIS=0 TO 300 BY 50 MIDPOINTS=0.05 TO 4.95 BY .1;

PROC UNIVARIATE;
```

Output 1.3 Sample from an Exponential Distribution

```
                     SAMPLE OF 1000 OBSERVATIONS FROM AN EXPONENTIAL DISTRIBUTION                  1

                                          FREQUENCY BAR CHART

FREQUENCY

   300 +
       |
       |
       |
       |
   250 +
       |
       |
       |
       |
   200 +
       |
       |
       |
       |
   150 +
       |
       |
       |
       |
   100 + *
       | *
       | * * *   *
       | * * * * *
       | * * * * *     *
    50 + * * * * * * * *
       | * * * * * * * * * * *
       | * * * * * * * * * * * *   *
       | * * * * * * * * * * * * * * *   * *       *
       | * * * * * * * * * * * * * * * * * * * * * * * * *   * * *   * * *   *           *                 *
       ---------------------------------------------------------------------------------------------------------
         0 0 0 0 0 0 0 0 0 0 1 1 1 1 1 1 1 1 1 1 2 2 2 2 2 2 2 2 2 2 3 3 3 3 3 3 3 3 3 3 4 4 4 4 4 4 4 4 4 4
         . . . . . . . . . . . . . . . . . . . . . . . . . . . . . . . . . . . . . . . . . . . . . . . . . .
         0 1 2 3 4 5 6 7 8 9 0 1 2 3 4 5 6 7 8 9 0 1 2 3 4 5 6 7 8 9 0 1 2 3 4 5 6 7 8 9 0 1 2 3 4 5 6 7 8 9
         5 5 5 5 5 5 5 5 5 5 5 5 5 5 5 5 5 5 5 5 5 5 5 5 5 5 5 5 5 5 5 5 5 5 5 5 5 5 5 5 5 5 5 5 5 5 5 5 5 5

                                                   X MIDPOINT
```

```
                     SAMPLE OF 1000 OBSERVATIONS FROM AN EXPONENTIAL DISTRIBUTION                  2

                                              UNIVARIATE

VARIABLE=X

              MOMENTS                                     QUANTILES(DEF=5)                          EXTREMES

N               1000  SUM WGTS        1000       100% MAX  6.639068     99%    5.044917        LOWEST   HIGHEST
MEAN        1.011762  SUM         1011.762        75% Q3   1.357334     95%    3.134823      .0005544 5.782202
STD DEV     1.043712  VARIANCE    1.089334        50% MED  .6895022     90%    2.378036      .0012478 6.006787
SKEWNESS    1.969631  KURTOSIS    4.801506        25% Q1   .2948144     10%    .1021901      .0022229 6.135398
USS         2111.908  CSS         1088.245         0% MIN  .0005544      5%     .051928      .0025333 6.608973
CV          103.1578  STD MEAN    .0330051                               1%    .0119559      .0039673 6.639068
T:MEAN=0    30.65475  PROB>|T|       .0001       RANGE     6.638513
SGN RANK      250250  PROB>|S|       .0001       Q3-Q1      1.06252
NUM ^= 0        1000                             MODE      .0005544
```

The next DATA step draws 1000 different samples from the same population as the previous DATA step. Each sample contains 10 observations. PROC MEANS computes the mean of each sample. In the data set created by PROC MEANS, each observation represents the mean of a sample of 10 observations from an exponential distribution. Thus, the data set is a sample from the sampling distribution of the mean for an exponential population.

PROC UNIVARIATE displays statistics for this sample of means. Notice that the mean of the sample of means is .99, almost the same as the mean of the original population. Theoretically, the standard deviation of the sampling distribution is $\sigma/\sqrt{n} = 1.00/\sqrt{10} = .32$, whereas the standard deviation of this sample from the sampling distribution is .31. The skewness (.55) and kurtosis (−.01) are closer to zero in the sample from the sampling distribution than in the original sample from the exponential distribution, since the sampling distribution is closer to a normal distribution than is the original exponential distribution. A histogram of the 1000 sample means is shown by PROC CHART. The shape of the histogram is much closer to a bell-like normal density, but it is still distinctly lopsided. See **Output 1.4** .

```
TITLE '1000 SAMPLE MEANS WITH 10 OBSERVATIONS PER SAMPLE';
TITLE2 'DRAWN FROM AN EXPONENTIAL DISTRIBUTION';
DATA SAMP10;
   DROP N;
   DO SAMPLE=1 TO 1000;
      DO N=1 TO 10;
         X=RANEXP(433879);
         OUTPUT;
         END;
      END;

PROC MEANS NOPRINT;
   OUTPUT OUT=MEAN10 MEAN=MEAN;
   VAR X;
   BY SAMPLE;

PROC CHART;
   VBAR MEAN/AXIS=0 TO 300 BY 50 MIDPOINTS=0.05 TO 4.95 BY .1;

PROC UNIVARIATE;
   VAR MEAN;
```

Output 1.4 Sample Drawn from an Exponential Distribution

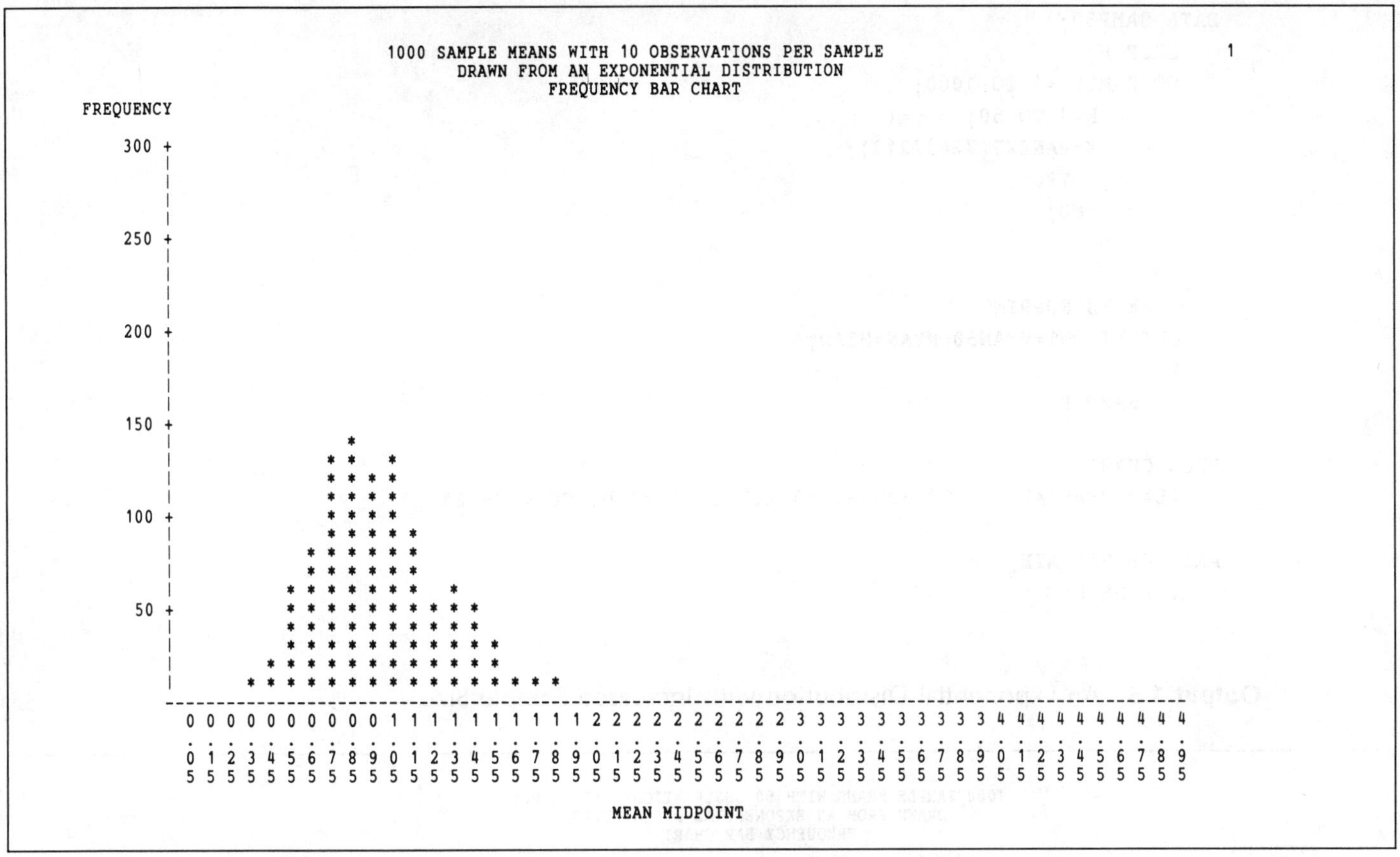


```
                        1000 SAMPLE MEANS WITH 10 OBSERVATIONS PER SAMPLE                    2
                               DRAWN FROM AN EXPONENTIAL DISTRIBUTION

                                             UNIVARIATE

VARIABLE=MEAN

                MOMENTS                                 QUANTILES(DEF=5)                        EXTREMES

N              1000  SUM WGTS        1000        100% MAX  2.053899    99%    1.827503      LOWEST  HIGHEST
MEAN       .9906857  SUM         990.6857         75% Q3   1.181006    95%    1.557175    .2560693 1.903374
STD DEV    .3073265  VARIANCE    .0944496         50% MED  .9561524    90%    1.416611    .3009028 1.913087
SKEWNESS   .5457562  KURTOSIS    -.006089         25% Q1   .7639726    10%    .6217868    .3437991  1.92148
USS        1075.813  CSS         94.35512          0% MIN  .2560693     5%    .5535677    .3642348 1.933354
CV         31.02159  STD MEAN    .0097185                               1%    .4338201    .3808081 2.053899
T:MEAN=0    101.938  PROB>|T|       .0001        RANGE     1.797829
SGN RANK     250250  PROB>|S|       .0001        Q3-Q1     .4170335
NUM ¬= 0       1000                              MODE      .2560693
```

In the following DATA step, the size of each sample is increased to 50. The standard deviation of the sampling distribution is smaller than in the previous example because the size of each sample is larger. Also, the sampling distribution is even closer to a normal distribution, as can be seen from the histogram and from the skewness. This example produces **Output 1.5**.

```
TITLE '1000 SAMPLE MEANS WITH 50 OBSERVATIONS PER SAMPLE';
TITLE2 'DRAWN FROM AN EXPONENTIAL DISTRIBUTION';
DATA SAMP50;
   DROP N;
   DO SAMPLE=1 TO 1000;
      DO N=1 TO 50;
         X=RANEXP(72437213);
         OUTPUT;
         END;
      END;

PROC MEANS NOPRINT;
   OUTPUT OUT=MEAN50 MEAN=MEAN;
   VAR X;
   BY SAMPLE;

PROC CHART;
   VBAR MEAN/AXIS=0 TO 300 BY 50 MIDPOINTS=0.05 TO 4.95 BY .1;

PROC UNIVARIATE;
   VAR MEAN;
```

Output 1.5 An Exponential Distribution with Increased Sample Size

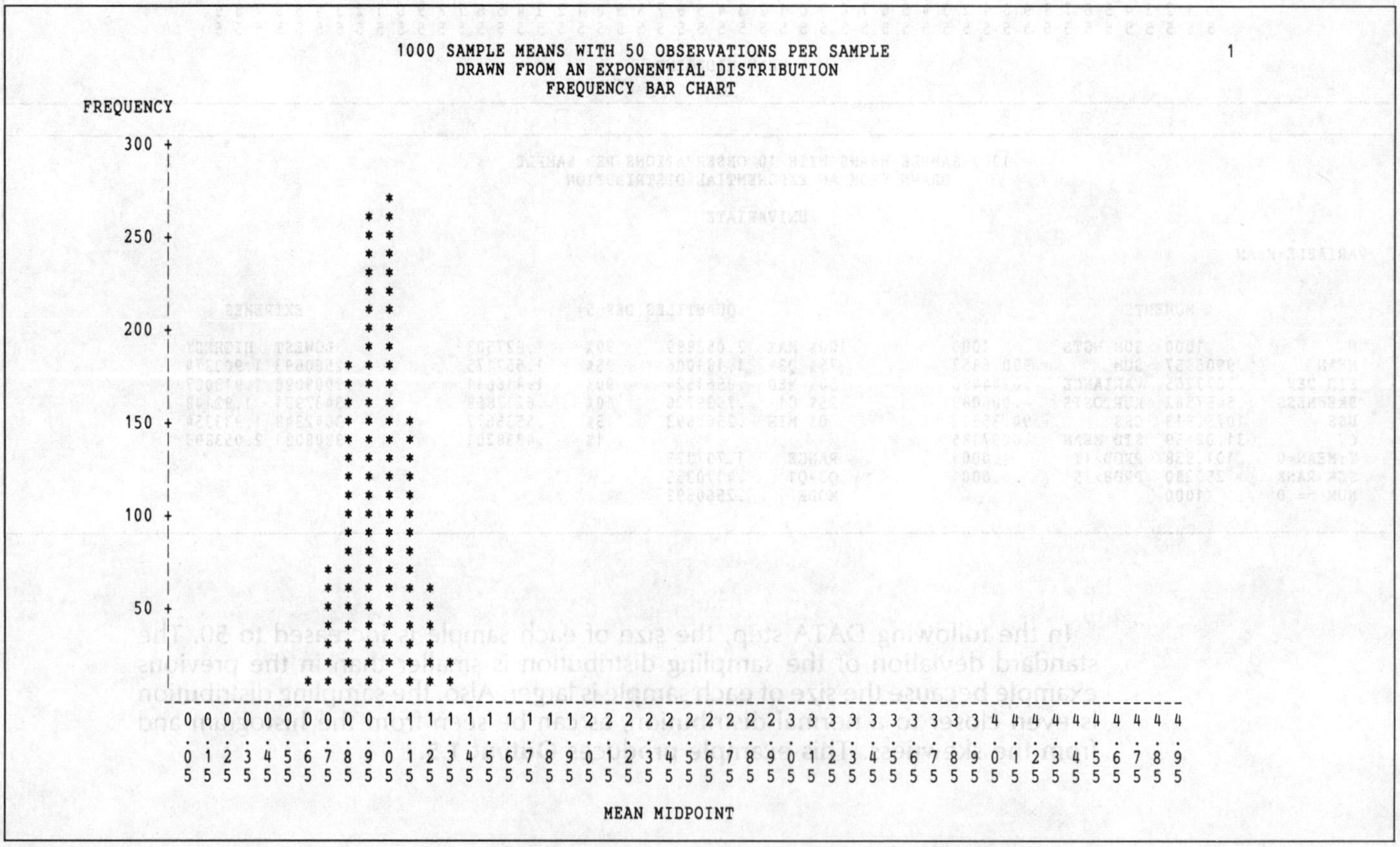

```
                 1000 SAMPLE MEANS WITH 50 OBSERVATIONS PER SAMPLE                          2
                         DRAWN FROM AN EXPONENTIAL DISTRIBUTION
                                           UNIVARIATE

VARIABLE=MEAN

                  MOMENTS                                 QUANTILES(DEF=5)                                  EXTREMES

 N              1000  SUM WGTS       1000      100% MAX 1.454957      99%    1.337016            LOWEST  HIGHEST
 MEAN        .996797  SUM         996.797       75% Q3  1.086515      95%    1.231508          .5845583 1.375359
 STD DEV     .138154  VARIANCE   .0190865       50% MED .9960226      90%    1.179223          .6702515 1.378008
 SKEWNESS   .1906263  KURTOSIS    -.14386       25% Q1   .896953      10%    .8149059          .6714301 1.391916
 USS        1012.672  CSS        19.06745        0% MIN .5845583       5%    .7807826          .6722099 1.403003
 CV          13.8598  STD MEAN   .0043688                              1%    .7065879           .680194 1.454957
 T:MEAN=0   228.1619  PROB>|T|      .0001       RANGE   .8703986
 SGN RANK     250250  PROB>|S|      .0001       Q3-Q1   .1895618
 NUM ¬= 0       1000                            MODE    .5845583
```

Testing Hypotheses

The purpose of the statistical methods discussed so far is to estimate a population parameter by means of a sample statistic. Another class of statistical methods is used for testing hypotheses about population parameters or for measuring the amount of evidence against a hypothesis.

Consider the aforementioned universe of students. Let the variable X be the number of pounds by which a student's weight deviates from the ideal weight for a person of the same sex, height, and build. You want to find out whether the population of students is, on the average, underweight or overweight. To this end, you have taken a random sample of X values from nine students, with results as given in the following DATA step:

```
DATA X;
   TITLE 'DEVIATIONS FROM NORMAL WEIGHT';
   INPUT X @@;
   CARDS;
-7 -2 1 3 6 10 15 21 30
;
```

You can define several hypotheses of interest. One hypothesis is that, on the average, the students are of exactly ideal weight. If μ represents the population mean of the X values, you can write this hypothesis, called the *null* hypothesis, as H_0: $\mu=0$. The other two hypotheses, called *alternative* hypotheses, are that the students are underweight on the average, H_1: $\mu<0$, and that the students are overweight on the average, H_2: $\mu>0$.

The null hypothesis is so called not because the hypothesized parameter value is zero, but because the hypothesis specifies a particular value for the parameter. The null hypotheses is not credible because the mean of a continuous variable is almost never exactly equal to any known value. The null hypothesis can be considered a straw man to be knocked down by statistical evidence, and you can decide between the alternative hypotheses according to which way it falls.

A naive way to approach this problem would be to look at the sample mean $\bar{x}$ and decide among the three hypotheses according to the following rule:

- if $\bar{x}<0$, decide on H_1: $\mu<0$
- if $\bar{x}=0$, decide on H_0: $\mu=0$
- if $\bar{x}>0$, decide on H_2: $\mu>0$.

The trouble with this approach is that there may be a high probability of making an incorrect decision. If H_0 is true, you are nearly certain to make a wrong decision because the chances of $\bar{x}$ being exactly zero are almost nil. If μ is slightly less than zero, so that H_1 is true, there may be nearly a 50% chance that $\bar{x}$ will be greater than zero in repeated sampling, so the chances of incorrectly choosing H_2 would also be nearly 50%. Thus, you have a high probability of making an error if $\bar{x}$ is near zero. In such cases, there is not enough evidence to make a confident decision, so the best response may be to reserve judgment until you can obtain more evidence.

The question is, how far from zero must $\bar{x}$ be for you to be able to make a confident decision? The answer can be obtained by considering the sampling distribution of $\bar{x}$. If X has a roughly normal distribution, then $\bar{x}$ has an approximately normal sampling distribution. The mean of the sampling distribution of $\bar{x}$ is μ. Assume temporarily that σ, the standard deviation of X, is known to be 12. Then the standard error of $\bar{x}$ for samples of nine observations is $\sigma/\sqrt{n} = 12/\sqrt{9} = 4$. You know that about 95% of the values from a normal distribution are within two standard deviations of the mean, so about 95% of the possible samples of nine X values have a sample mean $\bar{x}$ between $0-2 \times 4$ and $0+2 \times 4$, or between -8 and 8. Consider the chances of making an error with the following decision rule:

- if $\bar{x}<-8$, decide on H_1: $\mu<0$
- if $-8<=\bar{x}<=8$, reserve judgment
- if $\bar{x}>8$, decide on H_2: $\mu>0$.

If H_0 is true, then in about 95% of the possible samples $\bar{x}$ will be between the *critical values* -8 and 8, so you will reserve judgment. In these cases the statistical evidence is not strong enough to fell the straw man. In the other 5% of the samples you will make an error; in 2.5% you will incorrectly choose H_1, and in 2.5% you will incorrectly choose H_2.

If H_1 is true, you will make an error only if $\bar{x}$ is greater than 8. To calculate the chances of this occurrence you need to know the actual value of μ, but the chance of an error cannot exceed 2.5%. Similarly, the chance of an incorrect decision if H_2 is true cannot exceed 2.5%.

Thus, using this decision rule, you will make an incorrect decision in at most about 5% of the possible samples. The price you pay for controlling the chances of making an error is the necessity of reserving judgment when there is not sufficient statistical evidence to reject the null hypothesis.

Significance and power The probability of rejecting the null hypothesis if it is true is called the *significance* level of the statistical test. In this example, an $\bar{x}$ value less than -8 or greater than 8 is said to be *statistically significant* at the 5% level. You can adjust the significance level according to your needs by choosing different critical values. For example, critical values of -4 and 4 would produce a significance level of about 32%, while -12 and 12 would give a significance level of about 0.3%.

The decision rule stated above is a *two-tailed* test because the alternative hypotheses allow for population means either smaller or larger than the value specified in the null hypothesis. If you were interested only in the possibility of the students being overweight on the average, you could use a *one-tailed* test:

- if $\bar{x}<=8$, reserve judgment
- if $\bar{x}>8$, decide on H_2: $\mu>0$.

For this one-tailed test, the significance level is 2.5%, half that of the two-tailed test.

The probability of rejecting the null hypothesis if it is false is called the *power* of the statistical test. The power depends on the true value of the parameter. In the example, assume the population mean is 4. The power for detecting H_2 is the probability of getting a sample mean greater than 8. The critical value 8 is one standard error higher than the population mean 4. The chance of getting a value at least one standard deviation greater than the mean from a normal distribution is about 16%, so the power for detecting the alternative hypothesis H_2

is about 16%. If the population mean were 8, the power for H_2 would be 50%, whereas a population mean of 12 would yield a power of about 84%.

The smaller the significance level, the less the chance of making an incorrect decision, but the higher the chance of having to reserve judgment. In choosing a significance level, you should consider the resulting power for various alternatives of interest.

Student's t distribution Unfortunately, you could not really use the decision rule described above because you do not know the value of σ. You could, however, use *s* as an estimate of σ. Consider the following statistic:

$$t = (\bar{x} - \mu_0)/(s/\sqrt{n})$$

which is the difference between the sample mean and the hypothesized mean μ_0 divided by the estimated standard error of the mean. A *t* statistic for the null hypothesis that $\mu=0$ can be obtained along with related statistics from PROC MEANS:

```
PROC MEANS DATA=X N MEAN STD STDERR T PRT;
```

If the null hypothesis is true and the population is normally distributed, then the *t* statistic has what is called a *Student's t distribution* with *n-1 degrees of freedom*. This distribution looks very similar to a normal distribution, but the tails of the Student's *t* distribution are heavier. As the sample size gets larger, the sample standard deviation becomes a better estimator of the population standard deviation, and the *t* distribution gets closer to a normal distribution.

You can base a decision rule on the *t* statistic:

- if $t<-2.3$, decide on H_1: $\mu<0$
- if $-2.3<=t<=2.3$, reserve judgment
- if $t>2.3$, decide on H_2: $\mu>0$.

The value 2.3 was obtained from a table of Student's *t* distribution in a statistics text to give a significance level of 5% for 8 (that is, 9−1) degrees of freedom. If you do not have a statistics text handy, you can print a table of the *t* distribution using a DATA step. This example produces **Output 1.6** .

```
DATA _NULL_;
   TITLE;
   FILE PRINT;
   ARRAY P P1-P7;
   RETAIN P1 .10 P2 .05 P3 .025 P4 .01 P5 .005 P6 .0025 P7 .001;
   PUT '                TABLE OF STUDENT''S T DISTRIBUTION'
     / '                ----------------------------------'
    // '  DF                 TWO-TAILED SIGNIFICANCE LEVEL'
     / '  --   ------------------------------------------------------'
     / '      ' @;
   DO OVER P;
      PC=100*P;
      PUT PC BEST7. '%' @;
      END;
   PUT /;
   DO DF=1 TO 30, 35 TO 50 BY 5, 60 TO 100 BY 10, 200 TO 1000 BY 100;
      PUT DF 4. @;
      DO OVER P;
         B=BETAINV(P,DF/2,.5);
         F=DF*(1-B)/B;
```

```
        T=SQRT(F);
        PUT T 8.3 @;
        END;
     PUT;
     END;
```

In the current example, the value of the *t* statistic is 2.18, so using a 5% significance level you must reserve judgment. If you had elected to use a 10% significance level, the critical value of the *t* distribution would have been 1.86 and you could have rejected the null hypothesis. The sample size is so small, however, that the validity of your conclusion depends strongly on how close the distribution of the population is to a normal distribution.

Probability values Another way to report the results of a statistical test is to compute a *probability value* or *p-value*. A *p*-value gives the probability in repeated sampling of obtaining a statistic as far from the value specified in the null hypothesis as is the value actually observed. A two-tailed *p*-value for a *t* statistic is the probability of obtaining an absolute *t* value greater than the observed absolute *t* value. A one-tailed *p*-value for a *t* statistic for the alternative hypothesis $\mu>\mu_0$ is the probability of obtaining a *t* value greater than the observed *t* value. Once the *p*-value is computed, you can perform a hypothesis test by comparing the *p*-value with the desired significance level. If the *p*-value is less than the significance level of the test, the null hypothesis can be rejected. In the example, the two-tailed *p*-value, labeled PR> |T| on the PROC MEANS printout, is .0606, so the null hypothesis could be rejected at the 10% significance level but not at the 5% level.

Output 1.6 Output of a Table Showing the T Distribution

DEVIATIONS FROM NORMAL WEIGHT — 1

VARIABLE	N	MEAN	STANDARD DEVIATION	STD ERROR OF MEAN	T	PR>|T|
X	9	8.55555556	11.75915719	3.91971906	2.18	0.0606

TABLE OF STUDENT'S T DISTRIBUTION — 2

DF	TWO-TAILED SIGNIFICANCE LEVEL						
	10%	5%	2.5%	1%	0.5%	0.25%	0.1%
1	6.314	12.706	25.452	63.657	127.321	254.647	636.619
2	2.920	4.303	6.205	9.925	14.089	19.962	31.599
3	2.353	3.182	4.177	5.841	7.453	9.465	12.924
4	2.132	2.776	3.495	4.604	5.598	6.758	8.610
5	2.015	2.571	3.163	4.032	4.773	5.604	6.869
6	1.943	2.447	2.969	3.707	4.317	4.981	5.959
7	1.895	2.365	2.841	3.499	4.029	4.595	5.408
8	1.860	2.306	2.752	3.355	3.833	4.334	5.041
9	1.833	2.262	2.685	3.250	3.690	4.146	4.781
10	1.812	2.228	2.634	3.169	3.581	4.005	4.587
11	1.796	2.201	2.593	3.106	3.497	3.895	4.437
12	1.782	2.179	2.560	3.055	3.428	3.807	4.318
13	1.771	2.160	2.533	3.012	3.372	3.735	4.221
14	1.761	2.145	2.510	2.977	3.326	3.675	4.140
15	1.753	2.131	2.490	2.947	3.286	3.624	4.073
16	1.746	2.120	2.473	2.921	3.252	3.581	4.015
17	1.740	2.110	2.458	2.898	3.222	3.543	3.965

(continued on next page)

(continued from previous page)

18	1.734	2.101	2.445	2.878	3.197	3.510	3.922
19	1.729	2.093	2.433	2.861	3.174	3.481	3.883
20	1.725	2.086	2.423	2.845	3.153	3.455	3.850
21	1.721	2.080	2.414	2.831	3.135	3.432	3.819
22	1.717	2.074	2.405	2.819	3.119	3.412	3.792
23	1.714	2.069	2.398	2.807	3.104	3.393	3.768
24	1.711	2.064	2.391	2.797	3.091	3.376	3.745
25	1.708	2.060	2.385	2.787	3.078	3.361	3.725
26	1.706	2.056	2.379	2.779	3.067	3.346	3.707
27	1.703	2.052	2.373	2.771	3.057	3.333	3.690
28	1.701	2.048	2.368	2.763	3.047	3.321	3.674
29	1.699	2.045	2.364	2.756	3.038	3.310	3.659
30	1.697	2.042	2.360	2.750	3.030	3.300	3.646
35	1.690	2.030	2.342	2.724	2.996	3.258	3.591
40	1.684	2.021	2.329	2.704	2.971	3.227	3.551
45	1.679	2.014	2.319	2.690	2.952	3.203	3.520
50	1.676	2.009	2.311	2.678	2.937	3.184	3.496
60	1.671	2.000	2.299	2.660	2.915	3.156	3.460
70	1.667	1.994	2.291	2.648	2.899	3.137	3.435
80	1.664	1.990	2.284	2.639	2.887	3.122	3.416
90	1.662	1.987	2.280	2.632	2.878	3.111	3.402
100	1.660	1.984	2.276	2.626	2.871	3.102	3.390
200	1.653	1.972	2.258	2.601	2.839	3.062	3.340
300	1.650	1.968	2.253	2.592	2.828	3.049	3.323
400	1.649	1.966	2.250	2.588	2.823	3.043	3.315
500	1.648	1.965	2.248	2.586	2.820	3.039	3.310
600	1.647	1.964	2.247	2.584	2.817	3.036	3.307
700	1.647	1.963	2.246	2.583	2.816	3.034	3.304
800	1.647	1.963	2.246	2.582	2.815	3.033	3.303
900	1.647	1.963	2.245	2.581	2.814	3.032	3.301
1000	1.646	1.962	2.245	2.581	2.813	3.031	3.300

A *p*-value is a measure of the strength of the evidence against the null hypothesis. The smaller the *p*-value, the stronger the evidence for rejecting the null hypothesis.

Bivariate Measures

Bivariate statistics measure the degree of dependence between two variables. Bivariate measures for continuous variables are available in PROC CORR. These include correlations, rank correlations, and measures of concordance. These measures are discussed in detail in the CORR procedure description.

References

Ali, M.M. (1974), "Stochastic Ordering and Kurtosis Measure," JASA, 69, 543-545.

Fisher, R.A. (1973), *Statistical Methods for Research Workers*, 14th Edition, New York: Hafner Publishing Company.

Johnson, M.E., Tietjen, G.L., and Beckman, R.J. (1980), "A New Family of Probability Distributions With Applications to Monte Carlo Studies," JASA, 75, 276-279.

Kaplansky, I. (1945), "A Common Error Concerning Kurtosis," JASA, 40, 259-263.

Moore, D.S. (1979), *Statistics: Concepts and Controversies*, San Francisco: W.H. Freeman and Company.

Ott, L. (1977), *An Introduction to Statistical Methods and Data Analysis*, North Scituate, Mass.: Duxbury Press.

Snedecor, G.W. and Cochran, W.C. (1967), *Statistical Methods*, 6th Edition, Ames, Iowa: Iowa State University Press.

Chapter 2

SAS® Reporting Procedures

Introduction

Reporting procedures produce a display of information. The display can be a listing of data, an organized display of data, or a graphical display such as a bar chart or a scatter plot. Most descriptive and statistical procedures also produce reports to display results, but the procedures in this section are specialized for reporting.

PRINT	prints values from a SAS data set.
FORMS	prints mailing list labels or other data laid out in repetitive forms.
CHART	charts frequencies and other statistics with bar charts and other pictorial representations.
PLOT	plots variables in a scatter diagram.
CALENDAR	prints data in the form of a summary or schedule calendar.
TIMEPLOT	plots one or more variables over time intervals.

In addition to these procedures, the PUT statement in the DATA step can be used to program custom reports. (See the discussion of the PUT statement in *SAS Language Guide for Personal Computers*.)

The PRINT Procedure

The PRINT procedure is an easy procedure for listing the data in a SAS data set. The simplest invocation

```
PROC PRINT;
```

prints the most recently created SAS data set. Each variable in the data set forms a column of the report; each observation of the data set forms a row of the report. If you want variables to form rows and observations to form columns, use PROC TRANSPOSE to change variables into observations and vice versa before you print the data set.

PROC PRINT is able to

- use FORMAT statements to associate variables with formats

- use TITLE and FOOTNOTE statements to define up to ten title and ten footnote lines
- use LINESIZE= and PAGESIZE= system options to control size
- print any subset of the variables
- use an ID variable to identify observations
- divide the report into sections when there are too many variables to fit across the page
- separate groups of observations according to BY groups
- print totals and other statistics for all observations and BY groups
- print variable labels as column headings.

You tell PROC PRINT what to do, not how to do it. While other SAS reporting methods can require a lot of programming, no programming is required with PROC PRINT.

But the PRINT procedure may be too limited for some applications. It cannot select subsets of the observations to print, and almost all computations must be done ahead of time in DATA steps.

The following example creates a SAS data set and then prints it twice using PROC PRINT, once in a very simple manner and again using formats, totals, variable labels, and an ID variable. See **Output 2.1**.

```
DATA A;
   INPUT YEAR SALES COST;
   PROFIT=SALES-COST;
   CARDS;
1981 12132 11021
1982 19823 12928
1983 16982 14002
1984 18432 14590
;

PROC PRINT DATA=A;
   TITLE 'SIMPLE PROC PRINT REPORT';
PROC PRINT DATA=A SPLIT='*';
   LABEL SALES='SALES FOR *  YEAR'
      COST='TOTAL COST'
      PROFIT='PROFIT BEFORE *    TAXES';
   FORMAT SALES COST PROFIT DOLLAR10.2;
   ID YEAR;
   SUM SALES COST PROFIT;
   TITLE 'PROC PRINT WITH TOTALS, FORMATS, LABELS, AND ID VARIABLE';
```

Output 2.1 Two PROC PRINT Reports

```
                          SIMPLE PROC PRINT REPORT                                    1
                    OBS    YEAR    SALES    COST     PROFIT

                     1     1981    12132    11021     1111
                     2     1982    19823    12928     6895
                     3     1983    16982    14002     2980
                     4     1984    18432    14590     3842
```

```
          PROC PRINT WITH TOTALS, FORMATS, LABELS, AND ID VARIABLE                    2

              YEAR     SALES FOR        TOTAL        PROFIT BEFORE
                          YEAR          COST             TAXES

              1981    $12,132.00    $11,021.00       $1,111.00
              1982    $19,823.00    $12,928.00       $6,895.00
              1983    $16,982.00    $14,002.00       $2,980.00
              1984    $18,432.00    $14,590.00       $3,842.00
                      ==========    ==========      ==========
                      $67,369.00    $52,541.00      $14,828.00
```

The FORMS Procedure

The FORMS procedure is designed to print mailing labels and other types of repetitive forms. This example adds labeling variables to the data in order to identify the fields on the form units. The forms are laid out three units across the page, as shown in **Output 2.2**.

```
DATA B;
   SET A;
   TYEAR ='YEAR  = ';
   TSALES='SALES = ';
   TCOST ='COST  = ';
PROC FORMS W=20 D=1 NA=3 BETWEEN=5 DATA=B;
   FORMAT SALES COST COMMA10.2 YEAR 10.;
   LINE 1 TYEAR YEAR;
   LINE 2 TSALES SALES;
   LINE 3 TCOST COST;
```

Output 2.2 PROC FORMS Report

```
                                                                                      1

YEAR  =          1981     YEAR  =          1982     YEAR  =          1983
SALES =     12,132.00     SALES =     19,823.00     SALES =     16,982.00
COST  =     11,021.00     COST  =     12,928.00     COST  =     14,002.00

YEAR  =          1984
SALES =     18,432.00
COST  =     14,590.00
```

The CHART Procedure

The CHART procedure draws a variety of charts: horizontal and vertical bar charts, block charts, pie charts, and star charts. The procedure can chart counts, percentages, means, and sums. **Output 2.3** is a block chart of the PROFIT variable from the PRINT example.

```
PROC CHART DATA=A;
   TITLE 'PROC CHART REPORT ON PROFIT';
   BLOCK YEAR / SUMVAR=PROFIT DISCRETE SYMBOL='XOA';
```

Output 2.3 PROC CHART Report

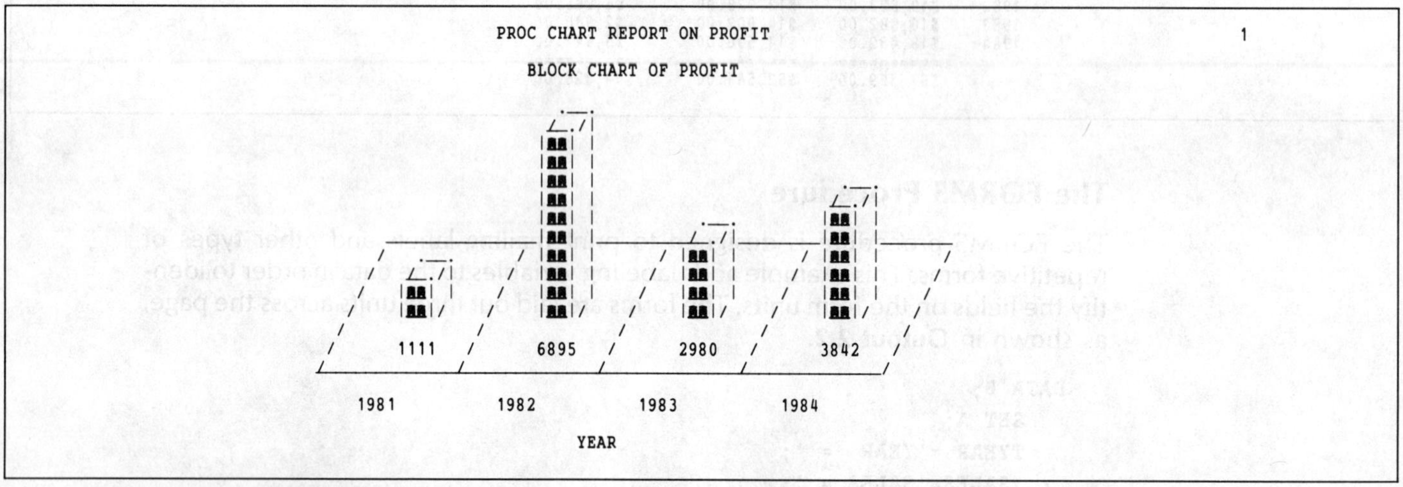

The PLOT Procedure

The PLOT procedure draws scatter plots. The following example plots three variables against YEAR. The three variables appear on the same plot, identified by different plotting characters. See **Output 2.4**.

```
PROC PLOT DATA=A;
   TITLE 'PROC PLOT REPORT: P=PROFIT S=SALES C=COST';
   PLOT PROFIT*YEAR='P'
        SALES*YEAR='S'
        COST*YEAR='C' / OVERLAY VPOS=20 HPOS=32;
```

Output 2.4 PROC PLOT Report

```
PROC PLOT REPORT: P=PROFIT S=SALES C=COST                                1

 PLOT OF PROFIT*YEAR      SYMBOL USED IS P
 PLOT OF SALES*YEAR       SYMBOL USED IS S
 PLOT OF COST*YEAR        SYMBOL USED IS C

 PROFIT |
        |
        |
 20000  +          S
        |                            S
        |                  S
        |
 15000  +                            C
        |                  C
        |S         C
        |C
 10000  +
        |
        |          P
        |
  5000  +
        |                            P
        |                  P
        |P
     0  +
       -+---------+---------+---------+-
       1981      1982      1983      1984

                     YEAR
```

The CALENDAR Procedure

Use the CALENDAR procedure if you have either daily data on some activity or data representing events, each of which is identified by a date. In both cases, CALENDAR displays the data in the form of a monthly calendar. You can specify formats for variables, missing value options, and customized borders for the calendar. You can also specify the calendar to cover all the days in a month or weekdays only (Monday-Friday). This procedure is useful for two main applications:

- daily reporting, such as daily tallies of sales or usage. You can also collect sums and means.
- scheduling, making calendars of events.

Output 2.5 is a summary calendar that displays telephone calls received by a library during daytime and evening hours. Variables are printed using picture formats created by PROC FORMAT, and sums and means of the variables appear in the legend.

```
DATA TEL;
   INPUT DATE : DATE. DAY NIGHT @@;
   CARDS;
 1OCT85 33 48   2OCT85 29 10   3OCT85 18 35   4OCT85 18 23
 5OCT85 36 45   6OCT85 25 44   7OCT85 28 40   8OCT85 29 49
 9OCT85 31 17  10OCT85 20 .   11OCT85 19 29  12OCT85 30 11
13OCT85 28 49  14OCT85 27 46  15OCT85 20 36  16OCT85 27 48
17OCT85 20 39  18OCT85 27 46  19OCT85 20 36  20OCT85 27 48
21OCT85 33 48  22OCT85 29 10  23OCT85 18 35  24OCT85 18 23
25OCT85 36 45  26OCT85 25 44  27OCT85 28 40  28OCT85 29 49
29OCT85 31 17  30OCT85 20 .   31OCT85 19 29
;
PROC FORMAT;
   PICTURE DDD OTHER='000 DAY';
   PICTURE NNN OTHER='000 NIGHT';
PROC CALENDAR HEADER=SMALL LEGEND;
```

```
ID DATE;
VAR DAY NIGHT;
SUM DAY NIGHT;
MEAN DAY NIGHT;
LABEL DAY='DAYTIME CALLS' NIGHT='NIGHT CALLS';
FORMAT DAY DDD. NIGHT NNN. ;
TITLE 'TELEPHONE CALLS RECEIVED AT CITY LIBRARY';
```

Output 2.5 PROC CALENDAR Report

```
                          TELEPHONE CALLS RECEIVED AT CITY LIBRARY                                1

                                        OCTOBER  1985

   -------------------------------------------------------------------------------------------
   |  SUNDAY   |  MONDAY   |  TUESDAY  | WEDNESDAY | THURSDAY  |  FRIDAY   | SATURDAY  |
   |-----------+-----------+-----------+-----------+-----------+-----------+-----------|
   |           |           |     1     |     2     |     3     |     4     |     5     |
   |           |           |           |           |           |           |           |
   |           |           | 33 DAY    | 29 DAY    | 18 DAY    | 18 DAY    | 36 DAY    |
   |           |           | 48 NIGHT  | 10 NIGHT  | 35 NIGHT  | 23 NIGHT  | 45 NIGHT  |
   |-----------+-----------+-----------+-----------+-----------+-----------+-----------|
   |     6     |     7     |     8     |     9     |    10     |    11     |    12     |
   |           |           |           |           |           |           |           |
   | 25 DAY    | 28 DAY    | 29 DAY    | 31 DAY    | 20 DAY    | 19 DAY    | 30 DAY    |
   | 44 NIGHT  | 40 NIGHT  | 49 NIGHT  | 17 NIGHT  |           | 29 NIGHT  | 11 NIGHT  |
   |-----------+-----------+-----------+-----------+-----------+-----------+-----------|
   |    13     |    14     |    15     |    16     |    17     |    18     |    19     |
   |           |           |           |           |           |           |           |
   | 28 DAY    | 27 DAY    | 20 DAY    | 27 DAY    | 20 DAY    | 27 DAY    | 20 DAY    |
   | 49 NIGHT  | 46 NIGHT  | 36 NIGHT  | 48 NIGHT  | 39 NIGHT  | 46 NIGHT  | 36 NIGHT  |
   |-----------+-----------+-----------+-----------+-----------+-----------+-----------|
   |    20     |    21     |    22     |    23     |    24     |    25     |    26     |
   | 27 DAY    | 33 DAY    | 29 DAY    | 18 DAY    | 18 DAY    | 36 DAY    | 25 DAY    |
   | 48 NIGHT  | 48 NIGHT  | 10 NIGHT  | 35 NIGHT  | 23 NIGHT  | 45 NIGHT  | 44 NIGHT  |
   |-----------+-----------+-----------+-----------+-----------+-----------+-----------|
   |    27     |    28     |    29     |    30     |    31     |           |           |
   | 28 DAY    | 29 DAY    | 31 DAY    | 20 DAY    | 19 DAY    |           |           |
   | 40 NIGHT  | 49 NIGHT  | 17 NIGHT  |           | 29 NIGHT  |           |           |
   -------------------------------------------------------------------------------------------

                         ---------------------------------------------
                         |    LEGEND     |    SUM    |     MEAN      |
                         |               |           |               |
                         | DAYTIME CALLS |       798 |     25.7419   |
                         | NIGHT CALLS   |      1039 |     35.8276   |
                         ---------------------------------------------
```

The TIMEPLOT Procedure

The TIMEPLOT procedure produces a plot and a listing of observations in the data set similar to that produced by the PLOT and PRINT procedures. However, a plot produced by TIMEPLOT has these features:

- The vertical axis always represents the sequence of observations in the data set; thus, if the observations are arranged chronologically, the vertical axis represents time.
- The horizontal axis contains values of the variables you are examining.
- A plot can occupy more than one page.
- Each observation appears on a separate line; no observations are hidden as can occur with PROC PLOT.
- Each observation in the plot is accompanied by a listing of the values plotted.

The following example overlays plots of U.S. and world cotton production on the same axes. A vertical reference line appears at the mean value of each variable, and a horizontal line connects the values within each observation. See **Output 2.6**.

```
DATA COTTON;
   INPUT YEAR US WORLD @@;
   LABEL US='US COTTON PRODUCTION'
      WORLD='WORLD COTTON PRODUCTION';
   CARDS;
1940 12.6 31.2 1975  8.3 54.0
1950 10.0 30.6 1976 10.6 57.4
1960 14.2 46.2 1977 14.4 63.5
1965 15.0 55.0 1978 10.9 60.2
1970 10.2 53.6 1979 14.6 65.7
1972 13.7 62.9 1980 11.1 65.5
1973 13.0 63.3 1981 15.6 70.8
1974 11.5 64.3 1982 12.0 67.4
;
PROC SORT;
   BY YEAR;
PROC TIMEPLOT;
   PLOT US WORLD / OVERLAY REF=MEAN(US WORLD) HILOC POS=64;
   ID YEAR;
   TITLE 'TRENDS IN COTTON PRODUCTION';
   TITLE2 'SELECTED YEARS 1940-1982';
   TITLE4 '(MILLIONS OF BALES)';
RUN;
```

Output 2.6 PROC TIMEPLOT Report

```
                                     TRENDS IN COTTON PRODUCTION                                     1
                                      SELECTED YEARS 1940-1982

                                        (MILLIONS OF BALES)

YEAR      US COTTON        WORLD COTTON      MIN                                                            MAX
         PRODUCTION         PRODUCTION       8.3                                                           70.8
                                             *----------------------------------------------------------------*
1940          12.60              31.20       |    U------------------W                          |             |
1950          10.00              30.60       |  U-|------------------W                          |             |
1960          14.20              46.20       |    | U--------------------------------W          |             |
1965          15.00              55.00       |    |  U----------------------------------------W |             |
1970          10.20              53.60       |  U-|-----------------------------------------W   |             |
1972          13.70              62.90       |    | U-------------------------------------------|-----W       |
1973          13.00              63.30       |    |U--------------------------------------------|-----W       |
1974          11.50              64.30       |   U|---------------------------------------------|------W      |
1975           8.30              54.00       |U---|------------------------------------------W  |             |
1976          10.60              57.40       |  U-|---------------------------------------------W             |
1977          14.40              63.50       |    | U-------------------------------------------|------W      |
1978          10.90              60.20       |   U|---------------------------------------------|--W          |
1979          14.60              65.70       |    | U-------------------------------------------|--------W    |
1980          11.10              65.50       |   U|---------------------------------------------|--------W    |
1981          15.60              70.80       |    |  U------------------------------------------|------------W|
1982          12.00              67.40       |    U---------------------------------------------|----------W  |
                                             *----------------------------------------------------------------*
```

Reports Written with PUT Statements

The PUT statement is a program statement used in a DATA step. Reports written with PUT statements use program statements to create the form of the report. You specify the column positions and program every calculation.

Using PUT statements for report writing is documented in detail in *SAS Language Guide for Personal Computers*. **Output 2.7** is an example of a report produced with PUT statements.

You want to print the observations as columns and the variables as rows in the report. This is most conveniently done with the N=PS feature (see the **FILE Statement** in *SAS Language Guide for Personal Computers*) and by computing column positions with program statements. The variable C indexes column positions corresponding to observations from the data and a column for the total.

```
DATA _NULL_;
   FILE PRINT N=PS;
   TITLE 'PUT STATEMENT REPORT';
   *---BRING IN THREE OBSERVATIONS PER PAGE---;
   DO C=25 TO 61 BY 12;      *---C WILL BE THE PRINTING COLUMN---;
      SET A END=EOF;         *---BRING IN AN OBSERVATION HERE----;
      *---COMPUTE GROSS PROFIT AND ACCUMULATE TOTALS---;
      TOTSALES+SALES;
      TOTCGS+COST;
      TOTPROF+PROFIT;
      *---PRINT OUT A COLUMN FOR THIS MONTH---;
      PUT #5
          'YEAR'                @C YEAR     10.
      // 'GROSS REVENUE'       @C SALES    10.2
       / 'COST OF GOODS SOLD'  @C COST      10.2
       /                       @C '=========='
       / 'GROSS PROFIT'        @C PROFIT 10.2;
      *---AT END OF DATA---;
      IF EOF THEN DO;
         C=C+12;
         *---COMPUTE MARGIN AND PRINT TOTALS---;
         PCTMARG=100*TOTPROF/TOTCGS;
         PUT #5 @C '   TOTAL'
              // @C TOTSALES   10.2
               / @C TOTCGS     10.2
               / @C '=========='
               / @C TOTPROF   10.2
              // 'PROFIT MARGIN PERCENT OF COST' @C PCTMARG 10.2;
         END;
      END;
```

Output 2.7 PUT Statement Report

```
                                  PUT STATEMENT REPORT                                   1


YEAR                        1981        1982        1983        1984      TOTAL

GROSS REVENUE           12132.00    19823.00    16982.00    18432.00   67369.00
COST OF GOODS SOLD      11021.00    12928.00    14002.00    14590.00   52541.00
                      ==========  ==========  ==========  ==========  ==========
GROSS PROFIT             1111.00     6895.00     2980.00     3842.00   14828.00

PROFIT MARGIN PERCENT OF COST                                              28.22
```

Chapter 3
SAS® Scoring Procedures

Scoring procedures are utilities that produce an output data set with new variables that are transformations of data in the old data set. PROC STANDARD transforms each variable individually. PROC RANK produces rank scores across observations. Both procedures produce an output data set, but no printed output.

STANDARD	standardizes variables to a given mean and standard deviation.
RANK	ranks the observations of each numeric variable from low to high and outputs ranks or rank scores.

Chapter 4

SAS® Utility Procedures

A utility procedure performs a specific type of intermediate processing or data manipulation. Following is a list and brief description of utility procedures, which are fully described in this book. If you are unable to find a utility procedure to do exactly what you want, you can probably program a DATA step to handle the task.

APPEND	appends data from one SAS data set to the end of another SAS data set.
CONTENTS	describes the contents of a SAS data library or specified members of the library.
COPY	copies a SAS data library or selected members of the library.
DATASETS	manages a SAS data library.
DBF	converts VisiCalc and Lotus 1-2-3 files to SAS data sets.
DIF	converts dBASE II and dBASE III files to SAS data sets.
DOWNLOAD	moves SAS data sets from a mainframe computer to a microcomputer.
FORMAT	defines output formats for value labeling.
SORT	sorts a SAS data set according to one or more variables.
TRANSPOSE	turns a SAS data set on its side, changing variables into observations and observations into variables.
UPLOAD	moves SAS data sets from a microcomputer to a mainframe computer.

Chapter 5

The APPEND Procedure

ABSTRACT

The APPEND procedure adds the observations from one SAS data set to the end of another SAS data set.

INTRODUCTION

The APPEND procedure operates only on SAS data sets (library members of DATA type). Refer to the "SAS Files" chapter in *SAS Language Guide for Personal Computers* to familiarize yourself with SAS data sets and related terminology.

Often you need to add new observations to a SAS data set. If you use a DATA step to concatenate two data sets, the SAS System must process all the observations in both data sets to create a new one. The APPEND procedure bypasses the processing of data in the original data set and adds new observations directly to the end of the original data set.

Another method of adding observations to the end of a SAS data set is available with the APPEND statement in PROC DATASETS (described later in this book).

SPECIFICATIONS

The PROC statement is the only statement associated with the APPEND procedure.

PROC APPEND BASE=*SASdataset options;*

PROC APPEND Statement

PROC APPEND BASE=*SASdataset options;*

BASE=*SASdataset*
OUT=*SASdataset*

names the data set to which you want to add observations. If APPEND cannot find an existing data set with this name, it creates a new data set. In other words, you can use PROC APPEND to create a data set by specifying a new data set name in BASE=. OUT= is equivalent to BASE=. Either BASE= or OUT= must be specified.

The APPEND procedure can be used with these options:

DATA=*SASdataset*
NEW=*SASdataset*

names the SAS data set containing observations to be added to the end of the SAS data set specified by BASE=. If DATA= is omitted, the most recently created SAS data set is used. NEW= is equivalent to DATA=.

FORCE

causes truncation of values if variables in the DATA= data set have longer lengths than the corresponding variables in the BASE= data set. FORCE also causes variables in the DATA= data set to be dropped if there are not corresponding variables in the BASE= data set. DATA= variables that do not match BASE= variables are assigned missing values in the output (BASE=) data set when FORCE is in effect. A mismatch occurs if a DATA= variable name or variable type (character or numeric) does not match a corresponding variable name or variable type in the BASE= data set. If DATA= variables are too long or do not match BASE= variables, the SAS System prints a message on the log and stops processing unless FORCE is specified.

DETAILS

Usage Notes

When the APPEND procedure has finished processing, the BASE= data set in its modified form becomes the current SAS data set.

Using PROC APPEND can be more efficient than using a SET statement in the DATA step to concatenate two data sets, especially if the BASE= data set is large. Consider the following example:

```
DATA LARGE;
   SET LARGE SMALL;
```

To perform this concatenation, the SAS System must read all observations in both the LARGE and SMALL data sets. With the APPEND procedure you can add the observations in the SMALL data set to the end of the LARGE data set without reading the observations in LARGE. For example, the statement

```
PROC APPEND BASE=LARGE DATA=SMALL;
```

offers a much more efficient way to concatenate the two data sets. The procedure is very useful if observations are frequently added to a SAS data set (for example, in production programs that are constantly appending data to a journal-type data set).

If all variables in the BASE= data set have the same length and relative position as the variables in the DATA= data set and if all variables exist in both data sets, the procedure executes faster. You can use PROC CONTENTS with the

POSITION option for each data set to see if the variable lengths and positions are identical.

If there is a system failure or if some other type of interruption occurs while the procedure is executing, the BASE= data set may not be properly updated; it is possible that not all, perhaps none, of the observations will be added to the BASE= data set.

Output Data Set

All observations from the DATA= data set are added to the BASE= data set. If the BASE= data set does not exist, APPEND creates a new SAS data set consisting of the observations in the DATA= data set. The output data set (BASE=) becomes the current SAS data set.

If there are variables in the BASE= data set that are not in the DATA= data set, those variables have missing values in the new observations.

Messages pertaining to procedure processing appear in the SAS log, but no printed output is produced.

EXAMPLES

Appending an Update File: Example 1

An update file called ADD contains information on average temperatures in cities around the country. It is appended to a master file, EXP.MASTER. PROC PRINT lists the master file before and after the execution of PROC APPEND.

```
DATA ADD;
   INPUT CITY $15. MONTH $15. TEMP;
   CARDS;
RALEIGH        JULY           77.5
RALEIGH        JANUARY        40.5
MIAMI          AUGUST         82.9
MIAMI          JANUARY        67.2
LOS_ANGELES    AUGUST         69.5
LOS_ANGELES    JANUARY        54.5
;
PROC PRINT DATA=EXP.MASTER;
   TITLE 'MASTER BEFORE ADD DATA APPENDED';
PROC APPEND BASE=EXP.MASTER DATA=ADD;
PROC PRINT DATA=EXP.MASTER;
   TITLE 'MASTER AFTER ADD DATA APPENDED';
RUN;
```

Output 5.1 The BASE= Data Set before and after the PROC APPEND Step

```
                    MASTER BEFORE ADD DATA APPENDED                              1

                   OBS       CITY         MONTH        TEMP

                    1      HONOLULU      AUGUST        80.7
                    2      HONOLULU      JANUARY       72.3
                    3      BOSTON        JULY          73.3
                    4      BOSTON        JANUARY       29.2
                    5      DULUTH        JULY          65.6
                    6      DULUTH        JANUARY        8.5
```

```
                    MASTER AFTER ADD DATA APPENDED                               2
                 OBS     CITY              MONTH        TEMP
                   1     HONOLULU          AUGUST       80.7
                   2     HONOLULU          JANUARY      72.3
                   3     BOSTON            JULY         73.3
                   4     BOSTON            JANUARY      29.2
                   5     DULUTH            JULY         65.6
                   6     DULUTH            JANUARY       8.5
                   7     RALEIGH           JULY         77.5
                   8     RALEIGH           JANUARY      40.5
                   9     MIAMI             AUGUST       82.9
                  10     MIAMI             JANUARY      67.2
                  11     LOS_ANGELES       AUGUST       69.5
                  12     LOS_ANGELES       JANUARY      54.5
```

Using PROC APPEND with FORCE: Example 2

This example illustrates one use of the FORCE option. Weather data is gathered each day and stored in a SAS data set named ACCUM.WEATHER. The following statements produce **Output 5.2**, which shows the information contained in ACCUM.WEATHER.

```
PROC PRINT DATA=ACCUM.WEATHER;
   FORMAT DATE DATE7.;
   TITLE 'WEATHER INFORMATION BEFORE APPEND';
RUN;
```

Output 5.2 Printed Output for ACCUM.WEATHER

```
                    WEATHER INFORMATION BEFORE APPEND                            1

                    OBS      DATE       TEMP       SUNHRS

                     1      01JAN84      35         9.30
                     2      02JAN84      34         9.33
                     3      03JAN84      37         9.35
                     4      04JAN84      38         9.39
```

The following program appends the weather information accumulated the next day to ACCUM.WEATHER and prints a copy of the results:

```
DATA DAILY;
   INPUT DATE MMDDYY8. TEMP SUNHRS PRECIP;
```

```
   CARDS;
01-05-84 35 9.40 0.00
;
PROC APPEND BASE=ACCUM.WEATHER FORCE;
PROC PRINT;
   FORMAT DATE DATE7.;
   TITLE 'WEATHER INFORMATION AFTER APPEND';
RUN;
```

Notice that the data set DAILY contains the additional variable PRECIP for which there is no corresponding variable in the BASE= data set. With FORCE in effect, the observation is appended to ACCUM.WEATHER, but the value for PRECIP is dropped. Also notice that the DATA= option is not necessary on the PROC statement because DAILY is the most recently created SAS data set before the PROC step executes.

Output 5.3 FORCE Option Causes Variable to Be Dropped

```
                    WEATHER INFORMATION AFTER APPEND                    1

                    OBS      DATE      TEMP     SUNHRS

                     1     01JAN84      35       9.30
                     2     02JAN84      34       9.33
                     3     03JAN84      37       9.35
                     4     04JAN84      38       9.39
                     5     05JAN84      35       9.40
```

Chapter 6

The CALENDAR Procedure

ABSTRACT

The CALENDAR procedure displays data from a SAS data set in a month-by-month calendar format.

INTRODUCTION

PROC CALENDAR produces either of two calendar formats: summary or schedule.

A summary calendar provides information about the same variables over time. For example, the summary calendar in **Output 6.1** displays the number of meals served daily in a hospital cafeteria during the month of December, 1985.

Output 6.1 Summary Calendar

```
                    MEALS SERVED IN COMMUNITY HOSPITAL CAFETERIA                               1

                                  DECEMBER  1985

 ---------------------------------------------------------------------------------------------
 |   SUNDAY    |   MONDAY    |   TUESDAY   |  WEDNESDAY  |  THURSDAY   |   FRIDAY    |  SATURDAY   |
 |-------------+-------------+-------------+-------------+-------------+-------------+-------------|
 |      1      |      2      |      3      |      4      |      5      |      6      |      7      |
 |             |             |             |             |             |             |             |
 |             |             |             |             |             |             |             |
 | 334 BRKFST  | 289 BRKFST  | 184 BRKFST  | 179 BRKFST  | 360 BRKFST  | 245 BRKFST  | 280 BRKFST  |
 | 484 LUNCH   | 501 LUNCH   | 352 LUNCH   | 228 LUNCH   | 450 LUNCH   | 440 LUNCH   | 399 LUNCH   |
 | 368 DINNER  | 380 DINNER  | 292 DINNER  | 212 DINNER  | 332 DINNER  | 386 DINNER  | 312 DINNER  |
 |-------------+-------------+-------------+-------------+-------------+-------------+-------------|
 |      8      |      9      |     10      |     11      |     12      |     13      |     14      |
 |             |             |             |             |             |             |             |
 |             |             |             |             |             |             |             |
 | 294 BRKFST  | 309 BRKFST  | 199 BRKFST  | 186 BRKFST  | 301 BRKFST  | 276 BRKFST  | 272 BRKFST  |
 | 489 LUNCH   | 569 LUNCH   |             | 294 LUNCH   | 511 LUNCH   | 488 LUNCH   | 460 LUNCH   |
 | 316 DINNER  | 449 DINNER  | 202 DINNER  | 260 DINNER  | 403 DINNER  | 365 DINNER  | 421 DINNER  |
 |-------------+-------------+-------------+-------------+-------------+-------------+-------------|
 |     15      |     16      |     17      |     18      |     19      |     20      |     21      |
 |             |             |             |             |             |             |             |
 |             |             |             |             |             |             |             |
 | 204 BRKFST  | 266 BRKFST  | 195 BRKFST  | 164 BRKFST  | 210 BRKFST  | 311 BRKFST  | 402 BRKFST  |
 | 356 LUNCH   | 480 LUNCH   | 388 LUNCH   | 280 LUNCH   | 394 LUNCH   | 595 LUNCH   | 654 LUNCH   |
 | 345 DINNER  | 470 DINNER  | 311 DINNER  | 234 DINNER  | 256 DINNER  | 541 DINNER  | 580 DINNER  |
 |-------------+-------------+-------------+-------------+-------------+-------------+-------------|
 |     22      |     23      |     24      |     25      |     26      |     27      |     28      |
 |             |             |             |*CHRISTMAS** |             |             |             |
 |             |             |             |             |             |             |             |
 | 420 BRKFST  | 339 BRKFST  | 201 BRKFST  | 160 BRKFST  | 412 BRKFST  | 292 BRKFST  | 309 BRKFST  |
 | 530 LUNCH   | 590 LUNCH   | 400 LUNCH   | 485 LUNCH   | 663 LUNCH   | 559 LUNCH   |             |
 | 501 DINNER  | 489 DINNER  | 266 DINNER  | 195 DINNER  | 581 DINNER  | 503 DINNER  | 552 DINNER  |
 |-------------+-------------+-------------+-------------+-------------+-------------+-------------|
 |     29      |     30      |     31      |             |             |             |             |
 |             |             |             |             |             |             |             |
 |             |             |             |             |             |             |             |
 | 330 BRKFST  | 321 BRKFST  | 220 BRKFST  |             |             |             |             |
 | 771 LUNCH   | 605 LUNCH   | 415 LUNCH   |             |             |             |             |
 | 495 DINNER  | 550 DINNER  |             |             |             |             |             |
 ---------------------------------------------------------------------------------------------

                    ----------------------------------------------------
                    |      LEGEND       |      SUM     |      MEAN     |
                    |                   |              |               |
                    | BREAKFASTS SERVED |        8464  |      273.032  |
                    | LUNCHES SERVED    |       13830  |      476.897  |
                    | DINNERS SERVED    |       11567  |      385.567  |
                    ----------------------------------------------------
```

In a summary calendar, each day is represented by one observation. Each piece of information for a given day is the value of a variable for that day. Variables displayed can be numeric or character and can be formatted. Sums and means for any of the numeric variables displayed can be collected; these are printed after the body of the calendar.

A schedule calendar displays the duration of an event by a continuous line through each day for the event. The example in **Output 6.2** is a planning calendar for the month of July, 1985.

Output 6.2 Schedule Calendar

```
                     SUMMER PLANNING CALENDAR: JULIA Q. WYDGET, PRESIDENT                                            1
                                     BETTER PRODUCTS INC.

------------------------------------------------------------------------------------------------------------------------
|                                                                                                                      |
|                                                     JULY  1985                                                       |
|                                                                                                                      |
|----------------------------------------------------------------------------------------------------------------------|
|     SUNDAY     |     MONDAY     |    TUESDAY     |   WEDNESDAY    |    THURSDAY    |     FRIDAY     |    SATURDAY    |
|----------------+----------------+----------------+----------------+----------------+----------------+----------------|
|                |       1        |       2        |       3        |       4        |       5        |       6        |
|                |                |                |                |**INDEPENDENCE**|                |                |
|                |                |                |                |                |                |                |
|                |                |                |                |                |+VIP BANQUET/JW+|                |
|                |+=========COMPUTER CAMP/BRIAN/SOUTHFIELD=========>|                |+====SALES_DRIVE/DISTRICT_6=====>|
|                |+===MGRS. MEETING/DISTRICT_6====+|                |                |+==TRADE SHOW/KNOX/LOS ANGELES==>|
|                |+DIST. MTG./ALL+|                |+INTERVIEW/TIME+|                |<COMPUTER CAMP/BRIAN/SOUTHFIELD=>|
|----------------+----------------+----------------+----------------+----------------+----------------+----------------|
|       7        |       8        |       9        |       10       |       11       |       12       |       13       |
|                |                |                |                |                |                |                |
|                |                |                |                |                |                |                |
|                |                |                |                |                |+SEMINAR/WHITE=+|                |
|<===============================================SALES_DRIVE/DISTRICT_6===============================================>|
|<TRADE SHOW/KNO+|                |                |                |+PLANNG COUNCIL+|+==TENNIS CLINIC/LLOYD/CHICAGO==+|
|<===========================================COMPUTER CAMP/BRIAN/SOUTHFIELD===========================================+|
|----------------+----------------+----------------+----------------+----------------+----------------+----------------|
|       14       |       15       |       16       |       17       |       18       |       19       |       20       |
|                |                |+==DENTIST/JW==+|                |                |                |                |
|                |+==============SHORT COURSE/CANNON===============+|+PLANNG COUNCIL+|                |                |
|                |+===================================VISIT/MORSE====================================+|                |
|                |+=============================VACATION/VIVIAN/HOUSTON=============================+|                |
|+CO. PICNIC/ALL+|+===MGRS. MEETING/DISTRICT_7====+|                |+NEWSLETR DEADL+|+SEMINAR/WHITE=+|                |
|<=============SALES_DRIVE/DISTRICT_6=============+|+========TOY SHOW/MARKS=========+|+====SALES_DRIVE/DISTRICT_7=====>|
|----------------+----------------+----------------+----------------+----------------+----------------+----------------|
|       21       |       22       |       23       |       24       |       25       |       26       |       27       |
|                |                |                |                |                |                |                |
|                |                |                |                |                |                |                |
|                |                |                |                |+==========GOLF TOURNAMENT/JW/PEBL BCH===========>|
|                |                |                |+BIRTHDAY/MARY=+|+PLANNG COUNCIL+|+=====INVENTORS SHOW/MELVIN=====>|
|+===============================================VACATION/PEARL/TORONTO===============================================>|
|<===============================================SALES_DRIVE/DISTRICT_7===============================================>|
|----------------+----------------+----------------+----------------+----------------+----------------+----------------|
|       28       |       29       |       30       |       31       |                |                |                |
|                |                |                |                |                |                |                |
|                |                |                |                |                |                |                |
|<INVENTORS SHOW+|                |                |                |                |                |                |
|<GOLF TOURNAMEN+|                |                |                |                |                |                |
|<VACATION/PEARL+|+=====CLOSE SALE/WYGIX CO.======+|                |                |                |                |
|<=============SALES_DRIVE/DISTRICT_7=============+|                |                |                |                |
------------------------------------------------------------------------------------------------------------------------
```

The line for an event begins and ends with a cross (+). If an event continues from one week to another or after one or more holidays, an arrow appears at the point of continuation. In a schedule calendar, each event is one observation, and a single day can display several events (observations) on successive lines. One event can also appear in several days, weeks, or months, depending on its duration.

PROC CALENDAR determines the amount of data that can be displayed with either calendar type from the number of lines available on the page (PAGESIZE= system option) and the line width (LINESIZE= system option). See "SAS System Options" in the *SAS Language Guide for Personal Computers* for more information on these options.

SPECIFICATIONS

The CALENDAR procedure is invoked by using the following statements:

PROC CALENDAR *options;*
BY *variables;*
ID *variable;*
VAR *variables;*
SUM *variables / option;*
MEAN *variables / option;*
DURATION *variable;*
HOLIDAYS *variables;*
HOLINAME *variable;*

PROC CALENDAR Statement

PROC CALENDAR *options;*

The following options can appear on the PROC CALENDAR statement and can be used with either a summary or a schedule calendar:

DATA=*SASdataset*
: gives the name of the SAS data set to be used by the CALENDAR procedure. If DATA= is omitted, the most recently created SAS data set is used.

HOLIDATA=*SASdataset*
: gives the name of the SAS data set that contains variables whose values are "holidays." The variables that contain holiday values are specified in the HOLIDAYS statement. See **HOLIDATA= Data Set** under **Details** for information on the HOLIDATA= data set.

SCHEDULE
: specifies that a schedule calendar is to be printed. A summary calendar is the default if no DURATION statement is specified.

FILL
: specifies that all months between the first and last observation dates inclusive are to be displayed even if no data are present for a particular month. By default, CALENDAR leaves out months with no data.

WEEKDAYS
: specifies that CALENDAR should display and use in calculations only weekdays (excluding Saturday and Sunday). The default displays and uses all days.

MISSING
: specifies for a summary calendar that when a day has no associated observation, the values of the VAR variables for that day are to be printed using the format specified for missing values. If MISSING is not given, the day contains only the date. For a schedule calendar, MISSING specifies that missing values for VAR variables appear in the label of an observation. If MISSING is not specified, missing values of VAR variables are ignored in labeling the observation.

DATETIME

specifies that the ID and HOLIDAYS variables contain SAS datetime values rather than SAS date values. PROC CALENDAR then uses only the date portion of the datetime value. Use this option if the ID and HOLIDAYS variables are associated with the DATETIME. informat. Both the ID and HOLIDAYS variables must contain the same type of value. By default, CALENDAR assumes that the ID and HOLIDAYS variables are SAS date values.

HEADER=LARGE
HEADER=SMALL

specifies the type of heading for CALENDAR to use in formatting the month name. HEADER=LARGE prints the month name 7 lines high with an additional blank line above and below the month name. The year is also printed if space is available (as determined by the LINESIZE= option). HEADER=SMALL prints the month and year on a single line like a regular printed title. By default, CALENDAR prints the month and year in a box 4 lines high.

FORMCHAR=*'string'*
FORMCHAR(*n* ...)=*'string'*

defines the set of characters used to draw the calendar outlines and the special characters used to represent events on a schedule calendar. If the FORMCHAR(*n* ...)=*'string'* form of the option is used, each *n* must represent a valid position in the FORMCHAR= string. See **Using the FORMCHAR= Option** below.

The following options can be used for a summary calendar (they are ignored if the SCHEDULE option is specified):

LEGEND

requests that CALENDAR print a legend block containing the label or name of each variable displayed on the calendar. The legend appears at the bottom of the page for each month or on a following page if there is insufficient room on the calendar page.

MEANTYPE=NOBS
MEANTYPE=NDAYS

gives the type of mean to be calculated for each month. MEANTYPE=NOBS specifies that the mean is to be calculated for the number of observations on the input data set for each month. MEANTYPE=NDAYS specifies that the mean is to be calculated for the number of days displayed in the month (the number of days displayed depends on the WEEKDAYS option). The default MEANTYPE is NOBS.

BY Statement

BY *variables;*

A BY statement can be used with PROC CALENDAR to obtain separate calendars for observations in groups defined by the BY variables. When a BY statement appears, the procedure expects the input data set to be sorted in order of the BY variables, in addition to the ID variable. If your input data set is not sorted in ascending order, use the SORT procedure with a similar BY statement to sort the data, or, if appropriate, use the BY statement options NOTSORTED or DESCENDING. For more information, see the discussion of the BY statement in the *SAS Language Guide for Personal Computers*.

ID Statement

ID *variable;*

The ID statement is required, and the ID variable must contain either SAS date values or SAS datetime values. If the values are datetime values, specify the DATETIME option in the PROC CALENDAR statement. The input data set must be sorted by the ID variable (within any BY variables). If a HOLIDAYS statement is present, the ID variable values and the HOLIDAYS variable values must contain the same type of information (either date or datetime).

For a summary calendar, the ID statement specifies the variable to be used as the date of each observation. There should be only one observation per day in the input data set; if multiple observations for the same day appear, only the last is used. Observations with missing values for the ID variable are ignored.

For a schedule calendar, the ID statement specifies the variable used as the beginning date for the observation (event). Several observations may have the same ID value.

VAR Statement

VAR *variables;*

For a summary calendar, the VAR statement specifies the variables in the input data set to be displayed on the calendar for each day. Variables can be either character or numeric. If no VAR statement is used, all variables in the data set (excluding BY and ID variables) are displayed. Note that the number of lines available per page determines the actual number of variables that a summary calendar displays.

For a schedule calendar, the values of the VAR variables label each observation and are printed in the middle of the line for a given observation. VAR variables can be character or numeric. The number of VAR variable values that can be printed for a given observation depends on the number of days that observation occupies, that is, the length of the observation's line.

SUM Statement

SUM *variables / option;*

The SUM statement specifies for a summary calendar the variables to be totaled for each month. If a variable specified in the SUM list is not in the VAR list, it is added to the VAR list. Multiple SUM statements can be used.

The SUM statement is valid only for a summary calendar; if the SCHEDULE option is specified, SUM statements are ignored.

The following option can be used with the SUM statement:

FORMAT=*formatname*
F=*formatname*

names a SAS or user-defined format to be used in displaying the sums requested. The default uses the BEST. format for the sums.

MEAN Statement

MEAN *variables / option;*

The MEAN statement specifies for a summary calendar the variables for which a mean value is to be calculated for each month. If a variable specified in the MEAN list is not in the VAR list, SAS adds that variable to the VAR list. Multiple MEAN statements can be used.

The MEAN statement is valid only for a summary calendar; if the SCHEDULE option is specified, MEAN statements are ignored.

The following option can be used with the MEAN statement:

FORMAT=*formatname*
F=*formatname*
: names a SAS or user-defined format to be used in displaying the means requested. The default uses the BEST. format for the means.

DURATION Statement

DURATION *variable*;

The DURATION (or DUR) statement specifies for a schedule calendar the variable containing the duration of each event in days. The DUR statement is required for a schedule calendar, and using a DUR statement causes SAS to produce a schedule calendar.

Duration is measured inclusively from the first day of an event (given in the ID variable). For example, the line for an event with an ID value of 1JUL85 and a DUR value of 3 appears in July 1, July 2, and July 3 of a schedule calendar. Any noninteger portion of the DURATION variable value is truncated, and any observation with a missing value or a value less than or equal to 0 is skipped. If a HOLIDAYS statement is present, the DUR value does not include any holidays within the duration. Thus, if 4JUL85 is a holiday, an event with an ID value of 1JUL85 and a DUR value of 4 appears in July 1, 2, 3, and 5. If you use the WEEKDAYS option, CALENDAR assumes that DUR refers to the number of weekdays. Specifying the WEEKDAYS option causes an event with an ID value of 1JUL85 and a DUR value of 31 to extend into August.

HOLIDAYS Statement

HOLIDAYS *variables*;

The HOLIDAYS statement specifies a list of variables in the HOLIDATA= data set to be treated as "holidays." For a schedule calendar, a holiday is defined as a day to be excluded from an event. If an event spans a holiday, it is simply continued past the holiday. For a summary calendar, the holiday name is placed above the values for the holiday. If multiple observations or variables in the HOLIDATA= data set have the same value, the last value encountered is used.

HOLINAME Statement

HOLINAME *variable*;

The HOLINAME statement specifies a variable in the HOLIDATA= data set whose formatted value in each observation labels all holidays specified in the HOLIDAYS statement for that observation. The variable can be either character or numeric. If no HOLINAME statement is used, the holiday is labeled with the variable label, if present, or the name of the HOLIDAYS variable that contributed the date.

DETAILS

Input Data Set

The data set must be sorted by the ID variable (within any BY variables).

For a summary calendar the input data set should consist of one observation per day. If multiple observations for one day are encountered, only the last is used. You can use PROC SUMMARY or a DATA step to collapse the data by day.

For a schedule calendar the input data set should contain one observation per event.

HOLIDATA= Data Set

The HOLIDATA= data set contains variables to identify and, optionally, label days to be considered holidays in the calendar. You can treat any day as a holiday.

Variables that identify holidays must contain either SAS date or SAS datetime values. In PROC CALENDAR, specify these variables in the HOLIDAYS statement. The data set does not have to be sorted by the HOLIDAYS variables.

Specify the variable that labels the holidays in the HOLINAME statement. The HOLINAME variable labels holidays for all variables in the HOLIDAYS statement for each observation. If the value of the HOLINAME variable is too long for a calendar cell, the value is truncated.

These statements create the HOLIDATA= data set shown in **Output 6.3**:

```
DATA HOL;
   INPUT HDAY : DATE7. HNAME & $12.;
   CARDS;
1JAN85  NEW YEAR'S
4JUL85  INDEPENDENCE
2SEP85  LABOR DAY
25DEC85 CHRISTMAS
3APR85  CONVENTION
4APR85  CONVENTION
5APR85  CONVENTION
30JUN85 TAKEINVENTRY
;
PROC PRINT;
   ATTRIB HDAY FORMAT=DATE7.;
RUN;
```

Output 6.3 HOLIDATA= Data Set

```
                         HOLIDATA= DATA SET                              1

                   OBS     HDAY       HNAME

                    1     01JAN85    NEW YEAR'S
                    2     04JUL85    INDEPENDENCE
                    3     02SEP85    LABOR DAY
                    4     25DEC85    CHRISTMAS
                    5     03APR85    CONVENTION
                    6     04APR85    CONVENTION
                    7     05APR85    CONVENTION
                    8     30JUN85    TAKEINVENTRY
```

Missing Values

Table 6.1 shows how CALENDAR handles missing values of various types.

Limitations

Since PROC CALENDAR attempts to fit the calendar within a single page, the page dimensions determine the number of variables and observations that can be displayed. You should carefully select the values for the system options PAGESIZE= and LINESIZE=. CALENDAR prints a message on the SAS log if one or more events is omitted for lack of space on a schedule calendar or if one or more variables is omitted for a summary calendar.

Using the FORMCHAR= Option

PROC CALENDAR uses the FORMCHAR= values to produce the calendar outlines and the event representation lines on a schedule calendar. The boxing characters (characters 1 to 11 in the FORMCHAR= string) are used to generate the calendar outlines. The vertical thick character (character 12) is the starting or ending character for an event line. The horizontal thick character (character 13) is the fill character for the event line. The slash (character 16) separates the variable values in the event line label. The left and right arrows (characters 18 and 19) indicate the continuation of an event line. The bullet (character 20) highlights a holiday name.

You can change the FORMCHAR= characters with the system option FORMCHAR= or the FORMCHAR= option in the PROC CALENDAR statement. Use FORMCHAR=*'string'*to change all the characters or a group of consecutive characters beginning with the first. UseFORMCHAR(*n* . . .)= *'string'* to change only the characters at positions *n*. . . . For example,FORMCHAR(18 19)='XX' changes the left and right arrows to X. The default value of the FORMCHAR= option is '|----|+|---+=| −/\<>*'.

Table 6.2 shows the characters produced by the default value and their hexadecimal equivalents. You can substitute any character or hexadecimal string for those given here to customize the appearance of the calendar.

Table 6.1 Treatment of Missing Values in PROC CALENDAR

Type of Missing Data	Action: Summary	Action: Schedule
No observation for day	MISSING option specified: Variables represented by missing values MISSING option not specified: day in calendar contains only date	
Missing value for ID variable	Observation ignored	Observation ignored
Missing value for DUR variable		Observation ignored
Missing value for HOLIDAYS variable	Value not treated as a holiday	Value not treated as a holiday
Missing value for HOLINAME variable	Day labeled with missing value	Day labeled with missing value
Missing value for VAR variable	Value represented by a missing value for that day; treatment of other VAR variables for that day not affected	MISSING option specified: variables represented by missing values MISSING option not specified: missing value ignored in labeling event lines
Missing value for SUM variable	Value ignored in calculating sum	
Missing value for MEAN variable	Value included in calculating mean unless ID variable missing	

Table 6.2 Characters Used with the FORMCHAR= Option

Name	Position	Default
Vertical bar	1	| 7C
Horizontal bar	2	– 2D
Upper left	3	– 2D
Upper middle	4	– 2D
Upper right	5	– 2D
Middle left	6	| 7C
Middle middle	7	+ 2B
Middle right	8	| 7C
Lower left	9	– 2D
Lower middle	10	– 2D
Lower right	11	– 2D
Vertical thick	12	+ 2B
Horizontal thick	13	= 3D
Vertical dash	14	| 7C

Continued on next page

Table 6.2 *Continued*

Name	Position	Default
Horizontal dash	15	- 2D
Slash	16	/ 2F
Backslash	17	\ 5C
Left arrow	18	< 3C
Right arrow	19	> 3E
Bullet	20	* 2A

Printed Output

The printed output for a summary calendar consists of the following:

1. any titles specified
2. the month name and year heading
3. day of the week heading
4. data for each day listed week by week
5. a combination legend, sums, and means block if these are requested. The legend/summary block appears on a following page if it does not fit on the same page as the calendar.

The printed output for a schedule calendar consists of items 1 through 3 above and a week-by-week listing of the events on each day. Each event is represented by a continuous line through the days on which it occurs except for holidays. The values of the variables specified in the VAR list are used to label this line. An arrow at the right end of an event line indicates that the event continues into the next week or past the following holiday. An arrow at the left end of an event line indicates that the event continues from the previous day or week.

EXAMPLES

Summary Calendar: Example 1

The summary calendar shown in **Output 6.4** displays computer usage at the Dusty National Bank for the month of March, 1983. Note that the calendar records only use from Monday through Friday of each week (the WEEKDAYS option). The mean is calculated on the number of days displayed in the month (MEANTYPE=NDAYS). Values for March 4 (for which there is no observation) are printed using the format for missing values (the MISSING option).

```
OPTIONS LINESIZE=120 NODATE;
DATA CAL;
   INPUT OPDATE: DATE. JOBS ACT CPU;
   LIST;
   CARDS;
1MAR83 873 22.1 7.6
2MAR83 881 23.8 11.7
3MAR83 940 24.0 7.7
5MAR83 877 23.5 9.1
6MAR83 194 5.3 1.5
7MAR83 154 17.4 7.1
8MAR83 807 24 10.5
9MAR83 829 23.4 10.5
10MAR83 915 24 10.6
11MAR83 582 19.2 6.2
12MAR83 647 17.1 4.3
13MAR83 388 21 6.9
14MAR83 194 22.5 10.9
15MAR83 806 23.5 7.5
16MAR83 848 23.6 10.5
17MAR83 906 23 10.1
18MAR83 505 14.9 5.8
19MAR83 4 0.1 0
21MAR83 3 0.1 0
22MAR83 729 24 4.9
23MAR83 652 21.3 12.2
24MAR83 809 23.8 12.3
25MAR83 15 3.5 1.6
26MAR83 103 23.4 18.7
27MAR83 168 15.8 10.7
28MAR83 108 15.3 6
29MAR83 896 21.5 5.8
30MAR83 760 18.7 8
31MAR83 200 10 5
;
PROC FORMAT;
   PICTURE JFMT . ='    0 JOBS' (NOEDIT)
          OTHER=' 999 JOBS';
   PICTURE AFMT . ='    0 ACT    (NOEDIT)
          OTHER='99. 9 ACT ';
   PICTURE CFMT  ='    0 CPU ' (NOEDIT)
          OTHER='99. 9 CPU ';
  PROC CALENDAR WEEKDAYS HEADER=SMALL MEANTYPE=NDAYS MISSING;
   ID OPDATE;
   VAR JOBS ACT CPU;
   SUM JOBS ACT CPU;
   MEAN JOBS ACT CPU;
   FORMAT JOBS JFMT.
          ACT  AFMT.
          CPU  CFMT. ;
   LABEL JOBS = 'JOBS RUN DURING THE MONTH'
         ACT  = 'ACTIVE HOURS'
         CPU  = 'CPU HOURS';
   TITLE1 'SYSTEM PERFORMANCE SUMMARY';
   TITLE2 'DUSTY NATIONAL BANK COMPUTER CENTER';
```

Output 6.4 Summary Calendar

```
                         SYSTEM PERFORMANCE SUMMARY                                      1
                     DUSTY NATIONAL BANK COMPUTER CENTER

                                 MARCH  1983

        -----------------------------------------------------------------------
        |   MONDAY    |   TUESDAY    |  WEDNESDAY  |   THURSDAY   |    FRIDAY   |
        |-------------+--------------+-------------+--------------+-------------|
        |             |      1       |      2      |      3       |      4      |
        |             |              |             |              |             |
        |             |  873 JOBS    |  881 JOBS   |  940 JOBS    |    0 JOBS   |
        |             |  22. 1 ACT   |  23. 8 ACT  |  24. 0 ACT   |    0 ACT    |
        |             |  07. 6 CPU   |  11. 7 CPU  |  07. 7 CPU   |    0 CPU    |
        |-------------+--------------+-------------+--------------+-------------|
        |      7      |      8       |      9      |     10       |     11      |
        |             |              |             |              |             |
        |  154 JOBS   |  807 JOBS    |  829 JOBS   |  915 JOBS    |  582 JOBS   |
        |  17. 4 ACT  |  24. 0 ACT   |  23. 4 ACT  |  24. 0 ACT   |  19. 2 ACT  |
        |  07. 1 CPU  |  10. 5 CPU   |  10. 5 CPU  |  10. 6 CPU   |  06. 2 CPU  |
        |-------------+--------------+-------------+--------------+-------------|
        |     14      |     15       |     16      |     17       |     18      |
        |             |              |             |              |             |
        |  194 JOBS   |  806 JOBS    |  848 JOBS   |  906 JOBS    |  505 JOBS   |
        |  22. 5 ACT  |  23. 5 ACT   |  23. 6 ACT  |  23. 0 ACT   |  14. 9 ACT  |
        |  10. 9 CPU  |  07. 5 CPU   |  10. 5 CPU  |  10. 1 CPU   |  05. 8 CPU  |
        |-------------+--------------+-------------+--------------+-------------|
        |     21      |     22       |     23      |     24       |     25      |
        |             |              |             |              |             |
        |  003 JOBS   |  729 JOBS    |  652 JOBS   |  809 JOBS    |  015 JOBS   |
        |  00. 1 ACT  |  24. 0 ACT   |  21. 3 ACT  |  23. 8 ACT   |  03. 5 ACT  |
        |  00. 0 CPU  |  04. 9 CPU   |  12. 2 CPU  |  12. 3 CPU   |  01. 6 CPU  |
        |-------------+--------------+-------------+--------------+-------------|
        |     28      |     29       |     30      |     31       |             |
        |             |              |             |              |             |
        |  108 JOBS   |  896 JOBS    |  760 JOBS   |  200 JOBS    |             |
        |  15. 3 ACT  |  21. 5 ACT   |  18. 7 ACT  |  10. 0 ACT   |             |
        |  06. 0 CPU  |  05. 8 CPU   |  08. 0 CPU  |  05. 0 CPU   |             |
        -----------------------------------------------------------------------

              ---------------------------------------------------------
              |                            |      SUM    |    MEAN    |
              | JOBS RUN DURING THE MONTH  |     13412   |    583.13  |
              | ACTIVE HOURS               |     423.6   |   18.4174  |
              | CPU HOURS                  |     172.5   |       7.5  |
              ---------------------------------------------------------
```

Schedule Calendar: Example 2

The following SAS statements produced the schedule calendar shown as **Output 6.2** in the **Introduction**. The HOLIDATA= data set is shown in the **HOLIDATA= Data Set** section. Since the MISSING option is not specified, the missing values for WHERE are ignored in labeling the events.

```
DATA PLAN;
   INPUT DATE:DATE. HAPPEN $ 9-36 WHO $ 38-48 LONG 50-51 WHERE $ 53-70;
   CARDS;
1JUL85   DIST. MTG.                   ALL          1  CARY
1JUL85   MGRS. MEETING                DISTRICT_6   2
1JUL85   COMPUTER CAMP                BRIAN        12 SOUTHFIELD
5JUL85   TRADE SHOW                   KNOX         3  LOS ANGELES
12JUL85  TENNIS CLINIC                LLOYD        2  CHICAGO
16JUL85  DENTIST                      JW           1
18JUL85  NEWSLETR DEADLN              ALL          1
5JUL85   SALES_DRIVE                  DISTRICT_6   12
11JUL85  PLANNG COUNCIL               GROUP II     1
15JUL85  MGRS. MEETING                DISTRICT_7   2
15JUL85  VACATION                     VIVIAN       5  HOUSTON
15JUL85  VISIT                        MORSE        5
19JUL85  SALES_DRIVE                  DISTRICT_7   12
```

```
25JUL85 PLANNG COUNCIL                  GROUP IV    1
5JUL85  VIP BANQUET                     JW          1
15JUL85 SHORT COURSE                    CANNON      3
3JUL85  INTERVIEW                       TIMES       1
29JUL85 CLOSE SALE                      WYGIX CO.   2
16JUL85 BANK MTG.                       1ST NATL    1
24JUL85 BIRTHDAY                        MARY        1
17JUL85 TOY SHOW                        MARKS       2
26JUL85 INVENTORS SHOW                  MELVIN      3
14JUL85 CO. PICNIC                      ALL         1  PARK
19JUL85 SEMINAR                         WHITE       1
21JUL85 VACATION                        PEARL       8  TORONTO
25JUL85 GOLF TOURNAMENT                 JW          4  PEBL BCH
12JUL85 SEMINAR                         WHITE       1
18JUL85 PLANNG COUNCIL                  GROUP III   1
;
PROC SORT;
   BY DATE;
PROC CALENDAR SCHEDULE HOLIDATA=HOL;
   ID DATE;
   HOLIDAYS HDAY;
   HOLINAME HNAME;
   VAR HAPPEN WHO WHERE;
   DUR LONG;
TITLE 'SUMMER PLANNING CALENDAR: JULIA Q. WYDGET, PRESIDENT';
TITLE2 'BETTER PRODUCTS INC.';
```

Chapter 7
The CHART Procedure

ABSTRACT

The CHART procedure produces vertical and horizontal bar charts (also called *histograms*), block charts, pie charts, and star charts. These charts are useful for showing pictorially a variable's values or the relationships between two or more variables.

INTRODUCTION

Method

The appearance of a chart produced by PROC CHART is determined by three factors:

1. the method chosen to present the chart
2. the summary measures that are shown for the variable whose values are charted
3. features of the procedure that specify how the values are grouped.

You request each chart presentation method in PROC CHART with the following statements:

- vertical bar chart (VBAR statement)
- horizontal bar chart (HBAR statement)
- block chart (BLOCK statement)
- pie chart (PIE statement)
- star chart (STAR statement).

In each case, the variable listed (the chart variable) determines the values that label the bars or sections. Options are used to control the kind of statistics presented and any grouping that is done. For example, you use the TYPE= option to choose a measure to compute and display:

- frequency counts (TYPE=FREQ)
- percentages (TYPE=PCT)
- cumulative frequencies (TYPE=CFREQ)
- cumulative percentages (TYPE=CPCT)
- totals (TYPE=SUM)
- averages (TYPE=MEAN).

Among the characteristics that determine how values are grouped are

- the type of variable charted, numeric or character
- the DISCRETE option for categorical grouping variables
- the GROUP= option for side-by-side grouping
- the SUBGROUP= option for sub-grouping
- the MIDPOINTS= option to locate interval midpoints for continuous variables.

PROC CHART produces charts for both numeric and character variables. Character variables and formats cannot exceed a length of sixteen. For continuous numeric variables, CHART automatically selects display intervals, although you can explicitly define interval midpoints. If a value falls exactly halfway between two midpoints, the procedure puts the value in the higher interval. For character variables and discrete numeric variables, which contain several distinct values rather than a continuous range, the data values themselves define the intervals.

Introductory Examples

To give you an idea of PROC CHART's capabilities, the kinds of charts that you can produce are described below. If you have a specific chart in mind, glance through the following examples for a similar one. Many other charts can be produced by combining the options. The SAS statements needed to produce the following charts are found in the **Examples** section.

Frequency bar charts When you want to divide your data into groups based on the values of a variable, frequency bar charts are useful. For example, say you have a data set containing information about employees. You want a bar chart comparing the number of male employees and the number of female employees. This chart is a frequency chart since it shows the number of employees (observations) of each sex. The following SAS code produces the vertical frequency chart shown in **Output 7.1**:

```
PROC CHART;
   VBAR SEX;
```

Output 7.1 Vertical Frequency Bar Chart: The CHART Procedure

```
            EMPLOYEE DATA                                          1

       FREQUENCY BAR CHART
FREQUENCY

       |                    *****
       |                    *****
       |                    *****
    90 +                    *****
       |                    *****
       |                    *****
       |                    *****
    80 +                    *****
       |                    *****
       |        *****       *****
       |        *****       *****
    70 +        *****       *****
       |        *****       *****
       |        *****       *****
       |        *****       *****
    60 +        *****       *****
       |        *****       *****
       |        *****       *****
       |        *****       *****
    50 +        *****       *****
       |        *****       *****
       |        *****       *****
       |        *****       *****
    40 +        *****       *****
       |        *****       *****
       |        *****       *****
       |        *****       *****
    30 +        *****       *****
       |        *****       *****
       |        *****       *****
       |        *****       *****
    20 +        *****       *****
       |        *****       *****
       |        *****       *****
       |        *****       *****
    10 +        *****       *****
       |        *****       *****
       |        *****       *****
       |        *****       *****
       --------------------------
                  F           M

                   SEX
```

At the bottom of the chart are the two values of SEX, F and M. The vertical axis represents the number of observations in the data set containing the value; seventy-five of the employees are females and ninety-seven are males.

If you prefer a horizontal bar chart, use the HBAR statement instead of the VBAR statement. You can use the keyword HBAR in any of the following examples instead of VBAR. The following SAS code produces the horizontal frequency bar chart shown in **Output 7.2**:

```
PROC CHART;
   HBAR SEX;
```

Output 7.2 Horizontal Frequency Bar Chart: The CHART Procedure

```
                                        EMPLOYEE DATA                                                    1
                                     FREQUENCY BAR CHART

SEX                                                                                  FREQ  CUM.  PERCENT    CUM.
                                                                                           FREQ             PERCENT
      |
F     |***************************************************************************   75    75    43.60    43.60
      |
M     |*************************************************************************************************   97   172    56.40   100.00
      |
      -----+----+----+----+----+----+----+----+----+----+----+----+----+----+----+----+----+----+----+--
           5   10   15   20   25   30   35   40   45   50   55   60   65   70   75   80   85   90   95

                                          FREQUENCY
```

Percentage bar charts These charts are handy for showing what percentage of the observations falls into different groups. For example, say you want to show the percentage of employees of each sex. The TYPE=PERCENT option produces the percentage bar chart. The following SAS code produces the percentage bar chart shown in **Output 7.3**:

```
PROC CHART;
   VBAR SEX / TYPE=PERCENT;
```

Output 7.3 Percentage Bar Chart: The CHART Procedure

```
                                EMPLOYEE DATA                                1

                            PERCENTAGE BAR CHART
                     PERCENTAGE

                           |                   *****
                           |                   *****
                           |                   *****
                        50 +                   *****
                           |                   *****
                           |                   *****
                           |      *****        *****
                           |      *****        *****
                        40 +      *****        *****
                           |      *****        *****
                           |      *****        *****
                           |      *****        *****
                           |      *****        *****
                        30 +      *****        *****
                           |      *****        *****
                           |      *****        *****
                           |      *****        *****
                           |      *****        *****
                        20 +      *****        *****
                           |      *****        *****
                           |      *****        *****
                           |      *****        *****
                           |      *****        *****
                        10 +      *****        *****
                           |      *****        *****
                           |      *****        *****
                           |      *****        *****
                           |      *****        *****
                           --------------------------
                                    F            M

                                         SEX
```

Cumulative frequency charts Sometimes you want a cumulative frequency chart where each bar represents the frequency of a given value plus the frequencies of all the values to its left in the chart. For example, using the data set containing employee information, you may want to show how many employees have not attended college. The TYPE=CFREQ option produces the cumulative frequency chart. The following SAS code produces the cumulative frequency bar chart shown in **Output 7.4**.

```
PROC CHART;
   VBAR EDUC / TYPE=CFREQ;
```

Output 7.4 Cumulative Frequency Bar Chart: The CHART Procedure

```
                                   EMPLOYEE DATA                                                       1

                           CUMULATIVE FREQUENCY BAR CHART
CUMULATIVE FREQUENCY
              |                                           *****       *****
              |                                           *****       *****
          160 +                                           *****       *****
              |                                           *****       *****
              |                                           *****       *****
              |                                           *****       *****
          140 +                                           *****       *****
              |                               *****       *****       *****
              |                               *****       *****       *****
              |                               *****       *****       *****
          120 +                               *****       *****       *****
              |                               *****       *****       *****
              |                               *****       *****       *****
              |                               *****       *****       *****
          100 +                               *****       *****       *****
              |                   *****       *****       *****       *****
              |                   *****       *****       *****       *****
              |                   *****       *****       *****       *****
           80 +                   *****       *****       *****       *****
              |                   *****       *****       *****       *****
              |                   *****       *****       *****       *****
              |                   *****       *****       *****       *****
           60 +                   *****       *****       *****       *****
              |                   *****       *****       *****       *****
              |                   *****       *****       *****       *****
              |                   *****       *****       *****       *****
           40 +                   *****       *****       *****       *****
              |                   *****       *****       *****       *****
              |                   *****       *****       *****       *****
              |                   *****       *****       *****       *****
           20 +                   *****       *****       *****       *****
              |                   *****       *****       *****       *****
              |       *****       *****       *****       *****       *****
              |       *****       *****       *****       *****       *****
              --------------------------------------------------------------
                       8TH       SOME HS     HS GRAD   SOME COLL   COLL GRAD

                                            EDUC
```

Output 7.4 shows that 135 employees have not attended college.

Cumulative percentage charts The bars of a cumulative percentage chart represent the percentage of the observations having a given value plus the percentages of all the values appearing to the left in the chart.

For example, suppose you want to represent the educational attainments of the employees in terms of percentages rather than frequencies. The TYPE=CPERCENT option produces the cumulative percentage chart. The following SAS code produces the cumulative percentage bar chart shown in **Output 7.5**:

```
PROC CHART;
   VBAR EDUC / TYPE=CPERCENT;
```

Output 7.5 Cumulative Percentage Bar Chart: The CHART Procedure

```
                              EMPLOYEE DATA                                    1

                     CUMULATIVE PERCENTAGE BAR CHART
CUMULATIVE PERCENTAGE

    100 +                                                   *****
        |                                       *****       *****
        |                                       *****       *****
        |                                       *****       *****
     90 +                                       *****       *****
        |                                       *****       *****
        |                                       *****       *****
        |                                       *****       *****
     80 +                                       *****       *****
        |                           *****       *****       *****
        |                           *****       *****       *****
        |                           *****       *****       *****
     70 +                           *****       *****       *****
        |                           *****       *****       *****
        |                           *****       *****       *****
        |                           *****       *****       *****
     60 +                           *****       *****       *****
        |                           *****       *****       *****
        |               *****       *****       *****       *****
        |               *****       *****       *****       *****
     50 +               *****       *****       *****       *****
        |               *****       *****       *****       *****
        |               *****       *****       *****       *****
        |               *****       *****       *****       *****
     40 +               *****       *****       *****       *****
        |               *****       *****       *****       *****
        |               *****       *****       *****       *****
        |               *****       *****       *****       *****
     30 +               *****       *****       *****       *****
        |               *****       *****       *****       *****
        |               *****       *****       *****       *****
        |               *****       *****       *****       *****
     20 +               *****       *****       *****       *****
        |               *****       *****       *****       *****
        |               *****       *****       *****       *****
        |               *****       *****       *****       *****
     10 +               *****       *****       *****       *****
        |               *****       *****       *****       *****
        |   *****       *****       *****       *****       *****
        |   *****       *****       *****       *****       *****
        ------------------------------------------------------------
             8TH       SOME HS     HS GRAD    SOME COLL   COLL GRAD

                                    EDUC
```

Bar charts of group totals These charts are like the frequency and percentage charts described earlier, but the vertical axis represents the group totals for another variable in the data set instead of frequencies or percentages. This variable is usually a continuous variable, such as SALES.

Suppose you have a data set that consists of twelve observations for each department. Each observation contains DEPT, the chart variable, which identifies the department, and the variable SALES, which gives each department's sales for that month. Suppose you want to see the total sales for the year for each department. You use the option SUMVAR= to specify SALES as the sum variable since you want the sum of each department's monthly sales for the chart. The following SAS code produces the bar chart of group totals shown in **Output 7.6**:

```
PROC CHART;
   VBAR DEPT / SUMVAR=SALES;
```

Output 7.6 Bar Chart of Group Totals: The CHART Procedure

```
                DEPARTMENT SALES FOR THE YEARS 1982-1984                                   1

                           BAR CHART OF SUMS
SALES SUM

      |               *****
      |               *****
35000 +               *****
      |               *****     *****
      |               *****     *****
      |               *****     *****
      |               *****     *****
30000 +               *****     *****
      |     *****     *****     *****
      |     *****     *****     *****
      |     *****     *****     *****
      |     *****     *****     *****
25000 +     *****     *****     *****
      |     *****     *****     *****
      |     *****     *****     *****
      |     *****     *****     *****
      |     *****     *****     *****
20000 +     *****     *****     *****
      |     *****     *****     *****
      |     *****     *****     *****
      |     *****     *****     *****
      |     *****     *****     *****
15000 +     *****     *****     *****
      |     *****     *****     *****
      |     *****     *****     *****
      |     *****     *****     *****
      |     *****     *****     *****
10000 +     *****     *****     *****
      |     *****     *****     *****
      |     *****     *****     *****
      |     *****     *****     *****
      |     *****     *****     *****
 5000 +     *****     *****     *****
      |     *****     *****     *****
      |     *****     *****     *****
      |     *****     *****     *****
      |     *****     *****     *****
--------------------------------------------
            PARTS    REPAIRS    TOOLS

                       DEPT
```

Suppose you have one observation per group—you already have each department's total sales and want to display them. You can use exactly the same statements as above:

```
PROC CHART;
   VBAR DEPT / SUMVAR=SALES;
```

Even though PROC CHART does not need to sum the SALES values, they do represent a sum, and, thus, SUMVAR=SALES is the correct option to use. The results are like the chart above, but marked as VALUE rather than SUM. You can use this technique to present any value that has been entered as the value of a variable, such as a mean, standard deviation, or percentage.

Bar charts for group means Bar charts of group means are like the bar chart of group totals described earlier. However, the vertical axis represents the means of another variable rather than the sums. For example, to show each department's average monthly sales, use these statements to produce the bar chart for group means shown in **Output 7.7**:

```
PROC CHART;
  VBAR DEPT / TYPE=MEAN SUMVAR=SALES;
```

Output 7.7 Bar Charts for Group Means: The CHART Procedure

```
    DEPARTMENT SALES FOR THE YEARS 1982-1984                                   1

               BAR CHART OF MEANS
SALES MEAN

        |                   *****
  12000 +                   *****
        |                   *****
        |                   *****
        |                   *****
  10000 +                   *****
        |                   *****
        |                   *****
        |                   *****
   8000 +                   *****
        |                   *****
        |                   *****
        |                   *****
   6000 +                   *****
        |                   *****       *****
        |                   *****       *****
        |                   *****       *****
   4000 +                   *****       *****
        |       *****       *****       *****
        |       *****       *****       *****
        |       *****       *****       *****
   2000 +       *****       *****       *****
        |       *****       *****       *****
        |       *****       *****       *****
        |       *****       *****       *****
        --------------------------------------
                PARTS     REPAIRS       TOOLS

                            DEPT
```

Subdividing the bars You can show the distribution of a second variable by using the first character of each of the values to print the bars. For example, say you want to compare the number of males and females in each of the three departments. You can ask PROC CHART to subdivide the bars using F and M with these statements:

```
PROC CHART;
   VBAR DEPT / SUBGROUP=SEX;
```

From **Output 7.8**, you can see that females represent about one-third of the PARTS employees, a very small percentage of the REPAIRS employees, and about one-fifth of the TOOLS employees.

Output 7.8 Subdividing a Frequency Bar Chart: The CHART Procedure

```
                    EMPLOYEE DATA                                                  1

              FREQUENCY BAR CHART
FREQUENCY

        I       MMMMM
        I       MMMMM                   MMMMM
        I       MMMMM                   MMMMM
    160 +       MMMMM                   MMMMM
        I       MMMMM                   MMMMM
        I       MMMMM                   MMMMM
        I       MMMMM                   MMMMM
    140 +       MMMMM                   MMMMM
        I       MMMMM                   MMMMM
        I       MMMMM                   MMMMM
        I       MMMMM                   MMMMM
    120 +       MMMMM                   MMMMM
        I       MMMMM                   MMMMM
        I       MMMMM                   MMMMM
        I       MMMMM       MMMMM       MMMMM
    100 +       MMMMM       MMMMM       MMMMM
        I       MMMMM       MMMMM       MMMMM
        I       MMMMM       MMMMM       MMMMM
        I       MMMMM       MMMMM       MMMMM
     80 +       MMMMM       MMMMM       MMMMM
        I       MMMMM       MMMMM       MMMMM
        I       MMMMM       MMMMM       MMMMM
        I       MMMMM       MMMMM       MMMMM
     60 +       MMMMM       MMMMM       MMMMM
        I       MMMMM       MMMMM       MMMMM
        I       FFFFF       MMMMM       MMMMM
        I       FFFFF       MMMMM       MMMMM
     40 +       FFFFF       MMMMM       MMMMM
        I       FFFFF       MMMMM       FFFFF
        I       FFFFF       MMMMM       FFFFF
        I       FFFFF       MMMMM       FFFFF
     20 +       FFFFF       MMMMM       FFFFF
        I       FFFFF       MMMMM       FFFFF
        I       FFFFF       MMMMM       FFFFF
        I       FFFFF       FFFFF       FFFFF
        -------------------------------------
                PARTS     REPAIRS       TOOLS

                         DEPT

              SYMBOL SEX     SYMBOL SEX

                F    F         M    M
```

You can use other options in addition to SUBGROUP= to produce more complicated charts. For example, say you want to compare the sales figures for each of the three departments over the past three years. Your data set contains nine observations, each having values of the variables YEAR, DEPT, and SALES. These statements produce the chart shown in **Output 7.9**:

```
PROC CHART;
   VBAR YEAR / SUBGROUP=DEPT SUMVAR=SALES DISCRETE;
```

You need the DISCRETE option to display three distinct YEAR values. When DISCRETE is omitted for a numeric variable, the procedure divides the values into intervals. If you specify YEAR as a character variable, DISCRETE can be omitted.

Output 7.9 Subdividing a Bar Chart of Sums: The CHART Procedure

```
     DEPARTMENT SALES FOR THE YEARS 1982-1984                                        1

                 BAR CHART OF SUMS
  SALES SUM

          |                               TTTTT
    40000 +                               TTTTT
          |                               TTTTT
          |                               TTTTT
          |                               TTTTT
          |                               TTTTT
    35000 +                               TTTTT
          |                   TTTTT       TTTTT
          |                   TTTTT       TTTTT
          |                   TTTTT       TTTTT
          |                   TTTTT       TTTTT
    30000 +                   TTTTT       TTTTT
          |                   TTTTT       TTTTT
          |                   TTTTT       TTTTT
          |                   TTTTT       TTTTT
          |       TTTTT       TTTTT       TTTTT
    25000 +       TTTTT       TTTTT       TTTTT
          |       TTTTT       TTTTT       RRRRR
          |       TTTTT       RRRRR       RRRRR
          |       TTTTT       RRRRR       RRRRR
          |       TTTTT       RRRRR       RRRRR
    20000 +       TTTTT       RRRRR       RRRRR
          |       RRRRR       RRRRR       RRRRR
          |       RRRRR       RRRRR       RRRRR
          |       RRRRR       RRRRR       RRRRR
          |       RRRRR       RRRRR       RRRRR
    15000 +       RRRRR       RRRRR       RRRRR
          |       RRRRR       RRRRR       RRRRR
          |       RRRRR       RRRRR       RRRRR
          |       RRRRR       RRRRR       RRRRR
          |       RRRRR       PPPPP       RRRRR
    10000 +       PPPPP       PPPPP       RRRRR
          |       PPPPP       PPPPP       RRRRR
          |       PPPPP       PPPPP       PPPPP
          |       PPPPP       PPPPP       PPPPP
          |       PPPPP       PPPPP       PPPPP
     5000 +       PPPPP       PPPPP       PPPPP
          |       PPPPP       PPPPP       PPPPP
          |       PPPPP       PPPPP       PPPPP
          |       PPPPP       PPPPP       PPPPP
          |       PPPPP       PPPPP       PPPPP
          -------------------------------------
                   1982        1983        1984

                           YEAR

SYMBOL DEPT        SYMBOL DEPT        SYMBOL DEPT

  P    PARTS         R    REPAIRS       T    TOOLS
```

Side-by-side charts Another way of comparing quantities is with side-by-side charts. You can show the information—total sales for the three departments over the past three years—with these statements:

```
PROC CHART;
   VBAR DEPT / SUMVAR=SALES GROUP=YEAR;
```

The result is shown in **Output 7.10**.

Output 7.10 Side-by-Side Charts: The CHART Procedure

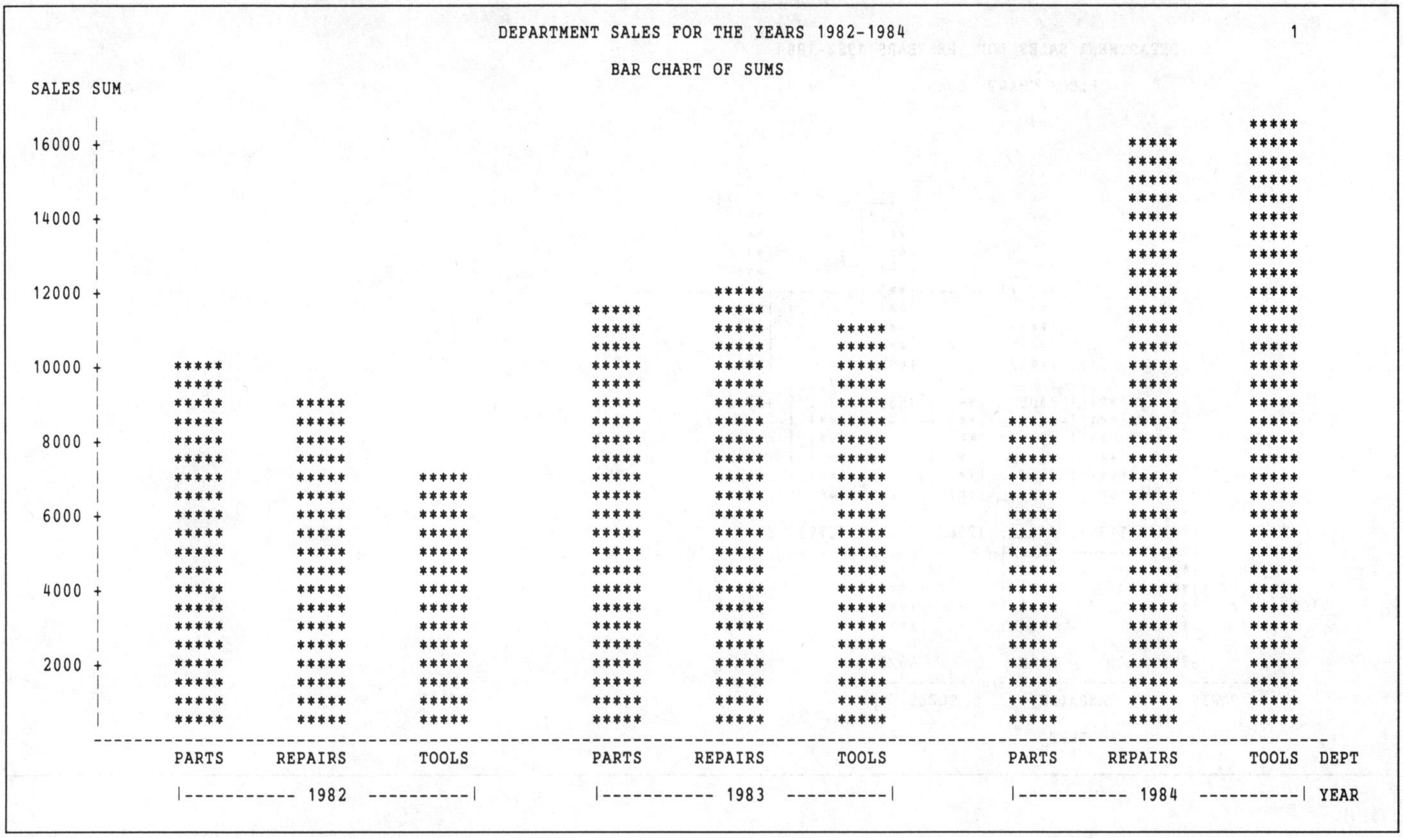

Block charts Another way you can show the sales information by department for each year is with a block chart. Block charts look like city blocks with a building drawn in each block. You can represent the frequency, mean, or sum by the height of the building. Use the following SAS code to produce a block chart like that shown in **Output 7.11**, which displays the same total sales as the VBAR chart presented earlier:

```
PROC CHART;
   BLOCK DEPT / SUMVAR=SALES GROUP=YEAR DISCRETE;
```

Output 7.11 Block Chart of Sales Sums: The CHART Procedure

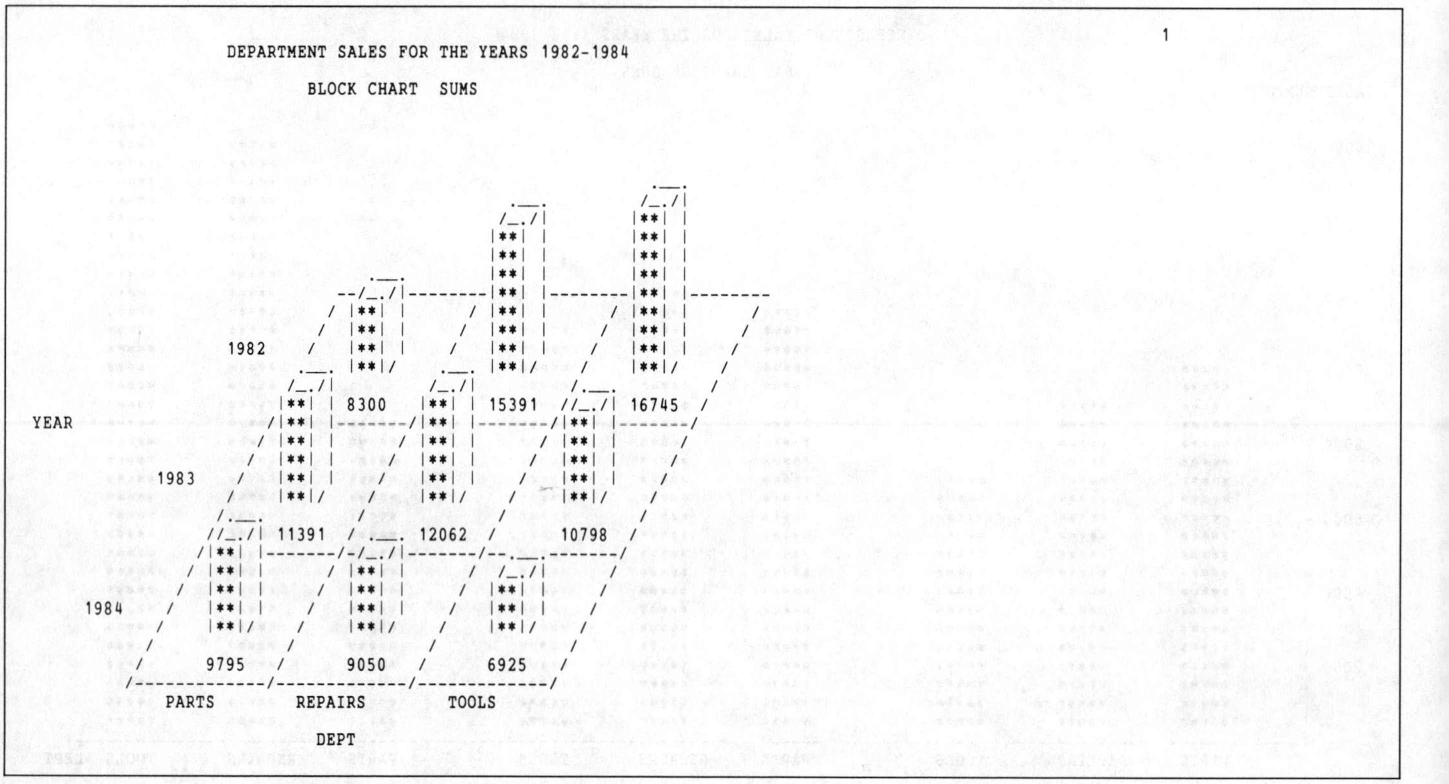

Pie charts You can also use the CHART procedure to draw a pie chart representing the distribution of a variable's values. For the example above where you want to show the total sales for each department over the three-year period, use these statements to produce the pie chart shown in **Output 7.12**:

```
PROC CHART;
   PIE DEPT / SUMVAR=SALES;
```

Output 7.12 Sum Pie Chart of Sales Grouped by Department: The CHART Procedure

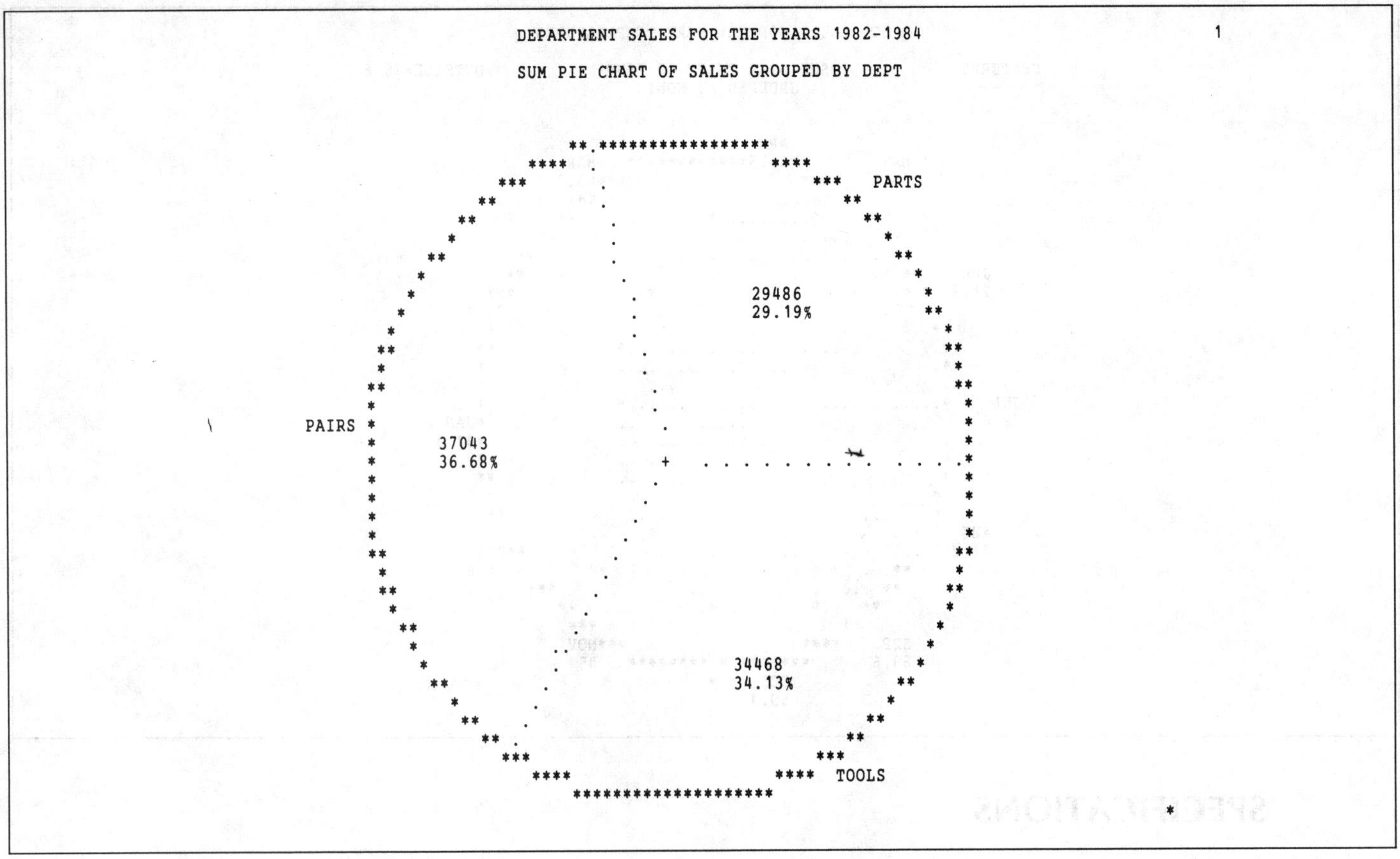

Star charts You can produce star charts showing group frequencies, totals, or means with PROC CHART. Star charts are appropriate for cyclical data, such as months of the year or hours of the day. The following SAS statements produce the star chart shown in **Output 7.13** that shows monthly temperature averages. (The star chart that results is like a vertical bar chart where the bars are wrapped around in a circle and connected.) The statements are

```
PROC FORMAT;
   VALUE _MON 1=JAN  2=FEB  3=MAR  4=APR  5=MAY  6=JUN
              7=JUL  8=AUG  9=SEP 10=OCT 11=NOV 12=DEC;
DATA MONTHLY;
   TITLE 'ST. LOUIS MONTHLY MEAN TEMPERATURES';
   DO MONTH=1 TO 12;
      INPUT TEMP @@;
      OUTPUT;
      END;
   FORMAT MONTH _MON.;
   CARDS;
31.3 35.1 43.3 56.5 65.8 74.9 78.6 77.2 69.6 59.1 45.0 34.6
;

PROC CHART;
   STAR MONTH / SUMVAR=TEMP DISCRETE;
```

Output 7.13 Star Chart of Temperature Grouped by Month: The CHART Procedure

```
               ST. LOUIS MONTHLY MEAN TEMPERATURES                               1

CENTER=0             SUM STAR CHART OF TEMP            OUTSIDE=78.6
                        GROUPED BY MONTH

                         APR
             MAY       **56.5************   MAR
             65.8   ****                 ***43.3
                  **                        ***
                **     *.........*            ***
              **   .....        ...             ***
             **  ....   .       . ...             **
     JUN    **...       ..      .   ..             **
     74.9  *.*.          ..     .     *             *FEB
          * .   ...       ..    .    . .             35.1
          *..     ...      ..   .  .    .             *
         *..        ....    ..  . ..    .*            **
         *.           ....   .. . ..  ....             *
         .                ............. .              *
  JUL    *...............................*             *
  78.6   .                   ...+...    ..             *JAN
         .                .............  .             *31.3
         *.           ....  .. . ..  ....              *
         *.        ....    ..  . ..    ..             **
          *.      ...      ..   .  .    .             *
          *.   ...        ..    .    . .             **
     AUG    *..          ..     .     *.            **
     77.2   ...         ..      .   ..             **DEC
             **...      .       .  ..             ** 34.6
              **  ..  ..        ...             ***
                **  ..*.........*.            ***
                  **                        ***
             SEP    ****                 ***NOV
             69.6      ********* ********   45
                         OCT    *
                         59.1
```

SPECIFICATIONS

The CHART procedure is controlled by the following statements:

PROC CHART *options;*
BY *variables;*
VBAR *variables / options;*
HBAR *variables / options;*
BLOCK *variables / options;*
PIE *variables / options;*
STAR *variables / options;*

Any number of chart request statements can follow a PROC CHART statement.

PROC CHART Statement

PROC CHART *options;*

The following options can be used in the PROC CHART statement:

DATA=*SASdataset*
: names the SAS data set to be used by PROC CHART. If DATA= is not specified, CHART uses the most recently created SAS data set.

LPI=*p*
: specifies the proportions of PIE and STAR charts. The value of LPI is

(lines per inch/columns per inch) * 10

and the default is LPI=6. For example, if you have a printer with 8 lines per inch and 12 columns per inch, specify LPI=6.6667.

BY Statement

BY *variables;*

A BY statement can be used with PROC CHART to obtain separate analyses on observations in groups defined by the BY variables. When a BY statement appears, the procedure expects the input data set to be sorted in order of the BY variables. If your input data set is not sorted in ascending order, use the SORT procedure with a similar BY statement to sort the data, or, if appropriate, use the BY statement options NOTSORTED or DESCENDING. For more information, see the discussion of the BY statement in *SAS Language Guide for Personal Computers.*

VBAR Statement

VBAR *variables / options;*

In the VBAR statement, list the variables for which you want vertical bar charts. (The options with VBAR are described later.) If you list X as one of the chart variables, then a vertical bar chart is produced with the values of X underneath the bars.

Each chart takes one page. Along the vertical axis, PROC CHART describes the chart frequency, cumulative frequency, percentage, cumulative percentage, sum, or mean. At the bottom of each bar, CHART prints a value. For character variables or discrete numeric variables, this value is the actual value represented by the bar. For continuous numeric variables, the value gives the midpoint of the interval represented by the bar.

PROC CHART can automatically scale the vertical axis, determine the bar width, and choose spacing between the bars. However, the options and parameters described below allow you to choose bar intervals and the number of bars, include missing values in the chart, produce side-by-side charts, and subdivide the bars.

The number of lines in the body of the VBAR chart is limited to sixty-six, regardless of the system PAGESIZE= option in effect. If the number of characters per line (LINESIZE) does not allow at least one blank space between bars, an error message is printed and PROC CHART produces an HBAR chart instead of a VBAR chart, unless the NOSPACE option is included.

HBAR Statement

HBAR *variables / options;*

The HBAR statement requests a horizontal bar chart for each variable listed. For example, the statements

```
PROC CHART;
   HBAR A X1 X2;
```

produce three horizontal bar charts. Each chart occupies one or more pages, depending on the number of levels; each bar is one line. (The options available in the HBAR statement are discussed later.)

BLOCK Statement

BLOCK *variables / options;*

In the BLOCK statement, list the variables for which you want block charts. Since each block chart must fit on one output page, there are some restrictions on the number of levels of the BLOCK and GROUP variables. (BLOCK statement options are described later.)

Table 7.1 shows the maximum number of levels of GROUP and BLOCK variables for selected LINESIZEs that can be represented in a block chart using a sixty-six-line page.

Table 7.1 Maximum Number of Levels of GROUP and BLOCK Variables: The CHART Procedure

groups	LS=132	LS=120	LS=105	LS=90	LS=76	LS=64
0,1	9	8	7	6	5	4
2	8	8	7	6	5	4
3	8	7	6	5	4	3
4	7	7	6	5	4	3
5,6	7	6	5	4	3	2

If the value of any GROUP level is longer than three characters, the maximum number of BLOCK levels that can be produced may be reduced by one. BLOCK level values are truncated to twelve characters. If these limits are exceeded, data are represented as an HBAR chart.

PIE Statement

PIE *variables / options;*

The PIE statement requests a pie chart for each variable listed. For example, the statements

```
PROC CHART;
   PIE A X1 X2;
```

produce three one-page pie charts. (Options available for PIE charts are discussed later.)

PROC CHART determines the number of slices for the pie in the same way that it determines the number of bars for VBAR charts. Any slices of the pie accounting for less than three print positions are lumped together into a slice called OTHER.

The pie's size is determined only by the LINESIZE= and PAGESIZE= system options. The pie looks elliptical if your printer does not print 6 lines per inch and 10 columns per inch. If your printer prints 8 lines per inch and 10 columns per inch, specify LPI=8 in the PROC CHART statement:

```
PROC CHART LPI=8;
```

If a PIE chart is requested for a variable with over fifty levels, an HBAR chart is produced instead.

STAR Statement

STAR variables / options;

The STAR statement requests a star chart for each variable listed. (Options in the STAR statement are discussed later.) For example, the statements

```
PROC CHART;
   STAR Z;
```

produce a one-page star chart for the variable Z.

The number of points in the star is determined in the same way as the number of bars for VBAR charts.

If all the data to be charted with a STAR statement are positive, the center of the star represents zero and the outside circle represents the maximum value. If negative values occur in the data, the center represents the minimum. See the AXIS= option below for more information about how to specify maximum and minimum values. If a STAR chart is requested for a variable with over twenty-four levels, an HBAR chart is produced instead.

Note: if you want different variables to form the rays of the star, use an OUTPUT statement in a DATA step to create new observations having one variable with values equal to the variables you want represented by the rays; create another variable whose values are the original variable names.

Options for VBAR, HBAR, BLOCK, PIE, and STAR Statements

If any of the options below are used, a slash (/) precedes the option keywords. The slash is not necessary if no options are specified.

The following options can be used with all the types of charts in the CHART procedure: vertical bar, horizontal bar, block, pie, or star charts.

MISSING

specifies that missing values are to be considered as valid levels for the chart variable.

DISCRETE

is used when the numeric chart variable specified is discrete rather than continuous. If DISCRETE is omitted, PROC CHART assumes that all numeric variables are continuous. If the MIDPOINTS= or LEVELS= options are not specified, the procedure automatically chooses the intervals for the chart.

TYPE=*type*

specifies what the bars or sections in the chart represent. If the TYPE= option is omitted, the default TYPE is FREQ. When SUMVAR= is specified, the default TYPE is SUM. You can specify one of the following keywords for *type*:

FREQ

makes each bar or section represent the frequency with which a value or range occurs for the chart variable in the data.

PERCENT or PCT

makes each bar or section represent the percentage of observations of the chart variable having a given value or falling into a given range.

CFREQ

makes each bar or section represent cumulative frequency, which is the frequency for the group plus all the frequencies shown to its left.

CPERCENT or CPCT

makes each bar represent the cumulative percentage of observations of the chart variable, which is the percentage of the group plus the percentages of the bars shown to its left.

SUM

makes each bar or section represent the sum of the SUMVAR= variable for observations having the bar's value. For example, the statement

```
VBAR DEPT / SUMVAR=SALES;
```

produces a chart with one bar or section for each DEPT value. The bar height for a given DEPT corresponds to the total of the SALES values for observations having that DEPT value.

MEAN

makes each bar or section represent the mean of the SUMVAR= variable for observations having the bar's value.

SUMVAR=*variable*

names the variable to collect summaries for means, sums, or frequencies. The SUMVAR= option is useful for producing bar charts showing total expenditures for each department, or means at each level of an experiment. For example, the statement

```
VBAR LOCATION / TYPE=MEAN SUMVAR=YIELD;
```

produces a chart showing the mean yield for each location. Another example

```
VBAR DEPT / SUMVAR=EXPEND;
```

charts total expenditures by department. If SUMVAR= is specified but TYPE= is not MEAN or SUM, then TYPE=SUM overrides whatever TYPE= value is specified.

MIDPOINTS=*values*

defines the range of values for the chart variable each bar or section represents by specifying the range midpoints. For example, the statement

```
VBAR X / MIDPOINTS=10 20 30 40 50;
```

produces a chart with five bars: the first bar represents the range of data values with a midpoint of ten; the second bar represents the range of data values with a midpoint of twenty; and so on. When the variables given in the VBAR statement are numeric, the midpoints must be given in ascending order, although they need not be uniformly distributed. For example, the statement

```
VBAR X / MIDPOINTS=10 100 1000 10000;
```

produces a chart of X with logarithmic intervals. Numeric MIDPOINTS lists of the form

```
MIDPOINTS=10 TO 100 BY 5
```

are also acceptable. For character variables, MIDPOINTS= can be specified in any order, which is useful in ordering the bars or in specifying a subset of the possible values. For example, you can give a list of the form

```
MIDPOINTS='JAN' 'FEB' 'MAR'
```

Without the MIDPOINTS= option, the values are displayed in sorted order.

FREQ=*variable*
is used when a variable in the data set represents a count (or weight) for each observation. Normally, each observation contributes a value of one to the frequency counts. When FREQ= appears, each observation contributes the FREQ= variable's value. If the FREQ= variable's values are not integers, they are truncated to integers. If the values are missing or negative, the contribution is zero. If SUMVAR= is specified, the sums are multiplied by the FREQ= value.

AXIS=*value*
specifies the maximum value to use in constructing the FREQ, PCT, CFREQ, CPCT, SUM, or MEAN axis. If the VBAR or HBAR chart is of TYPE=SUM or TYPE=MEAN and if any of the sums or means are less than zero, then a negative minimum value can also be specified in the AXIS= option. Otherwise, a minimum value of zero is always assumed. Counts or percentages outside the maximum (or minimum) override the AXIS= specification. If AXIS= is specified and a BY statement also appears, uniform axes are produced over BY groups. When AXIS= appears in a STAR statement, the first value specified is the center (minimum) of the star and the second value is the outside circle (maximum). If only one AXIS= value is specified in the STAR statement, PROC CHART assumes this value as the maximum and zero as the minimum. For example, the statements

```
PROC CHART;
   STAR A / SUMVAR=X TYPE=SUM AXIS=100 200;
```

produce a star chart for the sums of X classified by A and scaled from 100 at the center to 200 at the outside circle.

More Options for VBAR, HBAR, and BLOCK Statements

GROUP=*variable*
produces side-by-side charts, with each chart representing the observations having a given value of the GROUP= variable. The GROUP= variable can be character or numeric and is assumed to be discrete. For example, the statement

```
VBAR SEX / GROUP=DEPT;
```

produces a frequency bar chart for males and females in each department. Missing values for a GROUP variable are treated as valid levels when a chart is produced.

SUBGROUP=*variable*
requests that each bar be subdivided into characters that show the SUBGROUP= variable's contribution to the bar. For example, the statement

```
VBAR DEPT / SUBGROUP=SEX;
```

produces a chart with one bar for each department. The portion of each bar filled in with the character M represents those observations that have a SEX value of M.

The first character of the value is used to fill in the portion of the bar corresponding to the value, unless more than one value begins with the same first character. In that case, the letters A, B, C, and so on are used. The characters used in the chart and the values they represent are given in a table at the bottom of the chart.

Missing values for a SUBGROUP= variable are treated as valid levels when a chart is produced.

PROC CHART calculates the height of the bar for each subgroup individually and then rounds each bar's percentage of the total bar up or down. Thus, the total height of the bar may be higher or lower than the same bar without SUBGROUP=.

With both TYPE=MEAN and the SUBGROUP= option, PROC CHART first calculates the mean for each bar and then subdivides the bar into the percentages contributed by each subgroup.

LEVELS=*n*

specifies the number of bars representing each chart variable when the variables given in the VBAR statement are continuous.

SYMBOL=*'char'*

defines the symbol to be used in the body of standard HBAR and VBAR charts with no subgrouping. The default SYMBOL value is the asterisk (*).

NOSYMBOL

suppresses the subgrouping symbol table printed below the chart for VBAR and HBAR charts.

NOZEROS

specifies that any bar with zero value be suppressed.

G100

is used in conjunction with the GROUP= option to force the bars and statistics to add to 100% for each group.

Options for VBAR and HBAR Statements

ASCENDING

prints the bars and any associated statistics in ascending order of size within groups.

DESCENDING

prints the bars and any associated statistics in descending order of size within groups.

REF=*value*

requests that a single reference line be drawn on the response axis. For TYPE=FREQ or TYPE=CFREQ, this REF= value should be a frequency; for TYPE=PCT or TYPE=CPCT, the REF= value should be a percent between 1 and 100. For TYPE=SUM or TYPE=MEAN, the REF= value should be a sum or mean.

More HBAR Statement Options

These options are used only in the HBAR statement:

NOSTAT

specifies that no statistics be printed with a horizontal bar chart.

FREQ
: specifies for a horizontal bar chart that the frequency of each bar be printed to the side of the chart.

CFREQ
: specifies that the cumulative frequency be printed.

PERCENT
: specifies that the percentages of observations having a given value for the chart variable be printed.

CPERCENT
: specifies that the cumulative percentages be printed.

SUM
: specifies that the total number of observations that each bar represents be printed.

MEAN
: specifies that the mean of the observations represented by each bar be printed.

For charts produced with any TYPE= specification without a SUMVAR= variable, PROC CHART can print FREQ, CFREQ, PERCENT, and CPERCENT.

For TYPE=MEAN with a SUMVAR= variable, PROC CHART can print FREQ and MEAN. For a TYPE=SUM specification, PROC CHART can print FREQ and SUM.

Another VBAR Statement Option

This option is used only in the VBAR statement:

NOSPACE
: specifies that if the LINESIZE does not allow room for spaces between the bars, PROC CHART can print a VBAR chart without spaces between bars. If space is still insufficient, an HBAR chart is printed instead.

DETAILS

Missing Values

The way that PROC CHART treats missing values depends on whether or not the MISSING option is specified. See the section **Options for VBAR, HBAR, BLOCK, PIE, and STAR Statements** above.

EXAMPLES

Employee Sex and Education Level Data: Example 1

The statements below produced the data used in the CHART procedure for the charts on employee sex and education.

These statements include a DATA step to enter the values and the FORMAT procedure to define a format for the EDUC variable (for more information, see the chapter on PROC FORMAT):

```
PROC FORMAT;
   VALUE _E 1=8TH 2=SOME HS 3=HS GRAD 4=SOME COLL 5=COLL GRAD;
DATA WSEXED;
   TITLE 'EMPLOYEE DATA';
   INPUT SEX $ EDUC @@;
   FORMAT EDUC _E.;
   CARDS;
M 1  M 2  M 2  M 1  M 4  M 5  M 3  F 2  F 2  M 1  F 4
more data lines
;
```

Department Sales for the Years 1982-1984: Example 2

These statements produced the data for the charts on departmental sales:

```
DATA SALES;
   TITLE 'DEPARTMENT SALES FOR THE YEARS 1982-1984';
   INPUT DEPT :$7. SEX :$1. WT P82 P83 P84;
   YEAR=1982; SALES=P82; OUTPUT;
   YEAR=1983; SALES=P83; OUTPUT;
   YEAR=1984; SALES=P84; OUTPUT;
   CARDS;
PARTS    F 17    3500  2500   800
PARTS    M 21    3651  5391  4500
PARTS    M 21    2644  3500  3000
TOOLS    F 12    5672  6100  7400
TOOLS    M 45    1253  4698  9345
REPAIRS F  2     9050 12062 15931
more data lines
;
```

Sales Statistics from Summaries: Example 3

The statements below produce charts from summary statistics for three variables: PRODUCT with three levels, YEAR with three levels, and DATE. PROC CHART displays charts of a subset of the summary statistics contained in data set C.

The first chart, shown in **Output 7.14**, is a horizontal bar chart showing SALES for each PRODUCT by DATE. You need the DISCRETE option to display each value of DATE rather than the midpoints of the DATE values. The next chart is a block chart showing number of products by year. The pie chart of PRODUCT uses SALES as a weighting variable specified with the FREQ= option. The final vertical bar chart by YEAR shows number of products as the SUBGROUP= variable. You must specify DISCRETE so that the chart does not show YEAR with continuous values.

```
DATA C;
   SET B;
   IF _TYPE_=3;
PROC CHART;
   HBAR DATE / SUMVAR=SALES GROUP=PRODUCT DISCRETE;
   BLOCK PRODUCT / GROUP=YEAR;
   PIE PRODUCT / FREQ=SALES;
   VBAR YEAR / DISCRETE SUBGROUP=PRODUCT;
   TITLE 'RESULTS OF SALES DATA';
```

Output 7.14 Charts Showing Summaries

```
                                      RESULTS OF SALES DATA                                             1

                                        BAR CHART OF SUMS
            MIDPOINT
PRODUCT       DATE                                                                         FREQ   SALES SUM
                       |
4005        10APR79    |*******************************                                      6    308.0000
            17SEP79    |***********************                                              6    230.0000
            24FEB80    |*************************                                            5    251.0000
            02AUG80    |**********************                                               5    222.0000
            09JAN81    |*******************************                                      5    308.0000
            18JUN81    |**********************************************                       6    460.0000
            25NOV81    |*******************                                                  3    188.0000
                       |
8401        10APR79    |                                                                     0      0.0000
            17SEP79    |*******************************                                      6    314.0000
            24FEB80    |*****************************                                        5    290.0000
            02AUG80    |****************************                                         5    277.0000
            09JAN81    |*****************************                                        5    294.0000
            18JUN81    |********************************************************************  6    682.0000
            25NOV81    |*********************                                                3    205.0000
                       |
9054        10APR79    |***********                                                          6    109.0000
            17SEP79    |*************                                                        6    128.0000
            24FEB80    |*********************                                                5    213.0000
            02AUG80    |*********                                                            5     92.0000
            09JAN81    |*********                                                            5     87.0000
            18JUN81    |**********                                                           6    102.0000
            25NOV81    |**                                                                   3     21.0000
                       |
                       -----+----+----+----+----+----+----+----+----+----+----+----+----+---
                           50  100  150  200  250  300  350  400  450  500  550  600  650

                                             SALES SUM
```

```
                                      RESULTS OF SALES DATA                                             2

                                      FREQUENCY BLOCK CHART
```

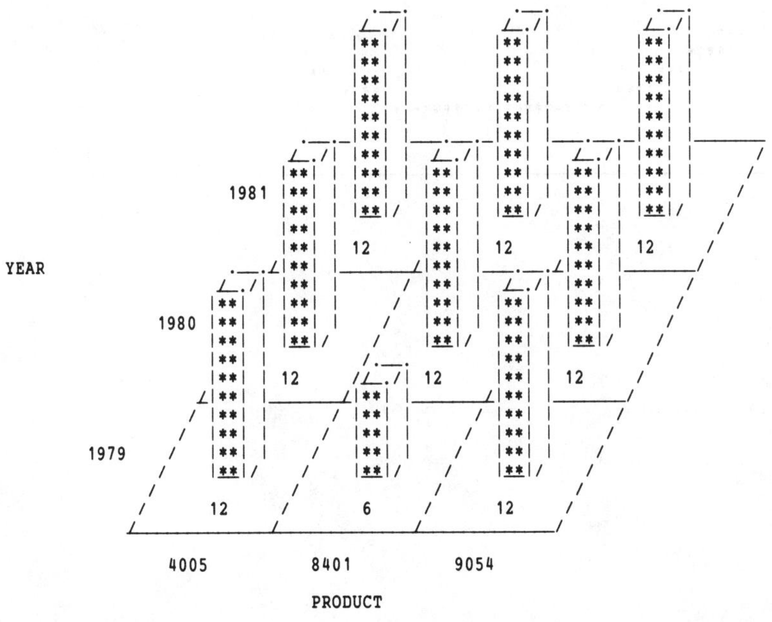

RESULTS OF SALES DATA 3

FREQ PIE CHART OF PRODUCT

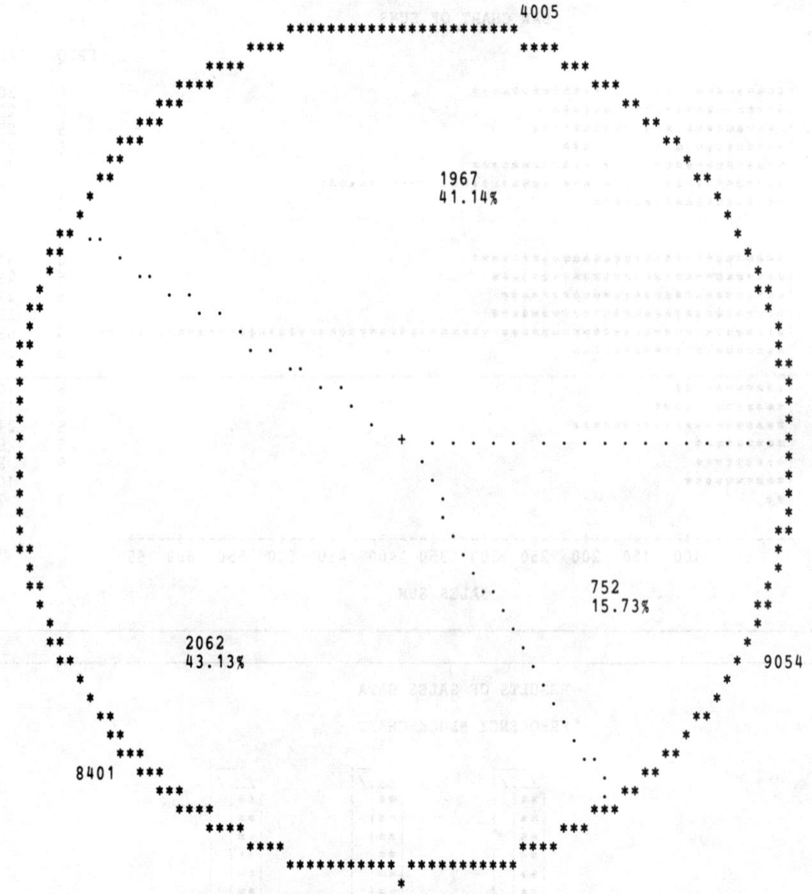

```
               RESULTS OF SALES DATA                                        4

                FREQUENCY BAR CHART
   FREQUENCY

          |                    99999       99999
       35 +                    99999       99999
          |                    99999       99999
          |                    99999       99999
          |                    99999       99999
          |                    99999       99999
       30 +       99999        99999       99999
          |       99999        99999       99999
          |       99999        99999       99999
          |       99999        99999       99999
          |       99999        99999       99999
       25 +       99999        99999       99999
          |       99999        88888       88888
          |       99999        88888       88888
          |       99999        88888       88888
          |       99999        88888       88888
       20 +       99999        88888       88888
          |       99999        88888       88888
          |       88888        88888       88888
          |       88888        88888       88888
          |       88888        88888       88888
       15 +       88888        88888       88888
          |       88888        88888       88888
          |       88888        88888       88888
          |       44444        44444       44444
          |       44444        44444       44444
       10 +       44444        44444       44444
          |       44444        44444       44444
          |       44444        44444       44444
          |       44444        44444       44444
          |       44444        44444       44444
        5 +       44444        44444       44444
          |       44444        44444       44444
          |       44444        44444       44444
          |       44444        44444       44444
          |       44444        44444       44444
          --------------------------------------
                    1979        1980        1981

                            YEAR

SYMBOL PRODUCT      SYMBOL PRODUCT     SYMBOL PRODUCT

  4    4005           8    8401           9    9054
```

Chapter 8
The COMPARE Procedure

ABSTRACT

PROC COMPARE compares the values of variables in two SAS data sets and reports the differences found. PROC COMPARE is especially useful in data base management applications (to verify data updates by comparing "before" and "after" images of a data base) and in forecasting (to compare forecasts made under different assumptions).

INTRODUCTION

The COMPARE procedure matches variables and observations in a base data set with those in a comparison data set. For numeric variables, PROC COMPARE computes the difference and percent difference of each pair of values, and if the difference is large enough, judges the pair to be unequal. PROC COMPARE then prints a list of variable pairs that were compared and found equal for all observations and a separate list of those with at least one unequal observation and the number of observations unequal for each. For each unequal variable pair, a report is printed showing the unequal values found. For numeric variables, the difference, percent difference, and summary statistics for each are shown.

Normally, the corresponding variables in the base and comparison data sets have the same names, but COMPARE can also compare variables with differing names. Different variables within one data set can also be compared.

COMPARE can also produce an output data set containing the differences or percent differences of the numeric variables compared.

SPECIFICATIONS

PROC COMPARE *options;*
VAR *variables;*
WITH *variables;*
ID *variables;*
BY *variables;*

PROC COMPARE Statement

PROC COMPARE *options;*

The following options can be used with the PROC COMPARE statement:

DATA=*SASdataset*
: names the data set to be used as the base data set for the comparison. If DATA= is omitted, the most recently created SAS data set is used.

COMPARE=*SASdataset*
: names the data set to be used as the comparison data set for the comparison. If COMPARE= is omitted, the DATA= data set is used and the comparison data set is the same as the base data set.

OUT=*SASdataset*
: requests that the differences for the numeric variables be written to a SAS data set. If OUT= is omitted, no output data set is created.

OUTPERCENT
: requests that the percent differences, instead of the differences, be written to the OUT= data set. OUTPERCENT is ignored unless OUT= is used.

OUTNOEQUAL
: requests that the differences or percent differences written to the OUT= data set be set to missing values for values that compared equal. OUTNOEQUAL is ignored unless OUT= is used.

CRITERION=*n*
: specifies the criterion for judging the equality of numeric values. See the section on **The Equality Criterion** in this chapter for details. The default value is CRITERION=.001.

METHOD=*name*
: specifies the method for judging the equality of numeric values. The methods available are RELATIVE, PERCENT, and ABSOLUTE. See the section on **The Equality Criterion** for details. The default is METHOD=RELATIVE.

ALLOBS
: requests that values and differences for all matching observations be printed. If ALLOBS is omitted, values are printed only for observations judged unequal.

NOOBS
: suppresses the listing of the value pairs and their differences.

ALLVARS
: requests that a detailed report of the value pairs be printed for each variable. (ALLVARS implies the ALLOBS option.) If ALLVARS is omitted, reports are generated only for variable pairs that compare unequal.

STATS
: requests the printing of summary statistics for the numeric variable pairs that compare unequal.

ALLSTATS
: requests the printing of summary statistics for all numeric variable pairs.

NOSUMMARY
: suppresses the printing of the summary notes, the list of variables that compare equal, and the list of variables that compare unequal.

NOLISTEQUAL
: suppresses the printing of the list of variables that compare equal.

NOPRINT
: suppresses all printed output. (Used in conjunction with the OUT= option.)

FUZZ=*n*
: requests that values of smaller magnitude than *n* not be printed on the reports. The default is FUZZ=1E−12.

NOMISSING or NOMISS
: specifies that missing values are to compare equal to any value. If NOMISSING is omitted, a missing value compares equal only to another missing value of the same kind.

NOMISS1
: specifies that the NOMISSING option is to apply for values in the base data set but not for values in the comparison data set.

NOMISS2
: specifies that the NOMISSING option is to apply for values in the comparison data set but not for values in the base data set.

VAR Statement

VAR *variables;*

The VAR statement lists the variables in the base data set to be compared with matching variables in the comparison data set. If no VAR statement is used, all variables in the base data set are compared except those appearing on the BY and ID statements. If no matching variable in the comparison data set is found for a variable in the VAR list, a warning is printed on the SAS log and the variable is ignored.

WITH Statement

WITH *variables;*

If the variables to be compared have different names in the comparison data set from those in the base data set, specify these names using the WITH statement. The first variable in the WITH statement list corresponds to the first variable in the VAR statement list, the second with the second, and so on. If the WITH list is shorter than the VAR list, the extra variables in the VAR list are assumed to have the same names in the comparison data set. If the WITH list is longer than the VAR list, the extra variables in the WITH list are ignored.

A VAR statement should be used when a WITH statement is used. If the WITH statement is omitted, the variables to be compared are assumed to have the same names in the comparison data set as in the base data set. If the COMPARE= option is omitted from the PROC COMPARE statement, a WITH statement **must** be used.

A variable name can appear any number of times in the VAR statement and in the WITH statement, and by selecting VAR and WITH lists, the variables can be compared in any permutation.

ID Statement

ID *variables;*

The ID statement lists variables that are used to match observations in the base data set with corresponding observations in the comparison data set. The ID statement variables are also used to identify observations on the reports listing variable values and differences. If an ID variable is not found in the comparison data set, a warning is printed on the SAS log and the variable is not used to match observations in the comparison data set. (It is used to identify observations on the reports and is output to the OUT= data set.) All of the ID variables must be in the base data set, and both data sets must be sorted by the ID variables in common (within the BY variables, if any).

If the ID statement is omitted, the first observation in the base data set is matched with the first observation in the comparison data set, the second with the second, and so on.

BY Statement

BY *variables;*

A BY statement can be used with PROC COMPARE. Both the base and comparison data sets must be sorted by the BY variables.

DETAILS

Output Data Set (OUT=)

The output data set contains the BY and ID variables and the numeric VAR statement variables for which matching variables were found in the comparison data set. Variable names and attributes in the output data set are taken from the base data set. The values of the VAR statement variables in the output data set are the differences (the comparison value less the base value), or the percent differences if the OUTPERCENT option is specified.

If the OUTNOEQUAL option is used, the special missing value *.E* will be output in place of differences that were judged "equal" (see below). The output data set contains an observation for each observation in the base data set for which a matching observation was found in the comparison data set. Nonmatching observations are not output.

The Equality Criterion

PROC COMPARE judges numeric values to be "equal" if their difference is sufficiently small relative to the CRITERION value. PROC COMPARE provides three methods for applying the CRITERION:

- The RELATIVE method uses the absolute relative difference.
- The PERCENT method uses the absolute percent difference.
- The ABSOLUTE method uses the absolute difference.

For a numeric variable compared, let *x* be its value in the base data set (DATA=), and let *y* be its value in the comparison data set (COMPARE=). If both *x* and *y* are nonmissing, the values are judged unequal according to the METHOD and CRITERION as described below.

- If METHOD=RELATIVE, the values are unequal if

  ```
  ABS(y-x)/((ABS(x)+ABS(y))/2) > CRITERION
  ```

  The values are equal if x=y=0.
- If METHOD=PERCENT, the values are unequal if

  ```
  ABS(y-x)/ABS(x)*100 > CRITERION        (for x¬=0)
  ```

  or

  ```
  y¬=0                                   (for x=0)
  ```
- If METHOD=ABSOLUTE, the values are unequal if

  ```
  ABS(y-x) > CRITERION
  ```

If *x* or *y* is missing, then the comparison depends on the NOMISSING option. If the NOMISSING option is in effect, a missing value will always compare equal to anything. Otherwise, a missing value is judged equal only to a missing value of the same type. (That is, .=., . ¬=.A, .A=.A, .A ¬=.B, and so on.)

If the CRITERION specified is negative, then the actual criterion used is made equal to the absolute value of the CRITERION option times a very small number ε that depends on the numerical precision of the computer. This number ε is defined as the smallest positive floating point value such that, using machine arithmetic, $1-\varepsilon<1<1+\varepsilon$. Round-off or truncation error in floating-point computations is typically a few orders of magnitude larger than ε. This means that CRITERION=−1000 will often provide a reasonable test of the equality of computed results at the machine level of precision.

For character variables, if one value has a greater length than the other, the shorter value is padded with blanks for the comparison. Nonblank character values are judged equal only if they agree at each character. If the NOMISSING option is in effect, blank character values compare equal to anything.

Difference and Percent Difference

For a numeric variable compared, let *x* be its value in the base data set and let *y* be its value in the comparison data set. If *x* and *y* are both nonmissing the difference and percent difference are defined as:

Difference $= y - x$

Percent Difference $= (y - x)/x * 100$, for $x \neg= 0$

or

$=$ missing, for $x = 0$

Memory Limitations

For each BY group, PROC COMPARE reads the values for the base variables into memory and then reads and matches the comparison values. Thus, when comparing very large data sets, memory limitation problems may occur. If you receive error messages for insufficient memory, move the first few ID variables to a BY statement to force PROC COMPARE to process the data in BY groups.

Reports Printed

PROC COMPARE can produce three kinds of reports:

1. A report containing summary notes for the comparisons and a listing of the variable pairs that compare equal and of those that compare unequal and the number of unequal observations (NDIF) found for each. This report is suppressed by the NOSUMMARY option.
2. Reports (printed separately for each variable pair) of the differences found at each observation. The report includes: the ID variable values for the observation, the value in the base data set, the value in the comparison data set, and, for numeric variables, the difference and percent difference. For character variables, only the first 20 characters of the values are printed. Unless the ALLOBS option is used, only the observations for which the values were judged unequal will be listed.
3. For numeric variables, a table of summary statistics is printed when the STATS or ALLSTATS option is used. First, the number of observations unequal (NDIF) and the percent of the matching observations unequal are printed. Second, the correlation of the base and comparison values (R) and the square of the correlation (RSQ) are printed. Next, descriptive statistics are printed for the base values, comparison values, differences, and percent differences.

   The statistics printed for each are N (number nonmissing), MEAN, STD, MAX, MIN, STDERR of MEAN, T ratio, and probability of greater |T| if true MEAN=0. These statistics are computed from all of the nonmissing matching observations for the item, but the R and RSQ statistics are computed from the matching observations that are nonmissing for **both** the base and comparison values. When the STATS option is used, summary statistics will be reported only for the variable pairs judged unequal.

   The summary statistics reports are combined with the listing of differences (described above) when both are produced. (Note that the statistics are calculated from all the nonmissing matching observations and not just from the unequal observations printed in the listing of differences.)

EXAMPLES

Finding the Differences between Two Data Sets: Example 1

Given monthly data sets ONE and TWO, find the differences between them for variables A, B, and C. The following statements produce **Output 8.1**.

```
PROC PRINT;
   TITLE 'DATA SET ONE';
PROC PRINT;
   TITLE 'DATA SET TWO';
PROC COMPARE DATA=ONE COMPARE=TWO;
   VAR A B C;
   ID YEAR MONTH;
   TITLE;
```

Output 8.1 Finding the Differences between Two Data Sets

```
                              DATA SET ONE                                    1

                 OBS    YEAR    MONTH    A     B   C

                  1     1984      1      1     2   JAN.
                  2     1984      2      4     5   FEB.
                  3     1984      3      7     8   MARCH
                  4     1984      4     10    11   APR.
                  5     1984      5     13    14   MAY
                  6     1984      6     16    17   JUNE
                  7     1984      7     19    20   JULY
                  8     1984      8     22    23   AUGUST
```

```
                              DATA SET TWO                                    2

              OBS    YEAR    MONTH     A          B     C

               1     1984      1       1     2.0000     JAN.
               2     1984      2       4     5.0000     FEB.
               3     1984      3       7     8.0989     MARCH
               4     1984      4      10    10.0157     +FOUR
               5     1984      5      13    15.4770     MAY
               6     1984      6      16    16.8609     XXXXX
               7     1984      7      19    20.4357     JULY
               8     1984      8      22    22.3798     AUGUST
```

```
                                                                              3
                             COMPARE PROCEDURE
                         COMPARISON OF ONE WITH TWO


                            COMPARISON SUMMARY

      DATASET            OBS  VARIABLES          COMPARISON RESULTS
      ONE                 8          5           EQUAL            1
      TWO                 8          5           UNEQUAL          2
      MATCHED             8          5           TOTAL            3



                            COMPARISONS EQUAL

        VARIABLE  TYPE  LEN   LABEL

        A         NUM     8   A NUMBERIC VARIABLE "A"



                           COMPARISONS UNEQUAL

        VARIABLE  TYPE  LEN   LABEL                         NDIF

        B         NUM     8                                    6
        C         CHAR    8   A CHARACTER VARIABLE "C"         2
```

```
                         COMPARE PROCEDURE                                               4
                   COMPARISON OF ONE WITH TWO

           ----------------------------------------------------------------------
                 YEAR       MONTH ||  VARIABLE    COMPARE
                                  ||         B          B      DIFF.     % DIFF
             --------   --------- ||  --------   --------   --------   --------
                                  ||
              1984.00     3.00000 ||   8.00000    8.09886    0.09886    1.23581
              1984.00     4.00000 ||  11.00000   10.01573   -0.98427   -8.94789
              1984.00     5.00000 ||  14.00000   15.47700    1.47700   10.55001
              1984.00     6.00000 ||  17.00000   16.86094   -0.13906   -0.81798
              1984.00     7.00000 ||  20.00000   20.43574    0.43574    2.17872
              1984.00     8.00000 ||  23.00000   22.37975   -0.62025   -2.69673
           ----------------------------------------------------------------------

           ----------------------------------------------------------------------
                                  ||  A CHARACTER VARIABLE "C"
                                  ||  VARIABLE              COMPARE
                 YEAR       MONTH ||  C                     C
             --------   --------- ||  --------              --------
                                  ||
              1984.00     4.00000 ||  APR.                  +FOUR
              1984.00     6.00000 ||  JUNE                  XXXXX
           ----------------------------------------------------------------------
```

Verifying Changes Made to a Master File: Example 2

Given a quarterly master file and a data set with update transactions, verify the changes made to the master file by the update. The following statements produce **Output 8.2**.

```
PROC COMPARE DATA=NEW COMPARE=DATABASE.MASTER NOMISS1;
   ID YEAR QTR;
   TITLE 'COMPARISON OF UPDATE DATA WITH DATA BASE BEFORE UPDATE';

DATA DATABASE.MASTER;
   UPDATE DATABASE.MASTER NEW;
   BY YEAR QTR;
```

Output 8.2 Verifying Changes Made to a Master File

```
               COMPARISON OF UPDATE DATA WITH DATA BASE BEFORE UPDATE                    1

                           COMPARE PROCEDURE
                  COMPARISON OF NEW WITH DATABASE.MASTER

                          COMPARISON SUMMARY

        DATASET           OBS  VARIABLES         COMPARISON RESULTS
        NEW                 1          5         EQUAL                1
        DATABASE.MASTER    16          5         UNEQUAL              2
        MATCHED             1          5         TOTAL                3

                          COMPARISONS EQUAL

                     VARIABLE  TYPE  LEN

                     A          NUM    8

                         COMPARISONS UNEQUAL

                     VARIABLE  TYPE  LEN  NDIF

                     B          NUM    8     1
```

(continued on next page)

(continued from previous page)

```
                          C              NUM      8      1

            COMPARISON OF UPDATE DATA WITH DATA BASE BEFORE UPDATE

                              COMPARE PROCEDURE
                       COMPARISON OF NEW WITH DATABASE.MASTER


     ---------------------------------------------------------------
                          ||   VARIABLE     COMPARE
         YEAR         QTR ||          B           B      DIFF.     % DIFF
     ---------   -------- ||  ---------   ---------  ---------  ---------
                          ||
      1982.00     2.00000 ||     999.00      342.99    -656.01  -65.66682
     ---------------------------------------------------------------

     ---------------------------------------------------------------
                          ||   VARIABLE     COMPARE
         YEAR         QTR ||          C           C      DIFF.     % DIFF
     ---------   -------- ||  ---------   ---------  ---------  ---------
                          ||
      1982.00     2.00000 ||   66.00000    17.88796  -48.11204  -72.89703
     ---------------------------------------------------------------
```

Comparing Variables within the Same Data Set: Example 3

Given a data set with variables X, Y, and Z, find the differences between X and Y, X and Z, and Y and Z, and print summary statistics for each comparison. The following statements produce **Output 8.3**.

```
PROC COMPARE STATS;
   VAR   X X Y;
   WITH  Y Z Z;
```

Output 8.3 Comparing Variables within the Same Data Set

```
                                                                          1
                              COMPARE PROCEDURE
                        COMPARISONS OF VARIABLES IN DATA1

                             COMPARISON SUMMARY

     DATASET              OBS   VARIABLES         COMPARISON RESULTS
     DATA1                 10           4         EQUAL              0
                                                  UNEQUAL            3
                                                  TOTAL              3




                          ALL COMPARISONS UNEQUAL

          VARIABLE   TYPE   LEN    COMPARE    LEN   NDIF

          X          NUM      8    Y            8     10
          X          NUM      8    Z            8      2
          Y          NUM      8    Z            8     10
```

COMPARE PROCEDURE 2
COMPARISONS OF VARIABLES IN DATA1

OBS	VARIABLE X	COMPARE Y	DIFF.	% DIFF
1	1.18496	2.49679	1.31183	110.71
2	2.97009	2.30604	-0.66405	-22.35778
3	3.39982	3.94087	0.54104	15.91382
4	4.25940	5.69862	1.43923	33.78940
5	5.92160	6.47501	0.55341	9.34558
6	6.96928	6.61771	-0.35157	-5.04451
7	7.54298	6.74075	-0.80223	-10.63547
8	8.53169	8.23654	-0.29515	-3.45945
9	9.04979	9.68850	0.63871	7.05773
10	10.06657	8.21800	-1.84856	-18.36340
NDIF	10	(100%)		
R, RSQ	0.943	0.888		
N	10	10	10	10
MEAN	5.98962	6.04188	0.05227	11.69523
STD	2.93879	2.47013	1.02655	38.59744
MAX	10.06657	9.68850	1.43923	110.71
MIN	1.18496	2.30604	-1.84856	-22.35778
STDERR	0.92933	0.78112	0.32462	12.20558
T	6.445	7.735	0.161	0.958
PROB>|T|	0.0001	0.0001	0.8756	0.3630

OBS	VARIABLE X	COMPARE Z	DIFF.	% DIFF
3	3.39982	5.44181	2.04198	60.06137
4	4.25940	5.16413	0.90473	21.24074
NDIF	2	(20%)		
R, RSQ	0.974	0.948		
N	10	10	10	10
MEAN	5.98962	6.28429	0.29467	8.13021
STD	2.93879	2.75159	0.67659	19.42946
MAX	10.06657	10.06657	2.04198	60.06137
MIN	1.18496	1.18496	0	0
STDERR	0.92933	0.87013	0.21396	6.14413
T	6.445	7.222	1.377	1.323
PROB>|T|	0.0001	0.0001	0.2017	0.2184

```
                         COMPARE PROCEDURE                                          3
                  COMPARISONS OF VARIABLES IN DATA1

         ____________________________________________________________
                 ||  VARIABLE    COMPARE
           OBS   ||         Y          Z      DIFF.       % DIFF
         _______ ||  _________  _________  _________   _________
                 ||
             1   ||   2.49679    1.18496   -1.31183   -52.54060
             2   ||   2.30604    2.97009    0.66405    28.79591
             3   ||   3.94087    5.44181    1.50094    38.08653
             4   ||   5.69862    5.16413   -0.53450    -9.37941
             5   ||   6.47501    5.92160   -0.55341    -8.54683
             6   ||   6.61771    6.96928    0.35157     5.31250
             7   ||   6.74075    7.54298    0.80223    11.90122
             8   ||   8.23654    8.53169    0.29515     3.58342
             9   ||   9.68850    9.04979   -0.63871    -6.59245
            10   ||   8.21800   10.06657    1.84856    22.49408
         _______ ||  _________  _________  _________   _________
                 ||
          NDIF   ||        10     (100%)
         R, RSQ  ||     0.931      0.868
           N     ||        10         10         10          10
          MEAN   ||   6.04188    6.28429    0.24241     3.31144
          STD    ||   2.47013    2.75159    1.00545    25.43798
          MAX    ||   9.68850   10.06657    1.84856    38.08653
          MIN    ||   2.30604    1.18496   -1.31183   -52.54060
         STDERR  ||   0.78112    0.87013    0.31795     8.04419
           T     ||     7.735      7.222      0.762       0.412
        PROB>|T| ||    0.0001     0.0001     0.4653      0.6902
         ____________________________________________________________
```

Plotting the Percent Differences of Variables: Example 4

Given yearly data sets ONE and TWO, plot the percent differences of the variables X1-X10 against time. Note: output for this example has been omitted.

```
PROC COMPARE DATA=ONE COMPARE=TWO OUT=THREE OUTPERCENT NOPRINT;
   VAR X1-X10;
   ID  YEAR;
PROC PLOT DATA=THREE;  PLOT ( X1-X10 ) * YEAR;
```

This could also have been done with a DATA step (using ARRAYs and a RENAME= data set option), but using PROC COMPARE is easier.

Chapter 9

The CONTENTS Procedure

ABSTRACT

The CONTENTS procedure prints descriptions of the contents of one or more files from a SAS library.

INTRODUCTION

Refer to the chapter on "SAS Files" in *SAS Language Guide for Personal Computers* to familiarize yourself with the basic features of SAS libraries and the types of files (or members) that can reside in them, or if you need help with the terminology used in this procedure description.

PROC CONTENTS provides information about SAS data libraries and about individual SAS files in a SAS data library. It is particularly useful for documenting permanent SAS data sets (library members of DATA type).

Specific information pertaining to the physical characteristics of a member depends on whether the file is a SAS data set or another type of SAS file.

SPECIFICATIONS

The PROC statement is the only statement associated with the CONTENTS procedure.

PROC CONTENTS *options;*

PROC CONTENTS Statement

PROC CONTENTS *options;*

You can specify the following options in the PROC CONTENTS statement.

DATA=*libref.member* | *member*

refers to an entire library or to a specific member within a library. If you use a two-level name, *libref* refers to the SAS library, and *member* is either the name of a member in the library or the keyword _ALL_. If you use a one-level name, *member* is either the name of a member in the WORK library or the keyword _ALL_.

When you specify the name of a member, you get a report on that member. When you specify _ALL_, you get information about all members having the type or types specified by MEMTYPE=.

For example, to print a description of all the members in the SAS library referenced by the libref STUDY, use the statement:

```
PROC CONTENTS DATA=STUDY._ALL_ MEMTYPE=ALL;
```

To obtain the contents of one member named HTWT of type DATA from the same library, use the statement:

```
PROC CONTENTS DATA=STUDY.HTWT MEMTYPE=DATA;
```

If you do not specify the DATA= option, PROC CONTENTS describes the most recently created member.

DIRECTORY

prints the list of members contained in the specified SAS library. This option is useful when you are printing the contents of just one file and when you also want to see the directory for the library. (When _ALL_ is specified in the DATA= option, the directory is automatically printed.)

MEMTYPE=*membertype*
MTYPE=
MT=

specifies the types of members that are available for processing. The following values can be specified:

ALL	all of the following types
CAT	catalog
DATA	SAS data set
FORMAT	format catalog

If MEMTYPE= is not specified, the default value is ALL. If you have files with the same name but different types, such as a type DATA file STUDY.INFO and a type CAT file STUDY.INFO, the following statement

```
PROC CONTENTS DATA=STUDY.INFO;
```

produces a report on both types.

You can specify more than one type by enclosing the list of types in parentheses. For example,

```
PROC CONTENTS DATA=STUDY._ALL_ MEMTYPE=(DATA CAT);
```

produces descriptions of all DATA and CAT types in the library.

NODS

suppresses printing the contents of individual files when _ALL_ is specified in the DATA= option. Only the SAS library directory is printed.

NOPRINT

specifies that you do not want the CONTENTS procedure output to be printed. The OUT= option should also be specified when this option is used. This option is for SAS data sets only.

OUT=*SASdataset*

gives the name of an output SAS data set. The output SAS data set contains the same information that is given in the variable description section in the printed output of CONTENTS. See the **OUT= SAS Data Set** section for more details. This option is for SAS data sets (DATA type) only.

POSITION output data set

prints a second list of the variable names in the order of their position in the data set. By default, the variables are listed in alphabetical order. This option is for SAS data sets (DATA type) only.

SHORT

prints only the list of variable names in the SAS data set. This option is for SAS data sets (DATA type) only.

DETAILS

OUT= SAS Data Set

The output SAS data set optionally produced by PROC CONTENTS contains information on the variables in the individual SAS data set or for all data sets in the library based on the DATA= value. The variables in the output data set are

FORMAT	variable format (blank if none given)
FORMATD	number of decimals for format (0 if none given)
FORMATL	format width (0 if none given)
INFORMAT	variable informat (blank if none given)
INFORMD	number of decimals for informat (0 if none given)
INFORML	informat width (0 if none given)
JUST	justification (0=left, 1=right)
LABEL	variable label (blank if none given)
LENGTH	variable length
LIBNAME	libref used for the data library
MEMLABEL	data set label for this member (blank if no label)
MEMNAME	member in which the variable is located
NAME	variable name
NOBS	number of observations in data set
NPOS	relative position in the data set input buffer
TYPE	1=numeric 2=character
TYPEMEM	TYPE= value for this member (blank if no TYPE= value)
VARNUM	variable number in data set.

For each SAS data set reported (identified by MEMNAME), the variable names are sorted. Note that they are sorted so that the values X1, X2, and X10 come out in that order, not the true collating sequence of X1, X10, X2. Therefore, if you want to use a BY statement on MEMNAME in subsequent steps, you should run a PROC SORT on the output data set first.

Printed Output

The amount of information and the appearance of the output depend on the type of member being described and the options you specify on the PROC CONTENTS statement. For members of type FORMAT and CAT, PROC CONTENTS gives the file name and file type.

For SAS data sets, PROC CONTENTS produces the following information:

- the number of OBSERVATIONS
- the number of variables
- the record length
- the TYPE of SAS data set
- data set LABEL, if one exists
- an alphabetic list of variables that includes the following:
    1. #, the position of the variable in the data set
    2. the VARIABLE name
    3. the TYPE of the variable (character or numeric)
    4. the variable's LENGTH
    5. the starting POSITION of the variable in the observation
    6. the variable's FORMAT and INFORMAT (if any)
    7. the variable's LABEL, if there is one.

EXAMPLE

The following program uses PROC CONTENTS to describe a SAS data set named GRDATA in a library referenced by the libref MYLIB:

```
LIBNAME MYLIB '\DIR';
PROC CONTENTS DATA=MYLIB.GRDATA;
RUN;
```

Output for this program is shown in **Output 9.1**.

Output 9.1 PROC CONTENTS Output

```
                                  PROC CONTENTS OUTPUT                                  1

                                  CONTENTS PROCEDURE

DSNAME=MYLIB.GRDATA
DATA SET LABEL: old graph data
NUMBER OF OBSERVATIONS: 45                                  NUMBER OF VARIABLES: 5
MEMTYPE:    DATA


                      ----ALPHABETIC LIST OF VARIABLES AND ATTRIBUTES-----
#  VARIABLE   TYPE LENGTH POSITION  FORMAT         INFORMAT  LABEL
1  COLOR      NUM       3        4                           COLOR FOR THIS OBSERVATION
2  LENGTH     NUM       3        7                           LENGTH OF THIS OBSERVATION
4  PART1      CHAR    200       13                           FIRST HALF OF DATA
5  PART2      CHAR    200      213                           LAST HALF OF DATA
3  PICTURE    NUM       3       10                           PICTURE NUMBER
```

Chapter 10

The COPY Procedure

ABSTRACT

The COPY procedure copies an entire SAS data library or selected members of the library. Optional features allow you to limit processing to specific types of library members.

INTRODUCTION

Refer to chapters on the DATA step and PROC step to acquaint yourself with general terminology used in this procedure description. Also see the "SAS Files" chapter in *SAS Language Guide for Personal Computers* for a discussion of the different types of files (or members) that can reside in a SAS data library.

The COPY procedure is a general utility for copying SAS data libraries from one device to another or from one file to another. You can copy the entire library or you can select or exclude members of specific types.

SPECIFICATIONS

PROC COPY IN=*libref* **OUT=***libref options;*
  SELECT *members... / option;*
  EXCLUDE *members... / option;*

PROC COPY Statement

PROC COPY IN=*libref* OUT=*libref options;*

where

IN=*libref*
INDD=*libref*

refers to the SAS data library containing members to be copied. IN= must be specified. IN= and INDD= are equivalent.

OUT=*libref*
OUTDD=*libref*

refers to the SAS data library into which members are copied. OUT= must be specified. OUT= and OUTDD= are equivalent.

You can use the following options in the PROC COPY statement:

MEMTYPE=*membertype*
MTYPE=
MT=

specifies one or more types of members that are to be moved or copied. Valid *membertype* values are

ALL	all member types (default)
CAT	full-screen catalogs
DATA	SAS data sets
FORMAT	SAS format catalogs.

If you specify more than one type, the list must be enclosed in parentheses. For example:

```
PROC COPY IN=DS1 OUT=DS2 MEMTYPE=(DATA CAT);
```

If MEMTYPE= is not specified, all (ALL) types of members in the library are available for processing.

MOVE

causes each member of the input library (IN=) to be deleted after it has been successfully copied. For example, the statement

```
PROC COPY IN=OLD OUT=NEW MOVE;
```

copies members of the SAS library referenced by OLD into the SAS library referenced by NEW and deletes the OLD library.

SELECT Statement

If you want to copy only selected members, use the SELECT statement to list the names of the members to be copied. The general form of the SELECT statement is

SELECT *member... / option;*

where *member* names one or more SAS files selected from the SAS library specified by IN= in the PROC statement and copied to the SAS library specified by OUT= in the PROC statement.

There are several ways to specify member names in the SELECT statement, as described in **Specifying Member Names** below.

You can use the following option in the SELECT statement:

MEMTYPE= *membertype*

specifies types of members to be selected. Valid values are the same as those shown above for the MEMTYPE= option in the PROC statement.

Types specified with MEMTYPE= on the SELECT statement override the MEMTYPE= specification on the PROC statement. For example, the following statements

```
PROC COPY IN=ORIG OUT=NEW MEMTYPE=(FORMAT DATA);
   SELECT MATH LANG GEO / MEMTYPE=CAT;
```

copy members named MATH, LANG, and GEO of type CAT. No other members are copied.

If you do not specify MEMTYPE= on the SELECT statement, those types specified with MEMTYPE= in the PROC statement are available to be selected. For example,

```
PROC COPY IN=ORIG OUT=NEW MEMTYPE=(FORMAT DATA);
   SELECT MATH LANG GEO;
```

copies the members MATH, LANG, and GEO of types FORMAT and DATA.

If MEMTYPE= is not specified in the PROC statement or the SELECT statement, MEMTYPE=ALL is in effect.

EXCLUDE Statement

If you want to copy most of the members in a library, use the EXCLUDE statement to specify the names of those to be excluded from the copy operation. The general form of the EXCLUDE statement is

EXCLUDE *member ... / option;*

where *member* names one or more SAS files (or members) to be excluded from the SAS library specified by OUT= in the PROC statement. See **Specifying Member Names** below.

You can specify the following option in the EXCLUDE statement:

MEMTYPE=*membertype*
: specifies the types of members that are to be excluded. Valid values for *membertype* are the same as those shown above for the MEMTYPE= option in the PROC statement.

  Any types specified with MEMTYPE= in the EXCLUDE statement must have been previously specified in the PROC statement or a SELECT statement.

Specifying Member Names

As shown in the examples above, you can select or exclude one member by giving the name in the SELECT or EXCLUDE statement. You can select or exclude more than one by giving a list of names. You can also select or exclude an abbreviated list of members. For example, this statement

```
SELECT TABS TEST1-TEST3;
```

selects members TABS, TEST1, TEST2, and TEST3. Also, you can select a group of members whose names begin with the same letter or letters by entering the common letter(s) followed by a colon (:). For example, you can select the four members shown in the previous example and all other members having names that begin with the letter T by specifying

```
SELECT T:;
```

Remember that the MEMTYPE= option affects which types of members are available to be selected. Therefore, if MEMTYPE=ALL is in effect, this example selects all member types having names beginning with the letter T.

You specify members to be EXCLUDEd the same way that you specify those to be SELECTed. That is, you can list individual member names, use an abbreviated list, or specify a common letter or letters followed by a colon (:). For example,

```
EXCLUDE STATS TEAMS1-TEAMS4 RBI:;
```

excludes the members STATS, TEAMS1, TEAMS2, TEAMS3, TEAMS4, and all the members beginning with the letters RBI from the copy operation. Again, keep in mind that all types having the specified names are excluded if MEMTYPE=ALL (the default) is in effect.

Note: only members named in a SELECT statement or selected by default can be excluded. If you attempt to exclude a member that is not eligible for copying, you will get an error message. For example, if you enter the following statements

```
SELECT GRADES1-GRADES3;
EXCLUDE GRADES4-GRADES5;
```

COPY will copy the selected members and issue an error message for the members listed in the EXCLUDE statement.

Output

A note appears on the SAS log as each data set is successfully copied. No printed output is produced.

EXAMPLES

Copying a SAS Data Library: Example 1

This example copies all members in the SAS data library referenced by the libref MISC to a library referenced by the libref NEW. Since MEMTYPE= is not specified, all types are copied:

```
PROC COPY IN=MISC OUT=NEW;
```

Copying Selected Members of a SAS Data Library: Example 2

In this example, selected members in the library referenced by the libref MISC are copied to a library referenced by the libref NEW. Notice that only SAS data sets (DATA types) are initially available for processing.

```
PROC COPY IN=MISC OUT=NEW MOVE MEMTYPE=DATA;
   SELECT MLIST;
   SELECT GTEST: / MEMTYPE=CAT;
   EXCLUDE GTEST3 / MEMTYPE=CAT;
```

The first SELECT statement copies SAS data set MLIST . The second SELECT statement copies all members having names beginning with letters GTEST of type CAT except the one named GTEST3 that is listed in the EXCLUDE statement. All of the selected members are copied to the SAS library referenced by NEW and deleted from the library referenced by OLD.

Chapter 11

The CORR Procedure

ABSTRACT

The CORR procedure computes correlation coefficients between variables, including Pearson product-moment and weighted product-moment correlations. CORR also computes some univariate descriptive statistics.

INTRODUCTION

Correlation measures the closeness of a linear relationship between two variables. If one variable x can be expressed exactly as a linear function of another variable y, then the correlation is 1 or −1, depending on whether the two variables are directly related or inversely related. A correlation of zero between two variables means that each variable has no linear predictive ability for the other. If the values are normally distributed, then a correlation of zero means that the variables are independent of one another.

The true product-moment correlation (Pearson), denoted ρ_{xy}, is defined:

$$\rho_{xy} = \mathrm{cov}(x,y)/\sqrt{\mathrm{var}(x)\mathrm{var}(y)}$$

$$= E((x - Ex)(y - Ey))/\sqrt{(E(x - Ex)^2 E(y - Ey)^2)}\ .$$

The sample correlation estimates the true correlation. It is computed:

$$r_{xy} = \Sigma(x - \bar{x})(y - \bar{y})/\sqrt{(\Sigma(x - \bar{x})^2 \Sigma(y - \bar{y})^2)}$$

where $\bar{x}$ and $\bar{y}$ are the sample means of x and y. The full name of this statistic is the *Pearson product-moment correlation*.

Output 11.1 below is a scatterplot of the variables x and y; its correlation is close to zero, specifically r=.02:

Output 11.1 Scatterplot Showing Variables with a Correlation r of .02: PROC CORR

```
  PLOT OF Y*X    LEGEND: A = 1 OBS, B = 2 OBS, ETC.
 Y
 4 +
   |                   A
   |
 3 +
   |                         A
   |                    A    A   B A A
 2 +                  A A  A  A BAB
   |                A A CBC BC AAAC AB A
   |               A A   AA DADDBCCA A A
 1 +            A    A CACBBCBCACAABA AAA
   |                 AD BBAACBEBFACBAACC A
   |                 A ACD FBDCGECECF A  AAA
 0 +            A  A CD BDDCBFFDEDBDAACAA A
   |          A       FBCHDEAGDEDDCEABB AA
   |             AB C BBBCBAIGGBFDBBACDBAA
-1 +              A   BBC BBCEACAACF BA A
   |                   ABAAACBACCAABBBA
   |              A  AB A    AA B  B   A
-2 +                A   BAC BA  AAA        A
   |                        A
   |                          A           A
-3 +
   |
   |
-4 +
   --+----+----+----+----+----+----+----+----+----+-
    -5   -4   -3   -2   -1    0    1    2    3    4

                          X
```

When variables are highly correlated, their points tend to fall on or near a line of fit. In **Output 11.2** x and z have a correlation r of .81.

If the variables are negatively correlated, the line of fit has a negative slope; in other words, the variables are related inversely so that high values of one variable tend to occur with low values of the other. This is the case with z and y, which have a correlation r of $-.57$, as shown in **Output 11.3**.

Output 11.2 Scatterplot Showing Variables with a Correlation *r* of .81: PROC CORR

```
  PLOT OF Z*X    LEGEND: A = 1 OBS, B = 2 OBS, ETC.
 Z
 4 +
   |
   |                                      AA
 3 +
   |
   |                                  AAA
 2 +                              AAABAAABAA
   |                          A  AAEADDABAA
   |                            DACFADEA A
 1 +                        BAACCDBGD CCA
   |                      B ADCEIGFEDABB
   |                    BABBGJIGHDHBBA A
 0 +                    BAACILGJICACAB
   |                AABBDCEFCFHBDDF  A
   |                  DDDKFFDDEEB AA
-1 +              A C FAFGBCFCB BC
   |              A  CDACBBACAA
   |             ABA BDCADCA B
-2 +                 A  C
   |          A A  A AA A
   |                A A
-3 +            A
   |                   A
   |
-4 +
   --+----+----+----+----+----+----+----+----+----+-
    -5   -4   -3   -2   -1    0    1    2    3    4

                          X
```

Output 11.3 Scatterplot Showing Variables with a Correlation *r* of −.57: PROC CORR

```
  PLOT OF Z*Y    LEGEND: A = 1 OBS, B = 2 OBS, ETC.
 Z
 4 +
   |
   |             A  A
 3 +
   |
   |                  AA A
 2 +               A A BAAABAA  A
   |             A   AACCBFA B  B
   |                 BAAADEBCBCA  A
 1 +              A B ABDACBDCACACB A
   |                ABAADBFEGEBFDB AAA
   |                CA DCEHFEGEFCBEA A A
 0 +                  AAABCGEJDIEDDAD AB
   |               A  CABAECBEDCEECBDCDA  A
   |                     CBDGHFCDCAEBEAAA A
-1 +                 A    C CF FDBCDBDB BBA
   |                      A  AEB ADB BBB
   |                      BA A A E CB EB  AA
-2 +                              A   AB
   |                        A A     AAA   A
   |                                  A  A
-3 +                               A
   |                                            A
   |
-4 +
   --+--------------+--------------+--------------+-
    -5             -2              1              4

                          Y
```

Correlations among a set of variables are statistics that contain sufficient information for computing regressions, partial correlations, canonical correlations, factor patterns, principal component coefficients, and many other statistics.

SPECIFICATIONS

The following statements can be used in the CORR procedure:

PROC CORR *options;*
  VAR *variables;*
  WEIGHT *variable;*
  FREQ *variable;*
  BY *variables;*

The PROC CORR statement invokes the procedure. The VAR statement is used to specify variables for the analysis. WEIGHT, FREQ, and BY statements are optional. There is no fixed order for statements following the PROC CORR statement.

PROC CORR Statement

PROC CORR *options;*

The options that can appear in the PROC CORR statement are given below. If no options are specified, CORR calculates Pearson product-moment correlations and significance probabilities, printing them in a rectangular table along with univariate statistics.

DATA=*SASdataset*
: specifies the name of the SAS data set to be used by PROC CORR. If it is omitted, the most recently created SAS data set is used.

RANK
: requests that the correlation coefficients for each variable be printed in order from highest to lowest in absolute value. When RANK is omitted, the correlations are printed in a rectangular table defined by variable names at the top and side.

BEST=*n*
: prints the *n* correlations for each variable with the largest absolute values; the coefficients are printed in descending order.

VARDEF=*divisor*
: specifies the divisor to be used in the calculation of variances and covariances. Possible values for *divisor* are N, DF, WEIGHT or WGT, and WDF. VARDEF=N requests that the number of observations be used as the divisor. VARDEF=DF requests that the error degrees of freedom, $n-1$, be used. VARDEF=WEIGHT or WGT requests that the sum of the weights be used. VARDEF=WDF requests that the sum of the weights minus one be used. The default value is DF.

NOSIMPLE
: suppresses printing the simple descriptive statistics for each variable.

NOPRINT
: suppresses printing the correlations. This option is used when the only purpose of using CORR is to create an output data set containing correlations.

NOPROB

suppresses the printing of significance probabilities associated with the correlations.

NOMISS

specifies that an observation with a missing value for any variable previously used in the analysis be dropped from all calculations. Otherwise, CORR includes observations that have nonmissing values for pairs. Specifying NOMISS can be much faster and cheaper.

SSCP

requests that the uncorrected sums of squares and cross products (SSCP) be printed. If both SSCP and OUT= (below) are specified, the output data set contains the SSCP matrix as well as the correlation matrix. For the SSCP observations, the _TYPE_ variable's value is SSCP.

CSS

requests that the corrected sums of squares and cross products (CSS) be printed. If both CSS and OUT= (below) are specified, the output data set contains the CSS matrix as well as the correlation matrix. For the CSS observations, the _TYPE_ variable's value is CSS.

COV

requests that covariances be printed. If COV and OUT= (below) are both specified, the output data set contains the covariance matrix, as well as the correlation matrix. For the observations containing the covariance matrix, the _TYPE_ variable's value is COV.

NOCORR

specifies that correlations not be output to the output data set. If NOCORR is specified, the data set does not contain correlations, but PROC CORR still makes the data set TYPE=CORR. You can change the data set type to COV or SSCP by using the TYPE= data set option, which is described in *SAS Language Guide for Personal Computers*.

```
PROC CORR NOCORR COV OUT=B(TYPE=COV);
```

OUT=*SASdataset*

requests that CORR create a new SAS data set containing Pearson correlations. The new data set is TYPE=CORR and includes means, standard deviations, simple statistics, and correlation coefficients. The example at the end of this chaper lists a TYPE=CORR data set. If you want to create a permanent SAS data set, you must specify a two-level name (see *SAS Language Guide for Personal Computers* for more information on permanent SAS data sets.) Also see **Output Data Set** at the end of this chapter for a complete description of the data set's structure.

VAR Statement

VAR *variables;*

The names of the variables to be correlated are listed in the VAR statement. If you omit the VAR statement, CORR calculates correlations between all the numeric variables in the input data set.

For example, the statements

```
PROC CORR;
   VAR A B C;
```

produce correlation coefficients between three pairs of variables: A and B, A and C, B and C.

WEIGHT Statement

WEIGHT *variable;*

If you want to compute weighted product-moment correlation coefficients, give the name of the weighting variable in a WEIGHT statement.

FREQ Statement

FREQ *variable;*

If one variable in your input data set represents the frequency of occurrence for values of another variable in the observation, include the variable's name in a FREQ statement. CORR then treats the data set as if each observation appeared *n* times, where *n* is the value of the FREQ variable for the observation. The total number of observations is considered equal to the sum of the FREQ variable when CORR calculates significance probabilities. WEIGHT and FREQ statements have similar effects except in calculating degrees of freedom.

BY Statement

BY *variables;*

A BY statement can be used with PROC CORR to obtain separate analyses on observations in groups defined by the BY variables. When a BY statement appears, the procedure expects the input data set to be sorted in order of the BY variables. If your input data set is not sorted in ascending order, use the SORT procedure with a similar BY statement to sort the data, or, if appropriate, use the BY statement options NOTSORTED or DESCENDING. For more information, see the discussion of the BY statement in *SAS Language Guide for Personal Computers.*

DETAILS

Missing Values

The default method of handling missing values is to use all the nonmissing pairs of values for each pair of variables. This means that some correlations are computed using more observations than others.

An alternative method is available with the NOMISS option, which uses an observation only if none of the variables is missing.

There are two reasons for specifying NOMISS and avoiding the pairwise default method. First, this method is more efficient computationally. Second, if the correlations are used as input to regression or other statistical procedures, a pairwise-missing correlation matrix leads to several statistical difficulties. Pairwise correlation matrices may not be positive definite. The pattern of missing values may bias the results.

Output Data Set

An output data set is requested by the OUT= specification in the PROC CORR statement. The data set is marked with the special data set type, TYPE=CORR. This type of data set is recognized by many SAS/STAT™ procedures, including REG and FACTOR.

The variables in the data set are

- BY variables
- _TYPE_, identifying the type of observation
- _NAME_, identifying variable names
- the variables listed in the VAR statement.

The observations, as identified by _TYPE_, are

- MEAN, the mean of each variable
- STD, the standard deviation of each variable
- N, the number of nonmissing observations for each variable
- SUMWGT, the sum of the weights for each variable, but only if a WEIGHT statement is specified.

The following kinds of observations are further identified by the combination of the variables _TYPE_ and _NAME_.

- SSCP, the uncorrected cross products (if the SSCP option is given)
- CSS, the corrected cross products (if the CSS option is given)
- COV, the covariances (if the COV option is given)
- CORR, a sequence of observations containing correlations.

Computer Resources

The only factor limiting the number of variables used by PROC CORR is the required computer resources. For efficient processing, the amount of memory needed for temporary storage depends on the options specified. If both NOMISS and NOSIMPLE options are specified, the minimum temporary storage needed in bytes to process the data is

$$24 * (V + K)$$

where

V	is the number of variables in the VAR list (or the number of numeric variables if the VAR list is omitted)
K (= V*(V+1)/2)	is the number of correlations to be computed.

Without the NOMISS option, an additional 52K bytes of memory for temporary storage is needed. If the NOSIMPLE option is not specified, the temporary storage must be increased by 16 * V + 52 bytes. When the options RANK or BEST=*n* are specified, increase the temporary storage by 8 * (V + K) bytes.

Let N denote the number of observations. Then the CPU time required varies as N * K. The required CPU time is much smaller if the NOMISS option is specified than if it is not specified. Without the NOMISS option, processing is much faster if most of the observations have no missing values.

Printed Output

For each variable, CORR prints:

1. the VARIABLE name
2. N, the number of observations having nonmissing values of the variable
3. the MEAN
4. STD DEV, the standard deviation
5. the SUM
6. the MINIMUM value
7. the MAXIMUM value.

For each pair of variables, CORR prints:

8. the Pearson coefficient.
9. N, the number of observations used to calculate the coefficient, under the null hypothesis that the correlation is zero. If a FREQ statement is used, this number is the sum of the frequency variable.
10. PROB> |R|, the significance probability of the correlation under the null hypothesis that the correlation is zero.

Among its optional features, CORR can

11. print only the correlations requested with no simple statistics (the NOSIMPLE option)
12. print the correlations for each variable in descending order of their absolute values (the RANK or BEST= options)
13. print the uncorrected cross products (the SSCP option), the corrected cross products (the CSS option), and the covariance matrix (the COV option)
14. produce a specially structured SAS data set containing a correlation matrix, which can be used as input to some SAS/STAT™ software procedures.

EXAMPLE

Three Uses of PROC CORR

You can use PROC CORR to

- show the simple descriptive statistics for each variable and correlation matrix
- show the correlations for each variable in descending order of their absolute values
- obtain an output data set with covariances as well as correlations.

The following example produces **Output 11.4 – 11.6.**

```
*---DATA COURTESY A.C. LINNERUD, N.C.STATE UNIV.;
DATA SKINFOLD;
   INPUT CHEST ABDOMEN ARM @@;
   CARDS;
09.0 12.0 3.0  20.0 20.0 7.5  10.0 23.0 6.0  12.0  6.0 5.0
08.5 15.0 3.0  12.0 17.0 4.0  11.0 13.0 6.0  05.0 14.0 3.0
13.0 19.0 3.0  22.0 20.0 6.0  10.5 12.0 3.5  17.0 15.0 4.5
10.0  7.0 4.0  17.0 28.0 5.5  15.0 15.5 3.0  16.0 11.0 3.0
07.0 13.0 2.5  16.0 18.0 3.0  09.0 12.5 5.0  17.5 18.0 3.0
15.5 28.5 5.0  21.0 27.5 6.0  23.0 24.0 6.5  11.5 15.0 3.0
22.5 20.0 4.5  13.0 14.0 4.0  14.0 21.0 2.5  04.0  3.0 2.0
05.5  8.5 3.0  21.0 13.0 9.0  16.0 11.0 3.0  17.5 15.0 4.5
25.0 35.0 6.5  21.0  6.0 3.5  16.5 17.0 4.0  09.5 11.5 2.5
15.0 19.0 4.0  13.5  6.5 3.5  16.0 15.0 3.0  26.0 38.0 4.0
12.5 20.0 3.0  05.0  7.5 3.5  12.0 15.0 3.5  15.0 13.0 4.5
17.0 19.5 5.0  16.0 20.0 5.5  09.0  4.0 2.0  19.0 12.0 3.0
16.0 17.5 6.0  14.5 14.5 4.0
;

PROC CORR DATA=SKINFOLD;
   VAR CHEST ABDOMEN ARM;
   TITLE 'DESCRIPTIVE STATISTICS AND CORRELATION MATRIX';

PROC CORR DATA=SKINFOLD RANK NOSIMPLE;
   TITLE 'RANKED CORRELATIONS';

PROC CORR DATA=SKINFOLD COV OUT=CORROUT;
   VAR CHEST ABDOMEN ARM;
TITLE 'COVARIANCES AND CORRELATIONS';
PROC PRINT DATA=CORROUT;
TITLE2 'OUTPUT DATASET FROM PROC CORR';
```

Output 11.4 Producing Descriptive Statistics and Correlation Matrix, Ranked Correlations, and an Output Data Set

```
                                                                                      1

                          DESCRIPTIVE STATISTICS AND CORRELATION MATRIX

VARIABLE ❶     N ❷           MEAN ❸          STD DEV ❹            SUM ❺        MINIMUM ❻        MAXIMUM ❼

CHEST          50           14.41   5.256376108681565            720.5               4                26
ABDOMEN        50           16.01   7.190902699428847            800.5               3                38
ARM            50            4.15   1.485473881648959            207.5               2                 9

               CORRELATION COEFFICIENTS / PROB > |R| UNDER HO: RHO=0 / N = 50 ❾

                                   CHEST   ABDOMEN       ARM

                    CHEST        1.00000   0.61986   0.52973 ❽
                                  0.0000    0.0001    0.0001 ❿

                    ABDOMEN      0.61986   1.00000   0.42925
                                  0.0001    0.0000    0.0019

                    ARM          0.52973   0.42925   1.00000
                                  0.0001    0.0019    0.0000
```

Output 11.5 Producing Ranked Correlations

```
                                                                          2

                    ⓫ RANKED CORRELATIONS

      CORRELATION COEFFICIENTS / PROB > |R| UNDER HO: RHO=0 / N = 50

                  CHEST
                           CHEST   ABDOMEN      ARM
                         1.00000   0.61986   0.52973 ⓬
                          0.0000    0.0001    0.0001

                  ABDOMEN
                         ABDOMEN     CHEST      ARM
                         1.00000   0.61986   0.42925
                          0.0000    0.0001    0.0019

                  ARM
                             ARM     CHEST   ABDOMEN
                         1.00000   0.52973   0.42925
                          0.0000    0.0001    0.0019
```

Output 11.6 Producing an Output Data Set with Covariances and Correlations

```
                                                                       3
                     COVARIANCES AND CORRELATIONS

                     ⓭ COVARIANCE MATRIX

       COV               CHEST            ABDOMEN            ARM

       CHEST          27.629489796      23.429489796      4.1362244898
       ABDOMEN        23.429489796      51.709081633      4.5852040816
       ARM            4.1362244898      4.5852040816      2.2066326531

                     COVARIANCES AND CORRELATIONS

VARIABLE     N          MEAN           STD DEV             SUM         MINIMUM        MAXIMUM

CHEST       50         14.41   5.256376108681565          720.5              4             26
ABDOMEN     50         16.01   7.190902699428847          800.5              3             38
ARM         50          4.15   1.485473881648959          207.5              2              9

       CORRELATION COEFFICIENTS / PROB > |R| UNDER HO: RHO=0 / N = 50

                             CHEST   ABDOMEN      ARM

               CHEST       1.00000   0.61986   0.52973
                            0.0000    0.0001    0.0001

               ABDOMEN     0.61986   1.00000   0.42925
                            0.0001    0.0000    0.0019

               ARM         0.52973   0.42925   1.00000
                            0.0001    0.0019    0.0000
```

⓮ COVARIANCES AND CORRELATIONS 4
OUTPUT DATASET FROM PROC CORR

OBS	_TYPE_	_NAME_	CHEST	ABDOMEN	ARM
1	COV	CHEST	27.62948979592	23.42948979592	4.136224489796
2	COV	ABDOMEN	23.42948979592	51.70908163265	4.585204081633
3	COV	ARM	4.136224489796	4.585204081633	2.206632653061
4	MEAN		14.41	16.01	4.15
5	STD		5.256376108682	7.190902699429	1.485473881649
6	N		50	50	50
7	CORR	CHEST	1	.6198591072548	.5297276579659
8	CORR	ABDOMEN	.6198591072548	1	.4292499347199
9	CORR	ARM	.5297276579659	.4292499347199	1

Chapter 12

The DATASETS Procedure

ABSTRACT

PROC DATASETS performs data management utility functions on the members of a SAS library. PROC DATASETS can

- list, rename, and delete all types of members
- alter and list variable names and related variable information in SAS data sets
- copy and concatenate SAS data sets.

INTRODUCTION

See the "SAS Files" chapter in *SAS Language Guide for Personal Computers* for information about SAS data libraries, especially the types of files (or members) that can reside in a SAS data library.

Use the DATASETS procedure to manage a SAS data library. With PROC DATASETS you can list, rename, and delete all types of members in a SAS data library. For SAS data sets (members of DATA type) PROC DATASETS can change variable names and related variable information, such as informats, formats, or labels.

The APPEND, CONTENTS, and COPY statements allow you to perform these utility functions within the DATASETS procedure rather than using the APPEND, CONTENTS, and COPY procedures in separate PROC steps.

You specify changes to library members in associated procedure statements, such as DELETE, EXCHANGE, and MODIFY statements. Changes are effective at the end of the PROC step if no errors are encountered in the step or if the FORCE option is in effect. Changes to variables in a SAS data set (named in the MODIFY statement) take effect when PROC DATASETS processes all FORMAT, INFORMAT, LABEL, and RENAME statements specified for that SAS data set.

SPECIFICATIONS

The following statements can be used in the DATASETS procedure:

PROC DATASETS *options;*
  AGE *currentname name2 name3 ... lastname (option) / option;*
  APPEND BASE= *SASdataset options;*
  CHANGE *oldname*=*newname ... / option;*
  CONTENTS *options;*
  COPY OUT= *libref options;*
    EXCLUDE *member member1-membern member:;*
    SELECT *member ... member1-membern member:;*
  DELETE *members (option) ... / option;*
  EXCHANGE *name*=*anothername ... / option;*
  MODIFY *SASdataset (options);*
    FORMAT *variable ... format. variable ... format. ...;*
    INFORMAT *variable ... informat. variable ... informat. ...;*
    LABEL *variable*=*newlabel ...;*
    RENAME *variable*=*newname ...;*
  SAVE *members (option) ... / option;*

PROC DATASETS Statement

PROC DATASETS *options;*

Use the following options in the PROC DATASETS statement:

LIBRARY=*libref*
DDNAME=

refers to the SAS data library to be processed. If LIBRARY= is not specified, the current default SAS library (usually the WORK library) is processed. DDNAME= is equivalent to LIBRARY=.

MEMTYPE=*membertype*
MTYPE=
MT=

specifies one or more member types that are available for processing. Valid *membertype* values are

ALL	all member types (default)
CAT	catalogs
DATA	SAS data sets
FORMAT	format catalogs.

In the PROC statement, the MEMTYPE= option limits the procedure processing to those types specified. For example, if the library being processed contains SAS data sets and catalogs, you can limit processing to SAS data sets with the MEMTYPE= option, as follows:

```
PROC DATASETS LIBRARY=REF1 MEMTYPE=DATA;
```

To specify more than one type, enclose the list in parentheses. For example,

```
PROC DATASETS LIBRARY=REF1 MEMTYPE=(DATA CAT);
```

If not specified, MEMTYPE=ALL is in effect. (For more information on types of members that can reside in a SAS data library, see the "SAS Files" chapter in *SAS Language Guide for Personal Computers*.)

You can also specify MEMTYPE= in most PROC DATASETS statements. For details refer to **Using MEMTYPE= in Associated Statements** below.

KILL

deletes **all** members in the SAS library.

FORCE

updates the SAS library even if errors are encountered during execution of any procedure statements.

Note: if the NOREPLACE system option has been specified, the FORCE option is ignored, and the library is not updated.

NOLIST

suppresses listing the members that are available for processing on the SAS log.

NOWARN

suppresses the warning message that is issued if a member specified in a DELETE or SAVE statement, or listed as the last member in an AGE statement, is not in the SAS library currently being processed.

Using MEMTYPE= in associated statements Using MEMTYPE= in an associated statement is slightly different from using MEMTYPE= in the PROC statement. You can specify only one type with MEMTYPE= in an associated statement. If MEMTYPE= is specified in the PROC statement, you must use one of those previously specified values with MEMTYPE= in the associated statement; otherwise, use any valid MEMTYPE= value in the associated statement. MEMTYPE=ALL is in effect for associated statements if MEMTYPE= is not specified in the PROC statement and an associated statement.

As illustrated in **Specifications** above, many of the statements allow you to specify MEMTYPE= as an option either in parentheses or after a slash, or both. If specified after the /, the MEMTYPE= value applies to all members listed in the statement. If specified in parentheses after a member name(s), the MEMTYPE= value overrides one specified after the /. Also, note that a MEMTYPE= value in parentheses applies to all preceding members in the list. For example, in the following statements

```
PROC DATASETS LIBRARY=libref;
   DELETE member1 member2 (MEMTYPE=ALL) member3 (MEMTYPE=DATA);
```

the value ALL applies to *member1* and *member2*; DATA applies to *member3*. Use of the MEMTYPE= option is discussed further with each of the following statements.

AGE Statement

AGE *currentname name2 name3 ... lastname (option) / option;*

You can use the AGE statement to rename a group of related members in a library so that programs can then access the latest addition to the group using one name that does not change.

When an AGE statement is used, the name of the first member is changed to the second name; the name of the second member is changed to the third name, and so on until the name of the next-to-last member is changed to the last name. The last member is then deleted.

For example, each day you run a SAS program that creates the SAS data set TODAY. You keep that SAS data set in a SAS library with seven other members. Each time you want to create a new SAS data set, the oldest SAS data set must be deleted and the remaining members renamed, leaving the name TODAY available for the new SAS data set. You can delete and rename the members using PROC DATASETS with the AGE statement:

```
PROC DATASETS LIBRARY=DAILY;
   AGE TODAY DAY1-DAY7 (MEMTYPE=DATA);
```

After PROC DATASETS executes, the SAS data set originally named TODAY is renamed DAY1; the SAS data set originally named DAY1 is renamed DAY2; and so on. The SAS data set originally named DAY6 is renamed DAY7, and the SAS data set originally named DAY7 is deleted. Since there is no longer a member named TODAY, the name TODAY is available for the new SAS data set.

Notice that the above example uses an abbreviated SAS data set list, DAY1-DAY7.

Use the MEMTYPE= option to specify one type of member to age.

If the first member named in the AGE statement is not in the SAS library, the AGE statement does not execute. If other members listed are not present, the SAS System prints a note on the log and renames all the members that are present.

APPEND Statement

APPEND BASE=*SASdataset options;*

Use the APPEND statement to append observations from one SAS data set to the end of another. This statement can be used only with SAS data sets (library members of DATA type).

BASE=*SASdataset*
OUT=*SASdataset*

names the data set to which you want to add observations. If APPEND cannot find an existing data set with this name, it creates a new data set. In other words, you can use the APPEND statement to create a data set by specifying a new data set name in BASE=. OUT= is equivalent to BASE=. Either BASE= or OUT= must be specified.

APPEND statement options are:

DATA=*SASdataset*
NEW=*SASdataset*

names the SAS data set containing observations you want to add to the end of the SAS data set specified by BASE=. If DATA= is omitted, the most recently created SAS data set is used. NEW= is equivalent to DATA=.

FORCE

causes truncation of values if variables in the DATA= data set have longer lengths than the corresponding variables in the BASE= data set. FORCE also causes variables in the DATA= data set to be dropped if there are not corresponding variables in the BASE= data set. DATA= variables that do not match BASE= variables are assigned missing values in the output (BASE=) data set when FORCE is in effect. A mismatch occurs if a DATA= variable name or variable type (character or numeric) does not match a corresponding variable name or variable type in the BASE= data set. If DATA= variables are too long or do not match BASE= variables, the SAS System prints a message on the log and stops processing unless FORCE is specified.

The APPEND statement performs functions similar to those performed by the APPEND procedure (described in an earlier chapter).

CHANGE Statement

CHANGE *oldname=newname ... / option;*

Use the CHANGE statement to rename one or more members. Specify the old member name on the left side of the equal sign and the new member name on the right. For example, the statements

```
PROC DATASETS LIBRARY=OIL MEMTYPE=DATA;
   CHANGE PERSIA=IRAN RUSSIA=USSR;
```

change the name of the SAS data set PERSIA to IRAN and RUSSIA to USSR.

Use the MEMTYPE= option to restrict name changes to one type of member. If MEMTYPE= is not specified in the CHANGE statement, types specified by MEMTYPE= in the PROC statement can be changed. If MEMTYPE= is not specified in the PROC statement and the CHANGE statement, the default value is ALL.

CONTENTS Statement

CONTENTS *options;*

Use the CONTENTS statement to describe one or more members of a SAS data library.

CONTENTS statement options are:

DATA=*member* | _ALL_

specifies a member to be described by CONTENTS or specifies that all members in the library are to be described if the keyword _ALL_ is used. If DATA= is not specified, CONTENTS describes the last library member to be modified.

To describe the contents of one SAS data set named HTWT in the library referenced by STUDY, use the following statements

```
PROC DATASETS LIBRARY=STUDY MEMTYPE=DATA;
   CONTENTS DATA=HTWT;
```

POSITION

prints a second list of the variable names in the order of their position in the data set. By default, the variables are listed in alphabetical order.

SHORT

prints only the list of variable names in the SAS data set. This option is for SAS data sets (DATA type) only.

The CONTENTS statement performs functions similar to those performed by the CONTENTS procedure (described in an earlier chapter).

COPY Statement

COPY OUT=*libref options;*

Use the COPY statement and options when you want to copy members from one library to another.

OUT=*libref*

specifies the output library into which members are copied. OUT= must be specified.

The following options can be specified in the COPY statement:

IN=*libref*

specifies an alternate input library. For example, the following program copies all of the members from the WORK library into the TEST library.

```
PROC DATASETS LIBRARY=TEST;
   COPY IN=WORK OUT=TEST;
```

If you do not specify IN=, the library referenced by the LIBRARY= option in the PROC DATASETS statement is used as the input library.

MEMTYPE=*membertype*
MTYPE=
MT=

specifies one or more types of members that are to be moved or copied. If you specify more than one type, the list must be enclosed in parentheses. For example:

```
PROC DATASETS LIBRARY=DS1;
     COPY OUT=DS2 MEMTYPE=(DATA CAT);
```

If MEMTYPE= is not specified, then the COPY operation is limited by the MEMTYPE= values specified in the PROC DATASETS statement. If not specified on the COPY and PROC statement, MEMTYPE=ALL is in effect.

MOVE

causes each member of the input library to be deleted after it has been successfully copied. For example, the following statements

```
PROC DATASETS LIBRARY=OLD;
     COPY OUT=NEW MOVE;
```

copy the members of the SAS library referenced by OLD into the SAS library referenced by NEW and delete the OLD library.

You can use the SELECT and EXCLUDE statements in association with the COPY statement.

EXCLUDE Statement

EXCLUDE *member member1-membern member:;*

The EXCLUDE statement names one or more SAS files (or members) that are not copied to the output library.

For example, the following program

```
PROC DATASETS LIBRARY=STUDY;
   COPY OUT=CONTROL;
   EXCLUDE GROUP1-GROUP3;
```

copies all of the files (members) from the library referenced by STUDY to the library referenced by CONTROL except GROUP1, GROUP2, and GROUP3.

The COPY statement performs functions similar to those performed by the COPY procedure (described in an earlier chapter).

SELECT Statement

SELECT *member... member1-membern member:;*

Use the SELECT statement to name one or more SAS files (or members) to be copied from the input library to the output library. For example, the following program

```
PROC DATASETS LIBRARY=STUDY;
   COPY OUT=CONTROL;
   SELECT GROUP1-GROUP3;
```

copies SAS data sets GROUP1, GROUP2, and GROUP3 from the SAS library referenced by STUDY to the SAS library referenced by CONTROL.

DELETE Statement

DELETE *members (option) ... / option;*

Use the DELETE statement to specify members to be deleted from the SAS library. For example, say you want to delete the members ONE and TWO from the SAS library referenced by the libref DIGIT:

```
PROC DATASETS LIBRARY=DIGIT;
   DELETE ONE TWO;
```

You can use an abbreviated member list where appropriate. For example:

```
DELETE RDU1-RDU5;
```

Use MEMTYPE= in the DELETE statement to restrict processing to one type. If MEMTYPE= is specified in the PROC statement, use MEMTYPE= in the DELETE statement to further restrict processing to one of those previously specified types. For example, the MEMTYPE= option is used in both the PROC statement and the DELETE statement in the following program:

```
PROC DATASETS LIBRARY=FOOD MEMTYPE=(DATA CAT);
   DELETE MEATS DAIRY / MEMTYPE=CAT;
```

When this program executes, only MEATS and DAIRY of type CAT are deleted. If MEMTYPE= had not been specified on the DELETE statement, SAS data sets (DATA type) and CAT members named MEATS and DAIRY would have been deleted.

If MEMTYPE= is not specified on the DELETE statement and the PROC statement, the default value is ALL.

If you attempt to delete members of a type that has not been specified on the PROC statement, you will receive an error message that the member cannot be found.

EXCHANGE Statement

EXCHANGE *name=anothername ... / option;*

Use the EXCHANGE statement to exchange the names of two members in the SAS library. For example, if your SAS library contains the members A and Z, the statements

```
PROC DATASETS LIBRARY=MYLIB;
   EXCHANGE A=Z;
```

would change the name of the member originally called A to Z, and Z to A.

More than one pair of member names can be changed with one EXCHANGE statement.

Use the MEMTYPE= option to restrict name exchanges to one type of member. If MEMTYPE= is not specified on the EXCHANGE statement and the PROC statement, ALL is the default value.

MODIFY Statement

MODIFY *SASdataset (options);*

Use the MODIFY statement and options when you want to change attributes in the specified SAS data set (library member of DATA type). You can specify only one SAS data set name in each MODIFY statement, and you cannot specify the same data set name in more than one MODIFY statement in a given PROC step.

The MODIFY statement is used in conjunction with other procedure statements (described below) to change variable names, labels, informats, or formats in the specified SAS data set.

The following options can be specified in the MODIFY statement. Options must be enclosed in parentheses.

(LABEL=*'newlabel'*)
(LABEL=' ')

specifies a *newlabel* or removes a label for the SAS data set named in the MODIFY statement. A new label cannot be longer than 40 characters and must be enclosed in single quotes.

If you enter LABEL= with no value, the old label is removed but not replaced. For example:

```
PROC DATASETS LIBRARY=TEST;
   MODIFY EXP1 (LABEL=' ');
   MODIFY EXP2 (LABEL='TESTS ON THREE YEAR OLDS');
```

The first MODIFY statement removes the label of the SAS data set TEST.EXP1, and the second MODIFY statement changes the label of TEST.EXP2.

(TYPE=*type*)

assigns or changes the type of SAS data set. Most SAS data sets are TYPE=DATA. However, a number of special SAS data sets can be created by some SAS procedures (for example, PROC CORR and PROC FACTOR) or in a DATA step.

Valid *types* are DATA, CORR, COV, SSCP, EST, and FACTOR. See the "SAS Files" chapter in *SAS Language for Personal Computers* for a discussion of special SAS data sets.

Note: do not confuse TYPE= with MEMTYPE=. TYPE= specifies a type of special SAS data set. MEMTYPE= specifies one or more types of members in a SAS data library.

You must be sure that the specified value of TYPE= corresponds to the actual SAS data set type. The SAS data set type specified by TYPE= is not validated by SAS (except to check if it is a length of eight characters or less). SAS does not verify that the SAS data set's structure is appropriate for the type you have designated, or even that you have specified a valid special type.

When you specify both options, separate them with one blank and enclose them with parentheses, for example:

```
MODIFY EXP3 (LABEL= 'TESTS FOR ALL AGES'  TYPE=CORR);
```

Use the following statements to change variable labels, names, informats, and formats in a SAS data set named in the MODIFY statement.

FORMAT Statement

FORMAT *variable ... format. variable ... format. ...;*

Variable formats in the SAS data set specified by the MODIFY statement can be changed or removed with the FORMAT statement. To change a format, specify the name of the variable and then the new format. When the variable name is given, but there is no accompanying format, the old format is removed, and not replaced. Multiple variables can be used, and abbreviated variable lists, such as X1-X5, can be used where appropriate. You can change as many formats as you want with one FORMAT statement. Here is an example:

```
PROC DATASETS LIBRARY=STUDY;
   MODIFY GROUP1;
   FORMAT X1-X3 4.1 TIME HHMM2.2 AGE;
```

Variables X1, X2, and X3 are assigned the 4.1 format; the variable TIME is assigned the HHMM *w.d* format; and the format of the variable AGE is removed.

Any variables whose formats are to be removed must be listed last in the FORMAT statement; otherwise, they are assigned the first format that follows. For example, if you write the FORMAT statement shown above as follows,

```
FORMAT X1-X3 4.1 AGE TIME HHMM2.2;
```

the variable AGE would have its format changed to HHMM2.2, rather than removed.

INFORMAT Statement

INFORMAT *variable ... informat. variable ... informat. ...;*

Informats in the SAS data set specified by the MODIFY statement can be changed or removed using the INFORMAT statement. To change an informat, specify the name of the variable and then the new informat. When a variable name is specified but with no accompanying informat, the old informat is removed.

Multiple variables and abbreviated variable lists can be used. For example, in the SAS data set GROUP1, the variables A, B, and X1-X3 are assigned new informats and the variable C has its informat removed with these statements:

```
PROC DATASETS LIBRARY=STUDY;
   MODIFY GROUP1  ;
   INFORMAT A B 2. X1-X3 4.1 C;
```

Any variables whose informats are to be removed must be listed last in the INFORMAT statement; otherwise, they are assigned the first informat that follows. For example, the following INFORMAT statement,

```
INFORMAT A B C 2. X1-X3 4.1;
```

changes the informat for variable C to 2.

LABEL Statement

LABEL *variable=newlabel ...;*

The LABEL statement changes or removes variable labels in the SAS data set specified by the MODIFY statement. You can use as many variables as you want in the LABEL statement, as long as each variable name is followed by an equal sign. To specify a new label, follow the equal sign with a new label. To remove a label do not specify anything after the equal sign. If the new label includes a right parenthesis, equal sign, or semicolon, it must be enclosed in single quotes. If a single quote appears in the label, it must be written as two single quotes in the LABEL statement. The new label can be up to 40 characters long.

The following statements

```
PROC DATASETS LIBRARY=STUDY;
   MODIFY GROUP1 ;
   LABEL X1='Score 1=' X2='Score 2=' A=;
```

change the labels for variables X1 and X2 and remove the label for variable A in SAS data set GROUP1.

RENAME Statement

RENAME *variable=newname ...;*

Variables can be assigned new names using the RENAME statement. The new name must be a valid SAS name. There is no limit to the number of variables that you can rename in one statement. For example,

```
RENAME DAY1=TIME1 DAY2=TIME2;
```

SAVE Statement

SAVE *members (option) ... / option;*

If you want to **delete** most of the members of a SAS data library, specify the names of the members you want to keep in the SAVE statement.

Because the SAVE statement provides a simple way to delete many members in one operation, be sure that you understand how the MEMTYPE= option affects which member types are saved and which types are deleted. The MEMTYPE= option in the SAVE statement specifies the type(s) of members that are deleted. The members named in the SAVE statement are saved while all other members of the specified type are deleted. For example, suppose you have a SAS data library containing members of type DATA, CAT, and FORMAT. The following program

```
PROC DATASETS LIBRARY=FRUIT;
   SAVE APPLES ORANGES PEARS (MEMTYPE=CAT);
```

deletes all members of CAT type except APPLES, ORANGES, and PEARS. No members of any other type are deleted.

If you do not specify MEMTYPE= in the PROC statement and in the SAVE statement, MEMTYPE=ALL is in effect. For example,

```
PROC DATASETS LIBRARY=FRUIT;
   SAVE APPLES ORANGES PEARS;
```

deletes all members in the library (referenced by FRUIT) except those named APPLES, ORANGES, and PEARS.

If you specify MEMTYPE= in the PROC statement, the MEMTYPE= value in the SAVE statement must be one of those previously specified types. For example,

```
PROC DATASETS LIBRARY=FRUIT MEMTYPE=(DATA CAT);
   SAVE APPLES ORANGES PEARS (MEMTYPE=CAT);
```

deletes all members of DATA type and all members of CAT type except APPLES, ORANGES, and PEARS. If MEMTYPE=CAT had not been specified in the SAVE statement in this example, all members of CAT type except APPLES, ORANGES, and PEARS and all members of DATA type except APPLES, ORANGES, and PEARS would have been deleted.

Abbreviated member lists (for example, STUDY1-STUDY10) can be used with the SAVE statement.

Output

The DATASETS procedure lists the members in the SAS library before and after the library is updated unless the NOLIST option is specified. The list is written on the SAS log. If the MEMTYPE= option is used, only specified types are listed.

EXAMPLE

This program processes a SAS library referenced by libref MISC. Since the MEMTYPE= option is specified in the PROC2 statement, only DATA types (SAS data sets) are available for processing. First, DATASETS produces a list of SAS data sets on the SAS log. Then the procedure deletes a SAS data set named GEORGIA, changes a SAS data set name from GDPSTATS to ECONOMIC, and modifies characteristics of two SAS data sets. The contents of the modified data set named COFFEE are listed on the SAS log and the data sets COFFEE and TEA are copied to the library DRINK. DATASETS then writes the updated SAS data set list on the SAS log.

```
PROC DATASETS LIBRARY=MISC MEMTYPE=DATA;
   DELETE GEORGIA;
   CHANGE GDPSTATS=ECONOMIC;
   MODIFY CARS(LABEL=CARS RATED ON SIX SCALES);
      RENAME NOISE=QUIET;
      LABEL ACCEL=ACCELERATION
         VISIBLE=VISIBILITY
         CARGO=CARGO SPACE;
   MODIFY COFFEE(TYPE=CORR);
      FORMAT DEEP BREWED HEARTY PURE ROASTED FRESH 4.2;
   CONTENTS DATA=COFFEE;
   COPY OUT=DRINK;
      SELECT COFFEE TEA;
```

If you do not specify MEMTYPE= in the PROC statement and in the SAVE statement, MEMTYPE=ALL is in effect. For example,

```
PROC DATASETS LIBRARY=FRUIT;
   SAVE APPLES ORANGES PEARS;
```

deletes all members in the library referenced by FRUIT except those named APPLES, ORANGES, and PEARS.

If you specify MEMTYPE= in the PROC statement, the MEMTYPE= value in the SAVE statement must be one of those previously specified types. For example,

```
PROC DATASETS LIBRARY=FRUIT MEMTYPE=(DATA CAT);
   SAVE APPLES ORANGES PEARS (MEMTYPE=CAT);
```

deletes all members of DATA type and all members of CAT type except APPLES, ORANGES, and PEARS. If MEMTYPE=CAT had not been specified in the SAVE statement in this example, all members of CAT type except APPLES, ORANGES, and PEARS and all members of DATA type except APPLES, ORANGES, and PEARS would have been deleted.

Abbreviated member lists (for example, STUDY1-STUDY10) can be used with the SAVE statement.

Output

The DATASETS procedure lists the members in the SAS library before and after the library is updated unless the NOLIST option is specified. The list is written on the SAS log. If the MEMTYPE= option is used, only specified types are listed.

EXAMPLE

This program processes a SAS library referenced by libref MISC. Since the MEMTYPE= option is specified in the PROC statement, only DATA type SAS files (SAS data sets) are available for processing. First, DATASETS produces a list of SAS data sets on the SAS log. Then the procedure deletes a SAS data set named GEORGIA, changes a SAS data set name from GDPSTATS to ECONOMIC, and modifies characteristics of two SAS data sets. The contents of the modified data set named COFFEE are listed on the SAS log and the data sets COFFEE and TEA are copied to the library DRINK. DATASETS then writes the updated SAS data set list on the SAS log.

```
PROC DATASETS LIBRARY=MISC MEMTYPE=DATA;
   DELETE GEORGIA;
   CHANGE GDPSTATS=ECONOMIC;
   MODIFY CARS(LABEL=CARS RATED ON SIX SCALES);
      RENAME NOISE=QUIET;
      LABEL ACCEL=ACCELERATION
            VISIBLE=VISIBILITY
            CARGO=CARGO SPACE;
   MODIFY COFFEE(TYPE=CORR);
      FORMAT DEEP BREWED HEARTY PURE ROASTED FRESH 4.2;
   CONTENTS DATA=COFFEE;
   COPY OUT=DRINK;
      SELECT COFFEE TEA;
```

Chapter 13

The DBF Procedure

ABSTRACT

The DBF procedure converts dBASE II and dBASE III files to SAS data sets that are compatible with the current release of the SAS System. This procedure can also be used to convert SAS data sets to dBASE II and dBASE III files.

INTRODUCTION

DBF produces one output file, but no printed output. The output file contains the same information as the input file; exceptions are noted below under **Details.**

The DBF procedure supports the following versions of dBASE files:

- Version 2.4 of dBASE II
- Version 1.0 of dBASE III
- Version 1.1 of dBASE III.

dBASE II and dBASE III are products of Ashton-Tate. Future versions of dBASE II and dBASE III files may not be compatible with the current version of the DBF procedure. SAS Institute cannot be responsible for upgrading DBF to support these changes to dBASE software; however, attempts will be made to support new versions of dBASE II and dBASE III files with each new version of the SAS System.

SPECIFICATIONS

PROC DBF *options*;

The DBF statement is the only statement associated with the DBF procedure.

PROC DBF Statement

PROC DBF *options*;

The options below can appear in the PROC DBF statement. Only one of the two options specifying a dBASE file can be given.

DB2=*fileref*

specifies the fileref of a dBASE II file. Unless a FILENAME statement is specified before the procedure statement, the second level of the referenced dBASE II file must be DBF and the file must be located in your current directory.

DB3=*fileref*

specifies the fileref of a dBASE III file. Unless a FILENAME statement is specified before the procedure statement, the second level of the referenced dBASE III file must be DBF and the file must be located in your current directory.

DATA=*libref.member*

names the input SAS data set. Use this option if you are creating a dBASE II or dBASE III file from a SAS data set. If you use the DATA= option, do not use the OUT= option. If you omit the DATA= option, the SAS System creates an output SAS data set from the dBASE II or dBASE III file.

OUT=*libref.member*

names the SAS data set created to hold the converted data. Use this option only if you do not specify the DATA= option. If OUT= is omitted, the SAS System creates a temporary data set named _DATA_. If OUT= is omitted or if you do not specify a two-level name in the OUT= option, the SAS data set created by DBF is not permanently saved.

DETAILS

Conversion of dBASE II and dBASE III Variables to SAS Variables

Numeric variables are stored in character form by dBASE II and dBASE III. These numeric variables become SAS numeric variables when converting from a dBASE file to a SAS data set. Character variables become SAS character variables; any character variable of a length greater than 200 is truncated to 200. dBASE logical variables become SAS character variables with a length of 1. Date variables allowed by dBASE III become SAS date variables. When converting a dBASE III file to a SAS data set, memo fields supported by dBASE III are ignored.

dBASE II and dBASE III allow 10-character variable names. Variable names will be truncated to a length of 8 when converting a dBASE file to a SAS data set.

Missing values in dBase ⇒ '0' in SAS

Conversion of SAS Variables to dBASE II and dBASE III Variables

Numeric variables are stored in character form by dBASE II and dBASE III. SAS numeric variables become dBASE numeric variables with a length of 16 when converting from a SAS data set to a dBASE file. If the number of digits, including a possible decimal point, exceeds 16, a warning message is issued and the dBASE numeric field is filled with the character '9'. All SAS character variables become dBASE variables of the same length. When converting from a SAS data set to a dBASE III file, SAS date variables become dBASE III date variables. When converting from a SAS data set to a dBASE II file, SAS date variables become dBASE II character variables of the form YYYMMDD.

Missing Values

dBASE II and dBASE III do not have a designated missing value. If a SAS numeric value is missing, the corresponding dBASE numeric field is filled with the character '9'.

EXAMPLES

Conversion of a dBASE II File to a SAS Data Set: Example 1

In the example below, a dBASE II file named EMPLOYEE.DBF is converted to a SAS data set. Since no FILENAME statement is specified, the last level of the filename is assumed to be DBF and the file is assumed to be in your current directory.

```
PROC DBF DB2=EMPLOYEE OUT=SAVE.EMPLOYEE;
RUN;
```

Conversion of a SAS Data Set to a dBASE III File: Example 2

In this example, a SAS data set is converted to a dBASE III file. A FILENAME statement is used to specify a fileref that names the dBASE III file. The FILENAME statement must come before the PROC DBF statement.

```
FILENAME MAIL '\ROOT\SUBDIR\MAIL.DBF';
PROC DBF DB3=MAIL DATA=SAVE.MAIL;
RUN;
```


Chapter 14

The DIF Procedure

ABSTRACT

The DIF procedure converts Data Interchange Format (DIF) files to SAS data sets that are compatible with the current release of the SAS System. This procedure can also be used to convert SAS data sets to DIF files. Software Arts, Inc., developed the Data Interchange Format to be used as a common language for data. Many software packages, VisiCalc and Lotus 1-2-3 for example, use the DIF.

INTRODUCTION

PROC DIF produces one output file, but no printed output. The output file contains the same information as the input file; exceptions are noted below under **Details.**

It is important to remember that any DIF file that you plan to convert to a SAS data set should be in a tabular form; that is, all items in a given column should represent the same type of data. When converting from a DIF file to a SAS data set, each row of the DIF file becomes an observation in the SAS data set. Conversely, when converting a SAS data set to a DIF file, each SAS observation becomes a row in the DIF file.

SPECIFICATIONS

The DIF statement is the only statement associated with the DIF procedure.

PROC DIF *options;*

PROC DIF Statement

PROC DIF *options;*

The options below can appear in the PROC DIF statement.

DIF=*fileref*
: specifies the fileref of a DIF file. Unless a FILENAME statement was specified, the second level of the referenced DIF file must be DIF, and the file must be located in your current directory.

DATA=*libref.member*
: names the input SAS data set. Use this option if you are creating a DIF file from a SAS data set. If you use this option, do not use the OUT= option. If you omit the DATA= option, the SAS System creates an output SAS data set from the DIF file.

OUT=*libref.member*
: names the SAS data set to hold the converted data. Use this option only if you do not specify the DATA= option. If OUT= is omitted, the SAS System creates a temporary data set named _DATA_. If OUT= is omitted or if you do not specify a two-level name in the OUT= option, the SAS data set created by PROC DIF is not permanently saved.

LABELS
: causes PROC DIF to write the names of the SAS variables as the first row of the DIF file and a row of blanks as the second row of the DIF file. The actual data portion of the DIF file begins in the third row. The LABELS option is allowed only when converting a SAS data set to a DIF file.

PREFIX=*name*
: specifies a prefix to be used in constructing SAS variable names when converting a DIF file to a SAS data set. For example, if PREFIX=VAR, the new variable names are VAR1, VAR2,...,VAR*n* . If you do not specify the PREFIX= option, PROC DIF assigns the names COL1, COL2, ..., COL*n* to the variables in the output SAS data set.

SKIP=*n*
: specifies the number of rows, beginning at the top of the DIF file, to be ignored when converting a DIF file to a SAS data set. For example, suppose the first row of your DIF file contains column headings and the second row of your DIF file is a blank row. The actual data in your DIF file begin in row 3. You should specify SKIP=2 so that PROC DIF ignores the nondata portion of your DIF file. Alternatively, you could delete the first two rows of your DIF file before using PROC DIF.

DETAILS

Conversion of DIF Variables to SAS Variables

Character variables in a DIF file (sometimes referred to as string values) become SAS character variables of length 20. If a DIF character variable's value is longer than 20 characters, it is truncated to a length of 20 in the SAS output data set. The quotation marks that normally enclose character variable values in a DIF file are removed when the value is converted to a SAS character value.

Numeric variables, which can be represented in either integer or scientific notation in a DIF file, become SAS numeric variables when a DIF file is converted to a SAS data set.

Conversion of SAS Variables to DIF Variables

Character variables in a SAS data set become character variables of the same length in a DIF file. The quotation marks that normally enclose character variable values in a DIF file are added when a SAS character variable is converted to a DIF character variable.

SAS numeric variables become DIF numeric variables with a length of 16 when a SAS data set is converted to a DIF file. If a numeric variable in your SAS data set is formatted to have positions to the right of the decimal point, the decimal point is inserted in the DIF numeric value at the appropriate position. If the number of digits, including a possible decimal point, exceeds 16, SAS stores the numeric variable in the BESTw. format. The BESTw. format chooses the notation that gives the most information about the value within the number of columns that are available to write the value.

Caution

It is important to remember that any DIF file that you plan to convert to a SAS data set should be in a tabular form; that is, all items in a given column should represent the same type of data. When converting from a DIF file to a SAS data set, each row of the DIF file becomes an observation in the SAS data set. If there are any rows in your DIF file that contain inconsistent data, for example, a row of underscores, dashes, or blanks, delete these rows before converting the DIF file to a SAS data set. If your DIF file contains title or heading lines, you can either delete these rows or use the SKIP= option to make PROC DIF ignore them.

Missing Values

The developers of the Data Interchange Format (DIF) suggest treating all numeric values that have a value indicator other than V as missing values. PROC DIF follows this convention. When a DIF file is converted to a SAS data set, any numeric value with a value indicator other than V becomes a SAS missing value.

When a SAS data set that has missing values for some numeric variables is converted to a DIF file, the following assignments are made in the DIF file for the variables with missing values:

- the type indicator field value is set to 0
- the number field value contains a string of 16 blanks
- the value indicator is set to NA.

Conversion of SAS Data Sets to Lotus 1-2-3 Worksheet Files

Conversion of SAS data sets to Lotus 1-2-3 worksheet files is a two-step process. First run PROC DIF to convert your SAS data set to a DIF file. Then use the Lotus 1-2-3 Translate Utility to translate the DIF file to a 1-2-3 worksheet file.

To access the Translate Utility, select Translate from the Lotus Access System menu. When the utility is loaded, a menu appears that lists the types of translations available. Select the DIF to WKS choice. The system then displays the list of your files that have the extension, DIF. Select the appropriate file. The Translate Utility creates a new worksheet file with the same file name as the DIF file from which it was translated. The new worksheet has the file extension, WKS. See the *Lotus 1-2-3 User's Manual* for additional information on the Translate Utility.

Conversion of Lotus 1-2-3 Worksheet Files to SAS Data Sets

Conversion of Lotus 1-2-3 worksheet files to SAS data sets is a two-step process. First use the Lotus 1-2-3 Translate Utility to translate the 1-2-3 worksheet file to a DIF file. Then run PROC DIF to convert your DIF file to a SAS data set.

Before translating your 1-2-3 worksheet file to a DIF file, delete all extraneous rows in your WKS file. It is important to remember that any 1-2-3 worksheet file that you plan to convert to a SAS data set should be in tabular form; that is, all items in a given column should represent the same type of data. When you convert a 1-2-3 worksheet file to a SAS data set, each row of the worksheet file becomes an observation in the SAS data set.

To access the Translate Utility, select Translate from the Lotus Access System menu. When the utility is loaded, a menu appears that lists the types of translations available. Select the WKS to DIF choice. The system then displays the list of your files that have the extension, WKS. Select the appropriate file. The Translate Utility creates a new DIF file with the same file name as the WKS file from which it was translated. The new DIF has the file extension, DIF. See the *Lotus 1-2-3 User's Manual* for additional information on the Translate Utility.

EXAMPLES

Conversion of a DIF File to a SAS Data Set: Example 1

In the example below, a DIF file named EMPLOYEE.DIF is converted to a SAS data set. Since no FILENAME statement is specified, the last level of the file name is assumed to be DIF, and the file is assumed to be in your current directory.

```
PROC DIF DIF=EMPLOYEE OUT=SAVE.EMPLOYEE;
RUN;
```

Conversion of a SAS Data Set to a DIF File: Example 2

In this example, a SAS data set is converted to a DIF file. A FILENAME statement is used to specify a fileref that names the DIF file. The FILENAME statement must come before the PROC DIF statement.

```
FILENAME MAIL '\ROOT\SUBDIR\MAIL.DIF';
PROC DIF DIF=MAIL DATA=SAVE.MAIL;
RUN;
```

REFERENCE

"Programmer's Guide to the DIF," *Software Arts Technical Notes* (SATN-18).

Chapter 15

The DOWNLOAD Procedure

ABSTRACT

The micro-to-mainframe link allows you to use mainframe capabilities when you need them under PC DOS. You can use your PC as a development system and choose either local (on the PC) or remote (on the mainframe) processing for your SAS programs. In addition, you can easily transfer SAS data sets between systems with utilities that the micro-to-mainframe link provides.

This chapter documents one part of the link, the DOWNLOAD procedure. (See also "The UPLOAD Procedure.")

INTRODUCTION

You should be familiar with the SAS System for PC DOS before using PROC DOWNLOAD. If you need more information about the SAS System for PC DOS, see *SAS Introductory Guide for Personal Computers*.

The DOWNLOAD procedure copies a SAS data set stored on the remote mainframe system to the local PC system. After you have downloaded the data set to the PC, you can process it just as if it had been created entirely on the PC.

PROC DOWNLOAD executes only under SAS Display Manager. There are two Display Manager commands you need to know about in order to use the DOWNLOAD procedure:

SIGNON — If you have not already established the micro-to-mainframe link, issue the Display Manager SIGNON command. The SIGNON command establishes the link between your PC and the remote mainframe system. See *SAS Language Guide for Personal Computers* for details on the SIGNON command.

RSUBMIT / RSUB — The RSUBMIT, or RSUB, command (for remote submit) sends the program statements in the Program Edit window to the remote mainframe system for execution. See *SAS Language Guide for Personal Computers* for details on the RSUBMIT command. Even though the program executes in the remote mainframe environment, the information that displays on your PC is the same as if you had executed the program locally on the PC.

SPECIFICATIONS

The only statement used with the DOWNLOAD procedure is

PROC DOWNLOAD [*options*]**;**

PROC DOWNLOAD Statement

The following options can be used in the PROC DOWNLOAD statement:

DATA=*input SASdataset*
names the SAS data set that you want to download, or copy, from the mainframe to the PC. When you do not specify the DATA= option, the SAS System copies the last data set created on the mainframe in your SAS program.

OUT=*output SASdataset*
names the SAS data set to which you want the copied data set written. When you do not specify the OUT= option, the SAS System creates a temporary WORK data set.

EXAMPLE

It is easy to extract a subset of a large mainframe SAS data set in a SAS DATA step. You can then copy the subset SAS data set from the mainframe to the PC environment with PROC DOWNLOAD. For example, the following program extracts only the observations with odd numeric values for the variable X from the SAS data set MAIN.

```
DATA SUBSET;
   SET MAIN;
   IF MOD(X,2) = 1;

PROC DOWNLOAD DATA=SUBSET OUT=SUB;
RUN;
```

Remember that you must use the RSUBMIT command for PROC DOWNLOAD because the program executes in the remote mainframe environment.

Chapter 16

The FORMAT Procedure

ABSTRACT

Use the FORMAT procedure to define your own output formats for character or numeric values. These formats can be associated with variables in

- DATA step PUT or FORMAT statements and PUT functions
- a PROC step with a FORMAT statement.

See "SAS Informats and Formats" and also the **FORMAT Statement** in *SAS Language Guide to Personal Computers* for general information on how informats and formats are used with the SAS System.

INTRODUCTION

You can define formats to your own specifications with the FORMAT procedure. PROC FORMAT produces two kinds of formats:

- Value-labeling formats associate labels with values. The VALUE statement generates these formats. For example, you might store SEX as a numeric code, 1 or 2, but print it as a character value using the following statement:

  ```
  VALUE SEX 1='MALE' 2='FEMALE';
  ```

  Both character and numeric variables can have value-labeling formats.
- Picture formats specify templates for printing numbers, giving specifics such as leading zeros, comma and decimal punctuation, fill characters,

prefixes, and negative number representation. For example, you might want to define a picture format for phone numbers with the following statement:

```
PICTURE PHONENUM LOW-HIGH='000/000-0000';
```

Picture formats are for numeric values only.

Background

User-written formats created by PROC FORMAT are stored in a special SAS file called a *format catalog*. A format catalog's second-level name is always FORMATS. (The PC DOS file name is FORMATS.SFL.) A format catalog contains one or more formats. The formats in a catalog are identified by the format name, which is assigned with the PICTURE or VALUE statement.

User-written formats are either temporary or permanent, depending on whether they are stored in a temporary or permanent format catalog. You can use temporary formats only in the same SAS program in which they are created. Permanent formats can be used in the program that creates them and in subsequent SAS programs. For more information on storing and using formats, see the **Details** section of this chapter.

Formats, whether standard SAS formats or those created with PROC FORMAT, are used in PUT and FORMAT statements in a DATA step and in various procedures in a FORMAT statement. If you use a format in a PROC step, the procedure then uses the format to print the variable's values. For example:

```
PROC PRINT;
   VAR PHONE;
   FORMAT PHONE PHONENUM.;
```

The values of the variable PHONE are printed according to the specifications of the PHONENUM. format. Note that in some cases variables with formats are classified according to formatted values rather than internal values.

Format names, whether standard SAS formats or those created with PROC FORMAT, **must** end with a period. User-written formats can have width specifications like SAS-provided formats (for example, DOLLAR10.2). Formats with width and decimal specifications do not need an additional period after the format name; the decimal specification is sufficient, as it is in SAS-provided formats. A decimal specification is ignored in formats created by PROC FORMAT.

Do not confuse the FORMAT procedure with the FORMAT statement. PROC FORMAT creates user-defined formats. The FORMAT statement associates an existing format (either standard SAS or user-defined) with one or more variables. The FORMAT statement can be used in either a DATA or a PROC step. When used in the DATA step that creates a SAS data set, the FORMAT statement associates the format permanently with a variable. The FORMAT statement in a PROC step associates the format with a variable only for the duration of that step.

Note: permanently associating a format with a variable does not permanently **store** the format. Serious complications arise if you do **not** save the format for a permanent data set variable. Be sure you permanently store all formats associated with permanent data set variables. See **Temporary and Permanent Formats** in the **Details** section for more information.

The following example uses PROC FORMAT to define picture formats and then uses the formats with a PUT statement and PROC PRINT.

```
PROC FORMAT;
   PICTURE PHONENUM OTHER='000/000-0000';
   PICTURE SSNUM OTHER='999-99-9999';
```

```
DATA A;
   INPUT PHONE SS;
   PUT PHONE PHONENUM.;
   FORMAT SS SSNUM.;
   CARDS;
9194678000 333221111
9198344381 555667777
;
PROC PRINT;
   FORMAT PHONE PHONENUM.;
```

The results of the PUT statement are printed on the log:

```
919/467-8000
919/834-4381
```

The FORMAT statement in the PROC PRINT step indicates that the procedure is to use the format PHONENUM. to print PHONE values. Because the SSNUM. format is associated with the SS variable by a FORMAT statement within a DATA STEP, the association is permanent. The PRINT procedure prints both SS and PHONE values with the picture formats created for them by PROC FORMAT. The output from PROC PRINT looks like this:

```
OBS      PHONE           SS

 1   919/467-8000   333-22-1111
 2   919/834-4381   555-66-7777
```

The PHONE values print on the log in the pattern specified by PHONENUM. However, the PHONENUM. format is not permanently associated with PHONE the way SSNUM. is associated with SS. This FORMAT statement in the DATA step associates the PHONENUM. format with the PHONE variable permanently:

```
FORMAT SS SSNUM. PHONE PHONENUM.;
```

Value-labeling formats are especially useful when data are stored with uninformative values. For example, suppose you are analyzing the results of a questionnaire. One variable in your data set is PARTY, which represents the political party of the respondent. PARTY'S values are 1 for DEMOCRAT, 2 for REPUBLICAN, 3 for INDEPENDENT, and 4 for OTHER. Whenever values of the variable PARTY are printed, you want the name of the party substituted for the corresponding number. PROC FORMAT gives the appropriate directions for printing the party names. These SAS statements read the political questionnaire data, define a format called P., associate the P. format with the PARTY variable, and then produce a crosstabulation table of AGE by PARTY:

```
DATA POLIT;
   INPUT NAME $ ID AGE PARTY;
   CARDS;
JOHN  191 18 1
JOYCE 218 19 2
HARRY 923 21 4
JAMES 432 20 3
;
PROC FORMAT;
   VALUE P 1='DEMOCRAT'
           2='REPUBLICAN'
           3='INDEPENDENT'
           4='OTHER';
```

```
PROC PRINT;
   TITLE 'WITHOUT FORMAT';
PROC PRINT;
   TITLE 'WITH FORMAT';
   FORMAT PARTY P.;
PROC FREQ;
   TABLES PARTY*AGE;
   FORMAT PARTY P.;
```

SPECIFICATIONS

The FORMAT procedure is controlled by the following statements:

PROC FORMAT *option;*
  VALUE *name (options)*
    range=label
    ...;
  PICTURE *name (options)*
    range=picture (options)
    ...;

Each new VALUE or PICTURE statement defines a format. You can specify as many formats as you want in a PROC FORMAT step, with one format per VALUE or PICTURE statement.

PROC FORMAT Statement

PROC FORMAT *option;*

The following option can be used in the PROC FORMAT statement:

LIBRARY=*libref*

specifies the libref for a directory containing a permanent FORMATS catalog. (If the directory does not already contain a FORMATS catalog, SAS sets up one automatically.) Before you invoke PROC FORMAT, use a LIBNAME statement to associate the libref with the directory for the FORMATS catalog. We recommend that you use LIBRARY as the libref. Use the LIBRARY= option only when you want to store permanent formats.

See **Temporary and Permanent Formats** in the **Details** section for more information.

VALUE Statement

VALUE *name (options)*
  range1=label1
  range2=label2
  ... ;

The elements of the VALUE statement are

name names the format being created. You **must** specify a name in the VALUE statement. The name must be a valid SAS name up to eight characters long, not ending in a number. If the format is for character variables, the first character must be a dollar sign ($), while the remaining seven characters must follow the rules for a valid SAS name. The name must not be a reserved SAS word. Refer to the format later by using the name followed by a period. (Do **not** put a period after the format name in the VALUE statement.)

options are enclosed in parentheses and follow the format name. Valid options are MAX=, MIN=, DEFAULT=, and FUZZ=. They are described in detail in **Format Options (for VALUE or PICTURE)**.

ranges specifies a range of values, a list of values, or a list of ranges. You **must** specify one or more ranges in the VALUE statement. The syntax is

value	(single values)
value-value	(a range of values)
range,range	(list of ranges or values)

Do not overlap the values in ranges or value lists.

The appropriate label is the one associated with the range in which the character or number falls. For example:

```
VALUE ABC 1='A' 2='B' 3='C';
VALUE AGEFMT 0-12='CHILD'
             13-19='TEEN'
             20-HIGH='ADULT';
VALUE SEXFMT 1='FEMALE'
             2='MALE'
             0,3-9='MISCODED';
```

The first example uses single values, the second uses ranges, and the third uses both single values and ranges.

A noninclusive range can be specified. For example,

```
VALUE XXX 1-2='X1' 2-3='X2';
```

is confusing because the value 2 could be part of the first or second range. You can specify

```
VALUE XXX 1-<2='X1' 2-3='X2';
```

and the value 2 goes only with the second range. The notation

```
number1 <- number2
```

indicates that the first number is not part of the range. The notation

```
number1 -< number2
```

indicates that the second number is not part of the range. Also, if a range such as

```
VALUE XXX 1-2='X1' 2-3='X2';
```

is specified, the range is automatically changed to

```
VALUE XXX 1-2='X1' 2<-3='X2';
```

to avoid confusion. The first occurrence of a value is always chosen to be the inclusive one.

Formats may include the keywords LOW and HIGH in a range specification. In the AGEFMT. example above, the range 20-HIGH refers to all values from 20 through the largest value of the variable. (The LOW keyword does not include missing values.)

The keyword OTHER may be used on the left side of the equal sign to mean all values not given in any other range or value specification for the format. In the SEXFMT. example above, OTHER=MISCODED could be substituted for 0,3−9=MISCODED to mean that all values other than 1 and 2 are to have a printed value of MISCODED:

```
VALUE SEXFMT 1='FEMALE'
             2='MALE'
         OTHER='MISCODED';
```

Character values must be enclosed in single quotes.

labels value labels can be up to forty characters. (However, some procedures use only the first eight or sixteen characters of a label.) All labels must be in quotes. For example,

```
VALUE XXX 1='YES' 2='NO';
VALUE $XXX 'A'='GOOD' 'B'='BAD';
```

If a label contains a single quote, write it as two separate single quotes:

```
VALUE SECT 1='SMITH''S CLASS'
           2='DOE''S CLASS';
```

If a VALUE statement does not include all of a variable's values, those in the VALUE statement are printed with the specified format, while other values are printed with a default format. For example, these statements

```
PROC FORMAT;
   VALUE TEMP 98.6='NORMAL';
DATA A;
   INPUT T;
   PUT T TEMP6.1;
   CARDS;
98.4
98.6
101.2
;
```

produce these lines

```
  98.4
NORMAL
 101.2
```

Note: a numeric value with a default format is right-aligned in a field with a width equal to that given in the PUT statement. If a field width is not given, the default width of the format is used. Character values using a default format are left-aligned.

PICTURE Statement

PICTURE *name (options)*
range1=picture1 (options)
range2=picture2 (options)
... ;

The elements of the PICTURE statement are listed below.

name names the new format. You **must** specify a name in the PICTURE statement. The name must be a valid SAS name up to eight characters long, not ending in a number. Refer to the format later by using the name followed by a period. (Do **not** put a period after the format name in the PICTURE statement.)

options are enclosed in parentheses and follow the format name. The valid options are MAX=, MIN=, DEFAULT=, and FUZZ=. They are described in detail below.

ranges specifies a range of values, a list of values, or a list of ranges. The syntax is

value	(single values)
value-value	(a range of values)
range,range	(list of ranges or values)

The appropriate picture is the one associated with the range in which the value falls. For example:

```
PICTURE FM LOW -< 0 = '99999-'
            0 -HIGH = '99999+';
```

LOW and HIGH are keywords representing the largest negative and positive numbers, respectively. The "-< 0" indicates that the LOW range is **not** to include zero. The special range OTHER can be used to collect numbers not included in any other range. Missing values are represented with a period (.).

pictures specifies a template for printing numbers. The picture is a sequence of characters in single quotes. The maximum length for a picture is twenty-four characters. Pictures are specified with two types of characters: digit selectors and message characters.

Digit selectors are characters that define positions for numeric values. The digit selectors can be either 0, or the numbers 1 through 9. If the picture is specified with zeros, and the number to be formatted contains leading zeros, the leading zeros are not formatted into the field. To print leading zeros, you may use any digit 1 through 9 to define the positions. All digits, even leading zeros, are formatted. The picture cannot begin with a message character. (See the PREFIX and FILL options.)

Message characters are non-numeric characters that are printed just as they appear in the picture. They are inserted into the picture after the numeric digits are formatted. For example, this PICTURE statement:

```
PICTURE DAY 01-31='00';
```

causes the value 02 to be printed like this:

```
2
```

This PICTURE statement:

```
PICTURE DAY 01-31='99'
                OTHER='99-ILLEGAL DAY VALUE';
```

prints the values 02 and 67 as

```
02
67-ILLEGAL DAY VALUE
```

In this PICTURE statement, the characters 99 are digit selectors, and the characters -ILLEGAL DAY VALUE are message characters.

options are enclosed in parentheses and specify fill characters, prefix characters, and multipliers, described below. This field is optional.

PICTURE Options

These options can be specified for each picture in a picture format.

FILL='*character*' specifies a fill character. This character replaces the leading characters of the picture until a significant digit is encountered. The default is FILL=' ' (blank). The specified character must be enclosed in single quotes. One use of the FILL= option is to prevent a number with leading blanks from being altered, for example, on a check. (See the example below, following the PREFIX description.)

PREFIX='*character*' is a one- or two-character prefix placed in front of the first significant digit of the value. The default is no prefix. The specified character must be enclosed in single quotes. The prefix occupies positions within the picture, not additional positions. Thus, if the picture is not wide enough to contain both the value and the prefix, the prefix is truncated or omitted. The PREFIX= option is often used for leading dollar signs and minus signs. For example, the picture

```
PICTURE PAY OTHER='00,000,000.00'
    (FILL='*' PREFIX='$');
```

prints the value 25500 as

```
***$25,500.00
```

MULTIPLIER=*n*
MULT=*n* specifies a number to be multiplied by a value before it is formatted. The main use of the MULT= option is to get a data value containing decimal points into a form that will fit into the picture template correctly since picture format decimal points are part of the template, not part of the data value. For example, to

have 1600000 print as $1.6M use these PREFIX= and MULTIPLIER= specifications:

```
PICTURE MILLION LOW-HIGH='00.0M'
   (PREFIX='$' MULT=.00001);
```

If you do not specify a value for MULT=, the procedure uses a default value of 10^n, where *n* is the number of digits after the first decimal point in the picture. For example, suppose your data contain a value 123.456 and you want to print it using a picture of '999.999'. FORMAT multiplies 123.456 by 10^3 to obtain a value of 123456; it then fits this value into the picture template to produce 123.456.

NOEDIT forces the format to treat the picture as a value label rather than as a picture specification. This means that numbers are message characters rather than digit selectors; that is, the numbers in the picture are printed as they appear. For example, the statements

```
PROC FORMAT;
   PICTURE MILES 1-99='000000'
       100-HIGH='>100 MILES' (NOEDIT);

DATA TEMP;
   INPUT NAME $ DISTANCE 3.;
   CARDS;
JOHN 300
MARY 600
DAVID 27
ANN 2
;
PROC PRINT;
   FORMAT DISTANCE MILES.;
```

produce this output:

```
OBS  NAME    DISTANCE
 1   JOHN   >100 MILES
 2   MARY   >100 MILES
 3   DAVID          27
 4   ANN             2
```

Format Options (for VALUE or PICTURE)

A format is stored with width attribute information. You may sometimes find that you need one of the following format attributes:

MIN=*n* specifies a minimum width for the format. If MIN= is not given, the length of the longest picture or value label is the minimum default width.

MAX=*n* specifies a maximum width for the format. This can be larger than the picture or value label since picture formats can pad with fill characters on the left. The maximum MAX= width allowed is 40. If MAX= is not given, the default is 40.

DEFAULT=*n* specifies the default width if the format does not have a width specification. The default value for DEFAULT is the length of the longest picture or value.

FUZZ=*n* specifies a fuzz factor. If a number does not match a value or fall in a range exactly, but comes within the fuzz value, it is considered a match. For example

```
PROC FORMAT;
   VALUE ABC (FUZZ=.5) 1='A' 2='B' 3='C';
```

FUZZ=.5 means that if a variable value falls within .5 of a value specified in the VALUE statement, the corresponding label is used to print the value. So using the ABC. format to print a value of 1.2 produces an A, the value 1.7 produces a B, and the value 2.8 produces a C.

Only VALUE formats use FUZZ=; PICTURE formats do not. The default FUZZ value is 1E-12.

DETAILS

Character Data Limitations

The VALUE statement of PROC FORMAT processes character values with a maximum of sixteen characters. If a value has more than sixteen characters, the procedure truncates the value and processes the first sixteen characters. If more than one character value in a VALUE statement has the same first sixteen characters, the SAS System issues an error message indicating that the value is a duplicate. The labels specified by a VALUE statement can have a maximum of forty characters.

PICTURE Logic

The SAS System uses the following logic when printing a value with a PICTURE format. For illustration, suppose you define this format

```
PICTURE MILLION LOW-HIGH = '00.0M'
   (PREFIX='$' MULT=.00001);
```

and you are formatting the value 23468977.

1. Locate the picture associated with the corresponding range for the number to be formatted. If there is no range for the number, use the OTHER specification. If there is no OTHER specification, use the standard SAS numeric format.
2. If the picture contains only message characters (that is, it does not have digit selectors), or has the NOEDIT option, then output the label and ignore the rest of the steps.
3. Multiply the number by the multiplier. In our example, the multiplier is .00001, giving a result of 234.68977.
4. Take the absolute value, that is, ignore the sign.
5. Truncate the value to an integer. If the number is within 10^{-8} of a higher integer, round up. In other words, if the result is between 1 and .00000001, round up to the next integer value and truncate. In our example, the rounded and truncated value is 235.
6. Convert the number to a string of digits, the "source string." That is,

convert the number from floating point to character string representation.
7. Point to the digit corresponding to the high-order (left-most) digit selector in the picture. If the number is too large to fit into the picture, ignore the high-order digits, that is, truncate on the left. This has the effect of converting from a floating point number to a standard number. There is no error condition for this "overflow," although you can use special error ranges to control it.
8. Turn the significance switch off. The significance switch is an indicator of whether or not a digit is significant.

Now the format starts scanning the picture and source strings.

1. With a message (non-numeric) picture character, when the significance switch is off, the fill character is put into the result. If the significance switch is on, the message character is placed in the result.
2. With a digit selector (numeric) picture character, a digit is retrieved from the source string. When either the picture character is nonzero or the source string digit is nonzero, the significance switch is turned on. If the significance switch is on, the source digit is placed in the result. Otherwise, when the picture character and the source string digit are zero, the fill character is placed in the result.

   In our example, the picture character is a zero digit selector, and the source string digit is nonzero. Therefore, the significance switch is on, and the source digit is placed in the result.
3. Now the number is edited. Prefix characters are placed before the first nonfill character in the result. If the format width is larger than the picture length, the result is padded on the left with one fill character and the rest blanks. If the format width is smaller than the picture, the result is truncated on the left.

   In our example, the prefix character '$' is placed before the first digit, and the message character 'M' is the last character in the result:

```
$23.5M
```

Temporary and Permanent Formats

Formats are temporary when you do **not** specify the LIBRARY= option in the PROC FORMAT statement because they are stored in a temporary format catalog named WORK.FORMATS. To retrieve a temporary format for writing a variable value, simply include the format's name in the appropriate SAS statement. The SAS System automatically looks for the format in the WORK.FORMATS catalog.

To create permanent formats, you must:

1. If you do not already have a permanent format catalog, choose a directory in which to store the permanent format catalog.
2. Use a LIBNAME statement to associate a libref with that directory. We recommend that you use the word LIBRARY as the libref.
3. Specify the LIBRARY= option in the PROC FORMAT statement. When you have assigned LIBRARY as the libref, your PROC statement is

```
PROC FORMAT LIBRARY=LIBRARY;
```

When you follow these steps, any formats you create in the same SAS program are stored in a permanent format catalog called LIBRARY.FORMATS.

To use permanent formats in a later program, you **must first** issue a LIBNAME statement assigning the libref LIBRARY to the directory in which you stored the formats.

If you do not specify LIBRARY as the libref, the SAS System cannot find the formats because SAS looks in only two places for user-written formats. The SAS System first looks for the format in the temporary WORK library's format catalog. If the format is not in WORK.FORMATS, SAS then looks in the FORMATS catalog located in a directory referenced by the libref LIBRARY.

For example, suppose you create a permanent format named ANSWER. and store it in the FORMATS catalog in a directory named SASFILES. Later, when you want to use the ANSWER. format with the PRINT procedure, you need to issue a LIBNAME statement before the PROC PRINT step, as shown in the example below:

```
LIBNAME LIBRARY '\SASFILES';
PROC PRINT DATA=TVSURVEY;
   VAR ID WEEK Q1 Q2 Q3;
   FORMAT Q1 Q2 Q3 ANSWER.;
```

When SAS processes the FORMAT statement, it first looks for the ANSWER. format in the current WORK library's format catalog. If the format is not there, SAS then looks for it in the SASFILES directory.

Note that because the libref must be LIBRARY to retrieve formats stored in a permanent format catalog, you cannot use formats from more than one permanent format catalog in a given DATA or PROC step. If you want to create new formats in one format catalog, and write values with formats retrieved from another format catalog, use LIBRARY as the libref for the catalog containing the formats needed for writing values. Assign a libref other than LIBRARY to the catalog in which you are planning to store the new formats created with PROC FORMAT.

When you create a permanent SAS data set and assign user-written formats to any of its variables, be sure to store the formats permanently. Serious complications arise if you do **not** save the format for a permanent data set variable. The data set directory marks the variable as having a format, but when the variable is referenced in later jobs, the SAS System cannot find that format because it has not been saved.

EXAMPLES

The VALUE Statement Used with PROC FORMAT: Example 1

The following three format definitions are useful for transforming state codes or abbreviations into the state names. The $ZIPST. format corresponds to the ZIPNAME function; $STATE. to STNAME; and STATE. to FIPNAME. These formats are useful because you can access them in a PROC step, whereas you must use a DATA step to use the state functions. In addition, you can use these formats with the PUT function in the DATA step to create variables. For example, in this DATA step:

```
DATA NEW;
   INPUT ZIP $ ABBREV $ CENSUSBU;
   STATE1=PUT(ZIP,$ZIPST.);
   STATE2=PUT(ABBREV,$STATE.);
   STATE3=PUT(CENSUSBU, STATE.);
   CARDS;
27511 NC 37
;
```

STATE1, STATE2, and STATE3 all have a value of NORTH CAROLINA. See **Output 16.1** for state code and abbreviation formats.

```
PROC FORMAT;

  *-----$ZIPST: CONVERTS CHARACTER ZIP CODES TO STATE NAMES-----;
  VALUE $ZIPST
     00600-00999='PUERTO RICO'    01000-02799='MASSACHUSETTS'
     02800-02999='RHODE ISLAND'   03000-03899='NEW HAMPSHIRE'
     03900-04999='MAINE'          05000-05999='VERMONT'
     06000-06999='CONNECTICUT'    07000-08999='NEW JERSEY'
     09000-14999='NEW YORK'       15000-19699='PENNSYLVANIA'
     19700-19999='DELAWARE'       20000-20599='DISTRICT OF COLUMBIA'
     20600-21999='MARYLAND'       22000-24699='VIRGINIA'
     24700-26899='WEST VIRGINIA'  27000-28999='NORTH CAROLINA'
     29000-29999='SOUTH CAROLINA' 30000-31999='GEORGIA'
     32000-33999='FLORIDA'        35000-36999='ALABAMA'
     37000-38599='TENNESSEE'      38600-39799='MISSISSIPPI'
     40000-42799='KENTUCKY'       43000-45899='OHIO'
     46000-47999='INDIANA'        48000-49999='MICHIGAN'
     50000-52899='IOWA'           53000-54999='WISCONSIN'
     55000-56799='MINNESOTA'      57000-57799='SOUTH DAKOTA'
     58000-58899='NORTH DAKOTA'   59000-59999='MONTANA'
     60000-62999='ILLINOIS'       63000-65899='MISSOURI'
     66000-67999='KANSAS'         68000-69399='NEBRASKA'
     70000-71499='LOUISIANA'      71600-72999='ARKANSAS'
     73000-74999='OKLAHOMA'       75000-79999='TEXAS'
     80000-81699='COLORADO'       82000-83199='WYOMING'
     83200-83899='IDAHO'          84000-84799='UTAH'
     85000-86599='ARIZONA'        87000-88499='NEW MEXICO'
     89000-89899='NEVADA'         90000-96699='CALIFORNIA'
     96700-96899='HAWAII'         96900-96999='GUAM'
     97000-97999='OREGON'         98000-99499='WASHINGTON'
     99500-99999='ALASKA'
     ;
  *-----$STATE: CONVERTS STATE ABBREV. TO STATE NAMES------;
  VALUE $STATE
     'AL'='ALABAMA' 'AR'='ARKANSAS' 'AZ'='ARIZONA' 'CA'='CALIFORNIA'
     'IL'='ILLINOIS' 'KS'='KANSAS' 'CO'='COLORADO' 'ID'='IDAHO'
     'WI'='WISCONSIN' '99'='FOREIGN' 'GA'='GEORGIA' 'NJ'='NEW JERSEY'
     'VA'='VIRGINIA' 'SC'='SOUTH CAROLINA' 'IN'='INDIANA'
     'IA'='IOWA' 'MO'='MISSOURI' 'MD'='MARYLAND' 'NB'='NEBRASKA'
     'DC'='DISTRICT OF COLUMBIA' 'NY'='NEW YORK' 'OH'='OHIO"
     'MN'='MINNESOTA' 'PA'='PENNSYLVANIA' 'TX'='TEXAS' 'FL'='FLORIDA'
     'NC'='NORTH CAROLINA' 'OK'='OKLAHOMA' 'WV'='WEST VIRGINIA'
     'TN'='TENNESSEE' 'DE'='DELAWARE' 'KY'='KENTUCKY'
     'MS'='MISSISSIPPI' 'NM'='NEW MEXICO' 'ND'='NORTH DAKOTA'
     'MA'='MASSACHUSETTS' 'RI'='RHODE ISLAND' 'SD'='SOUTH DAKOTA'
     'LA'='LOUISIANA' 'UT'='UTAH' 'WA'='WASHINGTON'
     'MI'='MICHIGAN'
     ;
  *-----STATE: OFFICIAL CENSUS BUREAU CODES FOR STATE-----;
  VALUE STATE
     01='ALABAMA'            30='MONTANA'
     02='ALASKA'             31='NEBRASKA'
```

```
04='ARIZONA'          32='NEVADA'
05='ARKANSAS'         33='NEW HAMPSHIRE'
06='CALIFORNIA'       34='NEW JERSEY'
08='COLORADO'         35='NEW MEXICO'
09='CONNECTICUT'      36='NEW YORK'
10='DELAWARE'         37='NORTH CAROLINA'
11='D.C.'             38='NORTH DAKOTA'
12='FLORIDA'          39='OHIO'
13='GEORGIA'          40='OKLAHOMA'
15='HAWAII'           41='OREGON'
16='IDAHO'            42='PENNSYLVANIA'
17='ILLINOIS'         44='RHODE ISLAND'
18='INDIANA'          45='SOUTH CAROLINA'
19='IOWA'             46='SOUTH DAKOTA'
20='KANSAS'           47='TENNESSEE'
21='KENTUCKY'         48='TEXAS'
22='LOUISIANA'        49='UTAH'
23='MAINE'            50='VERMONT'
24='MARYLAND'         51='VIRGINIA'
25='MASSACHUSETTS'    53='WASHINGTON'
26='MICHIGAN'         54='WEST VIRGINIA'
27='MINNESOTA'        55='WISCONSIN'
28='MISSISSIPPI'      56='WYOMING'
29='MISSOURI'
;
```

Output 16.1 State Code and Abbreviation Formats

```
1       S A S   L O G    SAS VERSION 6.XX

NOTE: THE JOB X1FORMAT HAS BEEN RUN UNDER RELEASE 6.XX OF SAS AT SAS INSTITUTE INC. (BASE) (00000000).

NOTE: SAS OPTIONS SPECIFIED ARE:
      SORT=4

NOTE: THE INITIALIZATION PHASE USED 0.09 SECONDS.
           PROC FORMAT PRINT;
             *-----$ZIPST: CONVERTS CHARACTER ZIP CODES TO STATE NAMES-----;
             VALUE $ZIPST
                 00600-00999='PUERTO RICO'    01000-02799='MASSACHUSETTS'
                 02800-02999='RHODE ISLAND'   03000-03899='NEW HAMPSHIRE'
                 03900-04999='MAINE'          05000-05999='VERMONT'
                 06000-06999='CONNECTICUT'    07000-08999='NEW JERSEY'
                 09000-14999='NEW YORK'       15000-19699='PENNSYLVANIA'
                 19700-19999='DELAWARE'       20000-20599='DISTRICT OF COLUMBIA'
                 20600-21999='MARYLAND'       22000-24699='VIRGINIA'
                 24700-26899='WEST VIRGINIA'  27000-28999='NORTH CAROLINA'
                 29000-29999='SOUTH CAROLINA' 30000-31999='GEORGIA'
                 32000-33999='FLORIDA'        35000-36999='ALABAMA'
                 37000-38599='TENNESSEE'      38600-39799='MISSISSIPPI'
                 40000-42799='KENTUCKY'       43000-45899='OHIO'
                 46000-47999='INDIANA'        48000-49999='MICHIGAN'
                 50000-52899='IOWA'           53000-54999='WISCONSIN'
                 55000-56799='MINNESOTA'      57000-57799='SOUTH DAKOTA'
                 58000-58899='NORTH DAKOTA'   59000-59999='MONTANA'
                 60000-62999='ILLINOIS'       63000-65899='MISSOURI'
                 66000-67999='KANSAS'         68000-69399='NEBRASKA'
                 70000-71499='LOUISIANA'      71600-72999='ARKANSAS'
                 73000-74999='OKLAHOMA'       75000-79999='TEXAS'
NOTE: FORMAT $ZIPST HAS BEEN OUTPUT.
                 80000-81699='COLORADO'       82000-83199='WYOMING'
                 83200-83899='IDAHO'          84000-84799='UTAH'
                 85000-86599='ARIZONA'        87000-88499='NEW MEXICO'
                 89000-89899='NEVADA'         90000-96699='CALIFORNIA'
```

(continued on next page)

(continued from previous page)

```
                96700-96899='HAWAII'          96900-96999='GUAM'
                97000-97999='OREGON'          98000-99499='WASHINGTON'
                99500-99999='ALASKA' ;

          *-----$STATE: CONVERTS STATE ABBREV. TO STATE NAMES------;
          VALUE $STATE
        'AL'='ALABAMA' 'AR'='ARKANSAS' 'AZ'='ARIZONA' 'CA'='CALIFORNIA'
        'IL'='ILLINOIS' 'KS'='KANSAS' 'CO'='COLORADO' 'ID'='IDAHO'
        'WI'=WISCONSIN 99='FOREIGN' 'GA'='GEORGIA' 'NJ'='NEW JERSEY'
        'VA'='VIRGINIA' 'SC'='SOUTH CAROLINA' 'FL'='FLORIDA' 'IN'='INDIANA'
NOTE: FORMAT $STATE HAS BEEN OUTPUT.
        'IA'='IOWA' 'MO'='MISSOURI' 'MD'='MARYLAND' 'DC'='DISTRICT OF COLUMBIA'
        'NY'='NEW YORK' 'OH'='OHIO' 'NB'='NEBRASKA' 'MN'='MINNESOTA'
        'PA'='PENNSYLVANIA' 'TX'='TEXAS' 'NC'='NORTH CAROLINA' 'OK'='OKLAHOMA'
        'WV'='WEST VIRGINIA' 'TN'='TENNESSEE' 'DE'='DELAWARE' 'KY'='KENTUCKY'
        'MS'='MISSISSIPPI' 'NM'='NEW MEXICO' 'ND'='NORTH DAKOTA'
        'MA'='MASSACHUSETTS' 'RI'='RHODE ISLAND' 'SD'='SOUTH DAKOTA'
        'LA'='LOUISIANA' 'UT'='UTAH' 'WA'='WASHINGTON' 'MI'='MICHIGAN';

          *-----STATE: OFFICIAL CENSUS BUREAU CODES FOR STATE-----;
          VALUE STATE
           01='ALABAMA'        02='ALASKA'                          04='ARIZONA'
           05='ARKANSAS'       06='CALIFORNIA'                      08='COLORADO'
           09='CONNECTICUT'    10='DELAWARE'      11='D.C.'         12='FLORIDA'
           13='GEORGIA'                           15='HAWAII'       16='IDAHO'
           17='ILLINOIS'       18='INDIANA'       19='IOWA'         20='KANSAS'
           21='KENTUCKY'       22='LOUISIANA'     23='MAINE'        24='MARYLAND'
           25='MASSACHUSETTS'  26='MICHIGAN'      27='MINNESOTA'    30='MONTANA'
NOTE: FORMAT STATE HAS BEEN OUTPUT.
           29='MISSOURI'       28='MISSISSIPPI'   31='NEBRASKA'     32='NEVADA'
           33='NEW HAMPSHIRE'  34='NEW JERSEY'    35='NEW MEXICO'   36='NEW YORK'
           37='NORTH CAROLINA' 38='NORTH DAKOTA'  39='OHIO'         40='OKLAHOMA'
           41='OREGON'         42='PENNSYLVANIA'  44='RHODE ISLAND'
           45='SOUTH CAROLINA' 46='SOUTH DAKOTA'  47='TENNESSEE'    48='TEXAS'
           49='UTAH'           50='VERMONT'       51='VIRGINIA'
           53='WASHINGTON'     54='WEST VIRGINIA' 55='WISCONSIN'    56='WYOMING';
NOTE: SAS USED 616K MEMORY.

NOTE: SAS INSTITUTE INC.
      SAS CIRCLE
      PO BOX 8000
      CARY, N.C. 27511-8000
```

The PICTURE Statement Used with PROC FORMAT: Example 2

The ten formats in this example show the various features of picture formats. Note especially the specifications of the format, PROT, that establish error ranges so that numbers that do not fit the picture are flagged with an error message. The last value in the example shows that most of the formats produce a misleading value for an overflowed field. See **Output 16.2** for picture formats created with PROC FORMAT.

```
PROC FORMAT;

   PICTURE ACCT     LOW-0   = '000,009.99)' (PREFIX='(')
                    0-HIGH  = '000,009.99 ' ;

   PICTURE PROT     LOW-1E5= '-OVERFLOW'     (NOEDIT)
                    -99999.99-<0= '000,009.99 (PREFIX='-' FILL='*')
                    0-999999.99= '000,009.99' (FILL='*')
                    1E6-HIGH='OVERFLOW'        (NOEDIT);

   PICTURE DOL      LOW-0   = '000,009.99'  (PREFIX='⊖')
                    0-HIGH  = '000,009.99'  (PREFIX='$');

   PICTURE RSIGN    LOW-0   = '000,009.99-'
                    0-HIGH  = '000,009.00+';
```

```
   PICTURE CREDIT  LOW-0  = '00,009.99DR'
                   0-HIGH  = '00,009.99CR';

   PICTURE EUROPE  LOW-0  = '00.009,00'   (PREFIX='-' MULT=100)
                   0-HIGH  = '00.009,00'   (MULT=100);

   PICTURE BLANK   LOW-0  = '000 009.99'  (PREFIX='-')
                   0-HIGH  = '000 009.99';

   PICTURE THOUS   0-HIGH  = '00,009K'    (MULT=.001);

   PICTURE PHONE   LOW-HIGH = '000/000-0000';

   PICTURE SSNUM   LOW-HIGH = '999-99-9999';

DATA A;
   INPUT X PHONE SSN;
   ACCT=X; PROT=X; DOL=X; RSIGN=X; CREDIT=X; EUROPE=X; BLANK=X; THOU=X;
   FORMAT ACCT ACCT.  PROT PROT.  DOL DOL.  RSIGN RSIGN.
      CREDIT CREDIT.  EUROPE EUROPE.  BLANK BLANK.  THOU THOUS.
      PHONE PHONE.  SSN SSNUM.  X 12.2;
   CARDS;
12345   9194678000 123456789
0       4678000    987654321
-12345  .          .
-187.65 9194678000 111111111
187.65  .          .
.23     .          .
101.23  .          .
1.1E6
;
PROC PRINT; ID X;
   VAR ACCT PROT DOL RSIGN CREDIT EUROPE BLANK THOU PHONE SSN;
   TITLE 'PRINT THE FORMATS CREATED WITH PROC FORMAT';
```

Output 16.2 Picture Formats Created with PROC FORMAT

1

PRINT THE FORMATS CREATED WITH PROC FORMAT

X	ACCT	PROT	DOL	RSIGN	CREDIT	EUROPE	BLANK	THOU	PHONE	
12345.00	12,345.00	*12,345.00	$12,345.00	12,345.00+	12,345.00CR	12.345,00	12 345.00	12K	919/467-8000	123-45-
0.00	0.00	******0.00	$0.00	0.00+	0.00CR	0,00	0.00	0K	467-8000	987-65-
-12345.00	(12,345.00)	-12,345.00	-12,345.00	12,345.00-	12,345.00DR	12.345,00	-12 345.00	-12345	.	
-187.65	(187.65)	***-187.65	$-187.65	187.65-	187.65DR	-187,65	-187.65	-187.65	919/467-8000	111-11-
187.65	187.65	****187.65	$187.65	187.65+	187.65CR	187,65	187.65	0K	.	
0.23	0.23	******0.23	$0.23	0.23+	0.23CR	0,23	0.23	0K	.	
101.23	101.23	****101.23	$101.23	101.23+	101.23CR	101,23	101.23	0K	.	
1100000.00	100,000.00	OVERFLOW	100,000.00	100,000.00+	0.00CR	0,00	100 000.00	1,100K	.	

Chapter 17
The FORMS Procedure

ABSTRACT

The FORMS procedure can produce labels for envelopes, mailing labels, external tape labels, file cards, and any other printer forms that have a regular pattern.

INTRODUCTION

For each observation in the input SAS data set, PROC FORMS prints data in a rectangular block called a **form unit**. For example, a mailing label is a form unit.

The results can be routed to a specified external file or printed in the SAS print file. For external files, carriage controls can be used or suppressed.

Form layout The size and spacing of the forms are controlled by options as illustrated in **Figure 17.1**. The keyword options for the PROC FORMS statement are shown with their abbreviations in uppercase.

```
+-----------------Form Page---------------------------------+
|                 |                                          |
|               Down                                         |
|                 |                                          |
|        +---------------+        +---------------+          |
|-Indent-|--Width-|------|--Between-|   form unit   |         |
|        |        |      |        |               |         P
|        |      Lines    |        | NAcross,number|         a
|        |        |      |        |  of units     |         g
|        |        |      |        |across the page|         e
|        +---------------+        +---------------+         S
|                 |                                          i
|               Skip                                         z
|                 |                                          e
|        +---------------+        +---------------+          |
|        |   form unit   |        |   form unit   |          |
|        |               |        |               |          |
|        | NDown, number |        |               |          |
|        |   of units    |        |               |          |
|        | down the page |        |               |          |
|        +---------------+        +---------------+          |
|                                                            |
+-----------------------------------------------------------+
```

Figure 17.1 Sample PROC FORMS Placement

The values specified in LINE statements are formatted into a form unit that is WIDTH columns wide and LINES lines long. Values that do not fit into WIDTH columns are truncated. NACROSS form units are printed across the page, with BETWEEN columns between adjacent form units. The forms are indented INDENT spaces from the left margin. SKIP blank lines are printed between form units down the page.

PROC FORMS has two modes of operation: continuous mode and page mode. Page-mode operation is used if NDOWN= or PAGESIZE= options are specified or if the SAS print file is used rather than a FILE= file.

Continuous-mode operation For continuous-mode operation, the procedure first skips DOWN= spaces, then alternately prints LINES= print lines and SKIP= blank lines until all the data are printed. No carriage control characters are used to skip to the top of the form. Continuous-mode operation is suitable for most forms unless the distance between form units changes between pages.

Page-mode operation First, PROC FORMS goes to the start of a new page and then prints DOWN= blank lines (see **Carriage Control** below). Then NDOWN= sets of form units are printed down the page. If the NDOWN= option is not specified, the number of sets of form units is set to the maximum allowed by the PAGESIZE= value specified or assumed.

If the SAS print file is used (which occurs if FILE= is not specified), all the page calculations are done with respect to the lines remaining on the page after the title lines are printed.

Carriage control When you route the forms to an external file specified by the FILE= option, you must choose whether to use carriage control characters. A carriage control is an extra character prefixed to each record that controls the printer for line spacing and top-of-form ejection. If you want PROC FORMS to use carriage controls, you must choose the CC option in the PROC FORMS statement and an appropriate specification for the record format of the print file. If you do not use carriage controls, PROC FORMS prints blank lines to align form units correctly on the page.

If you are using page-mode printing with the CC option, PROC FORMS uses the top-of-form carriage control to start each page. For page-mode operation without CC, PAGESIZE= must be correct since FORMS uses it to calculate the number of blank lines to print at the bottom of a page to get to the next page.

Multiple Copies

Three features in PROC FORMS provide for multiple copies of forms. If you want the whole list repeated as a unit, use the SETS= option. If you want each observation repeated in adjacent form units, use the COPIES= option. If you want a variable number of copies depending on a variable in a data set, use the FREQ statement. These options can be used separately or together.

SPECIFICATIONS

The statements used to control PROC FORMS are

PROC FORMS *options;*
  LINE *linenumber variables / options;*
  FREQ *variable;*
  BY *variables;*

PROC FORMS Statement

PROC FORMS *options;*

The options listed below can appear in the PROC FORMS statement:

DATA=*SASdataset*
: names the input data set for PROC FORMS. If DATA= is omitted, the most recently created SAS data set is used.

FILE=*fileref*
DDNAME=*fileref*
DD=*fileref*
: specifies an external file where PROC FORMS writes the forms. If the FILE= option is not specified, PROC FORMS uses the SAS print file.

Options to control form placement

WIDTH=*number*
W=*number*
: specifies the number of print positions across the form unit. The minimum is 1, the maximum is 255, and the default is the width of the widest forms unit.

LINES=*number*
L=*number*
: specifies the number of lines on a form unit. The minimum is 1, the maximum is 255, and the default is the maximum LINE statement number.

DOWN=*number*
D=*number*
specifies the number of lines to skip on a page before printing the first line. The minimum is 0, the maximum is 200, and the default is 0.

SKIP=*number*
S=*number*
specifies the number of lines to skip between form units. The minimum is 0, the maximum is 200, and the default is 1.

NACROSS=*number*
NA=*number*
specifies the number of form units across the page. The minimum is 1, the maximum is 200, and the default is 1.

BETWEEN=*number*
B=*number*
specifies the number of print positions between form units. The minimum is 0, the maximum is 200, and the default is 1.

INDENT=*number*
I=*number*
specifies the number of positions to indent the first form unit across the page. The minimum is 0, the maximum is 200, and the default is 0.

Page layout options

NDOWN=*number*
ND=*number*
specifies the number of form units printed down the page. This option triggers page-mode operation. The default is

FLOOR((PAGESIZE-DOWN+SKIP)/(LINES+SKIP))

PAGESIZE=*number*
P=*number*
specifies the number of lines on a form page. This information is needed for page-mode operation only if CC is not specified. The minimum is DOWN+LINES, the maximum is 255, and the default is 66 if FILE= is specified; otherwise the number of lines is inferred from SAS print file characteristics and titling information. This option triggers page-mode operation.

Other options

CC
requests that the procedure add carriage control characters to the beginning of each print line. This option is relevant only if the FILE= option is specified.

COPIES=*number*
C=*number*
specifies that *number* copies be produced for each observation in the input data set. The copies are produced together rather than in separate sets (as in the SETS= option). In adjacent form units, the number of copies produced is the product of the value of the COPIES= option multiplied by the FREQ variable.

SETS=*number*

specifies that *number* multiple copies of the entire list be printed. For page-mode operation, PROC FORMS skips to a new page to start each set. This option is different from COPIES=, which prints the multiples in adjacent positions.

ALIGN=*number*

controls the number of XXXX form units printed so that the printer can be aligned. The default is 8 if FILE= is specified; otherwise it is 0.

LINE Statement

LINE *linenumber variables / options;*

LINE statements come directly after the PROC FORMS statement and specify the information to be printed on each line of the form unit.

The *linenumber* value gives the number of the line, and it must be an integer from 1 to the value of the LINES= option specified in the PROC FORMS statement. A LINE statement need not be given for a blank line.

Values of the *variables* specified in the LINE statement are printed on the specified line of the form unit. One blank space is inserted between each value. If the length of the values is longer than the WIDTH= value specified in the PROC FORMS statement, the field is truncated to the WIDTH= value specified. The PACK option can squeeze out extra blanks to get more fields onto a small form unit. However, if you must squeeze fields onto a form unit, it is better to use a FORMAT statement to truncate each field individually, rather than risk losing an entire field. For example,

```
FORMAT CITY $20. STATE $2.;
```

reduces the defined width of variables CITY and STATE to 20 and 2 columns, respectively.

The options below can appear in LINE statements after a slash (/).

INDENT=*number*
I=*number*

specifies that the line is to be indented by the value of *number*. This indent is done within the form unit (in contrast to the INDENT= option for the PROC FORMS statement).

PACK
P

removes extra blanks from the line so that all the values are separated by one space. For example, if a variable NAME has a length of 20 and the value of NAME is 'SMITH', the PACK option removes the extra 15 blanks.

LASTNAME
L

looks for commas in a character variable containing a name and rotates the words after the comma if it finds one. For example, a variable NAME might have the value 'SMITH, JAMES P.'. If the LASTNAME option is given, the value is printed 'JAMES P. SMITH'.

REMOVE
R

deletes the entire line if the values of the variables are all blanks or missing values.

FREQ Statement

FREQ *variable;*

When a FREQ statement is included, the value of the frequency variable determines the number of form units printed for each observation.

The variable given in the FREQ statement must be numeric. If the value is not an integer, the integer portion of the value determines the number of form units printed. If the value is less than 1 or is missing, one form unit is printed for each observation.

The actual number of copies produced in adjacent form units is the product of the FREQ variable multiplied by the value of the COPIES= option. For example, if the FREQ variable is 3 and the COPIES= value is 2, then 6 copies are printed.

BY Statement

BY *variables;*

A BY statement can be used with PROC FORMS to force new pages to be started (in page-mode operation) when the BY values change. When a BY statement appears, the procedure expects the input data set to be sorted in order of the BY variables. If your input data set is not sorted in ascending order, use the SORT procedure with a similar BY statement to sort the data, or, if appropriate, use the BY statement options NOTSORTED or DESCENDING. For more information, see the discussion of the BY statement in *SAS Language Guide for Personal Computers*.

DETAILS

Missing Values

PROC FORMS prints missing values as blanks.

Compatibility Features

PROC FORMS is similar to an earlier FORMS procedure in the SUGI supplemental library. The following options are still maintained to ensure compatibility: NSKIP and NS for SKIP, NBETWEEN and NB for BETWEEN, NCOPIES and N for COPIES.

The former PROC FORMS options BURST, TRUNCATE, NOALIGN, and EIGHTLPI have been replaced by more efficient options. The DOWN option has been slightly modified.

EXAMPLE

Printing a List of Names and Addresses Using PROC FORMS

The job below prints a listing of a set of names and addresses.

```
DATA MAILLIST;
   INPUT NAME &$20. STREET &$20. CITY &$15. STATE :$2. ZIP :$5.;
   CARDS;
JOHN SMITH          202 MAIN ST.         ANYTOWN      IN  22432
JOE WILLIAMS        101 BROADWAY         GOTHAM       NY  32334
```

```
ALICE GORDON        55 HAZEL WAY        ATLANTA     GA  68549
GEORGE HAYES        2132 GOODVIEW       MUNCIE      IN  54345
PENELOPE PETERS     543 PEANUT CIRCLE   COLUMBIA    MD  53455
HARRISON HARRISON   898 7TH ST          BIG ROCK    AK  98733
BILL SMITH          123 STATE           ROCKFORD    IL  81522
WILL RED            544 HILLSIDE AV     ROCQUEFORT  KY  98783
ANN ANDERSON        5456 PLEASANT BLVD  SEATTLE     WA  49747
ARISTOTLE JOHNSON   234 PEACE           PHOENIX     AZ  77898
GARRY MILLER        7 GRAY DRIVE        ST. LOUIS   MO  26578
WINSTON MARTIN      34 RED ROAD         NEWTON      MA  34678
ALISON TOWSON       44 MARS HILL DR.    REDWOOD     CA  23432
MATHEW MACKEM       78 HIGHVIEW CT.     VIRGIL      VA  87373
;
PROC SORT;
   BY ZIP;
PROC FORMS WIDTH=25 LINES=3 DOWN=2 SKIP=2 NACROSS=3 BETWEEN=1;
   LINE 1 NAME;
   LINE 2 STREET;
   LINE 3 CITY STATE ZIP/PACK;
```

Output 17.1 Mailing List Produced by PROC FORMS

```
                                                                                  1

JOHN SMITH               ALISON TOWSON            GARRY MILLER             JOE WILLIAMS
202 MAIN ST.             44 MARS HILL DR.         7 GRAY DRIVE             101 BROADWAY
ANYTOWN IN 22432         REDWOOD CA 23432         ST. LOUIS MO 26578       GOTHAM NY 32334


WINSTON MARTIN           ANN ANDERSON             PENELOPE PETERS          GEORGE HAYES
34 RED ROAD              5456 PLEASANT BLVD       543 PEANUT CIRCLE        2132 GOODVIEW
NEWTON MA 34678          SEATTLE WA 49747         COLUMBIA MD 53455        MUNCIE IN 54345


ALICE GORDON             ARISTOTLE JOHNSON        BILL SMITH               MATHEW MACKEM
55 HAZEL WAY             234 PEACE                123 STATE                78 HIGHVIEW CT.
ATLANTA GA 68549         PHOENIX AZ 77898         ROCKFORD IL 81522        VIRGIL VA 87373


HARRISON HARRISON        WILL RED
898 7TH ST               544 HILLSIDE AV
BIG ROCK AK 98733        ROCQUEFORT KY 98783
```

Chapter 18

The FREQ Procedure

ABSTRACT

The FREQ procedure produces one-way to *n*-way frequency and crosstabulation tables. For two-way tables, PROC FREQ computes tests and measures of association. For *n*-way tables, PROC FREQ does stratified analysis, computing statistics within as well as across strata. Frequencies can also be output to a SAS data set.

INTRODUCTION

Frequency tables show the distribution of variable values. For example, if a variable A has six possible values, a frequency table for A shows how many observations in the data set have the first value of A, how many have the second value, and so on.

Crosstabulation tables show combined frequency distributions for two or more variables. For example, a crosstabulation table for the variables SEX and EMPLOY shows the number of working females, the number of non-working females, the number of working males, and the number of non-working males.

One-Way Frequency Tables

If you want a one-way frequency table for a variable, simply name the variable in a TABLES statement. For example, the statements

```
PROC FREQ;
   TABLES A;
```

produce a one-way frequency table giving the values of A and the frequency of each value.

Two-Way Crosstabulation Tables

If you want a crosstabulation table for two variables, give their names separated by an asterisk (*). Values of the first variable form the rows of the table, and values of the second variable form the columns. For example, the statements

```
PROC FREQ;
   TABLES A*B;
```

produce a crosstabulation table with values of A down the side and values of B across the top.

N-Way Crosstabulation Tables

If you want a three-way (or *n*-way) crosstabulation table, give the three (or *n*) variable names separated by asterisks in the TABLES statement. Values of the last variable form the columns of a contingency table; values of the next-to-last variable form the rows. Each level (or combination of levels) of the other variables form one stratum, and a separate contingency table is produced for each stratum. For example, the statements

```
PROC FREQ;
   TABLES A*B*C*D / CMH;
```

produce *k* tables, where *k* is the number of different combinations of values for the variables A and B. Each table has the values of C down the side and the values of D across the top.

Note: multi-way tables can generate a great deal of printed output. For example, if the variables A, B, C, D, and E each have ten levels, five-way tables of A*B*C*D*E could generate 4000 or more pages of output.

PROC FREQ Contrasted with Other SAS Procedures

Many other procedures in SAS can collect frequency counts. PROC FREQ is distinguished by its ability to compute chi-square tests and measures of association for two-way and *n*-way tables. Other procedures to consider for counting are the following: TABULATE for more general table layouts, SUMMARY for output data sets, and CHART for bar charts and other graphical representations.

SPECIFICATIONS

The statements available in PROC FREQ are

PROC FREQ *options;*
  TABLES *requests / options;*
  WEIGHT *variable;*
  BY *variables;*

PROC FREQ Statement

PROC FREQ *options;*

The options that can be used in the PROC FREQ statement are as follows:

DATA=*SASdataset*

specifies the data set to be used by PROC FREQ. If the DATA= option is omitted, FREQ uses the most recently created data set.

ORDER=FREQ
ORDER=DATA
ORDER=INTERNAL
ORDER=FORMATTED

specifies the order in which the variable levels are to be reported. If ORDER=FREQ, levels are ordered by descending frequency count so that the levels with the largest frequencies come first. If ORDER=DATA, levels are put in the order in which they first occur in the input data. If ORDER=INTERNAL, then the levels are ordered by the internal value. If ORDER=FORMATTED, levels are ordered by the external formatted value. If you omit ORDER= or give an unrecognized value, PROC FREQ orders by the internal value. The ORDER= option does not apply to missing values, which are always ordered first. The ORDER= option does not apply to observations with zero weights.

FORMCHAR(1,2,7)=*'string'*

defines the characters to be used for constructing the outlines and dividers for the cells of contingency tables. The string should be three characters long. The characters are used to denote (1) vertical divider, (2) horizontal divider, and (3) vertical-horizontal intersection. Any character or hexadecimal string can be used to customize table appearance. Specifying FORMCHAR(1,2,7)='   ' (3 blanks) produces tables with no outlines or dividers.

If you do not specify the FORMCHAR option, FREQ uses the default FORMCHAR(1,2,7)='|-+'. See the CALENDAR and TABULATE procedures for further information.

TABLES Statement

TABLES *requests / options;*

Any number of TABLES statements can be included in one execution of PROC FREQ. If there is no TABLES statement, FREQ does one-way frequencies for all of the variables in the data set.

If you request a one-way table for a variable and do not specify any options, FREQ produces frequencies, cumulative frequencies, percentages of the total frequency, and cumulative percentages for each level of the variable.

If you request a two-way table and do not specify any options, FREQ produces crosstabulation tables that include cell frequencies, cell percentages of the total frequency, cell percentages of row frequencies, and cell percentages of column frequencies. Missing levels of each variable are excluded from the table, but the total frequency of missing subjects is printed below each table.

For each frequency or crosstabulation table that you want, put a table request in the TABLES statement.

requests

are composed of one or more variable names joined by asterisks (*). A one-way frequency is generated by a single name. Two-way crosstabulations are generated by two variables joined with an asterisk. Any number of variables can be joined for a multi-way table. A grouping syntax is also available to make the specifications of many tables easier. Several variables can be put in parentheses and joined to other effects.

For example,

TABLES A*(B C);	is equivalent to	TABLES A*B A*C;
TABLES (A B)*(C D);	is equivalent to	TABLES A*C A*D B*C B*D;
TABLES (A B C)*D;	is equivalent to	TABLES A*D B*D C*D;
TABLES A–C;	is equivalent to	TABLES A B C;
TABLES (A--C)*D;	is equivalent to	TABLES A*D B*D C*D;
TABLES A--C*D;	is illegal.	

Any number of requests can be given in one TABLES statement.

The options below can be used in the TABLES statement after a slash (/):

General options

MISSING

requests FREQ to interpret missing values as nonmissing and to include them in calculations of percentages and other statistics.

LIST

prints two-way to *n*-way tables in a list format rather than as crosstabulation tables. The LIST option cannot be used when statistical tests or measures of association are requested. Expected cell frequencies are not printed when LIST is specified, even if EXPECTED is specified.

OUT=*SASdataset*

sets up an output SAS data set containing variable values and frequency counts. If more than one table request appears in the TABLES statement, the contents of the data set correspond to the last table request in the TABLES statement. For details on the output data set created by PROC FREQ, see **Output Data Set** below. If you want to create a permanent SAS data set, you must specify a two-level name. See *SAS Language Guide for Personal Computers* for more information on permanent SAS data sets.

Option to request statistical analysis

CHISQ

requests a chi-square (χ^2) test of homogeneity or independence for each stratum, together with measures of association based on chi-square. The tests include Pearson chi-square, likelihood ratio chi-square, and Mantel-Haenszel chi-square. The measures include the phi coefficient, the contingency coefficient, and Cramer's V. For 2 by 2 tables, Fisher's Exact Test is also included.

Options to request additional table information

EXPECTED

requests that the expected cell frequencies under the hypothesis of independence (or homogeneity) be printed.

DEVIATION
: requests that, for each cell, FREQ print the deviation of the cell frequency from the expected value.

CELLCHI2
: requests that FREQ print each cell's contribution to the total χ^2 statistic. This is computed as *(frequency−expected)***2/*expected*.

CUMCOL
: requests that cumulative column percentages be printed in the cells.

MISSPRINT
: asks FREQ to print missing value frequencies for all frequency tables, even though the frequencies are not used in the calculation of statistics.

SPARSE
: causes the procedure to write out or print information about all possible combinations of levels of the variables in the table request, even when some combinations of levels do not occur in the data. This option affects printouts under the LIST option and output data sets.

Options to suppress printing

NOFREQ
: suppresses printing of cell frequencies for a crosstabulation.

NOPERCENT
: suppresses printing of cell percentages for a crosstabulation.

NOROW
: suppresses printing of row percentages in cells of a crosstabulation.

NOCOL
: suppresses printing of column percentages in cells of a crosstabulation.

NOCUM
: suppresses printing of cumulative frequencies and cumulative percentages for one-way frequencies and for frequencies in list format.

NOPRINT
: suppresses printing of tables, but allows printing of the statistics specified by CHISQ, MEASURES, CMH, and ALL. (Complete descriptions of the CHISQ, MEASURES, CMH, and ALL options are given in the chapter "The FREQ Procedure" in *SAS/STAT™ Guide for Personal Computers*.)

WEIGHT Statement

WEIGHT *variable*;

Normally, each observation contributes a value of 1 to the frequency counts. (In other words, each observation represents one subject.) However, when a WEIGHT statement appears, each observation contributes the weighting variable's value for that observation. (For example, a weight of 3 means that the observation represents 3 subjects.) The values must be nonnegative, but they do not have to be integers. FREQ uses double precision floating point arithmetic to accumulate the counts or weights. Values are summed and then printed with decimal places, if appropriate.

Only one WEIGHT statement can be used, and that statement applies to counts collected for all tables.

For example, suppose a data set contains variables RACE, SEX, and HRSWORK. The statements

```
PROC FREQ;
   TABLES RACE*SEX;
```

produce a table showing how many nonwhite females, nonwhite males, white females, and white males are present. The statements

```
PROC FREQ;
   TABLES RACE*SEX;
   WEIGHT HRSWORK;
```

produce a table showing the number of hours worked by nonwhite females, by nonwhite males, and so on.

BY Statement

BY *variables;*

A BY statement can be used with PROC FREQ to obtain separate analyses for the groups defined by the BY variables. When a BY statement appears, the procedure expects the input data set to be sorted in order of the BY variables. If your input data set is not sorted in ascending order, use the SORT procedure with a similar BY statement to sort the data, or, if appropriate, use the BY statement options NOTSORTED or DESCENDING. For more information, see the discussion of the BY statement in *SAS Language Guide for Personal Computers*.

DETAILS

Missing Values

Missing value frequencies do not appear in contingency tables or frequency tables, but the total frequency of missing subjects is given below each table. In all cases, the statistics do not include missing values.

Missing value frequencies can be printed by specifying the MISSPRINT option in the TABLES statement; they can be included in the computation of statistics by specifying the MISSING option.

Limitations

Any number of TABLES statements can be included after the PROC FREQ statement. Since FREQ builds all the tables requested in all TABLES statements in one pass of the data, there is essentially no loss of efficiency from using multiple TABLES statements.

A TABLES statement can contain any number of table requests, and each request can include any number of variables. The maximum number of levels allowed for any one variable is 32,000. If you have a variable with more than 32,000 levels, use PROC SUMMARY and PROC PRINT or reduce the number of levels by using the FORMAT statement.

FREQ stores each combination of values in memory. When FREQ is compiling and developing multi-way tables or when some variables have many levels, you may run out of main storage. If increasing the region size is impractical, use PROC SORT to sort the data set by one or more of the variables and then use PROC FREQ with a BY statement that includes the sorted variables.

The FREQ procedure handles both internal and formatted values up to length 16 on both the printout and the output data set. Longer data values are truncated to sixteen characters, and a warning message is printed on the SAS log.

Frequency values with more than seven significant digits may be printed in scientific notation (E format), in which case only the first few significant digits of the mantissa are printed. If you need more significant digits than FREQ prints, you can specify an output data set with the OUT= option. Then use

```
PROC PRINT DATA=FREQDATA;
   FORMAT COUNT BEST32.;
```

where FREQDATA is the OUT= data set produced by PROC FREQ.

The variable COUNT, containing the frequency values, is then printed with additional significant digits.

Output Data Set

The new data set produced by PROC FREQ contains one observation for each combination of the variable values in the table request. Each observation contains these variables plus two new variables, COUNT and PERCENT, which give respectively the frequency and cell percentage for the combination of variable values.

For example, consider the statements

```
PROC FREQ;
   TABLES A A*B / OUT=D;
```

The output data set D corresponds to the rightmost table request, A*B. If A has two values (1 and 2) and B has three values (1, 2, and 3), the output data set D can have up to six observations, one for each combination of the A and B values. In observation 1, A=1 and B=1; in observation 2, A=1 and B=2; and so on. The data set also contains the variables COUNT and PERCENT. COUNT's value in each observation is the number of subjects that have the given combination of A and B values; PERCENT's value is the percent of the total number of subjects having that A and B combination.

When FREQ collects different class values into the same formatted level, it saves the smallest internal value to output in the output data set.

Computer Resources

For each variable, PROC FREQ stores all of the levels in memory, requiring 56 bytes for each level. If FREQ runs out of memory, it stops collecting levels on the variable with the most levels and returns the memory so that counting can continue. The procedure then builds the tables that do not contain the disabled variables.

For two-way and *n*-way tables, FREQ uses a utility file to store frequencies when the number of nonzero cells exceeds 63.

Grouping with Formats

When you use PROC FREQ, remember that FREQ groups the variables according to their formatted values. If you assign a format to a variable with a FORMAT statement, the variable's values are formatted for printing before FREQ divides the observations into groups for the frequency counts.

For example, say a variable X has the values 1.3, 1.7, and 2.0, among others. Each of these values appears as a level in the frequency table. If you want each value rounded to a single digit, you include the statement

```
FORMAT X 1.;
```

after the PROC FREQ statement. The frequency table levels are then 1 and 2.

Formatted character variables are treated in the same way: the formatted values are used to divide the observations into groups. For character variables, formatted or not, only the first sixteen characters are used to determine the groups.

You can also use the FORMAT statement to assign formats created by PROC FORMAT to variables. Formats created by PROC FORMAT can serve two purposes: they can define the levels, and they can label the levels. You can use the same data with different formats to collect counts on different partitions of the class values.

In frequency tables, values of both character and numeric variables appear in ascending order by the original (unformatted) values unless you specify otherwise with the ORDER= option.

Printed Output

For a one-way table showing the frequency distribution of a single variable, FREQ prints these items:

1. the name of the variable and its values
2. FREQUENCY counts giving the number of subjects that have each value
3. CUMULATIVE FREQUENCY counts, giving the sum of the frequency counts of that value and all other values listed above it in the table (the total number of nonmissing subjects is the last cumulative frequency)
4. percentages, labeled PERCENT, giving the percent of the total number of subjects represented by that value
5. CUMULATIVE PERCENT values, giving the percent of the total number of subjects represented by that value and all others previously listed in the table.

Two-way tables can be printed either as crosstabulation tables (the default) or as lists (when the LIST option is specified). Each cell of a crosstabulation table contains items 6 through 9.

6. FREQUENCY counts, giving the number of subjects that have the indicated values of the two variables
7. PERCENT, the percentage of the total frequency count represented by that cell
8. ROW PCT, or the row percentage, the percent of the total frequency count for that row represented by the cell
9. COL PCT, or column percent, the percent of the total frequency count for that column represented by the cell
10. if the EXPECTED option is specified, the expected cell frequency under the hypothesis of independence
11. if the DEVIATION option is specified, the deviation of the cell frequency from the expected value
12. if the CELLCHI2 option is specified, the cell's contribution to the total chi-square statistic
13. if two contingency tables can fit on a page, one table above the other, then the tables are printed in that manner. Similarly, a table and its corresponding statistics are printed on the same page, provided that they fit.
14. if the CHISQ option is specified, tests and measures of association are printed for each 2-way table.

EXAMPLE

Options Available Using PROC FREQ: Example 1

The following example demonstrates various options in the PROC FREQ and TABLES statements. These statements produce the output shown in **Output 18.1**.

```
DATA NEW;
   INPUT A B @@;
   CARDS;
1 2    2 1    . 2    . .    1 1    2 1
;
PROC FREQ;
   TITLE 'NO TABLES STATEMENT';
PROC FREQ;
   TABLES A / MISSPRINT;
   TITLE '1-WAY FREQUENCY TABLE WITH MISSPRINT OPTION';

PROC FREQ;
   TABLES A*B;
   TITLE '2-WAY CONTINGENCY TABLE';
PROC FREQ;
   TABLES A*B / MISSPRINT;
   TITLE '2-WAY CONTINGENCY TABLE WITH MISSPRINT OPTION';
PROC FREQ;
   TABLES A*B / MISSING;
   TITLE '2-WAY CONTINGENCY TABLE WITH MISSING OPTION';
PROC FREQ;
   TABLES A*B / CHISQ;
   TITLE '2-WAY CONTINGENCY TABLE WITH CHISQ OPTION';

PROC FREQ;
   TABLES A*B / LIST;
   TITLE '2-WAY FREQUENCY TABLE';
PROC FREQ;
   TABLES A*B / LIST MISSING;
   TITLE '2-WAY FREQUENCY TABLE WITH MISSING OPTION';
PROC FREQ;
   TABLES A*B / LIST SPARSE;
   TITLE '2-WAY FREQUENCY TABLE WITH SPARSE OPTION';
PROC FREQ ORDER=DATA;
   TABLES A*B / LIST;
   TITLE '2-WAY FREQUENCY TABLE, ORDER=DATA';

RUN;
```

Output 18.1 Options Available Using PROC FREQ

```
                    NO TABLES STATEMENT                                   1


                                CUMULATIVE  CUMULATIVE
A   FREQUENCY    PERCENT    FREQUENCY    PERCENT
------------------------------------------------
1           2     50.0            2       50.0
2           2     50.0            4      100.0

              FREQUENCY MISSING = 2


                                CUMULATIVE  CUMULATIVE
B   FREQUENCY    PERCENT    FREQUENCY    PERCENT
------------------------------------------------
1           3     60.0            3       60.0
2           2     40.0            5      100.0

              FREQUENCY MISSING = 1
```

```
         1-WAY FREQUENCY TABLE WITH MISSPRINT OPTION                      2
                                     ❸           ❺
❶     ❷           ❹         CUMULATIVE  CUMULATIVE
A   FREQUENCY    PERCENT    FREQUENCY    PERCENT
------------------------------------------------
.           2      .              .        .
1           2     50.0            2       50.0
2           2     50.0            4      100.0

              FREQUENCY MISSING = 2
```

```
                   2-WAY CONTINGENCY TABLE                                3

                      TABLE OF A BY B

        A          B

     ❻ FREQUENCY|❼
        PERCENT |
     ❽ ROW PCT  |
        COL PCT |❾       1|       2|  TOTAL
        --------+--------+--------+
               1|      1 |      1 |      2
                |  25.00 |  25.00 |  50.00
                |  50.00 |  50.00 |
                |  33.33 | 100.00 |
        --------+--------+--------+
               2|      2 |      0 |      2
                |  50.00 |   0.00 |  50.00
                | 100.00 |   0.00 |
                |  66.67 |   0.00 |
        --------+--------+--------+
        TOTAL          3        1        4
                   75.00    25.00   100.00

        FREQUENCY MISSING = 2
```

```
2-WAY CONTINGENCY TABLE WITH MISSPRINT OPTION                         4

               TABLE OF A BY B

A          B

FREQUENCY|
 PERCENT |
 ROW PCT |
 COL PCT |       .|       1|       2|  TOTAL
---------+--------+--------+--------+
       . |      1 |      0 |      1 |      .
         |      . |      . |      . |      .
         |      . |      . |      . |
         |      . |      . |      . |
---------+--------+--------+--------+
       1 |      0 |      1 |      1 |      2
         |      . |  25.00 |  25.00 |  50.00
         |      . |  50.00 |  50.00 |
         |      . |  33.33 | 100.00 |
---------+--------+--------+--------+
       2 |      0 |      2 |      0 |      2
         |      . |  50.00 |   0.00 |  50.00
         |      . | 100.00 |   0.00 |
         |      . |  66.67 |   0.00 |
---------+--------+--------+--------+
TOTAL           .        3        1        4
                .    75.00    25.00   100.00

FREQUENCY MISSING = 2
```

```
2-WAY CONTINGENCY TABLE WITH MISSING OPTION                           5

               TABLE OF A BY B

A          B

FREQUENCY|
 PERCENT |
 ROW PCT |
 COL PCT |       .|       1|       2|  TOTAL
---------+--------+--------+--------+
       . |      1 |      0 |      1 |      2
         |  16.67 |   0.00 |  16.67 |  33.33
         |  50.00 |   0.00 |  50.00 |
         | 100.00 |   0.00 |  50.00 |
---------+--------+--------+--------+
       1 |      0 |      1 |      1 |      2
         |   0.00 |  16.67 |  16.67 |  33.33
         |   0.00 |  50.00 |  50.00 |
         |   0.00 |  33.33 |  50.00 |
---------+--------+--------+--------+
       2 |      0 |      2 |      0 |      2
         |   0.00 |  33.33 |   0.00 |  33.33
         |   0.00 | 100.00 |   0.00 |
         |   0.00 |  66.67 |   0.00 |
---------+--------+--------+--------+
TOTAL           1        3        2        6
            16.67    50.00    33.33   100.00
```

```
⓭     2-WAY CONTINGENCY TABLE WITH CHISQ OPTION                                  6

                    TABLE OF A BY B

           A          B

           FREQUENCY|
            PERCENT |
            ROW PCT |
            COL PCT |       1|       2|  TOTAL
           ---------+--------+--------+
                  1 |      1 |      1 |      2
                    |  25.00 |  25.00 |  50.00
                    |  50.00 |  50.00 |
                    |  33.33 | 100.00 |
           ---------+--------+--------+
                  2 |      2 |      0 |      2
                    |  50.00 |   0.00 |  50.00
                    | 100.00 |   0.00 |
                    |  66.67 |   0.00 |
           ---------+--------+--------+
           TOTAL           3        1        4
                       75.00    25.00   100.00

           FREQUENCY MISSING = 2


                STATISTICS FOR TABLE OF A BY B
   ⓮
  STATISTIC                          DF       VALUE        PROB
  ------------------------------------------------------------
  CHI-SQUARE                          1       1.333       0.248
  LIKELIHOOD RATIO CHI-SQUARE         1       1.726       0.189
  CONTINUITY ADJ. CHI-SQUARE          1       0.000       1.000
  MANTEL-HAENSZEL CHI-SQUARE          1       1.000       0.317
  FISHER'S EXACT TEST (1-TAIL)                            0.500
                      (2-TAIL)                            1.000
  PHI                                        -0.577
  CONTINGENCY COEFFICIENT                     0.500
  CRAMER'S V                                 -0.577

  EFFECTIVE SAMPLE SIZE = 4
  FREQUENCY MISSING = 2
  WARNING:   33% OF THE DATA ARE MISSING.
  WARNING: 100% OF THE CELLS HAVE EXPECTED COUNTS LESS
             THAN 5. CHI-SQUARE MAY NOT BE A VALID TEST.
```

```
                    2-WAY FREQUENCY TABLE                                        7

                                           CUMULATIVE   CUMULATIVE
  A    B     FREQUENCY    PERCENT           FREQUENCY     PERCENT
  -----------------------------------------------------------------
  1    1             1      25.0                   1       25.0
  1    2             1      25.0                   2       50.0
  2    1             2      50.0                   4      100.0

                    FREQUENCY MISSING = 2
```

2-WAY FREQUENCY TABLE WITH MISSING OPTION 8

A	B	FREQUENCY	PERCENT	CUMULATIVE FREQUENCY	CUMULATIVE PERCENT
.	.	1	16.7	1	16.7
.	2	1	16.7	2	33.3
1	1	1	16.7	3	50.0
1	2	1	16.7	4	66.7
2	1	2	33.3	6	100.0

2-WAY FREQUENCY TABLE WITH SPARSE OPTION 9

A	B	FREQUENCY	PERCENT	CUMULATIVE FREQUENCY	CUMULATIVE PERCENT
1	1	1	25.0	1	25.0
1	2	1	25.0	2	50.0
2	1	2	50.0	4	100.0
2	2	0	0.0	4	100.0

FREQUENCY MISSING = 2

2-WAY FREQUENCY TABLE, ORDER=DATA 10

A	B	FREQUENCY	PERCENT	CUMULATIVE FREQUENCY	CUMULATIVE PERCENT
1	2	1	25.0	1	25.0
1	1	1	25.0	2	50.0
2	1	2	50.0	4	100.0

FREQUENCY MISSING = 2

Chapter 19
The MEANS Procedure

ABSTRACT

The MEANS procedure produces simple univariate descriptive statistics for numeric variables.

INTRODUCTION

PROC MEANS computes statistics for an entire SAS data set or for groups of observations in the data set. PROC MEANS is identical to PROC SUMMARY except for the default on the PRINT/NOPRINT option. You may refer to "The SUMMARY Procedure" chapter for more detailed information.

If you use a BY statement, PROC MEANS calculates descriptive statistics separately for groups of observations. Each group is composed of observations having the same values of the variables used in the BY statement. The groups can be further subdivided by the use of the CLASS statement. However, the BY statement requires that the input data set be sorted by the BY variables. No such restriction is imposed by the CLASS statement. MEANS can optionally create one or more SAS data sets containing the statistics calculated. If you want descriptive statistics in a data set and do not require printed output, set the NOPRINT option in the PROC MEANS statement.

Other SAS procedures also compute univariate statistics. Although MEANS is the easiest and most direct descriptive procedure, other procedures provide more features. See the UNIVARIATE, CHART, and TABULATE procedures.

Note: in this discussion, names of statistics refer to the sample estimates of the true parameters. Thus, the term *mean* refers to the sample mean, *variance* refers to the sample variance, and so forth.

SPECIFICATIONS

The procedure is controlled by the following statements:

PROC MEANS *options;*
VAR *variables;*
BY *variables;*
CLASS *variables;*
FREQ *variable;*
WEIGHT *variable;*
ID *variables;*
OUTPUT *options;*

There is no limit to the number of OUTPUT statements that can accompany a PROC MEANS statement.

PROC MEANS Statement

PROC MEANS *options;*

The options below can appear in the PROC MEANS statement:

DATA=*SASdataset*
: names the SAS data set to be analyzed by MEANS. If DATA= is omitted, the most recently created SAS data set is used.

NOPRINT
: specifies not to print any of the descriptive statistics. Use NOPRINT when the only purpose of using the procedure is to create new SAS data sets.

MAXDEC=*n*
: gives the maximum number of decimal places (0 to 8) for MEANS to use in printing results. The default is 2.

FW=*n*
: specifies the field width for MEANS to use in printing each statistic. The default is 12.

MISSING
: requests that MEANS treat missing values as valid subgroup values for the CLASS variables.

NWAY
: specifies that statistics for only the observation with the highest _TYPE_ value (highest level of interaction among CLASS variables) are to be output.

IDMIN
: specifies that the value of the ID variable should be its minimum rather than its maximum value for the corresponding observations of the input data set.

DESCENDING
: specifies that the output data set is to be ordered by descending _TYPE_ value (ascending is the default). This causes the overall

totals (_TYPE_=0) to be placed at the end of each BY group. This option has no effect if the NWAY option is also specified.

ORDER=FREQ
ORDER=DATA
ORDER=INTERNAL
ORDER=EXTERNAL | FORMATTED
specifies the order in which the class variable values are to be sorted for display or for the output data set. If ORDER=FREQ, the class values are ordered by descending frequency count so that class values occurring in the greatest number of observations come first. If ORDER=DATA, class values are kept in the order they were encountered in the data set. If ORDER=INTERNAL, the class values are ordered by the internal representation of the values. If ORDER=EXTERNAL or FORMATTED, the class values are ordered by the formatted (external) representation of the value. ORDER=INTERNAL is the default. The ORDER= option does not apply to missing values, which are always ordered first.

VARDEF=DF
VARDEF=WEIGHT | WGT
VARDEF=N
VARDEF=WDF
specifies the divisor to be used in the calculation of the variance. VARDEF=DF requests that the degrees of freedom (N-1) be used as the divisor. VARDEF=WEIGHT or WGT requests that the sum of the weights be used. VARDEF=N requests that the number of observations (N) be used. VARDEF=WDF requests that the sum of the weights minus one be used. The default is VARDEF=DF.

The statistics below can be requested with the MEANS procedure by giving the keyword names of the statistics in the PROC MEANS statement. These keywords are also used in the OUTPUT statement described below. The statistics are defined in the chapter "SAS Elementary Statistics Procedures."

N	number of observations in the subgroup with nonmissing values
NMISS	number of observations in the subgroup having missing values for the variable
MEAN	mean
STD	standard deviation
MIN	minimum value
MAX	maximum value
RANGE	range
SUM	sum
VAR	variance
USS	uncorrected sum of squares
CSS	corrected sum of squares
CV	coefficient of variation
STDERR	standard error of the mean
T	Student's *t* value for testing the hypothesis that the population mean is 0

PRT	probability of a greater absolute value for the Student's *t* value above
SUMWGT	sum of the WEIGHT variable values.

VAR Statement

VAR *variables;*

Statistics are calculated for each numeric variable listed in the VAR statement. If a VAR statement is not used, all numeric variables in the input data set, except for those listed in BY, ID, FREQ, or WEIGHT statements are analyzed. The results are printed in the order of the variables in the VAR statement.

BY Statement

BY *variables;*

A BY statement can be used with PROC MEANS to obtain separate analyses on observations in groups defined by the BY variables. When a BY statement appears, the procedure expects the input data set to be sorted in order of the BY variables. If your input data set is not sorted in ascending order, use the SORT procedure with a similar BY statement to sort the data, or, if appropriate, use the BY statement options NOTSORTED or DESCENDING. For more information, see the discussion of the BY statement in *SAS Language Guide for Personal Computers*.

CLASS Statement

CLASS *variables;*

In the CLASS statement you assign the variables used to form subgroups. The CLASS statement has an effect on the statistics computed similar to that of the BY statement. The differences are in the format of the printed output and in the BY statement sorting requirement. You can do analysis on larger data sets using the BY statement because the observations are previously sorted. The example **Univariate Statistics** at the end of this chapter illustrates the differences in printed output. You can use both statements together, each defining a different set of variables.

FREQ Statement

FREQ *variable;*

When a FREQ statement appears with PROC MEANS, each observation in the input data set is assumed to represent *n* observations in the calculation of statistics, where *n* is the value of the FREQ variable. If the value of the FREQ variable is less than 1 or is missing, the observation is not used in the calculations. If the value is not an integer, only the integer portion is used.

WEIGHT Statement

WEIGHT *variable;*

The WEIGHT statement specifies a numeric variable in the input SAS data set whose values are to be used to weight each observation. Only one variable can be specified. Both the FREQ and WEIGHT statements can be used. The WEIGHT variable values can be nonintegers and are used to calculate a weighted mean and a weighted variance. If the value of the WEIGHT variable is less than zero or is missing, a value of zero is assumed.

ID Statement

ID *variables;*

An ID statement can be used with PROC MEANS to include additional variables in the output data set.

If your ID statement names only one variable, the value of the ID variable for a given observation in the output data set is the maximum value it has in the corresponding observations of the input data set unless IDMIN is specified in the PROC statement. When your ID statement includes two or more variables, the maximum value is chosen as if the values of the ID variables were concatenated into one value for each observation. Thus the maximum value comes from only one of the corresponding observations in the input data set.

OUTPUT Statement

OUTPUT *options;*

The OUTPUT statement requests that MEANS output statistics to a new SAS data set. The options name the data set and the variables to be included.

OUT=*SASdataset*

If you want to create a permanent SAS data set, you must specify a two-level name (see *SAS Language Guide for Personal Computers* for more information on permanent data sets).

statistical keyword=names

specifies the statistics you want in the new data set and names the variables containing these statistics. Any of the statistics available for the PROC MEANS statement can be output by using the keyword for that statistic. The keywords are listed below.

N	NMISS	MEAN	STD	MIN	MAX
RANGE	SUM	VAR	USS	CSS	STDERR
CV	T	PRT	SUMWGT		

The list of variable names after the equal sign names statistics for respective variables in the VAR statement. This list can be shorter than the VAR list.

For example, consider these statements:

```
PROC MEANS;
   VAR X1 X2;
   BY GROUP;
   OUTPUT OUT=STATS MEAN=MA MB STD=SA;
```

If the BY variable, GROUP, has two values, A and B, the data set STATS contains two observations. Each of these observations contains the variables GROUP, MA, MB, and SA. MA and MB are the means of X1 and X2, respectively. SA is the standard deviation of X1. The standard deviation of X2 is not output. The statistics are printed since NOPRINT is omitted.

If the statistics option in the OUTPUT statement is omitted, MEANS creates a special SAS data set in which five records are generated for each group defined by the BY variables or the CLASS variables. The five records contain the following statistics: N, MIN, MAX, MEAN, and STD. If weight is specified, a sixth record containing the sum of weights (SUMWGT) is also output. Note that the statistic N is the number of observations on which calculations are based. See the section on **Missing Values** for details.

There is no limit to the number of OUTPUT statements you can use. Each OUTPUT statement should have the OUT= options. One SAS data set is created for each valid OUTPUT statement.

For more details on the OUTPUT statement, refer to the same section in "The SUMMARY Procedure" chapter.

DETAILS

Missing Values

The MEANS procedure excludes missing values before calculating statistics. Each variable is treated individually: a missing value in one variable does not affect the calculations for other variables. If any CLASS variable has a missing value for an observation, that observation is not used in MEANS unless the MISSING option is specified in the PROC MEANS statement. Missing values for a BY variable form a separate BY group and are treated in the same way as BY groups with nonmissing values. If the FREQ variable value is missing, the observation is skipped. If the WEIGHT variable value is missing, the observation is treated as zero.

Limitations

See "The SUMMARY Procedure."

Output Data Set

The number of observations in the output data set produced by MEANS depends on the number of distinct values or levels (for example, a, b, c) of the CLASS variables (A, B, C).

Observations in the data set produced by MEANS are identified by a variable named _TYPE_. Values of _TYPE_ indicate which subgroup (defined by values of the CLASS variables) produced the summary statistics in that observation in the output data set. For a detailed description on the output variables and observations, see "The SUMMARY Procedure."

Printed Output

When no statistics are specifically requested in the PROC MEANS statement, MEANS prints these statistics for each variable in the VAR statement:

1. N, the number of observations in the CLASS group for the given BY group
2. the name of the variable
3. the MINIMUM VALUE of the variable
4. the MAXIMUM VALUE of the variable
5. the MEAN or average of the variable
6. the STANDARD DEVIATION of the variable

If statistics are specifically requested in the PROC statement, only those statistics are printed. In addition to the statistics above, upon request, MEANS can print these statistics:

7. STD ERROR OF MEAN, the standard error of the mean
8. the SUM of all the values for a variable
9. the VARIANCE of each variable
10. C.V., or the coefficient of variation expressed as a percentage
11. N MISSING, the number of missing values for each variable
12. the RANGE of each variable
13. the UNCORRECTED SS, the raw sum of squares (not adjusted for the mean)
14. the CORRECTED SS, the sum of squares adjusted for the mean
15. T, the Student's *t* value for testing the hypothesis that the population mean is zero
16. PR > |T|, the probability of a greater absolute value for Student's *t* under the hypothesis that the mean is zero
17. SUMWGT, the sum of the WEIGHT variable values.

If a statistic cannot be computed because of insufficient or inappropriate data, the statistic is reported as missing. See the chapter "SAS Elementary Statistics Procedures."

If a BY statement is included, a line is drawn to separate the statistics for each BY group.

EXAMPLE

Univariate Statistics

The following example requests univariate statistics for two variables, RATING and EXCESS. The first PROC MEANS statement asks for statistics on all numeric variables (including DAY) for all observations.

The second PROC MEANS statement asks for the statistics that must be specifically requested.

The third PROC MEANS statement requests statistics for each combination of values of the variables PLACE and DAY with the CLASS statement. MAXDEC=3 requests that only three decimal places be used to print the results. FW=10 limits the field width to 10 positions.

The fourth PROC MEANS statement shows that exactly the same statistics as those of the previous statement can be obtained using the BY statement instead of the CLASS statement. However, note the use of PROC SORT prior to invoking PROC MEANS. MEANS creates an output data set that includes the means and standard errors of the means for the two variables. The PRINT procedure is used to print the new data set. These statements produce **Output 19.1**.

```
DATA A;
   INPUT RATING EXCESS PLACE $ DAY @@;
   CARDS;
04 54 S 1   07 70 N 1   10 69 N 2   04 52 S 1
07 70 S 2   08 74 N 1   04 60 S 1   07 62 S 2
07 80 N 1   06 61 S 2   06 77 N 2   08 75 N 2
;
PROC MEANS;
   TITLE 'STATISTICS FOR ALL NUMERIC VARIABLES';

PROC MEANS DATA=A MAXDEC=3 NMISS RANGE USS CSS T PRT SUMWGT;
```

```
   VAR RATING EXCESS;
   TITLE 'REQUESTING ASSORTED STATISTICS';

PROC MEANS MAXDEC=3 FW=10;
   CLASS PLACE DAY;
   VAR RATING EXCESS;
   TITLE 'STATISTICS WITH TWO CLASS VARIABLES';

PROC SORT;
   BY PLACE DAY;
PROC MEANS MAXDEC=3 FW=10;
   BY PLACE DAY;
   VAR RATING EXCESS;
   OUTPUT OUT=NEW MEAN=RMEAN EMEAN STDERR=RSE ESE;
   TITLE 'STATISTICS WITH TWO BY VARIABLES';
PROC PRINT;
   TITLE 'NEW DATA SET';
```

Output 19.1 Several Kinds of PROC MEANS Output

```
                        STATISTICS FOR ALL NUMERIC VARIABLES                                    1

❶  ❷                    ❸               ❹               ❺                 ❻
N VARIABLE             MIN             MAX            MEAN              STD
-------------------------------------------------------------------------------
12 RATING             4.00           10.00            6.50             1.83
   EXCESS            52.00           80.00           67.00             9.09
   DAY                1.00            2.00            1.50             0.52
-------------------------------------------------------------------------------
```

```
                        REQUESTING ASSORTED STATISTICS                                          2

                    ⓱               ⓭               ⓫               ⓬
N VARIABLE         SUMWGT            USS           NMISS            RANGE
-------------------------------------------------------------------------------
12 RATING          12.000          544.000              0            6.000
   EXCESS          12.000        54776.000              0           28.000
-------------------------------------------------------------------------------
                    ⓮               ⓯               ⓰
N VARIABLE           CSS               T             PRT
-----------------------------------------------------
12 RATING          37.000          12.277           0.000
   EXCESS         908.000          25.546           0.000
-----------------------------------------------------
```

STATISTICS WITH TWO CLASS VARIABLES 3

PLACE	DAY	N	VARIABLE	MIN	MAX	MEAN
N	1	3	RATING	7.000	8.000	7.333
			EXCESS	70.000	80.000	74.667
	2	3	RATING	6.000	10.000	8.000
			EXCESS	69.000	77.000	73.667
S	1	3	RATING	4.000	4.000	4.000
			EXCESS	52.000	60.000	55.333
	2	3	RATING	6.000	7.000	6.667
			EXCESS	61.000	70.000	64.333

PLACE	DAY	N	VARIABLE	STD
N	1	3	RATING	0.577
			EXCESS	5.033
	2	3	RATING	2.000
			EXCESS	4.163
S	1	3	RATING	0.000
			EXCESS	4.163
	2	3	RATING	0.577
			EXCESS	4.933

STATISTICS WITH TWO BY VARIABLES 4

-------------------------------- PLACE=N DAY=1 --------------------------------

N	VARIABLE	MIN	MAX	MEAN	STD
3	RATING	7.000	8.000	7.333	0.577
	EXCESS	70.000	80.000	74.667	5.033

STATISTICS BY PLACE AND DAY

-------------------------------- PLACE=N DAY=2 --------------------------------

N	VARIABLE	MIN	MAX	MEAN	STD
3	RATING	6.000	10.000	8.000	2.000
	EXCESS	69.000	77.000	73.667	4.163

STATISTICS BY PLACE AND DAY

-------------------------------- PLACE=S DAY=1 --------------------------------

N	VARIABLE	MIN	MAX	MEAN	STD
3	RATING	4.000	4.000	4.000	0.000
	EXCESS	52.000	60.000	55.333	4.163

(continued on next page)

(continued from previous page)

STATISTICS BY PLACE AND DAY

-------------------------------- PLACE=S DAY=2 --------------------------------

N	VARIABLE	MIN	MAX	MEAN	STD
3	RATING	6.000	7.000	6.667	0.577
	EXCESS	61.000	70.000	64.333	4.933

NEW DATA SET 5

OBS	PLACE	DAY	_TYPE_	_FREQ_	RMEAN
1	N	1	0	3	7.3333333333
2	N	2	0	3	8
3	S	1	0	3	4
4	S	2	0	3	6.6666666667

NEW DATA SET

OBS	EMEAN	RSE	ESE
1	74.666666667	.33333333333	2.905932629
2	73.666666667	1.1547005384	2.4037008503
3	55.333333333	0	2.4037008503
4	64.333333333	.33333333333	2.8480012484

Chapter 20

The PLOT Procedure

ABSTRACT

The PLOT procedure graphs one variable against another, producing a printer plot. The coordinates of each point on the plot correspond to the two variables' values in one or more observations of the input data set.

INTRODUCTION

The PLOT procedure takes the values that occur for each observation in an input SAS data set on two variables, say X and Y, and then represents the intersection of these values as points on the plot. All you need to do to produce a plot is to tell the procedure which variables to plot. For example, these statements

```
PROC PLOT;
   PLOT Y*X;
```

produce the simple plot shown in **Output 20.1**.

Output 20.1 Plotting Variables: PLOT Procedure

```
                                   Plot of Y*X    Legend: A = 1 obs, B = 2 obs, etc.                                 1

Y     |
      |
      |
 1.50 +
      |
      |
      |  A
 1.25 +
      |
      |
      |       A
 1.00 +                                                                                A
      |                                                                                      A
      |
      |
 0.75 +                                                                          A
      |              A                                                                             A
      |
      |
 0.50 +
      |
      |
      |                    A                                                                             A
 0.25 +                                                                    A
      |
      |
      |                          A
 0.00 +
      |                                                                                                        A
      |
      |                                A
-0.25 +
      |
      |
      |                                                              A
      |                                                                                                              A
-0.50 +
      |                                      A
      |
      |
-0.75 +
      |
      |
      |                                            A           A
-1.00 +
      |
      |                                                  A
      |
-1.25 +
      |
      |
      |
      ---+-----+-----+-----+-----+-----+-----+-----+-----+-----+-----+-----+-----+-----+-----+-----+-----+-----+-----+--
        1.0   1.5   2.0   2.5   3.0   3.5   4.0   4.5   5.0   5.5   6.0   6.5   7.0   7.5   8.0   8.5   9.0   9.5  10.0
                                                         X
```

Note that PROC PLOT automatically scales the values of X and Y on the plot. Or you can specify the tick marks (the lines on the axis marking specific values that you want). For example,

```
PROC PLOT;
   PLOT Y*X  / HAXIS=0 TO 12 BY 2;
```

produces the output shown in **Output 20.2**.

Output 20.2 Specifying Tick Marks: PLOT Procedure

```
                                     Plot of Y*X    Legend:  A = 1 obs, B = 2 obs, etc.

  Y   |
      |
 1.50 +
      |
      |            A
 1.25 +
      |
      |                A
 1.00 +                                                                             A
      |                                                                                  A
      |
 0.75 +                                                                        A
      |                      A                                                                A
      |
 0.50 +
      |
      |                          A                                                                 A
 0.25 +                                                                   A
      |
      |                                A
 0.00 +
      |                                                                                                  A
      |                                    A
-0.25 +
      |                                                              A
      |                                                                                                       A
-0.50 +
      |                                          A
      |
-0.75 +
      |                                               A         A
      |
-1.00 +
      |                                                    A
      |
-1.25 +
      |
      |
      ---+-------------------+-------------------+-------------------+-------------------+-------------------+-------------------+--
         0                   2                   4                   6                   8                  10                  12
                                                                     X
```

In this example, PROC PLOT uses the plotting character A to indicate that one observation occurs at each point, B to indicate two observations, and so on. **Output 20.3** illustrates how you can specify another symbol, like a plus sign (+), to be used as the plotting character.

```
PROC PLOT;
   PLOT Y*X='+' / HAXIS=0 TO 12 BY 2;
```

Output 20.3 Specifying Other Plotting Symbols: PLOT Procedure

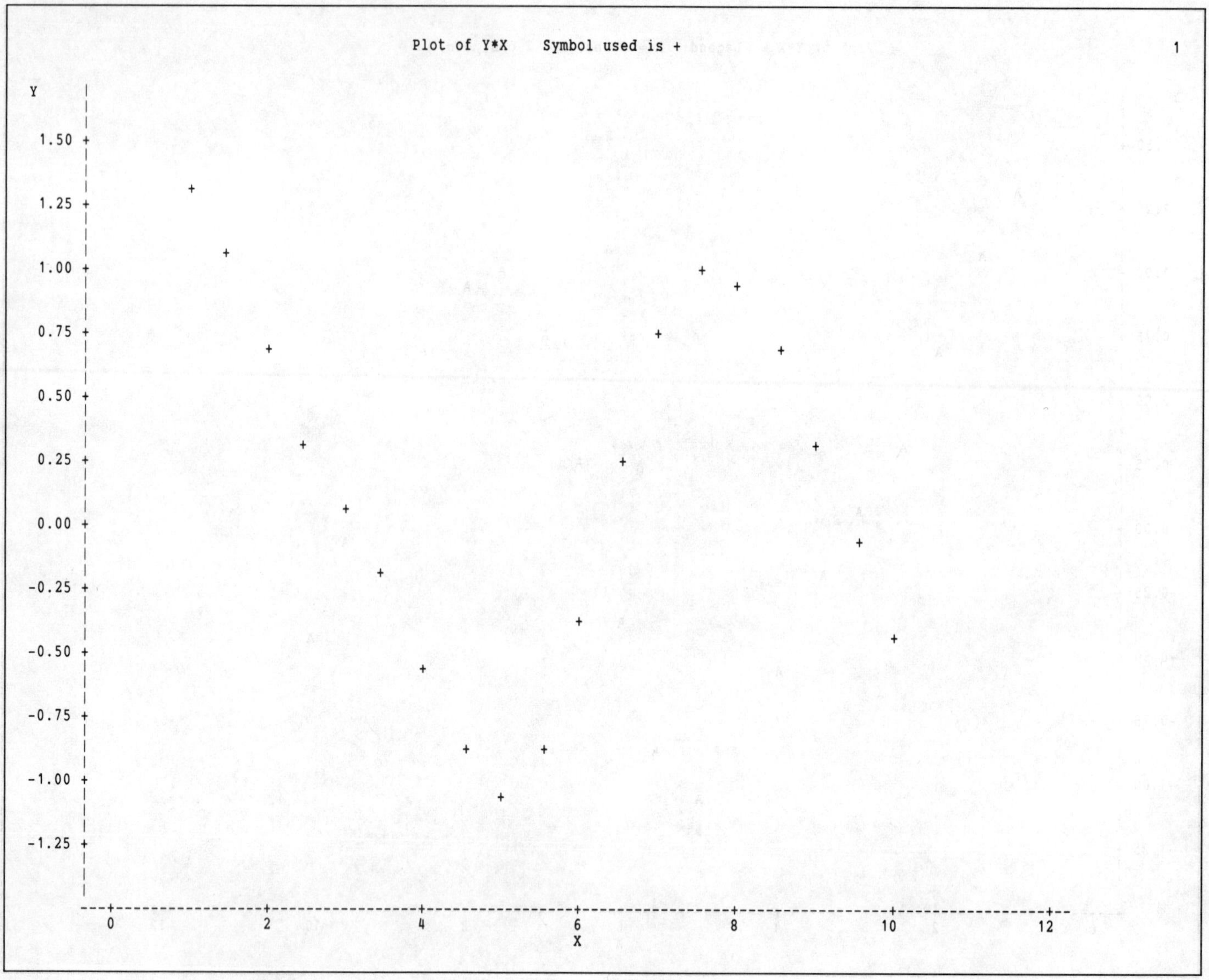

Output 20.4 shows how you can use the values of a third variable to determine the plotting character. For example, suppose another variable, Z, takes on the values 1, 2, and 3. These statements

```
PROC PLOT;
   PLOT Y*X=Z / HAXIS=0 TO 12 BY 2   BOX ;
```

indicate that the plotting character used for a particular observation is the value of Z for that observation. The BOX option causes PROC PLOT to draw a box all the way around the plot.

Output 20.4 Using the Values of a Third Variable to Determine Plotting Characters: PLOT Procedure

```
                                              Plot of Y*X      Symbol is value of Z                                                             1

       --+-------------------+-------------------+-------------------+-------------------+-------------------+-------------------+---
 Y     |                                                                                                                            |
       |                                                                                                                            |
       |                                                                                                                            |
  1.50 +                                                                                                                            +
       |                                                                                                                            |
       |                                                                                                                            |
       |           3                                                                                                                |
  1.25 +                                                                                                                            +
       |                                                                                                                            |
       |                                                                                                                            |
       |                1                                                                                                           |
  1.00 +                                                                            1                                               +
       |                                                                                 3                                          |
       |                                                                                                                            |
       |                                                                                                                            |
  0.75 +                                                                       3                                                    +
       |                     1                                                                2                                     |
       |                                                                                                                            |
       |                                                                                                                            |
  0.50 +                                                                                                                            +
       |                                                                                                                            |
       |                                                                                                                            |
       |                          1                                                                2                                |
  0.25 +                                                                  3                                                         +
       |                                                                                                                            |
       |                                                                                                                            |
       |                               2                                                                                            |
  0.00 +                                                                                                                            +
       |                                                                                                2                           |
       |                                                                                                                            |
       |                                    2                                                                                       |
 -0.25 +                                                                                                                            +
       |                                                                                                                            |
       |                                                             2                                                              |
       |                                                                                                     3                      |
 -0.50 +                                                                                                                            +
       |                                         3                                                                                  |
       |                                                                                                                            |
       |                                                                                                                            |
 -0.75 +                                                                                                                            +
       |                                                                                                                            |
       |                                              2         1                                                                   |
       |                                                                                                                            |
 -1.00 +                                                                                                                            +
       |                                                   3                                                                        |
       |                                                                                                                            |
       |                                                                                                                            |
 -1.25 +                                                                                                                            +
       |                                                                                                                            |
       |                                                                                                                            |
       |                                                                                                                            |
       --+-------------------+-------------------+-------------------+-------------------+-------------------+-------------------+---
         0                   2                   4                   6                   8                 10                  12
                                                                     X
```

Another way to enhance the information contained in the plot is to use reference lines at specific values. For example, for reference lines perpendicular to the horizontal axis, use these statements, which produce **Output 20.5**.

```
PROC PLOT;
   PLOT Y*X=Z / HAXIS=0 TO 12 BY 2 HREF=4 8;
```

Output 20.5 Specifying Reference Lines: PLOT Procedure

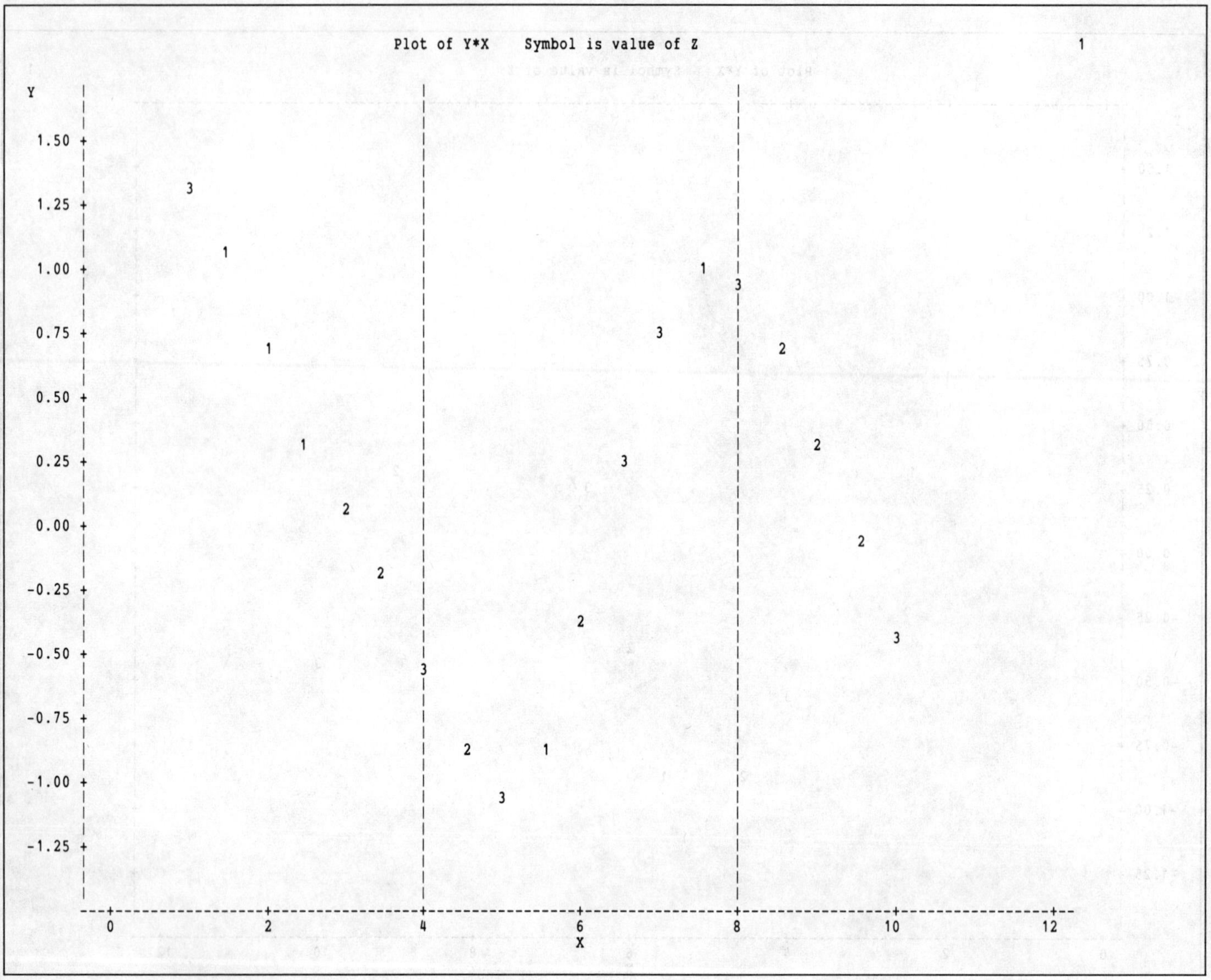

Output 20.6 shows that you can also superimpose two or more plots on the same axes.

```
PROC PLOT;
   PLOT Y*X=Z A*B / OVERLAY;
```

Output 20.6 Superimposing Two or More Plots on the Same Axes: PLOT Procedure

```
                                      Plot of Y*X     Symbol is value of Z                                                            1
                                      Plot of A*B     Legend:  A = 1 obs, B = 2 obs, etc.

     2.0 +                             A
         |
         |
         |                                                                 A
         |
         |
         |                                                                     A
     1.5 +                A
         |
         |
         |                   3
         |
         |
         |                        1
     1.0 +                                                                                   1
         |                                                                                        3
         |       A
         |         A                                                                    3
         |          A                                                     A                            2
         |                            1                       A
         |                                                 A
     0.5 +                            A A
         |                            A
         |                                  1                                                              2
         |                  A                                                      3
    Y    |
         |                                                       A
         |                   A                   2     A
     0.0 +                                     A   A
         |                                                                                                        2
         |
         |                                            2
         |
         |                                                                    2
         |                                                                                                           3
    -0.5 +
         |                                                 3
         |
         |
         |
         |                                                               1
         |                                                      2
    -1.0 +
         |                                                           3
         |
         |
         |
         |
         |
    -1.5 +
         -----+----+----+----+----+----+----+----+----+----+----+----+----+----+----+----+----+----+----+----+----+----+----
            -0.5  0.0  0.5  1.0  1.5  2.0  2.5  3.0  3.5  4.0  4.5  5.0  5.5  6.0  6.5  7.0  7.5  8.0  8.5  9.0  9.5 10.0
                                                                     X
```

You can also print multiple plots per page with PROC PLOT. For example, **Output 20.7** shows all six of the preceding plots on the same page. It was produced with the following statements:

```
PROC PLOT  HPERCENT=50  VPERCENT=33;
   TITLE 'MULTIPLE PLOTS PER PAGE';
   PLOT Y*X;
   PLOT Y*X / HAXIS=0 TO 12 BY 2;
   PLOT Y*X='+' / HAXIS=0 TO 12 BY 2;
   PLOT Y*X=Z / HAXIS=0 TO 12 BY 2  BOX;
   PLOT Y*Z=Z / HAXIS=0 TO 12 BY 2  HREF=4 8;
   PLOT Y*X=Z  A * B / OVERLAY;
```

Output 20.7 Multiple Plots per Page: PLOT Procedure

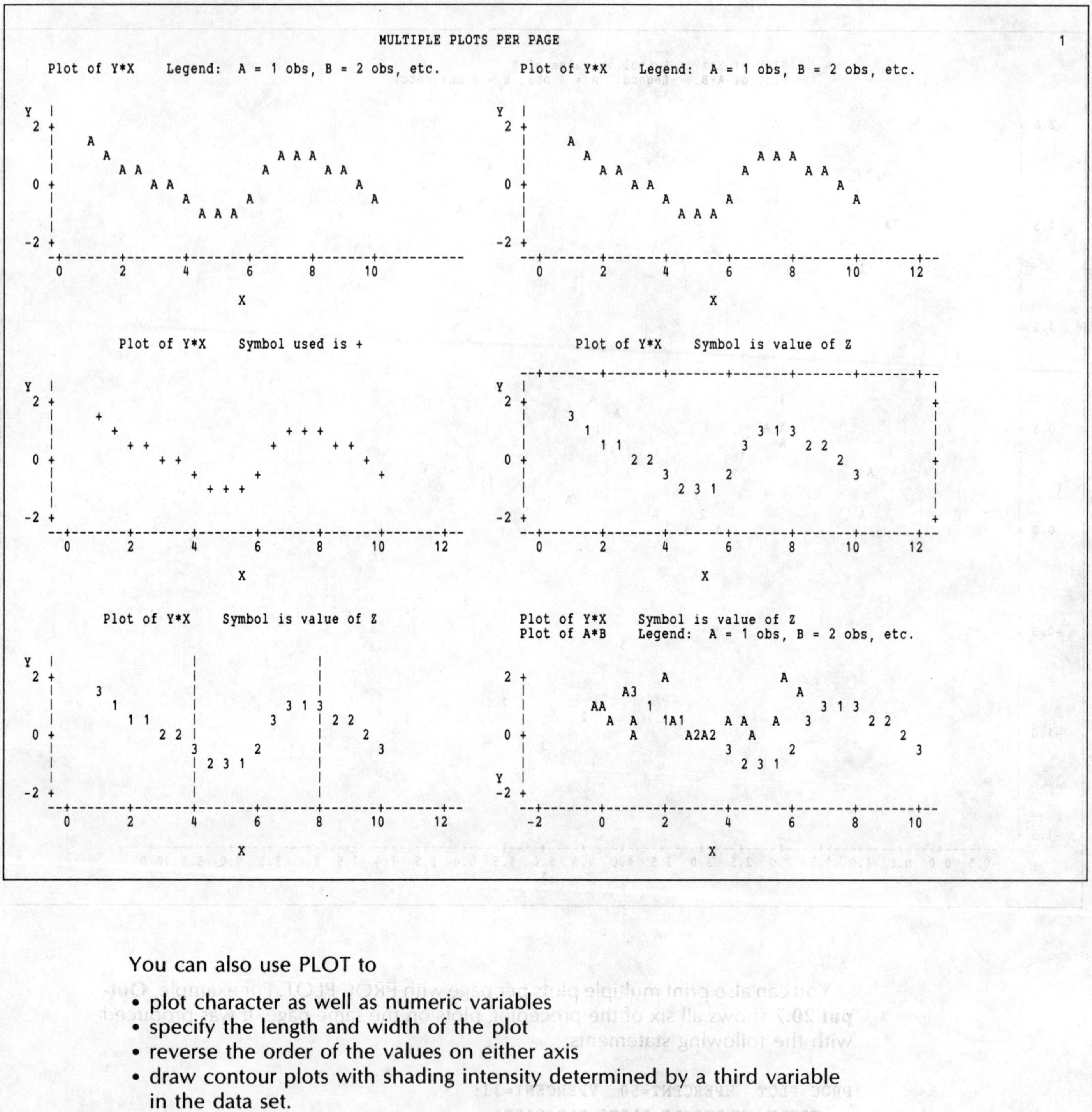

You can also use PLOT to

- plot character as well as numeric variables
- specify the length and width of the plot
- reverse the order of the values on either axis
- draw contour plots with shading intensity determined by a third variable in the data set.

The SAS statements that generated the data for the plots shown in this section are listed at the end of the chapter in **Examples of PROC PLOT Output**.

SPECIFICATIONS

The PLOT procedure is controlled by these statements:

PROC PLOT *options;*
BY *variables;*
PLOT *requests / options;*

A PLOT statement must be present to tell the procedure which variables to plot. Any number of PLOT statements can be specified each time the procedure is invoked, and any number of plots can be requested on one PLOT statement.

PROC PLOT Statement

PROC PLOT *options;*

The options below can appear in the PROC PLOT statement.

DATA=*SASdataset*
: names the input SAS data set to be used by PROC PLOT. When the DATA= option is omitted, PLOT uses the most recently created SAS data set.

UNIFORM
: requests uniform axis scaling across BY groups when a BY statement is used. The same scaling allows you to compare the plots for different levels of the BY variables directly.

NOLEGEND
: suppresses printing the legend at the top of each plot. The legend lists the names of the variables being plotted and the plotting characters used in the plot.

FORMCHAR (*index list*) ='*string*'
: defines the characters to be used for constructing the borders of the plot. The value is a string 11 characters long defining the two bar characters, vertical and horizontal, and the nine corner characters: upper left, upper middle, upper right, middle left, middle middle (cross), middle right, lower left, lower middle, and lower right. Of these, PROC PLOT uses only the horizontal and vertical bars, the four corners, and the cross. If the FORMCHAR= option in the PROC PLOT statement is not given, the value supplied, if any, with the system option FORMCHAR= will be used. The default value is FORMCHAR='|----|+|---'. Any character or hexadecimal string can be substituted to customize the table appearance. Use an index list to specify which default form character each supplied character replaces; or replace the entire default string by specifying the full 11 character replacement string with no index list. For example, change the four corners to asterisks by using

```
FORMCHAR(3 5 9 11)= '****'   .
```

Specifying

```
FORMCHAR='           ' (11 blanks)
```

produces plots with no borders.

PROC PLOT uses only the following FORMCHAR characters:

character	position	default
vertical bar	1	'|'
horizontal bar	2	'-'
upper left corner	3	'-'
upper right corner	5	'-'
cross (for tick marks)	7	'+'
lower left corner	9	'-'
lower right corner	11	'-'

For printing on the PC screen or to a printer with an IBM graphics character set (1 or 2), we recommend:

```
FORMCHAR='B3C4DAC2BFC3C5B4C0C1D9'X
```

VTOH=*value*
tells PROC PLOT the aspect ratio (vertical to horizontal) of the characters on the output device. If this option is specified, PROC PLOT will select spacing between tick marks so that the length of horizontal and vertical ticks are nearly equal. It is ignored on any plots for which both VSPACE and HSPACE are specified (see VSPACE and HSPACE options in the **PLOT statement**).

NOMISS
requests that observations for which either variable is missing be excluded from the axes calculations. Normally, the axes are drawn based on all the values of the variable being plotted, including points for which the other variable is missing. This option has no effect if you specify the plot axes. (See VAXIS and HAXIS options in the **Scale of axes** section.)

VPERCENT=*values*
requests PROC PLOT use the specified percentage(s) of the page, rather than exactly one page, for each plot. After reaching the end of this list, PROC PLOT cycles back to the beginning. PLOT tries to fit as many plots as possible per page when this option is used. For example,

```
VPERCENT=33
```

causes PROC PLOT to print three plots per page vertically, each of which is one third of a page long.

```
VPERCENT=50 25 25
```

also prints three plots per page, but the first one is twice as big as the other two.

By specifying a zero in the list, you can force PROC PLOT to go to a new page even though it could fit the next plot on the same page. For example,

```
VPERCENT=33 0
```

produces plots that are only one-third of a page long but only prints one plot per page.

This option can also be used to print very long plots. For example,

```
VPERCENT=300
```

produces plots three pages long.

At the beginning of every BY group and after each RUN statement, PROC PLOT returns to the beginning of the VPERCENT= list, and starts printing on a new page.

HPERCENT=*values*

specifies horizontal percentages for plot lengths, just as VPERCENT= specifies vertical percentages. If a percentage greater than 100 is used, sections of the plot are printed on successive pages.

BY Statement

BY *variables;*

A BY statement can be used with PROC PLOT to obtain separate plots on observations in groups defined by the BY variables. When a BY statement appears, the procedure expects the input data set to be sorted in order of the BY variables. If your input data set is not sorted in ascending order, use the SORT procedure with a similar BY statement to sort the data, or, if appropriate, use the BY statement options NOTSORTED or DESCENDING. PLOT produces a new page each time a new value of the BY variable is encountered in the data set. If a BY statement is used, it must be given before the first RUN statement.

PLOT Statement

PLOT *requests / options;*

The PLOT statement requests the plots to be produced by PROC PLOT. Remember that you can include many PLOT statements and specify many plot requests in one PLOT statement.

The *requests* in the PLOT statement specify the variables (vertical and horizontal) to be plotted and the plotting character to be used to mark the points on the plot. The request can take the following forms:

*vertical*horizontal*

names the variable to be shown on the vertical axis and the variable to be shown on the horizontal axis.

For example, the statements

```
PROC PLOT;
   PLOT Y*X;
```

request a plot of Y by X. Y appears on the vertical axis, X on the horizontal.

This form of the plot request uses the default method of choosing a plotting symbol to mark plot points. When a point on the plot represents the values of one observation in the data set, PROC PLOT puts the character A at that point. When a point represents the values of two observations, the character B appears. When a point represents values of three observations, the character C appears, and so on through the alphabet. The character Z is used for the occurrence of twenty-six or more observations at the same printing position.

*vertical*horizontal='character'*

names the variables to be shown on the vertical and horizontal axes and also specifies a character constant to mark each point on the plot. A single character is used to represent values from one or more observations.

For example, the statements

```
PROC PLOT;
   PLOT Y*X='+';
```

request a plot of Y by X, with each point on the plot represented by a plus sign (+).

*vertical*horizontal=variable*

names the variables to be plotted on the vertical and horizontal axes and also specifies a variable whose values are to mark each point on the plot. The variable can be either numeric or character. The first (left-most) nonblank character in the formatted value of the variable is used as the plotting symbol. When more than one observation maps to the same plotting position, the value from the first observation marks the point. For example, in the statements

```
PROC PLOT;
   PLOT HEIGHT*WEIGHT=SEX;
```

SEX is a character variable with values of FEMALE and MALE: the values F and M mark each observation on the plot.

Note: the plotting symbol is the first nonblank character of each value even if more than one value starts with the same letter.

To request two or more plots, write one request after another:

```
PROC PLOT;
   PLOT A*B R*S;
```

If you want to plot all the combinations of one set of variables with another, you can use a grouping specification. Enclose each set of variables in parentheses, joining them with an asterisk (*). For example, the following PLOT statements are equivalent:

```
PLOT (Y X)*(A B);
```

```
PLOT Y*A Y*B X*A X*B;
```

You can also abbreviate a variable list to request a number of plots:

```
PLOT Y*(A-Z);
```

If both the vertical and horizontal specifications request more than one variable, and a variable appears in both lists, it will not be plotted against itself. For example, the following statement plots all combinations of the variables A, B, and C with B, C, and D, but it does not plot B*B and C*C:

```
PLOT (A B C)*(B C D);
```

To plot all unique combinations of a list of variables, simply omit the second list. Thus, the following two statements are equivalent:

```
PLOT (A B C);
```

```
PLOT A*B A*C B*C;
```

The options below can appear in the PLOT statement. A slash (/) separates these options from the plot requests. No slash is needed if no options are specified.

Scale of axes

VAXIS=*values*

specifies the tick mark values to be equally spaced along the vertical axis. When the variable is numeric, VAXIS= values must be given in either ascending or descending order.

The statements

```
PROC PLOT;
   PLOT Y*X / VAXIS=10 TO 100 BY 5;
```

ask for a plot of Y by X, with tick marks at 10, 15, 20 and on up to 100 on the vertical axis.

Numeric values need not be uniformly distributed; a specification of the form

```
VAXIS=10 100 1000 10000
```

is valid and produces a logarithmic plot. If PROC PLOT cannot determine the function implied by the axis specification, it uses simple linear interpolation between the points.

To determine whether PLOT correctly interpolates a function you wish to use, you can generate data with the DATA step that determines the function and see whether it appears linear when plotted. For example, the following produces a linear plot:

```
DATA TEST;
DO X = 1 TO 3 BY .1;
   Y = 10**X;
   OUTPUT;
PROC PLOT;
   PLOT X*Y / HAXIS=10 100 1000 10000;
```

For character variables, the values can be given in any order.

In addition, the following VAXIS= specifications are valid

```
VAXIS='01JAN85'D TO '01JAN86'D BY MONTH
```

or

```
VAXIS='01JAN85'D TO '01JAN86'D BY QTR
```

In these examples, the FROM and TO values can be any of the valid SAS date, time, or datetime values described for the SAS functions INTCK and INTNX (see the chapter "SAS Functions" in *SAS Language Guide for Personal Computers*). The BY value can be any of the valid values listed for the *interval* argument in the SAS functions INTCK and INTNX. You must use a FORMAT statement to print the tick mark values in an understandable form.

HAXIS=*values*

specifies tick mark values for the horizontal axis. The HAXIS= option follows the same rules as the VAXIS= option above.

VZERO

requests that tick marks on the vertical axis begin in the first position with a zero. The VZERO request is ignored if the vertical variable has negative values or if an optional VAXIS= specification does not begin with zero.

HZERO

requests that tick marks on the horizontal axis begin in the first position with a value of zero. The HZERO request is ignored if the horizontal variable has negative values or if an optional HAXIS= specification does not begin with zero.

VREVERSE
: asks that the order of the values on the vertical axis be reversed.

HREVERSE
: asks that the order of the values on the horizontal axis be reversed.

VEXPAND
: requests that the vertical axis be expanded so it does not leave a great deal of white space. Depending on the data being plotted, it may or may not cause any difference in the appearance of the plot.

  Normally, PROC PLOT looks at the minimum difference between the five lowest ordered values of each variable (the *delta*) and insures that there is no more than one of these intervals per print position on the final scaled axis, if possible. If there is not enough room to do this, and if PLOT guesses that the data were artificially generated, it puts a fixed number of deltas in each print position. Otherwise it ignores the value. In most cases, this allows PROC PLOT to generate plots which are more accurate, but it can also cause more white space than would otherwise be necessary. This option causes PLOT to ignore delta, and thus to leave less white space on the vertical axis. It has no effect if delta was ignored already.

HEXPAND
: requests that the horizontal axis be expanded so as not to leave a great deal of white space. The behavior of HEXPAND is the same as that of VEXPAND, described above.

Reference lines

VREF=*values*
: requests that a horizontal line be drawn on the plot at the specified values on the vertical axis. If the VAXIS= option is not used, the points specified here will be included within the bounds of the axis generated.

VREFCHAR='*c*'
: gives the character to define the horizontal lines requested by the VREF= option. If you do not specify a character with VREFCHAR=, the horizontal bar character is used (default is '-'; see the FORMCHAR= option in the **PROC PLOT Statement**).

HREF=*values*
: requests that a vertical line be drawn on the plot at the specified values on the horizontal axis. For example, the statements

```
PROC PLOT;
     PLOT Y*X / HREF=5;
```

request a plot of Y by X with a vertical line at 5 on the horizontal axis. If the HAXIS= option is not used, the points specified here are included within the bounds of the axis generated.

HREFCHAR='*c*'
: specifies the character to define the vertical lines requested by the HREF= option. If you do not use HREFCHAR=, the horizontal bar character is used (default is '|'; see the FORMCHAR= option in the **PROC PLOT Statement**).

Appearance

BOX

requests that a border be drawn around the entire plot, rather than just on the left side and bottom.

Plot size Plots normally occupy one page each. You can use the options below to change the length and width of the plot. You can also use the system options LINESIZE= and PAGESIZE= and the PROC PLOT statement options VPERCENT= and HPERCENT= (see the **PROC PLOT Statement**) to change plot sizes.

VPOS=*n*

specifies the number of vertical print positions on the vertical axis. The maximum VPOS= must be at least eight less than the page size in order to fit; the exact number depends on the titles used, whether plots are overlaid, and whether CONTOUR is specified. If VPOS is too large to fit on the page, the plot spans more than one page.

HPOS=*n*

specifies the number of print positions on the horizontal axis. At least three additional positions are needed to print vertical axis information; the exact number depends on the number of characters in the vertical variable's values. If HPOS is too large to fit on a line, it will be ignored.

VSPACE=*n*

specifies the number of print lines to be used between tick marks on the vertical axis.

HSPACE=*n*

specifies the number of print positions to be used between tick marks on the horizontal axis.

Overlaying plots

OVERLAY

requests PROC PLOT combine the plots specified in the PLOT statement on one page. The variables in the first plot label the axes. Unless HAXIS= or VAXIS= is given, the axes are automatically scaled in the best way to fit all the variables, and the variable labels (if any) associated with the first pair of variables are printed next to the axes. When the SAS System option OVP is in effect and overprinting is allowed, the plots are superimposed; otherwise, when NOOVP is in effect, points appearing in more than one plot are represented by the value from the first plot.

Contour plots

CONTOUR=*value*

requests plotting symbols with varying degrees of shading where *value* is the number of levels for dividing the range of the response variable. The plot request must be of the form *vertical*horizontal*=*variable* where *variable* is a numeric variable in the data set. The intensity of shading is determined by the values of this variable. CONTOUR's value can range from one to ten.

For example, the statements

```
PROC PLOT;
    PLOT A*B=Z / CONTOUR=10;
```

request a plot whose points vary in darkness depending on the value of Z. Since the CONTOUR= value is ten, ten darkness levels are used.

Overprinting is used to produce the shading if it is allowed. Otherwise, single characters varying in darkness are used. The CONTOUR= option is most effective when the plot is dense.

S1=*'value'*
S2=*'value'*
...

specifies plotting symbols to use for each contour value in ascending order. When PROC PLOT produces contour plots, it automatically chooses the symbols to use for each level of intensity. It is possible to override these symbols and specify your own symbols for intensity levels using the S options. Up to three characters can be specified in quotes. If overprinting is not allowed, only the first character is used. For example, to specify three levels of shading for the Z variable, these statements can be used:

```
PROC PLOT;
    PLOT X*Y=Z / CONTOUR=3
          S1='A' S2='+' S3='X0A';
```

The symbols can be specified as hex constants.

```
PROC PLOT;
    PLOT X*Y=Z / CONTOUR=3
          S1='7A'X  S2='7F'X S3='A6'X;
```

This feature was designed especially for printers where the hex constants can represent grey-scale fill characters.

SLIST=*values*

is an alternative way of specifying symbols to use for each contour value in ascending order. It is often simpler to use. For example, the following statements are equivalent:

```
PLOT X*Y / CONTOUR=5  S1='.' S2=':' S3='!' S4='=' S5='+0';

PLOT X*Y / CONTOUR=5  SLIST='.' ':' '!' '=' '+0';
```

DETAILS

Missing Values

If values on either of the plotting variables are missing, PROC PLOT does not include the observation in the plot. However, in a plot of X*Y, values of X with corresponding missing values of Y are included in scaling the X axis, unless the NOMISS option is specified on the PROC PLOT statement.

Interactivity

PROC PLOT is an interactive procedure. Anytime you enter a RUN statement, PLOT executes all the statements entered so far, but it does not terminate. Each new group of statements executed this way begins on a new page and begins with the first item on the VPERCENT and HPERCENT lists, if any. If a BY statement is used, it must be specified before the first RUN. A QUIT statement stops the procedure without executing any statements entered since the last RUN. If another PROC or DATA step is encountered, or the SAS job is ended, all statements entered since the last RUN (or since the PROC PLOT statement, if a RUN was not used) are executed and then PLOT terminates.

Generating Data with Program Statements

When you generate data to be plotted, a good rule is to generate fewer observations than the number of positions on the horizontal axis. PROC PLOT then uses the increment of the horizontal variable as the interval between tick marks.

Since PROC PLOT prints one character for each observation, using SAS program statements to generate the data set for PLOT can enhance the effectiveness of continuous plots (see **Example 3**) and contour plots (see **Example 5**).

For example, suppose that you want to generate data in order to plot the equation

$$y = 2.54 + 3.83 * x$$

for *x* ranging from 0 to 100 with these statements:

```
OPTIONS LINESIZE=80;
DATA GENERATE;
   DO X=0 TO 100 BY 2;
      Y=2.54+3.83*X;
      OUTPUT;
      END;

PROC PLOT;
   PLOT Y*X;
```

If the plot is printed with a LINESIZE= value of eighty, about seventy-five positions are available on the horizontal axis for the X values. Thus, two is a good increment: fifty-one observations are generated, which is less than seventy-five.

However, if the plot is printed with a LINESIZE= value of 132, an increment of two produces a plot with a space between each plotting character. For a smoother line, a better increment is one, since 101 observations are generated.

Printed Output

Each plot uses one full page unless the plot's size is changed by the VPOS= and HPOS= options in the PLOT statement, the VPERCENT= or HPERCENT= options in the PROC PLOT statement, or the system options PAGESIZE= and LINESIZE=. Titles, legends, and variable labels are printed at the top of each page. Each axis is labeled with the variable name or the variable label, if one is specified.

Multiple plots per page Normally, PROC PLOT always begins a new plot on a new page. To print more than one plot on a single page, use the VPERCENT= and/or HPERCENT= options in the PROC PLOT statement. If the values supplied are small enough to allow it, PLOT prints more than one plot on a single page with these options. (See the VPERCENT= and HPERCENT= options in the PROC PLOT statement.) PROC PLOT always begins on a new page following a RUN statement and at the beginning of each new BY group.

EXAMPLES

Plotting Observed Data: Example 1

This example plots the two variables RATED and ACTUAL against each other. PROC PLOT uses an increment of ten for tick marks on the vertical axis; tick marks on the horizontal axis have an increment of four. Since two observations have a RATED value of 118 and an ACTUAL value of 121, PROC PLOT uses a B to represent the point corresponding to RATED=118 and ACTUAL=121. Other points are represented by As. The following example produces **Output 20.8**.

```
DATA SPEED;
   INPUT RATED ACTUAL;
   LABEL RATED='RATED SPEED'  ACTUAL='ACTUAL SPEED';
   CARDS;
 75  85
110 112
 75  81
105 108
112 115
 75  77
 90  89
 70  73
118 121
103 100
118 121
;
PROC PLOT;
   PLOT RATED*ACTUAL;
   TITLE 'RATED SPEED VS. ACTUAL SPEED';
```

Output 20.8 Plotting Observed Data: PLOT Procedure

```
                                   RATED SPEED VS. ACTUAL SPEED                                                    1

                         Plot of RATED*ACTUAL     Legend:  A = 1 obs, B = 2 obs, etc.

      |
      |
  120 +
      |
      |                                                                                                                   B
      |
      |
      |
      |
      |                                                                                                      A
      |
  110 +                                                                                               A
      |
      |
      |
      |                                                                                      A
      |
      |                                                                    A
      |
R     |
A 100 +
T     |
E     |
D     |
      |
S     |
P     |
E     |
E     |
D  90 +                                           A
      |
      |
      |
      |
      |
      |
      |
      |
   80 +
      |
      |
      |
      |                A        A        A
      |
      |
      |
      |
   70 +       A
      |
      -----+--------+--------+--------+--------+--------+--------+--------+--------+--------+--------+--------+--------+--------+----
          72       76       80       84       88       92       96      100      104      108      112      116      120      124
                                                                   ACTUAL SPEED
```

Using a Plot Character and Defining Tick Marks: Example 2

This example uses variables from an analysis of covariance: RESPONSE is the response variable, and NUISANCE is a presumed covariate. To keep track of which observations are associated with different values of the variable TREAT, values of TREAT are used for the plotting characters.

You can use the VAXIS= option to define tick marks for the vertical axis, beginning with 125 and going up to 185 by 5s. The following example produces **Output 20.9**.

```
DATA COVAR;
   INPUT TREAT $ RESPONSE NUISANCE;
   CARDS;
P 125 3.1
P 135 9.0
P 144 14.9
P 153 20.2
Q 136 2.0
```

```
Q 152 8.5
Q 160 12.6
Q 165 17.1
R 154 3.2
R 164 10.5
R 173 15.4
R 183 20.7
PROC PLOT;
   PLOT RESPONSE*NUISANCE=TREAT / VAXIS=125 TO 185 BY 5;
   TITLE 'RESPONSE VS. NUISANCE';
   TITLE2 'THREE TREATMENTS';
```

Output 20.9 Using a Plot Character and Defining Tick Marks: PLOT Procedure

```
                                                RESPONSE VS. NUISANCE                                                 1
                                                   THREE TREATMENTS

                                 Plot of RESPONSE*NUISANCE    Symbol is value of TREAT
185      +
         |
         |                                                                                                    R
         |
         |
180      +
         |
         |
         |
         |
175      +
         |
         |                                                                         R
         |
         |
170      +
         |
         |
         |
         |
165      +                                                                                  Q
         |                                                 R
         |
         |
         |
160      +                                                           Q
         |
         |
         |
         |
155      +
         |             R
         |
         |                                        Q                                                        P
RESPONSE |
150      +
         |
         |
         |
         |
145      +
         |                                                                       P
         |
         |
         |
140      +
         |
         |
         |
         |       Q
135      +                                         P
         |
         |
         |
         |
130      +
         |
         |
         |
         |
125      +             P
         --------+----+----+----+----+----+---+----+----+----+----+---+----+----+----+----+----+----+----+----+--------
                 2    3    4    5    6    7   8    9   10   11   12  13   14   15   16   17   18   19   20   21
                                                           NUISANCE
```

Plotting the Graph of an Equation: Example 3

In this example, program statements in the DATA step are used to create 115 observations to plot the equation

$$Y = X\ SIN(2X)$$

for values of X ranging from zero to five.

No INPUT statement is used; all the X and Y values are generated by the program statements, and the OUTPUT statement creates the observations. In the PLOT statement, an asterisk (*) is specified as the plotting character. The following example produces **Output 20.10**.

```
DATA PROGRAM;
   DO X=0 TO 5 BY .05;
      Y=X*SIN(2*X);
      OUTPUT;
      END;

PROC PLOT;
   PLOT Y*X='*';
   TITLE 'Y=X*SIN(2*X)';
```

Plotting Predicted vs. Actual Values: Example 4

It is often useful to plot the graph of an equation and the observed data for which the equation was developed.

In regression analysis you often want to plot the regression equation as well as the actual values. You can use the OUTPUT statement with PROC REG to produce a data set containing both observed and predicted values, and then use PROC PLOT to overlay plots of these values. Here is an example:

```
DATA HTWT;
   INPUT HEIGHT WEIGHT @@;
   CARDS;
69.0 112.5 56.5 84.0 65.3 98.0 62.8 102.5 63.5 102.5
57.3 83.0 59.8 84.5 62.5 112.5 62.5 84.0 59.0 99.5
51.3 50.5 64.3 90.0 56.3 77.0 66.5 112.0 72.0 150.0
64.8 128.0 67.0 133.0 57.5 85.0 66.5 112.0
;
PROC REG;
   MODEL HEIGHT=WEIGHT;
   OUTPUT OUT=BOTH P=PREDHT;

PROC PLOT DATA=BOTH;
   PLOT HEIGHT*WEIGHT PREDHT*WEIGHT='*' / OVERLAY;
   TITLE 'PREDICTED VS. ACTUAL';
```

Actual values are indicated with As, predicted values with asterisks (*). See **Output 20.11**.

Output 20.10 Plotting the Graph of an Equation: PLOT Procedure

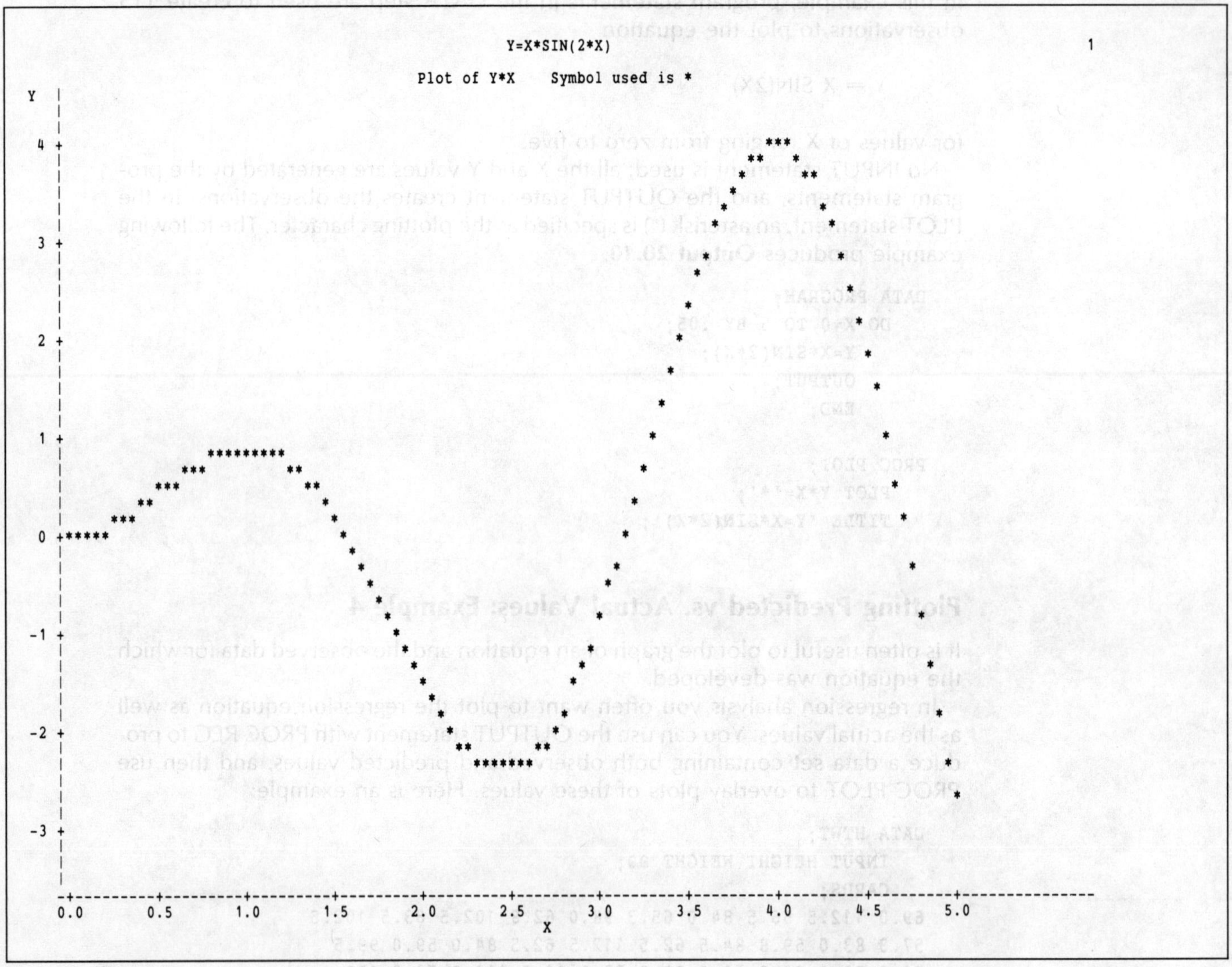

Output 20.11 Plotting Predicted vs. Actual Values: PLOT Procedure

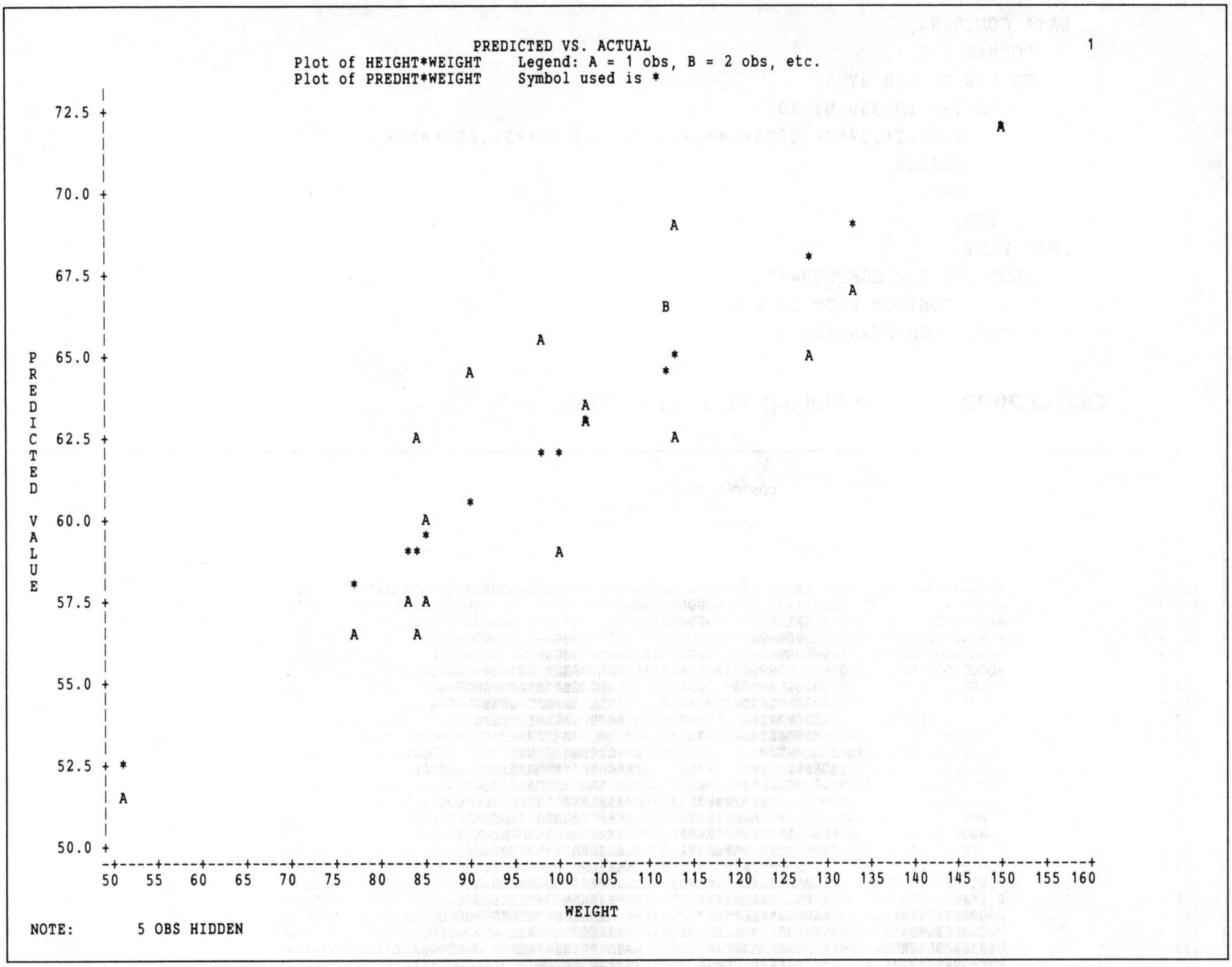

Contour Plotting: Example 5

It is possible to represent the values of three variables using a two-dimensional plot by setting one of the variables as the CONTOUR variable. When the value of that variable is high, it is represented by a dark point on the plot; when the value is low, it is represented by a light point.

In the example below, the three variables represented in the plot are X, Y, and Z. X and Y appear on the axes, and Z is the contour variable. You can see from the plot where high values of Z occur: if this were a three-dimensional plot, the dark areas would be a hilltop. Program statements are used to generate the observations for the plot, and the equation

$$Z=46.2 + .09X-.0005X^2 + .1Y-.0005Y^2 + .0004XY$$

describes the contour surface. Data set CONTOURS contains observations with values of X ranging from 0 to 400 by 5 and for values of Y ranging from 0 to 350 by 10.

The shadings associated with the values of Z appear at the bottom of the plot. See **Output 20.12**.

```
DATA CONTOURS;
   FORMAT Z 5.1;
   DO X=0 TO 400 BY 5;
      DO Y=0 TO 350 BY 10;
         Z=46.2+.09*X-.0005*X**2+.1*Y-.0005*Y**2+.0004*X*Y;
         OUTPUT;
         END;
      END;
PROC PLOT;
   PLOT Y*X=Z / CONTOUR=10;
   TITLE 'CONTOUR PLOT OF X VS. Y';
   TITLE2 'CONTOURS ARE Z';
```

Output 20.12 Contour Plotting: PLOT Procedure

```
CONTOUR PLOT OF X VS. Y                                  1
     CONTOURS ARE Z
   Contour Plot of Y*X
```

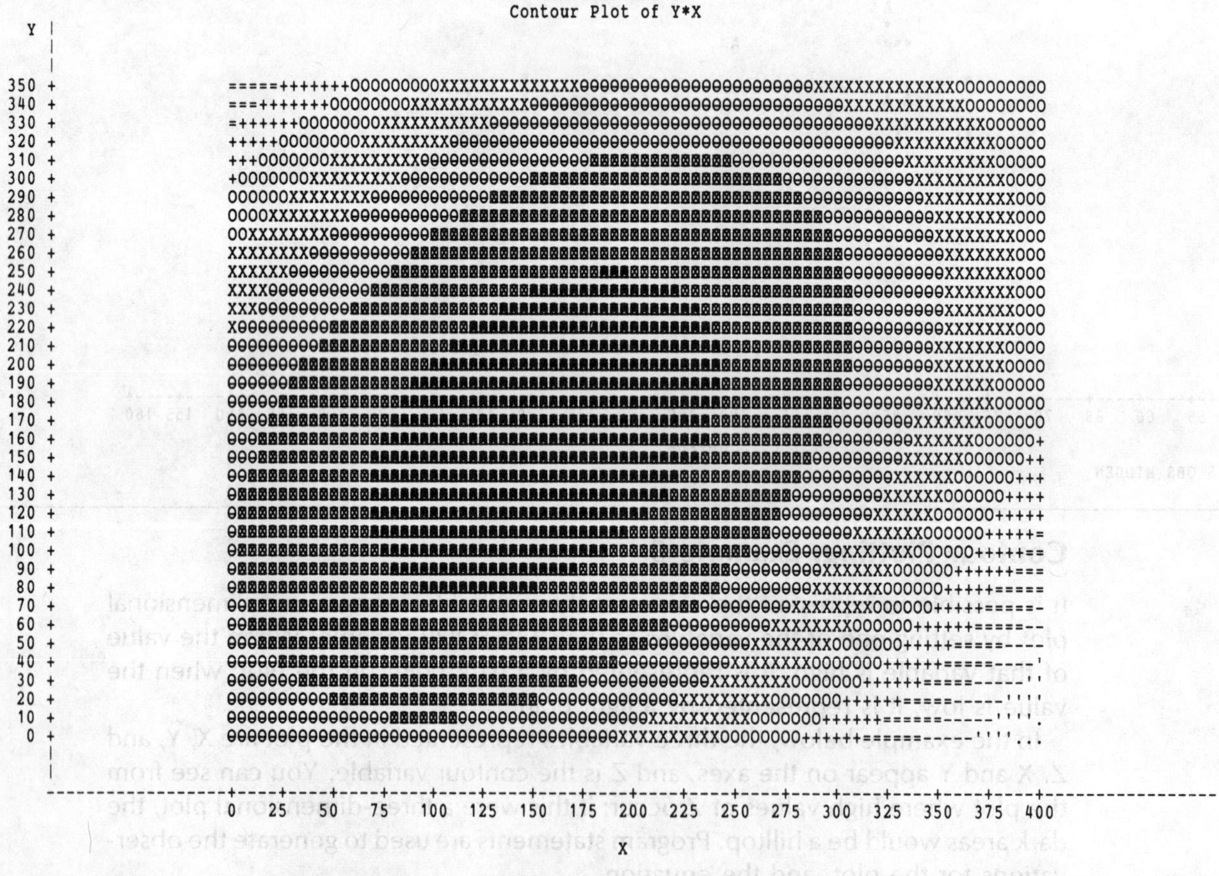

SYMBOL	Z	SYMBOL	Z	SYMBOL	Z	SYMBOL	Z	SYMBOL	Z
......	2.2 - 5.5	------	12.0 - 18.6	++++++	25.2 - 31.7	XXXXXX	38.3 - 44.9	▩▩▩▩▩▩	51.4 - 58.0
''''''	5.5 - 12.0	======	18.6 - 25.2	OOOOOO	31.7 - 38.3	ΘΘΘΘΘΘ	44.9 - 51.4	██████	58.0 - 61.3

Labeling an Axis with Date Values: Example 6

When you plot a variable against a date variable, you can label the tick marks on an axis with date values by using SAS date constants after the VAXIS= or HAXIS= option. (See "SAS Expressions" in *SAS Language Guide for Personal Computers* for a description of date, time, and datetime constants.) To cause the constants to be printed in an understandable form, specify a format for the date variable. This example uses date constants to label the tick marks on the horizontal axis with the first day of each month. Note that in order to have room on the axis for observations in the month of December, you must specify a tick mark for January of the following year. The following example produces **Output 20.13**.

```
DATA SAMPLE;
   INPUT DATE:DATE7. CALLS;
   LABEL DATE='DATE'
         CALLS='NUMBER OF CALLS';
   CARDS;
1APR82 134
2MAR82 289
3JUN82 184
4JAN82 179
5APR82 360
6MAY82 245
7JUL82 280
8AUG82 494
9SEP82 309
11APR82 384
21MAR82 201
13JUN82 152
14JAN82 128
15APR82 350
15DEC82 150
16MAY82 240
17JUL82 499
18AUG82 248
19SEP82 356
10OCT82 222
11NOV82 294
2DEC82  511
22DEC82 413
13FEB82 488
14MAR82 460
15APR82 356
16JUN82 480
17JUL82 388
17NOV82 328
18AUG82 280
19SEP82 394
23NOV82 590
24FEB82 201
25MAR82 183
26APR82 412
27MAY82 292
28JUN82 309
29JUL82 330
```

```
30AUG82 321
;

PROC PLOT;
   PLOT CALLS*DATE/HAXIS='1JAN82'D '1FEB82'D '1MAR82'D '1APR82'D
   '1MAY82'D '1JUN82'D '1JUL82'D '1AUG82'D '1SEP82'D '1OCT82'D
   '1NOV82'D '1DEC82'D '1JAN83'D;
   FORMAT DATE DATE7.;
   TITLE 'CALLS TO CITY EMERGENCY SERVICES NUMBER';
   TITLE2 'SAMPLE OF DAYS FOR 1982';
```

Output 20.13 Labeling an Axis with Data Values: PLOT Procedure

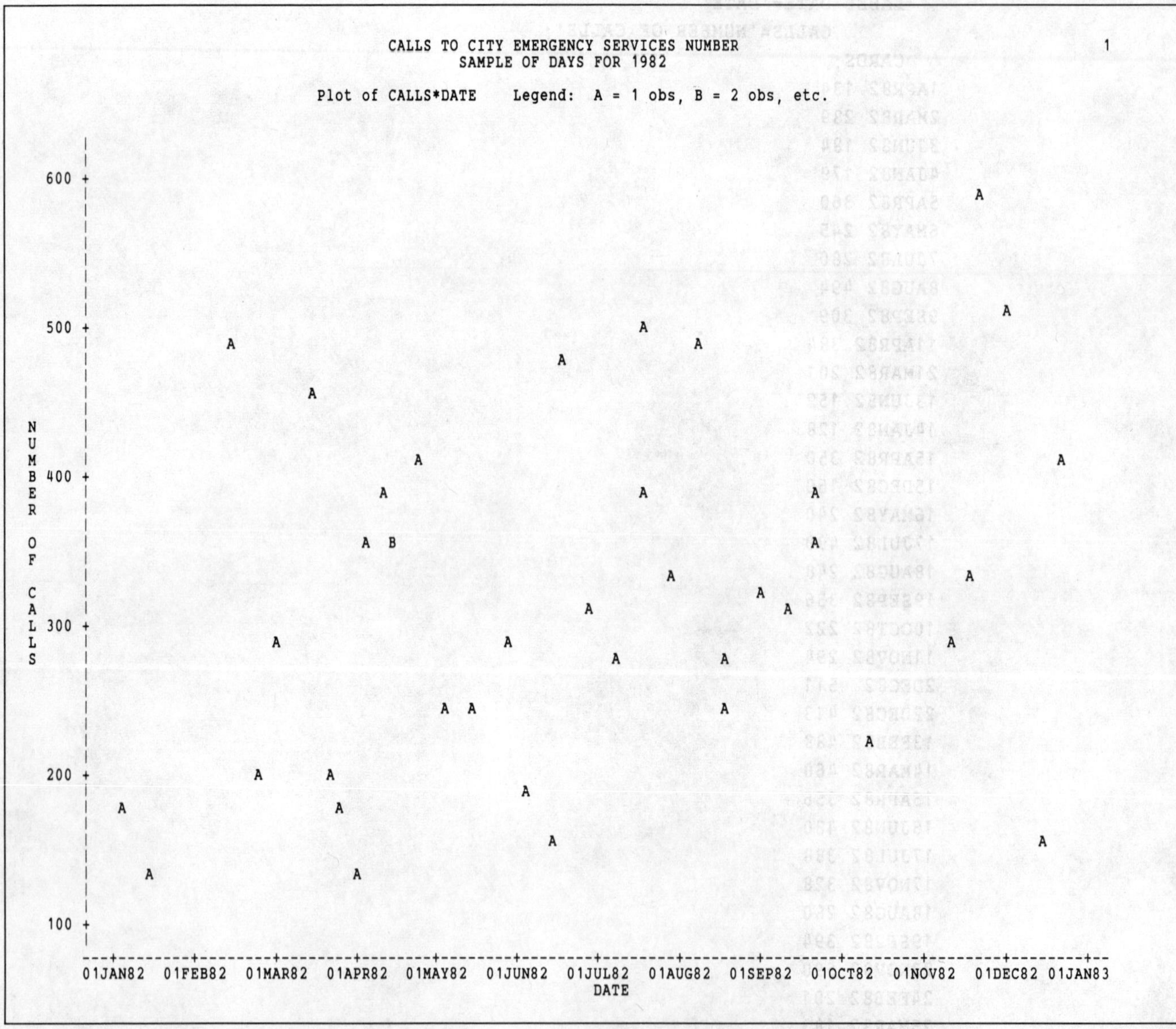

The Effect of the HEXPAND Option: Example 7

The HEXPAND option causes the PLOT procedure to ignore information about the spacing of the data. This tends to produce plots that are less accurate but have less wasted space. For this example, evenly spaced data are plotted against both with and without the HEXPAND option. Since the data generated require just more than half the available space to print evenly, there is a great deal of white space on the edges of the plot when the HEXPAND option is not used. However, the linear relationship of the data is obvious. With HEXPAND, on the other hand, there is not so much space but the perfectly linear relationship less clear. The following example produces **Output 20.14**.

```
DATA EVEN;
   DO A=1 TO 30;
      OUTPUT;
      END;
PROC PLOT  HPERCENT=50  VPERCENT=50;
   TITLE 'USING THE HEXPAND OPTION';
   PLOT A*A;
   PLOT A*A / HEXPAND
RUN;
```

Output 20.14 The Effect of the HEXPAND Option: PLOT Procedure

```
                                 USING THE HEXPAND OPTION                                                        1

   Plot of A*A     Legend:  A = 1 obs, B = 2 obs, etc.

 A |
   |
   |
30 +                              A
28 +                           AA
26 +                         AA
24 +                       AA
22 +                     AA
20 +                   AA
18 +                 AA
16 +               AA
14 +             AA
12 +           AA
10 +         AA
 8 +       AA
 6 +     AA
 4 +   AA
 2 + AA
 0 +
   -+----+----+----+----+----+----+----------------------
    0    5   10   15   20   25   30

                            A

   Plot of A*A     Legend:  A = 1 obs, B = 2 obs, etc.

 A |
   |
   |
30 +                                               A
28 +                                            A A
26 +                                         A A
24 +                                     AA
22 +                                  AA
20 +                               A A
18 +                            A A
16 +                         A A
14 +                     AA
12 +                   AA
10 +              A A
 8 +           A A
 6 +        A A
 4 +     AA
 2 +  AA
 0 +
   -+-------+-------+-------+-------+-------+-------+----
    0       5       10      15      20      25      30

                            A
```

The Effect of the NOMISS Option: Example 8

This example shows the effect of the NOMISS option. The data show sales for a firm over a 15-year period. Since part of the period lies in the future, the SALES data are missing for those years. They are plotted once with NOMISS and once without it. In order to fit both plots on a page, the system option PAGESIZE=40 is used. The following statements produced the plots shown in **Output 20.15**.

```
OPTIONS PAGESIZE=40;
DATA FIRM;
   INPUT YEAR SALES;
   CARDS;
1974  3825
1975  4000
1976  4578
1977  5103
1978  5732
1979  6295
1980  6728
1981  2917
1982  2898
1983  3745
1984  4207
1985   .
1986   .
1987   .
1988   .
;
PROC PLOT;
   TITLE 'PLOT WITH MISSING VALUES INCLUDED';
   PLOT SALES*YEAR;
RUN;
PROC PLOT  NOMISS;
   TITLE 'PLOT WITH MISSING VALUES EXCLUDED';
   PLOT SALES*YEAR;
RUN;
```

Examples of PROC PLOT Output

The data for the examples in the earlier section of this chapter were generated with the following SAS statements.

```
DATA GENERATE;
   DO X=1 TO 10 BY .5;
      Y=SIN(X) + SIN(2*X)/(X+1);
      Z=CEIL(UNIFORM(13131)*3);
      A=2*MOD(X,Y);
      B=3*(1-MOD(Y,X));
      OUTPUT;
      END;
```

Output 20.15 The Effect of the NOMISS Option: PLOT Procedure

```
                              PLOT WITH MISSING VALUES INCLUDED                                  1

                     Plot of SALES*YEAR    Legend:  A = 1 obs, B = 2 obs, etc.

SALES |
 7000 +
      |                                                A
      |
      |
      |                                        A
 6000 +
      |                                A
      |
      |
      |                        A
 5000 +
      |
      |                A
      |
      |                                                                                A
 4000 +        A
      |A                                                                       A
      |
      |
      |
 3000 +                                                        A
      |                                                                A
      |
      |
      |
 2000 +
      |
      -+-------+-------+-------+-------+-------+-------+-------+-------+-------+-------+-------+-------+-------+-------+
     1974    1975    1976    1977    1978    1979    1980    1981    1982    1983    1984    1985    1986    1987    1988

                                                 YEAR
NOTE:     4 obs had missing values
```

```
                                                                                                     2

                              PLOT WITH MISSING VALUES EXCLUDED

                     Plot of SALES*YEAR    Legend:  A = 1 obs, B = 2 obs, etc.

SALES |
 7000 +
      |                                                                   A
      |
      |
      |                                                        A
 6000 +
      |                                             A
      |
      |
      |                                  A
 5000 +
      |
      |                       A
      |
      |                                                                                                               A
 4000 +            A
      | A                                                                                                  A
      |
      |
      |
 3000 +                                                                              A
      |                                                                                         A
      |
      |
      |
 2000 +
      |
      --+----------+----------+----------+----------+----------+----------+----------+----------+----------+----------+-
      1974       1975       1976       1977       1978       1979       1980       1981       1982       1983       1984

                                                  YEAR
```

Output 20.15 The Effect of the NOMISS Option: PLOT Procedure

Chapter 21

The PRINT Procedure

ABSTRACT

The PRINT procedure prints the observations in a SAS data set, using all or some of the variables. Totals and subtotals for numeric variables can also be printed.

INTRODUCTION

PROC PRINT prints a listing of the values of some or all of the variables in a SAS data set. You can produce customized reports using procedure options and statements; for example, with a BY statement, PROC PRINT separates observations into groups defined by the BY variables. Numeric variable totals are printed if a SUM statement is used.

SPECIFICATIONS

The following statements can be used with PROC PRINT:

PROC PRINT *options;*
VAR *variables;*
ID *variables;*
BY *variables;*
PAGEBY *byvariable;*

SUM *variables;*
SUMBY *byvariable;*

PROC PRINT Statement

PROC PRINT *options;*

The options below can be specified in the PROC PRINT statement:

DATA=*SASdataset*
: names the SAS data set to be used by PROC PRINT. If DATA= is omitted, the most recently created data set is used.

N
: requests that the number of observations be printed at the end of the data set. If a BY statement is used, the number of observations in each BY group is printed at the end of the BY group.

DOUBLE
D
: causes the printed output to be double-spaced.

ROUND
: rounds values to the number of decimal places specified for a variable in a FORMAT statement or, if no format is specified, to two decimal places. The only variables whose values are rounded are those being summed (see the SUM and SUMBY statements, below). Values are rounded before printing, and the rounded values are accumulated for printing of totals.

LABEL
: uses variables' labels as column headings. Labels can be specified in LABEL statements in the DATA step that creates the data set or in the PROC PRINT step. See *SAS Language Guide for Personal Computers*, for a description of the LABEL statement. If LABEL is not specified, PROC PRINT splits labels if necessary in order to conserve space. Labels are printed for BY variables but are not printed in SUM lines (see the example output at the end of this chapter).

SPLIT=*'splitchar'*
: splits labels used as column headings where the split character appears. When you define the value of the split character, you must enclose it in single quotes. It is not necessary to use both the LABEL and SPLIT= options since SPLIT= implies that labels are to be used. For example, with the statements

```
PROC PRINT DATA=CLASS SPLIT='*';
   LABEL X='THIS IS*A LABEL';
```

the label for X prints like this:

```
THIS IS
A LABEL
```

The split character is not printed. Blanks in the label are permitted. Up to three lines of labels are allowed; that is, no more than two split characters can be used. To print a column with no heading, use the split character as the variable's label. For example, these statements:

```
DATA TEST;
   INPUT X $ @@;
   LABEL X='*';
   CARDS;
   AAA BBB CCC DDD
   ;
PROC PRINT DATA=TEST SPLIT='*';
```

produce this output:

```
OBS
 1    AAA
 2    BBB
 3    CCC
 4    DDD
```

Labels of BY variables are not split, even if SPLIT= is specified. The split character is printed as part of the label.

NOOBS
: causes the observation number to be suppressed. The NOOBS option produces the same effect as the ID statement. It is most useful when you do not want to use an ID statement, but you do not want the observation numbers to be printed.

VAR Statement

VAR *variables;*

The VAR statement names the variables to be printed. The variables are printed in the order in which they appear in the VAR statement. If no VAR statement is used, all variables in the data set are printed.

ID Statement

ID *variables;*

The formatted values of the variables in the ID statement are used instead of observation numbers to identify observations in the output. More than one variable can be specified. When an observation is too long to print on one line, the values of the ID variables are printed at the beginning of every line containing data values for the observation. The ID variables can be up to one-half the width of the page, which usually has a default value of 132 or 80, depending on the output device.

BY Statement

BY *variables;*

A BY statement can be used with PROC PRINT to obtain separate analyses on observations in groups defined by the BY variables. When a BY statement appears, the procedure expects the input data set to be sorted in order of the BY variables. If your input data set is not sorted in ascending order, use the SORT procedure with a similar BY statement to sort the data, or, if appropriate, use the BY statement options NOTSORTED or DESCENDING. For more information, see the discussion of the BY statement in *SAS Language Guide for Personal Computers*.

The LABEL and SPLIT= options have no effect on BY variables since the BY variable values are printed in a dashed line above the remaining printed output for the BY group.

PAGEBY Statement

PAGEBY *variable;*

The PAGEBY statement causes PROC PRINT to begin printing a new page when the specified BY variable changes value or when any BY variable listed before it in the BY statement changes value. For example,

```
PROC PRINT;
   BY X Y Z;
   PAGEBY Y;
```

causes SAS to print a new page when X or Y changes value, but not when Z changes value.

A BY statement is required with the PAGEBY statement.

SUM Statement

SUM *variables;*

The SUM statement specifies variables whose values are to be totaled. You can specify a variable in the SUM statement that is not listed on the VAR statement, and the procedure adds the variable to the VAR list. PRINT ignores requests for totals on BY and ID variables.

When a BY statement is used and only one BY variable is specified, the SUM variable is totaled for each BY group (subtotaled) containing more than one observation. Consider this example:

```
DATA A;
   INPUT X Y Z @@;
   CARDS;
1 1 1 1 1 2 2 1 1 2 1 2 3 1 1 3 3 1 3 3 2 3 4 1
;
PROC PRINT;
   BY X;
   SUM Z;
   TITLE 'ACCORDING TO VARIABLE X BY GROUPS';
```

Data set A is created and then printed with the Z variable values subtotaled according to variable X BY groups. Since the observations are already in sorted order by the X and Y values, it is not necessary to use PROC SORT. Subtotals are printed for each BY group because they all contain more than one observation. See **Output 21.1**.

Output 21.1 Variable Values Subtotaled According to Variable X BY Groups

```
                     ACCORDING TO VARIABLE X BY GROUPS                                1
------------------------------------------------X=1------------------------------------------------

                                     OBS     Y     Z

                                      1      1     1
                                      2      1     2
                                      -            -
                                      X            3

------------------------------------------------X=2------------------------------------------------

                                     OBS     Y     Z

                                      3      1     1
                                      4      1     2
                                      -            -
                                      X            3

------------------------------------------------X=3------------------------------------------------

                                     OBS     Y      Z

                                      5      1      1
                                      6      3      1
                                      7      3      2
                                      8      4      1
                                      -            --
                                      X             5
                                                   ==
                                                   11
```

When a BY statement is used and multiple BY variables are specified, subtotals are printed for a BY variable only when it changes value and there is more than one observation with that value. (Any BY variables listed after a given BY variable change value when that BY variable changes value. This is shown in **Output 21.2**; when X changes value, Y changes value also.) For example, suppose the data set A (above) is printed with X and Y as BY variables:

```
PROC PRINT;
   BY X Y;
   SUM Z;
   TITLE 'ACCORDING TO VARIABLE X AND Y BY GROUPS';
```

The output produced by these statements is shown in **Output 21.2**.

Output 21.2 Variable Values Subtotaled According to Variable X and Y BY Groups

```
                         ACCORDING TO VARIABLE X AND Y BY GROUPS                          1

----------------------------------------------X=1 Y=1---------------------------------------

                                      OBS    Z

                                       1     1
                                       2     2
                                       -     -
                                       Y     3
                                       X     3

----------------------------------------------X=2 Y=1---------------------------------------

                                      OBS    Z

                                       3     1
                                       4     2
                                       -     -
                                       Y     3
                                       X     3

----------------------------------------------X=3 Y=1---------------------------------------

                                      OBS    Z

                                       5     1

----------------------------------------------X=3 Y=3---------------------------------------

                                      OBS    Z

                                       6     1
                                       7     2
                                       -     -
                                       Y     3

----------------------------------------------X=3 Y=4---------------------------------------
                                      OBS    Z
                                       8     1
                                       X     5
                                            11
```

SUMBY Statement

SUMBY *byvariable;*

The SUMBY statement is used to print totals when the specified BY variable changes value or when any BY variable listed before it in the BY statement changes value. A BY statement is required with the SUMBY statement.

The variables that are totaled are those that appear in the SUM statement. If there is no SUM statement, the procedure totals all numeric variables in the data set except those listed in a BY statement.

These statements:

```
PROC PRINT;
   SUM A B C;
   BY X Y Z;
   SUMBY Y;
```

total the variables A, B, and C when either X or Y changes value, but not when Z changes value.

The effect of the SUMBY statement is to limit the printing of subtotals for BY groups; without it, subtotals are printed when any BY variable changes value and there is more than one observation with the value.

DETAILS

Usage Notes

Formats If you provide formats for the numeric variables (for example, with FORMAT statements), decimal points are not shifted each time a value is printed (that is, they align in the column). Numeric values not associated with a specific format are given a maximum width of 12 columns. (The FORMAT statement is described in *SAS Language Guide for Personal Computers*.)

Page format PROC PRINT uses an identical format for each page printed. First, it attempts to print observations on a single line. If it cannot do so, the observations are split into two or more sections per page, and the observation number or ID variable(s) is printed at the beginning of each line. Column headings are printed horizontally across the top of each section.

The data width of an unformatted character variable is its length or the pagesize minus the length of the ID variable, whichever is less. The width of an unformatted numeric variable is 12.

Printed Output

The printed output for PROC PRINT includes:

1. OBS, the number of each observation in the data set, appears in the leftmost column of the output. (OBS is not a variable in the data set; it is only used by the procedure to identify observations when the ID statement is not used or when NOOBS is not used.) If an ID variable is used, ID values rather than observation numbers are printed, and the column is headed with the name of the ID variable.
2. the names or labels of all variables that are printed.
3. the current value(s) of the BY variable, if any, above each section.
4. totals for the specified variables.

EXAMPLE

Printing Reports

A company's sales and expense reports for four regions of the United States are printed in three different ways in this example. The data set is first created and a simple listing of the data is printed.

```
DATA BRANCH;
   INPUT REGION $ STATE $ MONTH MONYY5.
         HEADCNT EXPENSES REVENUE;
   FORMAT MONTH MONYY5.;
   CARDS;
EASTERN  VA FEB78  10  7800 15500
SOUTHERN FL MAR78   9  9800 13500
SOUTHERN GA JAN78   5  2000  8000
NORTHERN MA MAR78   3  1500  1000
SOUTHERN FL FEB78  10  8500 11000
NORTHERN NY MAR78   5  6000  5000
EASTERN  VA MAR78  11  8200 16600
PLAINS   NM MAR78   2  1350   500
SOUTHERN FL JAN78  10  8000 10000
NORTHERN NY FEB78   4  3000  4000
SOUTHERN GA FEB78   7  1200  6000
;
PROC PRINT;
   TITLE 'PROC PRINT PROVIDES A LISTING';
```

Output 21.3 A Listing of the Data Set

```
                          PROC PRINT PROVIDES A LISTING                        1

         OBS    REGION      STATE    MONTH    HEADCNT    EXPENSES    REVENUE   ❷

   ❶      1     EASTERN     VA       FEB78      10         7800       15500
          2     SOUTHERN    FL       MAR78       9         9800       13500
          3     SOUTHERN    GA       JAN78       5         2000        8000
          4     NORTHERN    MA       MAR78       3         1500        1000
          5     SOUTHERN    FL       FEB78      10         8500       11000
          6     NORTHERN    NY       MAR78       5         6000        5000
          7     EASTERN     VA       MAR78      11         8200       16600
          8     PLAINS      NM       MAR78       2         1350         500
          9     SOUTHERN    FL       JAN78      10         8000       10000
         10     NORTHERN    NY       FEB78       4         3000        4000
         11     SOUTHERN    GA       FEB78       7         1200        6000
```

Now sort the data set and use PRINT to create a report showing revenue and expense totals.

```
PROC SORT;
   BY REGION STATE MONTH;
PROC PRINT SPLIT='*';
   LABEL REGION='SALES REGION'
         HEADCNT='SALES*PERSONNEL';
   BY REGION STATE;
   SUM REVENUE EXPENSES;
   TITLE 'REVENUE AND EXPENSE TOTALS';
```

Output 21.4 Sorted to Show Revenue and Expense Totals

```
        ❸  REVENUE AND EXPENSE TOTALS                                                       1
--------------------------------------------SALES REGION =EASTERN STATE=VA--------------------------------------------

                    OBS      MONTH    SALES        EXPENSES     REVENUE
                                      PERSONNEL

                      1      FEB78     10            7800        15500
                      2      MAR78     11            8200        16600
                   ------                           -----        -----
                   STATE                            16000  .     32100
                   REGION                       ❹   16000        32100

--------------------------------------------SALES REGION =NORTHERN STATE=MA--------------------------------------------

                    OBS      MONTH    SALES        EXPENSES     REVENUE
                                      PERSONNEL

                      3      MAR78       3           1500        1000

--------------------------------------------SALES REGION =NORTHERN STATE=NY--------------------------------------------

                    OBS      MONTH    SALES        EXPENSES     REVENUE
                                      PERSONNEL

                      4      FEB78       4           3000         4000
                      5      MAR78       5           6000         5000
                   ------                           -----        -----
                   STATE                             9000         9000
                   REGION                           10500        10000

--------------------------------------------SALES REGION =PLAINS STATE=NM--------------------------------------------

                    OBS      MONTH    SALES        EXPENSES     REVENUE
                                      PERSONNEL

                      6      MAR78       2           1350          500

--------------------------------------------SALES REGION =SOUTHERN STATE=FL--------------------------------------------

                    OBS      MONTH    SALES        EXPENSES     REVENUE
                                      PERSONNEL

                      7      JAN78      10           8000        10000
                      8      FEB78      10           8500        11000
                      9      MAR78       9           9800        13500
                   ------                           -----        -----
                   STATE                            26300        34500
```

```
                              REVENUE AND EXPENSE TOTALS                                       2

-------------------------------------------SALES REGION =SOUTHERN STATE=GA---------------------------------------------

                    OBS       MONTH     SALES          EXPENSES     REVENUE
                                        PERSONNEL

                     10       JAN78       5              2000         8000
                     11       FEB78       7              1200         6000
                    ------                               -----        -----
                    STATE                                3200        14000
                    REGION                              29500        48500
                                                        =====        =====
                                                        57350        91100
```

A different type of summary report is printed when the same variables are specified in both ID and BY statements.

```
PROC PRINT SPLIT='*';
   LABEL REGION='SALES REGION'
         HEADCNT='SALES*PERSONNEL';
   BY REGION STATE;
   ID REGION STATE;  /* PUT EACH BY VARIABLE IN ID */
   SUM REVENUE EXPENSES;
   VAR REVENUE EXPENSES HEADCNT MONTH;
   FORMAT HEADCNT 3. REVENUE EXPENSES COMMA10.;
   TITLE 'BRANCH HEADCOUNT, SALES, AND EXPENSES';
```

Output 21.5 Branch Headcount, Sales, and Expenses

```
                          BRANCH HEADCOUNT, SALES, AND EXPENSES                              1

          SALES REGION    STATE       REVENUE    EXPENSES    SALES      MONTH
                                                             PERSONNEL

          EASTERN         VA           15,500       7,800       10      FEB78
                                       16,600       8,200       11      MAR78
          --------        --------   ----------  ----------
          EASTERN         VA           32,100      16,000
          EASTERN                      32,100      16,000

          NORTHERN        MA            1,000       1,500        3      MAR78

          NORTHERN        NY            4,000       3,000        4      FEB78
                                        5,000       6,000        5      MAR78
          --------        --------   ----------  ----------
          NORTHERN        NY            9,000       9,000
          NORTHERN                     10,000      10,500

          PLAINS          NM              500       1,350        2      MAR78

          SOUTHERN        FL           10,000       8,000       10      JAN78
                                       11,000       8,500       10      FEB78
                                       13,500       9,800        9      MAR78
          --------        --------   ----------  ----------
          SOUTHERN        FL           34,500      26,300

          SOUTHERN        GA            8,000       2,000        5      JAN78
                                        6,000       1,200        7      FEB78
          --------        --------   ----------  ----------
          SOUTHERN        GA           14,000       3,200
          SOUTHERN                     48,500      29,500
                                     ==========  ==========
                                       91,100      57,350
```

Chapter 22

The RANK Procedure

ABSTRACT

The RANK procedure computes ranks for one or more numeric variables across the observations of a SAS data set. The ranks are output to a new SAS data set. Alternatively, PROC RANK produces normal scores or other rank scores. RANK procedure

INTRODUCTION

The RANK procedure ranks values from smallest to largest, assigning the rank 1 to the smallest number, 2 to the next largest, and so on up to rank *n*, the number of nonmissing observations. Tied values are given averaged ranks. Several options are available to request other ranking and tie-handling rules.

Many nonparametric statistical methods use ranks rather than the original values of a variable. For example, a set of data can be passed through PROC RANK to obtain the ranks for a response variable that could then be fit to an analysis-of-variance model using the ANOVA or GLM procedure. =ANOVA procedure

Ranks are also useful for investigating the distribution of values for a variable. The ranks divided by n or $n+1$ form values in the range 0 to 1, and they estimate the cumulative distribution function. Inverse cumulative distribution functions can be applied to these fractional ranks to obtain probability quantile scores, which can be compared to the original values to judge the fit to the distribution. For example, if a set of data has a normal distribution, the normal scores should be a linear function of the original values, and a plot of scores versus original values should be a straight line.

PROC RANK is also useful for grouping continuous data into ranges. The GROUPS= option can break a population into approximately equal-sized groups.

SPECIFICATIONS

The following statements can be specified to invoke PROC RANK:

PROC RANK *options;*
VAR *variables;*
RANKS *names;*
BY *variables;*

PROC RANK Statement

PROC RANK *options;*

The options below can appear in the PROC RANK statement:

DATA=*SASdataset*
names the SAS data set to be used by PROC RANK. If DATA= is omitted, the most recently created SAS data set is used.

TIES=MEAN
TIES=HIGH
TIES=LOW
specifies which rank to report for tied values. TIES=MEAN requests that tied values receive the mean of the corresponding ranks (mid-ranks). The specification TIES=HIGH requests that the largest of the corresponding ranks be used. TIES=LOW requests that the smallest of the corresponding ranks be used. The default method is TIES=MEAN.

Table 22.1 illustrates the three options available for handling tied values. Consider the values of the variable WEIGHT and the ranks that are assigned for each TIES value:

Table 22.1 Options Available for Handling Tied Values

WEIGHT	TIES=MEAN	TIES=HIGH	TIES=LOW
107	1	1	1
110	2.5	3	2
110	2.5	3	2
121	4	4	4
125	6	7	5
125	6	7	5
125	6	7	5
132	8	8	8

DESCENDING
reverses the ranking from largest to smallest. The largest value is given a rank of 1, the next smallest a rank of 2, and so on. When DESCENDING is omitted, values are ranked from smallest to largest.

GROUPS=*n*

requests grouping scores, where *n* is the number of groups. The scores are the integers 0 to (*n*−1). The groups have equal or nearly equal numbers of observations. The lowest values are in the first group; the highest values are in the last group. The following are common GROUP values: 100 produces percentile ranks, 10 produces deciles, and 4 produces quartiles.

For example, if you want quartile ranks, you specify GROUPS=4. RANK then separates the values of the ranking variable into four groups according to size. The values in the group containing the smallest values receive a quartile value of 0, the values in the next group receive a value of 1, the values in the next group receive a value of 2, and the largest values receive the value 3.

The formula used to calculate the quantile rank of a value is

FLOOR (*rank***k*/(*n* + 1))

where *rank* is the value's rank, *k* is the number of groups specified with the GROUPS= option, and *n* is the number of observations having nonmissing values of the ranking variable.

FRACTION
F

requests fractional ranks. RANK divides each rank by the number of observations having nonmissing values of the ranking variable and expresses the ranks as fractions. If the TIES= option is omitted or if TIES=HIGH is specified, these fractional ranks can be considered values of a right-continuous empirical cumulative distribution function.

PERCENT
P

asks RANK to divide each rank by the number of observations having nonmissing values of the ranking variable and then to multiply the result by 100 to get percentages. Like the FRACTION option, the PERCENT option implies TIES=HIGH unless another TIES= value is specified.

Note: the PERCENT option does not give what are usually called *percentile ranks*. These are produced by specifying GROUPS=100.

NORMAL=BLOM
NORMAL=TUKEY
NORMAL=VW

requests normal scores to be computed from the ranks. The resulting variables appear normally distributed. If NORMAL= is specified, either BLOM, TUKEY, or VW must be given. The formulas are as follows:

BLOM $y_i = \Psi C(r_i - 3/8)/(n + 1/4)$

TUKEY $y_i = \Psi C(r_i - 1/3)/(n + 1/3)$

VW $y_i = \Psi C(r_i)/\ (n + 1)$

where ΨC is the inverse cumulative normal (PROBIT) function, r_i is the rank, and *n* is the number of nonmissing observations for the ranking variable. VW stands for van der Waerden, whose scores are used for a nonparametric location test.

These normal scores are approximations to the exact expected order statistics for the normal distribution, also called *normal scores.* The BLOM version appears to fit slightly better than the others (Blom 1958, Tukey 1962).

SAVAGE

requests Savage (or exponential) scores to be computed from the ranks. The scores are computed by this formula (Lehman 1975):

$$y_i = \left[\sum_{j=n-r_i+1}^{n} (1/j) \right] - 1$$

OUT=*SASdataset*

names the output data set created by PROC RANK to contain the resulting ranks. If you do not specify OUT=, the default name is OUT=_DATA_, which produces a name such as DATA*n*. If you want to create a permanent SAS data set, you must specify a two-level name (see "SAS Files" in *SAS Language Guide for Personal Computers* for more information on permanent SAS data sets). For details on the data set created by RANK, see **Output Data Set** below.

VAR Statement

VAR *variables;*

RANK computes ranks for the variables given in the VAR statement. These variables must be numeric. If the VAR statement is omitted, ranks are computed for all numeric variables in the data set. The VAR statement must be included if a RANKS statement (below) is used.

RANKS Statement

RANKS *names;*

If you want the original variables included in the output data set in addition to the ranks, use the RANKS statement to assign variable names to the ranks. First, name the rank corresponding to the first variable in the VAR statement, next name the rank that corresponds to the second variable in the VAR statement, and so on.

BY Statement

BY *variables;*

A BY statement can be used with PROC RANK to obtain separate analyses on observations in groups defined by the BY variables. When a BY statement appears, the procedure expects the input data set to be sorted in order of the BY variables. If your input data set is not sorted in ascending order, use the SORT procedure with a similar BY statement to sort the data, or, if appropriate, use the BY statement options NOTSORTED or DESCENDING. For more information, see the discussion of the BY statement in *SAS Language Guide for Personal Computers.*

DETAILS

Missing Values

Missing values are not ranked and are left missing when ranks or rank scores replace the other values of the ranking variable.

Output Data Set

RANK creates a new SAS data set containing the ranks or rank scores but no printed output.

The new output data set contains all the variables from the input data set plus the variables named in the RANKS statement if one is specified. If a RANKS statement is used, a VAR statement must also be included. If no RANKS statement is given, then the procedure stores the ranks in the output data set in the original variables that were ranked. If no VAR statement is included, the procedure ranks all numeric variables.

Nonparametric Statistics

Many nonparametric methods are based on taking the ranks of a variable and analyzing these ranks instead of the original values.

- A two-sample *t* test applied to the ranks is equivalent to a Wilcoxon rank sum test using the *t* approximation for the significance level. If the *t* test is applied to the normal scores rather than to the ranks, the test becomes equivalent to the van der Waerden test. If the *t* test is applied to median scores (GROUPS=2), the test becomes the median test.
- A one-way analysis of variance applied to ranks is equivalent to the Kruskal-Wallis *k*-sample test; the F test generated by the parametric procedure applied to the ranks is often better than the χ^2 approximation used by Kruskal-Wallis. This test can be extended to other rank scores (Quade 1966).
- Friedman's two-way analysis for block designs can be obtained by ranking within blocks (using a BY statement with PROC RANK) and then performing a main-effects analysis of variance on these ranks (Conover 1980).
- Regression relationships can be investigated using rank transformations with a method described by Iman and Conover (1979).

EXAMPLE

Ranking of Gain Values

This example uses PROC RANK to get the ranks of the variable GAIN. The RANKS statement assigns the name RANKGAIN to the variable containing the ranks in the output data set. Since OUT= is not specified, RANK creates a new data set using the DATA*n* naming rules. The PRINT procedure prints the contents of the output data set. The second execution of PROC RANK uses a BY variable.

The following statements produce **Output 22.1**.

```
DATA A;
   INPUT LOCATION GAIN;
   CARDS;
1 7.2
1 7.9
```

```
1 7.6
1 6.3
1 8.4
1 8.1
2 8.1
2 7.3
2 7.7
2 7.7
;
PROC RANK;
   VAR GAIN;
   RANKS RANKGAIN;
PROC PRINT;
   TITLE 'RANK THE GAIN VALUES';
PROC RANK DATA=A OUT=B;
   BY LOCATION;
   RANKS RGAIN;
   VAR GAIN;
PROC PRINT;
   BY LOCATION;
   TITLE 'RANKINGS WITHIN LOCATIONS';
```

Output 22.1 Data Sets Generated with PROC RANK and Reproduced Using PROC PRINT

```
                              RANK THE GAIN VALUES                              1

                         OBS   LOCATION   GAIN   RANKGAIN

                           1       1       7.2      2.0
                           2       1       7.9      7.0
                           3       1       7.6      4.0
                           4       1       6.3      1.0
                           5       1       8.4     10.0
                           6       1       8.1      8.5
                           7       2       8.1      8.5
                           8       2       7.3      3.0
                           9       2       7.7      5.5
                          10       2       7.7      5.5
```

```
                           RANKINGS WITHIN LOCATIONS                            2

--------------------------------------LOCATION=1--------------------------------------

                              OBS    GAIN    RGAIN

                               1      7.2      2
                               2      7.9      4
                               3      7.6      3
                               4      6.3      1
                               5      8.4      6
                               6      8.1      5

--------------------------------------LOCATION=2--------------------------------------

                              OBS    GAIN    RGAIN

                               7      8.1     4.0
                               8      7.3     1.0
                               9      7.7     2.5
                              10      7.7     2.5
```

REFERENCES

Blom, G. (1958), *Statistical Estimates and Transformed Beta Variables*, New York: John Wiley & Sons.

Conover, W.J. (1980), *Practical Nonparametric Statistics*, Second Edition, New York: John Wiley & Sons.

Conover, W.J. and Iman, R.L. (1976), "On Some Alternative Procedures Using Ranks for the Analysis of Experimental Designs," *Communications in Statistics*, A5, 14, 1348-1368.

Conover, W.J. and Iman, R.L. (1981) "Rank Transformations as a Bridge between Parametric and Nonparametric Statistics," *The American Statistician*, 35, 124-129.

Iman, R.L. and Conover, W.J. (1979), "The Use of the Rank Transform in Regression," *Technometrics*, 21, 499-509.

Lehman, E.L. (1975), *Nonparametrics: Statistical Methods Based on Ranks*, San Francisco: Holden-Day.

Quade, D. (1966), "On Analysis of Variance for the *k*-Sample Problem," *Annals of Mathematical Statistics*, 37, 1747-1758.

Tukey, John W. (1962), "The Future of Data Analysis," *Annals of Mathematical Statistics*, 33, 22.

Chapter 23

The SORT Procedure

ABSTRACT

The SORT procedure sorts observations in a SAS data set by one or more variables, storing the resulting sorted observations in a new SAS data set or replacing the original.

INTRODUCTION

PROC SORT is used most often for sorting a data set so that other SAS procedures can process it in subsets using BY statements. Data sets must also be sorted before they can be match-merged or updated.

PROC SORT rearranges the observations in the data set according to the values of the variables in the BY statement, which **must** accompany the PROC SORT statement (see below). Suppose you want to sort a data set by an ID value that occurs in every observation. PROC SORT rearranges the data set so that the observation with the lowest ID value is first, the observation with the second lowest ID value is second, and so on. PROC SORT can also arrange observations in descending order.

When you want to sort by two or more variables, PROC SORT first arranges the data set in the order of the first BY variable. Then SORT arranges the observations having the lowest value of the first variable (if several observations have the same value) in the order of the second variable. This continues for every BY variable specified. For example, if you sort a data set containing state and city information by state and then by city, SORT first arranges the data so that Alabama's observations are first, then Alaska's, and so on. Next, SORT arranges Alabama's observations by the city value, so that Birmingham's observations are followed by Dothan's, and so on.

For numeric variables, the smallest-to-largest comparison sequence is

SAS System missing value .
negative numeric values
zero
positive numeric values

SORT uses the ASCII collating sequence when it compares character values. From smallest to largest, this sequence is

blank!"#$%&'()*+,-./0123456789:;<=>?@
ABCDEFGHIJKLMNOPQRSTUVWXYZ [\] ^ _
abcdefghijklmnopqrstuvwxyz {|}~

SPECIFICATIONS

The statements used with PROC SORT are

PROC SORT *options;*
BY *option variable option variable ...;*

PROC SORT Statement

PROC SORT *options;*

The options below can appear in the PROC SORT statement.

DATA=*SASdataset*
: names the SAS data set that you want to sort. If DATA= is omitted, the most recently created SAS data set is used.

OUT=*SASdataset*
: specifies a name for the output data set. If OUT= is omitted, the DATA= data set is sorted and the sorted version replaces the original data set. If you want the OUT= data set to be permanent, specify a two-level name (see *SAS Language Guide for Personal Computers*).

NODUPKEY
: checks for and eliminates records with duplicate keys.
This option causes PROC SORT to compare all key variable values for each observation to the previous one written to the output data set. If an exact match is found, the record is not written to the output data set.

BY Statement

BY *option variable option variable ...;*

Any number of variables can be specified in the BY statement. A BY statement **must** be used with PROC SORT.

As described above, PROC SORT first arranges the observations in the order of the first variable in the BY statement; then it sorts observations with a given value of the first variable by the second variable, and so on. Note that PROC SORT always retains the same relative positions of observations with identical BY variable values.

The following option can be specified in the BY statement:

DESCENDING
sorts variables in descending order. Use the keyword DESCENDING before the name of each variable in the BY statement whose values are to be in descending order. For example, these statements:

```
PROC SORT DATA=RANDOM;
   BY DESCENDING SIZE AGE;
```

sort the RANDOM data set first by descending order of SIZE values, then by ascending order of AGE values. To sort by descending AGE values, the DESCENDING keyword would have to precede the AGE variable name.

Output Data Set

If an OUT= option appears in the PROC SORT statement, a new data set is created containing the sorted observations. Otherwise, the original data set is sorted and the sorted observations replace the original values **after** the procedure is executed without errors. As always, when a data set is replaced, there must be space in the data library for a second copy of the old data set when PROC SORT is invoked.

Multiple Sorts

When you know that you need to sort a data set for several purposes, you can sometimes plan ahead and reduce the number of sorts needed. For example, suppose you want to run a procedure for the same data set twice, once with the BY statement

```
BY STATE;
```

and again with the BY statement

```
BY STATE CITY;
```

You can sort the data set once and use it for both these runs if you use the statements

```
PROC SORT;
   BY STATE CITY;
```

It does not matter for the BY STATE; run that the data set is sorted by both state and city. If the first statement above were BY CITY;, you would need to sort the data twice.

EXAMPLE

Sorting Information

In the example below, a list of names, telephone extensions, and room numbers is sorted two different ways. PROC SORT first sorts the data alphabetically by name, then by room number and name. See **Output 23.1** and **Output 23.2**.

```
DATA PHONES;
   INPUT NAME $ PHONE ROOM;
   CARDS;
REBECCAH 424 112
CAROL 450 112
LOUISE 409 110
```

```
GINA 474 110
MIMI 410 109
ALICE 411 106
BRENDA 414 105
DAVID 438 141
BETTY 464 141
HOLLY 466 140
GRETEL 465 140
PROC SORT OUT=LIST1;
   BY NAME;
PROC PRINT;
   TITLE 'NAME ORDER';
PROC SORT OUT=LIST2;
   BY ROOM NAME;
PROC PRINT;
   TITLE 'ROOM NUMBER AND NAME ORDER';
```

Output 23.1 Data Set Sorted in Name Order

```
                          NAME ORDER                                          1

                   OBS    NAME        PHONE    ROOM

                    1     ALICE        411     106
                    2     BETTY        464     141
                    3     BRENDA       414     105
                    4     CAROL        450     112
                    5     DAVID        438     141
                    6     GINA         474     110
                    7     GRETEL       465     140
                    8     HOLLY        466     140
                    9     LOUISE       409     110
                   10     MIMI         410     109
                   11     REBECCAH     424     112
```

Output 23.2 Data Set Sorted by Room Number and by Name

```
                  ROOM NUMBER AND NAME ORDER                                  2
                   OBS    NAME        PHONE    ROOM

                    1     BRENDA       414     105
                    2     ALICE        411     106
                    3     MIMI         410     109
                    4     GINA         474     110
                    5     LOUISE       409     110
                    6     CAROL        450     112
                    7     REBECCAH     424     112
                    8     GRETEL       465     140
                    9     HOLLY        466     140
                   10     BETTY        464     141
                   11     DAVID        438     141
```

Chapter 24

The STANDARD Procedure

ABSTRACT

The STANDARD procedure standardizes some or all of the variables in a SAS data set to a given mean and standard deviation and produces a new SAS data set to contain the standardized values.

INTRODUCTION

Standardizing is a technique for removing location and scale attributes from a set of data. Sometimes you need to center the values on a variable to a mean of 0 and a standard deviation of 1. Some statistical techniques begin the analysis by standardizing the data in this way. If your data are normally distributed, standardizing is also studentizing since the result has a Student's *t* distribution.

SPECIFICATIONS

The statements that control PROC STANDARD are

PROC STANDARD *options;*
  VAR *variables;*
  FREQ *variable;*
  WEIGHT *variable;*
  BY *variables;*

PROC STANDARD Statement

PROC STANDARD *options;*

The options below can appear in the PROC STANDARD statement. At least one of the last three options must be specified to prevent your output SAS data set from becoming an exact copy of the input data set.

DATA=*SASdataset*

gives the name of the data set to be used by PROC STANDARD. If it is omitted, STANDARD uses the most recently created SAS data set.

OUT=*SASdataset*

gives the name of the new SAS data set to contain the standardized variables. If OUT= is omitted, SAS names the new data set using the DATA*n* convention. The OUT= data set contains all the variables from the input data set, including those not standardized. If you want to create a permanent SAS data set, you must supply a two-level name.

VARDEF=DF
VARDEF=WEIGHT | WGT
VARDEF=N
VARDEF=WDF

specifies the divisor to be used in the calculation of the variance. VARDEF=DF requests the degrees of freedom (N-1) be used as the divisor. VARDEF=WEIGHT or WGT requests the sum of the weights; VARDEF=N requests the number of observations (N); and VARDEF=WDF requests the sum of the weights minus one. The default divisor is VARDEF=DF.

MEAN=*m*
M=*m*

requests that all the variables in the VAR statement (or all the numeric variables if the VAR statement is omitted) be standardized to a mean of *m*. Without the MEAN= option, the mean of the output values is the same as the mean of the input values.

STD=*s*
S=*s*

requests that all the variables in the VAR statement (or all the numeric variables if the VAR statement is omitted) be standardized to a standard deviation of *s*. Without the STD= option, the standard deviation of the output values is the same as the standard deviation of the input values. The REPLACE option, below, does not affect STD's action.

REPLACE

requests that all missing values be replaced with the variable mean. If MEAN=*m* is also specified, missing values are set instead to *m*.

VAR Statement

VAR *variables;*

The VAR statement allows you to list the variables you want standardized. If the VAR statement is omitted, all the numeric variables in the data set are standardized.

FREQ Statement

FREQ *variable;*

The FREQ statement specifies a numeric variable in the input SAS data set. If a FREQ statement is used, each observation in the input data set is assumed to represent *n* observations, where *n* is the value of the FREQ variable. If the value is not an integer, it is truncated to the integer portion. An observation is skipped for the calculation of the mean and standard deviation if the FREQ value is less than one or is missing. However, the variables to be standardized for the observation are still adjusted.

WEIGHT Statement

WEIGHT *variable;*

The WEIGHT statement specifies a numeric variable in the input SAS data set, the values of which are used to weight each observation. Only one variable can be specified. The WEIGHT variable values can be nonintegers and are used to calculate a weighted mean and a weighted variance. If the value of the WEIGHT variable is less than zero or missing, a value of zero is assumed. Both FREQ and WEIGHT statements can be used.

BY Statement

BY *variables;*

A BY statement can be used with PROC STANDARD to obtain separate analyses on observations in groups defined by the BY variables. When a BY statement appears, the procedure expects the input data set to be sorted in order of the BY variables. If your input data set is not sorted in ascending order, use the SORT procedure with a similar BY statement to sort the data, or, if appropriate, use the BY statement options NOTSORTED or DESCENDING. For more information, see the discussion of the BY statement in *SAS Language Guide for Personal Computers.*

DETAILS

Missing Values

Missing values are excluded from the standardization process. Unless the REPLACE option is specified, missing values are left as missing in the output data set. When REPLACE is specified, missing values are replaced with the variable mean or with the mean specified by the MEAN= option in the PROC STANDARD statement.

Output Data Set

The STANDARD procedure produces an output SAS data set to contain the standardized variables.

Printed Output

The STANDARD procedure prints the input frequency, mean, and standard deviation for each variable standardized.

EXAMPLE

Standardizing Test Scores

The data in the example below consist of three test scores for students in two sections of a course. For each section, you want to standardize all three test scores to a mean of 80 and a standard deviation of 5. To keep the original test scores with the standardized scores in the same SAS data set, create the three variables STEST1-STEST3 to contain the test scores.

The PROC STANDARD statement includes the MEAN= and STD= options and gives the name NEW to the new SAS data set containing the standardized values. Since only STEST1-STEST3 appear in the VAR statement, they are the only variables standardized; the original variables TEST1-TEST3 are not standardized. The BY statement asks that the standardization be done for each section of the course separately. The PROC PRINT statement prints the new data set, and the PROC MEANS output shows that STEST1-STEST3 in both sections have (1) means of 80 and (2) standard deviations of 5. See **Output 24.1**.

```
DATA A;
   INPUT STUDENT SECTION TEST1-TEST3;
   STEST1=TEST1;
   STEST2=TEST2;
   STEST3=TEST3;
   CARDS;
238900545 1 94 91 87
254701167 1 95 96 97
238806445 2 91 86 94
999002527 2 80 76 78
263924860 1 92 40 85
459700886 2 75 76 80
416724915 2 66 69 72
999001230 1 82 84 80
242760674 1 75 76 70
990001252 2 51 66 91
;
PROC SORT;
   BY SECTION;
PROC STANDARD MEAN=80 STD=5 OUT=NEW;
   BY SECTION;
   VAR STEST1-STEST3;
PROC PRINT DATA=NEW;
   BY SECTION;
   TITLE 'STANDARDIZED TEST SCORES';
PROC MEANS DATA=NEW(DROP=STUDENT) MAXDEC=2 N MEAN STD;
   BY SECTION;
```

Output 24.1 Standardizing Test Scores: PROC STANDARD

```
                         STANDARDIZED TEST SCORES                                  1

------------------------------------------------SECTION=1------------------------------------------------

        OBS     STUDENT       TEST1    TEST2    TEST3    STEST1     STEST2     STEST3

         1      238900545      94       91       87      83.6634    83.0601    81.6187
         2      254701167      95       96       97      84.2358    84.1851    86.6772
         3      263924860      92       40       85      82.5186    71.5848    80.6070
         4      999001230      82       84       80      76.7945    81.4850    78.0778
         5      242760674      75       76       70      72.7876    79.6850    73.0193

------------------------------------------------SECTION=2------------------------------------------------

        OBS     STUDENT       TEST1    TEST2    TEST3    STEST1     STEST2     STEST3

         6      238806445      91       86       94      86.1022    87.3710    85.9656
         7      999002527      80       76       78      82.4542    80.9052    77.2884
         8      459700886      75       76       80      80.7959    80.9052    78.3730
         9      416724915      66       69       72      77.8112    76.3792    74.0344
        10      990001252      51       66       91      72.8365    74.4394    84.3386
```

```
                         STANDARDIZED TEST SCORES                                  2

              VARIABLE           N           MEAN        STANDARD
                                                         DEVIATION

              ----------------- SECTION=1 ------------------

              TEST1              5          87.60           8.73
              TEST2              5          77.40          22.22
              TEST3              5          83.80           9.88
              STEST1             5          80.00           5.00
              STEST2             5          80.00           5.00
              STEST3             5          80.00           5.00

              ----------------- SECTION=2 ------------------

              TEST1              5          72.60          15.08
              TEST2              5          74.60           7.73
              TEST3              5          83.00           9.22
              STEST1             5          80.00           5.00
              STEST2             5          80.00           5.00
              STEST3             5          80.00           5.00
```

Chapter 25

The SUMMARY Procedure

ABSTRACT

The SUMMARY procedure computes descriptive statistics on numeric variables in a SAS data set and outputs the results to a new SAS data set.

INTRODUCTION

The SUMMARY procedure creates a SAS data set containing summary statistics and can optionally display the computed statistics. Each observation in the new data set contains the statistics for a different subgroup of the observations in the input data set. These subgroups represent all possible combinations of the levels of the variables in the CLASS statement.

Similarly, PROC MEANS can also compute descriptive statistics as well as create a SAS data set. The only difference is in the default setting of the PRINT option. By default, SUMMARY does not produce printed output. MEANS always prints the computed statistics unless the NOPRINT option is explicitly specified in the PROC statement.

SPECIFICATIONS

The SUMMARY procedure is controlled by these statements:

PROC SUMMARY *options;*
CLASS *variables;*
VAR *variables;*
BY *variables;*
FREQ *variable;*
WEIGHT *variable;*
ID *variables;*
OUTPUT OUT=*SASdataset statistics;*

PROC SUMMARY Statement

PROC SUMMARY *options;*

The options below can appear in the PROC SUMMARY statement:

DATA=*SASdataset*
: names the data set to be used by SUMMARY. If DATA= is omitted, the most recently created SAS data set is used.

PRINT
: tells SUMMARY to print the descriptive statistics. The statistics keywords listed in the **OUTPUT Statement** section can be used in the PROC SUMMARY statement to request specific statistics to be displayed.

MAXDEC=*n*
: gives the maximum number of decimal places (0 to 8) for SUMMARY to use in printing results. The default is 2.

FW=*n*
: specifies the field width for SUMMARY to use in printing each statistic. The default is 12.

MISSING
: requests that SUMMARY treat missing values as valid subgroup values for the CLASS variables.

NWAY
: specifies that only the statistics for the observation with the highest _TYPE_ value (highest level of interaction among CLASS variables) are to be output.

IDMIN
: specifies that the value of the ID variable should be its minimum rather than its maximum value for the corresponding observations of the input data set.

DESCENDING
: specifies that the output data set is to be ordered by descending _TYPE_ value (ascending is the default). This causes the overall totals (_TYPE_=0) to be placed at the end of each BY group. This option has no effect if the NWAY option is also specified.

ORDER=FREQ
ORDER=DATA
ORDER=INTERNAL
ORDER=EXTERNAL | FORMATTED

specifies the order in which you want the values of the CLASS variables to be sorted in the output data set. If you specify ORDER=FREQ, the values are ordered by descending frequency count so that class values occurring in the most observations come first. If you specify ORDER=DATA, class values are kept in the order encountered in the input data set. If you specify ORDER=INTERNAL, the values are ordered by their internal representation. If you specify ORDER=EXTERNAL or FORMATTED, the class values are ordered by their formatted values (external representation). ORDER=INTERNAL is the default.

The ORDER= option does not apply to missing values, which are always ordered first.

VARDEF=DF
VARDEF=WEIGHT | WGT
VARDEF=N
VARDEF=WDF

specifies the divisor to be used in the calculation of the variance. VARDEF=DF requests that the degrees of freedom (N-1) be used as the divisor. VARDEF=WEIGHT or WGT requests that the sum of the weights be used. VARDEF=N requests that the number of observations (N) be used. VARDEF=WDF requests that the sum of the weights minus one be used. The default is VARDEF=DF.

CLASS Statement

CLASS *variables;*

In the CLASS statement you can name the variables to be used to form subgroups. The CLASS statement must be present to produce subgroup statistics. Without a CLASS statement, SUMMARY produces only one observation per BY group.

VAR Statement

VAR *variables;*

In the VAR statement, give the numeric variables for which you want summary statistics.

BY Statement

BY *variables;*

A BY statement can be used with PROC SUMMARY to obtain separate analyses on observations in groups defined by the BY variables. When a BY statement appears, the procedure expects the input data set to be sorted in order of the BY variables. If your input data set is not sorted in ascending order, use the SORT procedure with a similar BY statement to sort the data, or, if appropriate, use the BY statement options NOTSORTED or DESCENDING. For more information, see the discussion of the BY statement in *SAS Language Guide for Personal Computers.*

The BY statement is not often used in PROC SUMMARY since the CLASS statement serves a similar but more general role without the need to sort.

FREQ Statement

FREQ *variable;*

The FREQ statement specifies a numeric variable in the input SAS data set. If a FREQ statement is used, each observation in the input data set is assumed to represent *n* observations, where *n* is the value of the FREQ variable. If the value is not an integer, it is truncated to its integer portion. If the FREQ value is less than one or is missing, the observation is skipped.

WEIGHT Statement

WEIGHT *variable;*

The WEIGHT statement specifies a numeric variable in the input SAS data set whose values are to be used to weight each observation. Only one variable can be specified. Both the FREQ and WEIGHT statements can be used. The WEIGHT variable values can be nonintegers and are used to calculate a weighted mean and a weighted variance. If the value of the WEIGHT variable is less than zero or is missing, a value of zero is assumed.

ID Statement

ID *variables;*

The ID statement includes additional variables in the output data set. If your ID statement names only one variable, the value of the ID variable for a given observation in the output data set is the maximum value it has in the corresponding observations of the input data set unless IDMIN is specified in the PROC statement. When your ID statement includes two or more variables, the maximum value is chosen as if the values of the ID variables were concatenated into one value for each observation. Thus the maximum value comes from only one of the corresponding observations in the input data set.

OUTPUT Statement

OUTPUT OUT=*SASdataset statistics;*

An OUTPUT statement must be specified to create an output data set. The options below can appear in the OUTPUT statement:

OUT=*SASdataset*

If you want to create a permanent SAS data set, you must specify a two-level name. (See *SAS Language Guide for Personal Computers* for more information on permanent SAS data sets.)

statistics

specifies the statistics you want in the new data set and names the variables containing these statistics. Output requests have four forms:

keyword=names
keyword(variables)=names
keyword=
keyword(variables)=

Below is a list of the statistical keywords and corresponding definitions that can be specified in the output requests:

N number of observations in the subgroup with nonmissing values

NMISS	number of observations in the subgroup having missing values for the variable
MEAN	mean
STD	standard deviation
MIN	minimum value
MAX	maximum value
RANGE	range
SUM	sum
VAR	variance
USS	uncorrected sum of squares
CSS	corrected sum of squares
CV	coefficient of variation
STDERR	standard error of the mean
T	Student's *t* value for testing the hypothesis that the population mean is 0
PRT	probability of a greater absolute value for the Student's *t* value above
SUMWGT	sum of the WEIGHT variable values.

Formulas for these statistics are presented in "SAS Elementary Statistics Procedures." To request statistics, give any number of keywords in the OUTPUT statement. The form of the output request determines the name of the new variable containing the statistic. Four choices are described below.

Output Form 1

keyword=names

If you want the statistic's values to have names different from the names of the original variables, follow the equal sign with a list of new variable names. These names will then be used for the statistic's values in the new data set.

The first variable name following the equal sign is given to the corresponding statistic for the first variable in the VAR statement; the second name is given to the statistic for the second variable in the VAR statement; and so on.

For example, suppose that you want to calculate means for the variables PRE and POST. In the output data set named RESULTS, the variable containing the PRE mean is PREMEAN; the variable containing the POST mean is POSTMEAN.

```
PROC SUMMARY;
   CLASS TEACHER;
   VAR PRE POST;
   OUTPUT OUT=RESULTS MEAN=PREMEAN POSTMEAN;
```

Output Form 2

keyword(variables)=names

You can calculate a statistic for only certain variables in the VAR statement and give those statistics new names in the output data set. After the keyword name, list the variables for which you want statistics in parentheses. Then place the names you assign to those statistics after the equal sign.

For example, suppose you want to compute standard deviations for only the POST variable but want means for both variables. The following statements could be used to do this:

```
PROC SUMMARY;
    CLASS TEACHER;
    VAR PRE POST;
    OUTPUT OUT=RESULTS MEAN=PREMEAN POSTMEAN
        STD(POST)=STDPOST;
```

Output Form 3

keyword=

The statistic in the new data set will have the same name as the corresponding variable in the input data set if you simply follow the keyword with an equal sign.

For example, say you want the output data set to contain means for the variables PRE and POST, and the variables containing the means are also to be called PRE and POST. You can specify the following:

```
PROC SUMMARY;
    CLASS TEACHER;
    VAR PRE POST;
    OUTPUT OUT=RESULTS MEAN=;
```

Do not use this form or the next one for more than one keyword in the OUTPUT statement. Multiple statistics requests using this form or the next one would cause the output data set to contain two or more variables with the same name.

Output Form 4

keyword(variables)=

You can compute the statistic for a subset of the variables in the VAR statement. After the keyword name, list the variables for which you want the statistic in parentheses. When no new variable names follow the equal sign, the statistics will have the same names as the original variables. Do not use this method for more than one statistic.

For example, say that you want the output data set to contain the mean for the variable PRE but standard deviations for both PRE and POST. The mean will have the name PRE, but the standard deviations will have new names.

```
PROC SUMMARY;
    VAR PRE POST;
    OUTPUT OUT=RESULTS MEAN(PRE)=  STD=STDPRE STDPOST;
```

If the statistics option in the OUTPUT statement is omitted, SUMMARY creates a special SAS data set in which five records are generated for each subgroup defined by the CLASS variables in each BY group. The five records contain the following statistics : N, MIN, MAX, MEAN, and STD. If weight is specified, a sixth record containing the sum of weights (SUMWGT) is also output. Note that the statistic N here refers to the number of observations on which calculations are based.

DETAILS

Missing Values

If any CLASS variable has a missing value for an observation, that observation is not used in SUMMARY unless the MISSING option is specified in the PROC SUMMARY statement.

Limitations

The maximum number of combinations of CLASS levels is 32767 or $2^{15}-1$. Because of computer resource limits, the maximum number of CLASS variables is 24.

Printed Output

If the PRINT option is set but no statistics are requested in the PROC SUMMARY statement, SUMMARY prints these statistics for each variable in the VAR statement:

1. N, the number of observations in the CLASS group for the given BY group
2. the name of the variable
3. the MINIMUM VALUE of the variable
4. the MAXIMUM VALUE of the variable
5. the MEAN or average of the variable
6. the STANDARD DEVIATION of the variable.

If statistics are specifically requested in the PROC statement, only those statistics are printed. In addition to the statistics above, upon request SUMMARY can print these statistics:

7. STD ERROR OF MEAN, the standard error of the mean
8. the SUM of all the values for a variable
9. the VARIANCE of each variable
10. C.V., or the coefficient of variation expressed as a percentage
11. N MISSING, the number of missing values for each variable
12. the RANGE of each variable
13. the UNCORRECTED SS, the raw sum of squares (not adjusted for the mean)
14. the CORRECTED SS, the sum of squares adjusted for the mean
15. T, the Student's *t* value for testing the hypothesis that the population mean is zero
16. PR > |T|, the probability of a greater absolute value for Student's *t* under the hypothesis that the mean is zero
17. SUMWGT, the sum of the WEIGHT variable values.

If a statistic cannot be computed because of insufficient or inappropriate data, the statistic is reported as missing. See the chapter "SAS Elementary Statistics Procedures."

If a BY statement is included, a line is drawn to separate the statistics for each BY group.

Output Data Set

SUMMARY can create one or more output SAS data sets. The output data set's record contents are described below.

Variables Variables in the output data set are

- the BY variables, if a BY statement is used.
- the ID variables, if an ID statement is used.
- the CLASS variables, if a CLASS statement is used. When formats combine several internal values into one formatted value, the lowest internal value is output.
- a variable created by SUMMARY named _TYPE_, whose values contain information about the CLASS variables that define each subgroup.

- a variable created by SUMMARY named _FREQ_ that gives the number of observations (both missing and nonmissing) for the current subgroup.
- the variables containing the subgroup statistics requested by the keywords in the OUTPUT statement.

For example, consider the data set created by SUMMARY with these statements:

```
PROC SUMMARY;
   CLASS TMT;
   VAR X Y;
   OUTPUT OUT=STATS  MEAN=MX MY  N=NX NY;
```

The data set STATS contains these variables:

TMT _TYPE_ _FREQ_ MX MY NX NY

Observations The number of observations in the output data set produced by SUMMARY depends on the number of distinct values or levels (for example, a, b, c) of the CLASS variables (A, B, C).

Observations in the data set produced by SUMMARY are identified by the variable named _TYPE_. Values of _TYPE_ indicate which subgroup (defined by values of the CLASS variables) produced the summary statistics in that observation in the output data set.

Table 25.1 shows how values of _TYPE_ are determined for one CLASS variable (A), two CLASS variables (A and B), and three CLASS variables (A, B, C). The same logic can be extended to analyses by PROC SUMMARY with more than three CLASS variables. The table assumes that all combinations of class levels occur in the data.

Table 25.1 Observations in PROC SUMMARY's Output Data Set

three CLASS variables / two CLASS variables / one CLASS variable

C	B	A	_TYPE_	Subgroup Defined By	Number of Observations of this _TYPE_ in the Data Set	Total Number of Observations in the Data Set	
0	0	0	0	Total	1		one CLASS variable
0	0	1	1	A	a	1+a	
0	1	0	2	B	b		two CLASS variables
0	1	1	3	A*B	a*b	1+a+b+a*b	
1	0	0	4	C	c		three CLASS variables
1	0	1	5	A*C	a*c		
1	1	0	6	B*C	b*c	1+a+b+a*b+c	
1	1	1	7	A*B*C	a*b*c	+a*c+b*c+a*b*c	
Binary equivalent of _TYPE_ value				A ,B ,C=CLASS variables	a, b, c=number of levels of A, B, C respectively		

For a CLASS statement with one class variable,

```
CLASS A;
```

the output data set contains one observation for totals (_TYPE_=0) and an observation for each level of A (_TYPE_=1).

For a CLASS statement with two class variables,

```
CLASS B A;
```

an observation for each level of B (_TYPE_=2) and an observation for each level of A*B (_TYPE_=3) are added.

For a CLASS statement with three class variables,

```
CLASS C B A;
```

observations for levels of C (_TYPE_=4), levels of A*C (_TYPE_=5), B*C (_TYPE_=6), and A*B*C (_TYPE_=7) are added.

You can extend the table to an N-way analysis by adding columns to the table on the left. A value of one is entered in a column if that CLASS variable is involved in defining the subgroup, a zero otherwise. Note that the ones and zeros in the CLASS variable columns form binary numbers across the row for each subgroup.

The decimal equivalent of one of these binary numbers for a subgroup is the _TYPE_ value for that subgroup. There are 2^n different values of _TYPE_ produced by SUMMARY for a given analysis, where n is the number of CLASS variables. The number of observations of each _TYPE_ in the data set depends on the number of levels of the CLASS variables as shown in the table above.

Consider the case where the CLASS statement contains two variables, SEX and RACE. The variable SEX has the two values, F and M; the variable RACE has the two values B and W. The observations in the output data set are determined as in **Table 25.2**.

Table 25.2 Two CLASS Variables: PROC SUMMARY

Sex	Race	_TYPE_	Subgroup Defined By	Number of Observations of this _TYPE_ in the Data Set	Total Number of Observations in the Data Set
0	0	0	Total	1	
0	1	1	Race	2	
1	0	2	Sex	2	
1	1	3	Race*Sex	4	9

These statements

```
PROC SUMMARY;
   CLASS SEX RACE;
   VAR AGE;
   OUTPUT OUT=STATS MEAN=AGEMEAN;
```

produce the information shown in the data set in **Table 25.2**.

The _TYPE_=0 observation contains the overall means for the data set. The SEX and RACE values for this output observation are missing. The value of _FREQ_ is 10 because ten observations were used to form this group.

The _TYPE_=1 observation contains the group means for the rightmost variable in the CLASS statement, in this case RACE. The first of these contains the mean for the four observations having a value of B for RACE; the second contains the mean for the six observations having the value of W for RACE.

The _TYPE_=2 observations contain the means for the two groups of observations defined by the SEX values.

The _TYPE_=3 observations contain the means for the subgroups defined by the combinations of the RACE and SEX values. For example, the first observation in this set contains the mean for the two observations having a SEX value of F and a RACE value of B.

Usage Note: SAS Bit-Testing Feature

The _TYPE_ variable is a good candidate for use with the SAS bit-testing feature. For example, say that you want to print a report using just the observations with the B and C combinations:

```
PROC SUMMARY;
   CLASS A B C;
   VAR X Y Z;
   OUTPUT OUT=STATS MEAN= ;
DATA _NULL_;
   SET STATS;
   IF _TYPE_='011'B;
   .
   more SAS statements
;
```

The IF statement could also be written:

```
IF _TYPE_=3;
```

EXAMPLE

Sales Data

Below are the statements that ask SUMMARY to create an output data set containing summary statistics for two CLASS variables, PRODUCT and DATE. PROC PRINT prints the summary file. If the PRINT option was specified in the PROC SUMMARY step, the statistics discussed in the section **Printed Output** would appear. See **Output 25.1**.

```
PROC FORMAT;
   VALUE MMM 1='JAN' 2='FEB' 3='MAR' 4='APR' 5='MAY' 6='JUN'
             7='JUL' 8='AUG' 9='SEP' 10='OCT' 11='NOV' 12='DEC';
   more SAS statements
;
DATA SALES2;
   SET SALES;
   KEEP PRODUCT DATE YEAR UNITS;
PROC SUMMARY DATA=SALES;
   CLASS PRODUCT DATE;
   VAR UNITS;
   ID YEAR;
   OUTPUT OUT=B SUM=SALES;
PROC PRINT DATA=B;
```

Output 25.1 Output Data Set Containing Summary Statistics

1

OBS	PRODUCT	DATE	YEAR	_TYPE_	_FREQ_	SALES
1			1979	0	742	4781
2		01JAN79	1979	1	8	67
3		01FEB79	1979	1	10	69
4		01MAR79	1979	1	12	82
5		01APR79	1979	1	13	77
6		01MAY79	1979	1	10	67
7		01JUN79	1979	1	12	55
8		01JUL79	1979	1	22	108
9		01AUG79	1979	1	21	129
10		01SEP79	1979	1	22	125
11		01OCT79	1979	1	21	145
12		01NOV79	1979	1	19	90
13		01DEC79	1979	1	14	75
14		01JAN80	1980	1	26	144
15		01FEB80	1980	1	22	141
16		01MAR80	1980	1	22	161
17		01APR80	1980	1	26	173
18		01MAY80	1980	1	20	135
19		01JUN80	1980	1	20	105
20		01JUL80	1980	1	23	130
21		01AUG80	1980	1	21	96
22		01SEP80	1980	1	22	134
23		01OCT80	1980	1	23	126
24		01NOV80	1980	1	16	93
25		01DEC80	1980	1	19	118
26		01JAN81	1981	1	19	143
27		01FEB81	1981	1	21	135
28		01MAR81	1981	1	33	200
29		01APR81	1981	1	34	181
30		01MAY81	1981	1	27	181
31		01JUN81	1981	1	36	220
32		01JUL81	1981	1	30	254
33		01AUG81	1981	1	19	202
34		01SEP81	1981	1	26	206
35		01OCT81	1981	1	24	187

2

OBS	PRODUCT	DATE	YEAR	_TYPE_	_FREQ_	SALES
36		01NOV81	1981	1	14	113
37		01DEC81	1981	1	15	114
38	4005		1979	2	212	1967
39	8401		1979	2	270	2062
40	9054		1979	2	260	752
41	4005	01JAN79	1979	3	5	56
42	4005	01FEB79	1979	3	5	57
43	4005	01MAR79	1979	3	5	60
44	4005	01APR79	1979	3	5	51
45	4005	01MAY79	1979	3	5	49
46	4005	01JUN79	1979	3	5	35
47	4005	01JUL79	1979	3	5	36
48	4005	01AUG79	1979	3	5	42
49	4005	01SEP79	1979	3	5	34
50	4005	01OCT79	1979	3	5	48
51	4005	01NOV79	1979	3	5	41
52	4005	01DEC79	1979	3	5	29
53	4005	01JAN80	1980	3	5	37
54	4005	01FEB80	1980	3	6	49
55	4005	01MAR80	1980	3	6	63
56	4005	01APR80	1980	3	6	59
57	4005	01MAY80	1980	3	6	43
58	4005	01JUN80	1980	3	6	42
59	4005	01JUL80	1980	3	6	42
60	4005	01AUG80	1980	3	6	32
61	4005	01SEP80	1980	3	6	48
62	4005	01OCT80	1980	3	6	58
63	4005	01NOV80	1980	3	6	56
64	4005	01DEC80	1980	3	6	42
65	4005	01JAN81	1981	3	6	67
66	4005	01FEB81	1981	3	7	57
67	4005	01MAR81	1981	3	7	86
68	4005	01APR81	1981	3	7	70
69	4005	01MAY81	1981	3	7	81
70	4005	01JUN81	1981	3	7	56

3

OBS	PRODUCT	DATE	YEAR	_TYPE_	_FREQ_	SALES
71	4005	01JUL81	1981	3	7	84
72	4005	01AUG81	1981	3	7	87
73	4005	01SEP81	1981	3	7	82
74	4005	01OCT81	1981	3	7	81
75	4005	01NOV81	1981	3	6	64
76	4005	01DEC81	1981	3	6	43
77	8401	01JUL79	1979	3	8	44
78	8401	01AUG79	1979	3	9	65
79	8401	01SEP79	1979	3	8	68
80	8401	01OCT79	1979	3	10	75
81	8401	01NOV79	1979	3	7	27
82	8401	01DEC79	1979	3	5	35
83	8401	01JAN80	1980	3	7	60
84	8401	01FEB80	1980	3	5	39
85	8401	01MAR80	1980	3	7	60
86	8401	01APR80	1980	3	10	68
87	8401	01MAY80	1980	3	8	63
88	8401	01JUN80	1980	3	7	50
89	8401	01JUL80	1980	3	8	60
90	8401	01AUG80	1980	3	6	46
91	8401	01SEP80	1980	3	9	72
92	8401	01OCT80	1980	3	8	49
93	8401	01NOV80	1980	3	6	29
94	8401	01DEC80	1980	3	6	55
95	8401	01JAN81	1981	3	7	63
96	8401	01FEB81	1981	3	7	60
97	8401	01MAR81	1981	3	14	87
98	8401	01APR81	1981	3	17	91
99	8401	01MAY81	1981	3	14	87
100	8401	01JUN81	1981	3	18	134
101	8401	01JUL81	1981	3	13	151
102	8401	01AUG81	1981	3	10	110
103	8401	01SEP81	1981	3	12	109
104	8401	01OCT81	1981	3	11	96
105	8401	01NOV81	1981	3	6	44

4

OBS	PRODUCT	DATE	YEAR	_TYPE_	_FREQ_	SALES
106	8401	01DEC81	1981	3	7	65
107	9054	01JAN79	1979	3	3	11
108	9054	01FEB79	1979	3	5	12
109	9054	01MAR79	1979	3	7	22
110	9054	01APR79	1979	3	8	26
111	9054	01MAY79	1979	3	5	18
112	9054	01JUN79	1979	3	7	20
113	9054	01JUL79	1979	3	9	28
114	9054	01AUG79	1979	3	7	22
115	9054	01SEP79	1979	3	9	23
116	9054	01OCT79	1979	3	6	22
117	9054	01NOV79	1979	3	7	22
118	9054	01DEC79	1979	3	4	11
119	9054	01JAN80	1980	3	14	47
120	9054	01FEB80	1980	3	11	53
121	9054	01MAR80	1980	3	9	38
122	9054	01APR80	1980	3	10	46
123	9054	01MAY80	1980	3	6	29
124	9054	01JUN80	1980	3	7	13
125	9054	01JUL80	1980	3	9	28
126	9054	01AUG80	1980	3	9	18
127	9054	01SEP80	1980	3	7	14
128	9054	01OCT80	1980	3	9	19
129	9054	01NOV80	1980	3	4	8
130	9054	01DEC80	1980	3	7	21
131	9054	01JAN81	1981	3	6	13
132	9054	01FEB81	1981	3	7	18
133	9054	01MAR81	1981	3	12	27
134	9054	01APR81	1981	3	10	20
135	9054	01MAY81	1981	3	6	13
136	9054	01JUN81	1981	3	11	30
137	9054	01JUL81	1981	3	10	19
138	9054	01AUG81	1981	3	2	5
139	9054	01SEP81	1981	3	7	15
140	9054	01OCT81	1981	3	6	10
141	9054	01NOV81	1981	3	2	5
142	9054	01DEC81	1981	3	2	6

Chapter 26

The TABULATE Procedure

ABSTRACT

PROC TABULATE constructs tables of descriptive statistics from compositions of classification variables, analysis variables, and statistics keywords. Tables can have up to three dimensions: column, row, and page.

INTRODUCTION

PROC TABULATE displays descriptive statistics in hierarchical tables. Each table cell belongs to a particular category of observations composed by crossing variable names. The statistic associated with each cell is calculated on values from all observations in that category. The statistics that PROC TABULATE computes are many of the same statistics computed by other descriptive procedures such as MEANS, FREQ, and SUMMARY. PROC TABULATE provides

- simple but powerful methods to create user-defined tables
- a great degree of flexibility in classification hierarchies
- a variety of mechanisms for titling and formatting variables and procedure-generated statistics.

Introductory Example

A sample data set In the following examples, tables are presented that contain demographic information extracted from a data set containing the following variables:

Variable	Description
REGION	code for region of the country
CITYSIZE	code for relative population size (S=small, M=medium, L=large)
POP	urban population

Each observation contains data for one city.

In the examples below, table format is specified with the TABLE statement. (Most applications also use CLASS and VAR statements in addition to the PROC TABULATE statement.) The first example (**Output 26.1**) produces a single column with population figures for each region.

```
PROC TABULATE;
   TITLE 'REGION, POP';
   CLASS REGION;
   VAR POP;
   TABLE REGION, POP;
```

Output 26.1 Specifying TABLE REGION, POP

REGION, POP 1

	POP
	SUM
REGION	
NC	4650000.00
NE	6666000.00
SO	6864000.00
WE	8376000.00

The next example (**Output 26.2**) produces a cross-tabulation of population values for REGION by CITYSIZE. These values can also be obtained by using PROC FREQ with a WEIGHT statement.

```
PROC TABULATE;
   TITLE 'REGION, CITYSIZE*POP*SUM';
   CLASS REGION CITYSIZE;
   VAR POP;
   TABLE REGION, CITYSIZE*POP*SUM;
```

Output 26.2 Specifying TABLE REGION, CITYSIZE*POP*SUM

REGION, CITYSIZE*POP*SUM 1

	CITYSIZE		
	L	M	S
	POP	POP	POP
	SUM	SUM	SUM
REGION			
NC	3750000.00	750000.00	150000.00
NE	5022000.00	1422000.00	222000.00
SO	4488000.00	2088000.00	288000.00
WE	5592000.00	2592000.00	192000.00

By changing the TABLE statement, the same values can be displayed in one column as shown in **Output 26.3**.

```
TABLE REGION*CITYSIZE, POP*SUM;
```

Output 26.3 Specifying TABLE REGION*CITYSIZE, POP*SUM;

		POP
		SUM
REGION	CITYSIZE	
NC	L	3750000.00
	M	750000.00
	S	150000.00
NE	CITYSIZE	
	L	5022000.00
	M	1422000.00
	S	222000.00
SO	CITYSIZE	
	L	4488000.00
	M	2088000.00
	S	288000.00
WE	CITYSIZE	
	L	5592000.00
	M	2592000.00
	S	192000.00

See **Output 26.4** for the results of requesting MEAN as well as SUM to produce two columns.

```
TABLE REGION*CITYSIZE, POP*(SUM MEAN);
```

Output 26.4 Specifying TABLE REGION*CITYSIZE, POP*(SUM MEAN);

1

		POP	
		SUM	MEAN
REGION	CITYSIZE		
NC	L	3750000.00	625000.00
	M	750000.00	125000.00
	S	150000.00	25000.00
NE	CITYSIZE		
	L	5022000.00	837000.00
	M	1422000.00	237000.00
	S	222000.00	37000.00
SO	CITYSIZE		
	L	4488000.00	748000.00
	M	2088000.00	348000.00
	S	288000.00	48000.00
WE	CITYSIZE		
	L	5592000.00	932000.00
	M	2592000.00	432000.00
	S	192000.00	32000.00

Fundamentals

An understanding of the TABLE statement is fundamental to using TABULATE. The following are important elements of the TABLE statement:

- types of variables—classification and analysis
- TABLE statement operators—comma, blank space, asterisk, brackets, parentheses
- table dimensions—pages, rows, columns.

Types of variables PROC TABULATE operates on two types of variables: classification (or class) variables and analysis variables. Class variables typically have a few discrete or noncontinuous values that define the classification. In the sample data set referred to above, REGION and CITYSIZE are class variables. Analysis variables have values on which statistics are calculated. In the sample data set, POP is used as an analysis variable.

Table statement operators A table is an organized collection of cells. Four items define the contents of each cell:

- classification levels (from class variables)
- an analysis variable
- a statistic
- a format specification.

For example, a cell may contain the SUM (a statistic) of population values (an analysis variable) of small cities (CITYSIZE='S', a classification variable) in the South (REGION= 'SO', a classification variable). The cell value is formatted using the *w.d* specification 12.0. See **Specifications** for a discussion of the TABLE statement and a list of the statistic keywords. See **Details** for a discussion of format specifications.

You can define the cells of a table using the four items discussed above and the TABLE statement operators.

- Crossing (the * operator) compounds items into a hierarchy.
- Concatenation (the blank space operator) joins items one after another.
- Grouping (parentheses) controls the precedence of the other two operations.

The crossing operation arranges all levels of its second operand within each level of its first operand. For two class variables A and B, with A having two levels and B having three levels, "A crossed with B" is written **A*B** and produces the following:

1

A=1			A=2		
B=1	B=2	B=3	B=1	B=2	B=3

Using the same data levels, B crossed with A is written **B*A**, and produces the following hierarchy:

1

B=1		B=2		B=3	
A=1	A=2	A=1	A=2	A=1	A=2

The concatenation operation causes all levels of its second operand to follow all levels of its first operand. For the same class variables and levels used above, B concatenated with A (written **A B**) produces:

1

A=1	A=2	B=1	B=2	B=3

You can also write compound expressions, which involve several operations. For example, **A*B C** (where the class variable C has three levels) produces:

1

A=1			A=2					
B=1	B=2	B=3	B=1	B=2	B=3	C=1	C=2	C=3

In compound expressions the crossing operator (*) takes precedence over concatenation. You can use parentheses to alter the binding produced by this operator precedence. For example, the operations in the expression above are distributed differently if you write **A*(B C)**, which produces:

```
                                                                    1

 |                  A=1                  |                  A=2                  |
 |B=1 |B=2 |B=3 |C=1 |C=2 |C=3 |B=1 |B=2 |B=3 |C=1 |C=2 |C=3 |
```

Table dimensions TABULATE produces tables that can contain up to three dimensions:

- page (or wafer)
- row (or stub, side)
- column (or banner, top).

Each dimension is specified by an expression, and dimension expressions are separated by a comma. If all the dimensions are included, the first expression defines the page dimension, the second the row dimension, and the third the column dimension. You can also specify tables that contain only rows and columns or only columns.

Concatenation and crossing can be expressed in any of the three dimensions. For example, concatenation in the column dimension causes all values of the left name or crossing to be followed horizontally by all values of the name or crossing to its right. Thus, the concatenation **A B** produces:

```
                                                                    1

 |A=1 |A=2 |B=1 |B=2 |B=3 |
```

Crossing in the column dimension is expressed vertically. Therefore, **A B*C** produces:

```
                                                                    1

 |    |    |      B=1       |      B=2       |      B=3       |
 |A=1 |A=2 |C=1 |C=2 |C=3 |C=1 |C=2 |C=3 |C=1 |C=2 |C=3 |
```

Concatenation in the row dimension causes all values of the left name or crossing to be followed vertically by all values of the name or crossing to its right. In the row dimension, crossing is expressed horizontally, as shown in the next output.

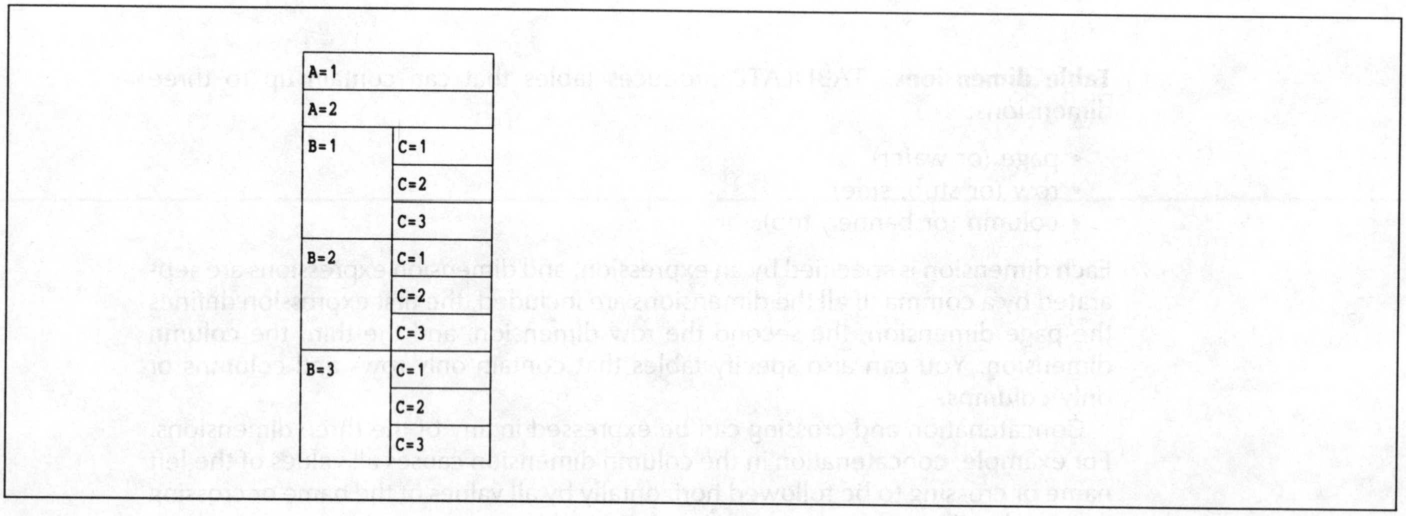

In the page dimension, a crossing specifies the set of class values, statistics, and variable information for each logical page. When any classification value, analysis variable, statistic, or class variable in the page dimension changes, TABULATE begins a new logical page. Therefore, crossing is expressed verbally in the page titles and concatenation is expressed by beginning a new logical page. Pages for the left name or crossing are followed by pages for the name or crossing to its right.

You can combine dimensions (for example, row * column) by crossing dimensions with each other, column within row and row within page, in the definition of individual table cell values. Each cell corresponds to one statistic calculated on all values of an analysis variable from observations sharing the same set of crossed class variable values. As this statement implies, you cannot cross an analysis variable with another analysis variable or a statistic with another statistic. These invalid crossings would result in two analysis variables or two statistics defining the same table cell. In the above examples, both the analysis variable and the statistic appear in the column dimension. The set of analysis variables and the set of statistics may appear together in any dimension. However, all statistics must appear in only one dimension, and all analysis variables must appear in only one dimension.

The following code and **Output 26.5** show the analysis variable in the column dimension and the statistics in the row dimension:

```
CLASS REGION CITYSIZE;
VAR POP;
TABLE REGION*CITYSIZE*(SUM MEAN), POP;
```

Output 26.5 Table with the Analysis Variable in the Column Dimension and the Statistics in the Row Dimension

1

REGION	CITYSIZE		
NC	L	SUM	3750000.00
		MEAN	625000.00
	M	SUM	750000.00
		MEAN	125000.00
	S	SUM	150000.00
		MEAN	25000.00
NE	CITYSIZE		
	L	SUM	5022000.00
		MEAN	837000.00
	M	SUM	1422000.00
		MEAN	237000.00
	S	SUM	222000.00
		MEAN	37000.00
SO	CITYSIZE		
	L	SUM	4488000.00
		MEAN	748000.00
	M	SUM	2088000.00
		MEAN	348000.00
	S	SUM	288000.00
		MEAN	48000.00
WE	CITYSIZE		
.			.
.			.
.			.

Next, add four additional variables to the example: PRODUCT and SALETYPE are class variables; QUANTITY and AMOUNT (price) are analysis variables.

The desired report (see **Output 26.6**) contains a one-page table for each product. The table provides an analysis of wholesale and retail sales by REGION and by CITYSIZE.

```
TABLE PRODUCT, REGION CITYSIZE, SALETYPE*(QUANTITY AMOUNT);
```

Output 26.6 Producing a One-page Table for Each Product

1

PRODUCT A100

	SALETYPE			
	R		W	
	QUANTITY	AMOUNT	QUANTITY	AMOUNT
	SUM	SUM	SUM	SUM
REGION				
NC	1250.00	31250.00	1250.00	25000.00
NE	1600.00	40000.00	1600.00	32000.00
SO	1880.00	47000.00	1880.00	37600.00
WE	1840.00	46000.00	1840.00	36800.00
CITYSIZE				
L	3190.00	79750.00	3190.00	63800.00
M	2440.00	61000.00	2440.00	48800.00
S	940.00	23500.00	940.00	18800.00

2

PRODUCT A200

	SALETYPE			
	R		W	
	QUANTITY	AMOUNT	QUANTITY	AMOUNT
	SUM	SUM	SUM	SUM
REGION				
NC	1295.00	32375.00	1295.00	25900.00
NE	1645.00	41125.00	1645.00	32900.00
SO	1925.00	48925.00	1925.00	38500.00
WE	1885.00	47125.00	1885.00	37700.00
CITYSIZE				
L	3250.00	81250.00	3250.00	65000.00
M	2500.00	63500.00	2500.00	50000.00
S	1000.00	24800.00	1000.00	20000.00

When you specify an analysis variable but no statistic, the default statistic is SUM. If you specify neither an analysis variable nor a statistic, the default statistic is N, the frequency of occurrence of an interaction of crossed class values.

In the table in **Output 26.6**, the page dimension is PRODUCT; the row dimension is REGION CITYSIZE, a concatenation; the column dimension is SALETYPE*(QUANTITY AMOUNT). The pages for the first two products are shown.

Important Features

The universal classifier ALL The universal class variable, ALL, represents a special class that has only one value. ALL is useful if you want to include statistics on totals and sub-totals within a classification group in a table. See **Details** for more information.

Percentages Percentages are calculated on two types of statistics. The two keywords are PCTN and PCTSUM. PCTN is calculated by dividing the frequency (N) for a subgroup of observations by the frequency of a containing group. PCTSUM is calculated by dividing the SUM of an analysis variable's values in a sub-group by the SUM of an analysis variable's values in a containing group. The two keywords PCTN and PCTSUM are used as if they were statistics keywords. It is not necessary to request N or SUM in order to request PCTN or PCTSUM. Each percentage is calculated on a denominator defined by crossings of classification and analysis variables. Denominator definitions follow the percent keyword in brackets (<>). See **Details** for more information. If percent keywords are labeled in the TABLE statement (see example below), the label specification follows the bracketed denominator definition list. For example, these statements produce **Output 26.7**.

```
TABLE (REGION*CITYSIZE ALL),
    (QUANTITY AMOUNT)*
      (SUM*F=8. PCTSUM<REGION*CITYSIZE ALL>='PERCENT'*F=8.2);
```

Output 26.7 Percents Calculated on Two Types of Statistics

1

		QUANTITY		AMOUNT	
		SUM	PERCENT	SUM	PERCENT
REGION	CITYSIZE				
NC	L	4544	11.38	102240	11.37
	M	2132	5.34	47920	5.33
	S	944	2.36	21240	2.36
NE	CITYSIZE				
	L	4842	12.13	108945	12.12
	M	3650	9.14	82125	9.14
	S	1246	3.12	28035	3.12
SO	CITYSIZE				
	L	4606	11.54	103635	11.53
	M	4298	10.77	97705	10.87
	S	2508	6.28	56230	6.25
WE	CITYSIZE				
	L	5310	13.30	119475	13.29
	M	4720	11.82	106200	11.81
	S	1122	2.81	25245	2.81
ALL		39922	100.00	898995	100.00

Titling and formatting There are four sources of text for page, row, and column titles:

- formatted class values
- literals attached to variable or keyword names in the TABLE statement
- variable names or labels (for both class and analysis variables)
- keyword names or labels (for statistics and ALL).

See **Details** for the use of each of these sources.

SPECIFICATIONS

The TABULATE procedure is controlled by the following statements:

PROC TABULATE *[options]*;
  CLASS *variable...*;
  VAR *variable...*;
  FREQ *variable*;
  WEIGHT *variable*;
  FORMAT *variables format. ...*;
  LABEL *variable=label...*;
  BY *variable...*;
  TABLE *[expression,][expression,]expression[/options]*;
  KEYLABEL *keyword= 'text'...*;

The PROC TABULATE statement is always accompanied by one or more TABLE statements specifying the tables to be produced. Classification variables used in TABLE statements must be specified in the CLASS statement. Analysis variables used in TABLE statements must appear in the VAR statement. A variable that appears in both a CLASS statement and a VAR statement is used as a CLASS variable only. The WEIGHT, FREQ, and BY statements are optionally specified once for the entire procedure step.

PROC TABULATE Statement

PROC TABULATE *options;*

The options below can appear on the PROC TABULATE statement:

DATA=*SASdataset*
: specifies the SAS data set to be used by TABULATE. If DATA= is not specified, TABULATE uses the most recently created SAS data set.

MISSING
: requests that missing values be considered as valid levels for the classification variables. Special missing values are considered as different level values. Unless MISSING is specified, TABULATE does not include observations with a missing value for one or more classification variables in the analysis.

FORMAT=*formatname*
: specifies a default format for formatting each table cell. You can use any valid SAS or user-defined format. If no value is specified, the default value is 12.2. The default format is always overridden by any formats specified in a TABLE statement. This option is especially useful for decreasing the number of print positions required to print a table.

ORDER=FREQ
ORDER=DATA
ORDER=INTERNAL
ORDER=FORMATTED

specifies the order in which the class variable values are displayed in each table. If ORDER=FREQ, the class values are ordered by descending frequency count so that class values occurring in the greatest number of observations come first. If ORDER=DATA, class values are kept in the order they were encountered in the data set. If ORDER=INTERNAL, the class values are ordered by the internal representation of the values. If ORDER=FORMATTED, the class values are ordered by the formatted (external representation) of the value. If you omit ORDER= or give an unrecognized value, TABULATE orders by the internal value.

FORMCHAR {*index list*}=*'string'*

defines the characters to be used for constructing the table outlines and dividers. The value is a string 11 characters long defining the two bar characters, vertical and horizontal, and the nine corner characters: upper left, upper middle, upper right, middle left, middle middle (cross), middle right, lower left, lower middle, and lower right. The default value is FORMCHAR='|----|+|---'. Any character or hexadecimal string can be substituted to customize the table appearance. Use an index list to specify which default form character each supplied character replaces; or replace the entire default string by specifying the full 11 character replacement string with no index list. For example, change the four corners to asterisks by using

```
FORMCHAR(3 5 9 11)= '****'
```

Specifying

```
FORMCHAR='           ' (11 blanks)
```

produces tables with no outlines or dividers.

NOSEPS

requests that no horizontal separator lines appear in the body of the table.

DEPTH=*number*

specifies the maximum depth of any crossing in a dimension. The default depth is 10. The depth of a crossing refers to the number of elements that are crossed with each other. For example, the depth of A*B is two and the maximum depth of the dimension A*(B*N ALL) is three since A*B*N has depth three.

CLASS Statement

CLASS *variables;*

The CLASS statement is used to identify variables in the input data set as classification variables. Any classification variable used in a TABLE statement must have been previously listed in the CLASS statement. The variables may have either numeric or character values. Normally each class variable has a small number of discrete values or unique levels. Continuous values for a numeric variable can be grouped into discrete levels by using PROC FORMAT.

VAR Statement

VAR *variables;*

The VAR statement is used to identify analysis variables in the input data set. Analysis variables must be numeric and may contain continuous values. All analysis variables used in TABLE statements must be included in this list.

FREQ and WEIGHT Statements

FREQ *variable;*
WEIGHT *variable;*

Both the FREQ and WEIGHT statements specify a numeric variable in the input SAS data set whose values are used to weight each observation. Only one variable can be used in each statement; both statements can be used.

If the FREQ statement is used, each observation in the input data set is assumed to represent *n* observations, where *n* is the value of the FREQ variable. If the value is not an integer, the value is truncated to the integer portion. If the FREQ variable has a value less than 1, the observation is skipped.

If the WEIGHT statement is used, TABULATE uses the value of the WEIGHT variable to calculate a weighted mean, a weighted variance, and a weighted sum. An observation with a WEIGHT value less than or equal to zero is skipped. Note that the WEIGHT variable value need not be an integer and does not affect the degrees of freedom.

FORMAT and LABEL Statements

FORMAT *variables format;*
LABEL *variable=label;*

The FORMAT and LABEL statements are especially useful with PROC TABULATE. You can use PROC FORMAT to specify discrete levels for a classification variable. The format specified is also used in any page, row, or column titles where the class variable appears. Any label text specified in a LABEL statement for a classification or analysis variable is used in any page, row, or column titles where that variable appears.

BY Statement

BY *variables;*

A BY statement can be used with PROC TABULATE to obtain separate analyses on observations in groups defined by the BY variables. When a BY statement appears, the procedure expects the input data set to have been sorted in order of the BY variables. If your input data set is not sorted in ascending order, use the SORT procedure with a similar BY statement to sort the data, or, if appropriate, use the BY statement options NOTSORTED or DESCENDING. For more information, see the discussion of the BY statement in *SAS Language Guide for Personal Computers*.

Note that the page dimension expression of a TABLE statement can have an effect similar to that of using a BY statement. The page dimension should be used in most cases where a new page is desired for a given level of a class variable or combination of variables.

Note that your input need not be sorted when the page dimension expression is used.

TABLE Statement

A TABLE statement consists of one to three dimension expressions separated by commas and followed by an option list. If all three dimensions are specified, the leftmost dimension defines pages, the middle dimension defines rows, and the rightmost dimension defines columns. If two dimensions are specified, the left defines rows and the right defines columns. If a single dimension is specified, it defines columns. A dimension expression consists of one or more operands. Valid operands are

- class variables (from the CLASS statement) or ALL
- analysis variables (from the VAR statement)
- statistics
- format specifications
- other expressions.

When an expression contains more than one operand, the operands are joined by operators. The operators and the effect they produce are listed below:

operator	**action**
asterisk (*)	subgroup or cross
blank space	concatenate tables together
parentheses ()	group or specify order

For example, you can design a table analyzing the total sum of units sold by each sales representative. In the TABLE statement, first list the class variable, then the analysis variable, then the statistic. Your PROC TABULATE statements read:

```
PROC TABULATE DATA=SASDATA.SALES;
   CLASS REPNAME;
   VAR NUMBER;
   TABLE REPNAME,NUMBER*SUM;
```

If both crossing and concatenation are used in an expression, the crossing operator takes precedence. Parentheses may be used to group expressions and alter the binding of operators to operands.

The following are examples of valid expressions using analysis variable X and class variables A, B, C, and D:

A	class variable
MEAN	statistic
X	analysis variable
A*B	class crossing
A*B*C	multiple class crossing
A*MEAN*X	mean for X within A
A B	class concatenation
A B*C	concatenation of A and B*C
(A B)*C	crossing of A B with C (equivalent to A*C B*C)
(A B)*(C D)*E	crossing of A B with C D, which is crossed with E.

If any analysis variables are specified, one or more of the following statistics can be requested:

N	number of observations with nonmissing analysis variable values in the subgroup determined by the combination of class variable values
NMISS	number of observations in the subgroup having missing values for the analysis variable
MEAN	mean
STD	standard deviation
MIN	minimum value
MAX	maximum value
RANGE	range of values
SUM	sum
USS	uncorrected sum of squares
CSS	sum of squares corrected for the mean
STDERR	standard error of the mean
CV	coefficient of variation
T	Student's *t* value for testing the hypothesis that the population mean is 0
PRT	probability of a greater absolute value for the Student's *t* value
VAR	variance
SUMWGT	sum of weight variable values
PCTN	the percentage of frequency (N)
PCTSUM	the percentage of SUM.

If no analysis variables are specified in the TABLE statement, either N or PCTN may be requested as a statistic. If analysis variables are specified, but no statistic, the statistic is SUM. If neither an analysis variable nor a statistic appears in the TABLE statement, each table cell will be the frequency count for a particular interaction of class variable values.

The set of analysis variables and the set of statistics can appear in the same dimension or in different dimensions. However, all analysis variables must appear together in one dimension and all statistic names must appear together in one dimension. You cannot cross an analysis variable with another analysis variable or a statistic with another statistic.

If a variable name (classification or analysis) and a statistic name are the same, specify the statistic name in single quotes. The ALL keyword can also be specified in this manner in case of a name conflict. (See **Details** below for a discussion of the keyword ALL.)

The form of the TABLE statement is

TABLE [*expression*,] [*expression*,] *expression* [/*options*];

where *expression* consists of an operand or more than one operand joined by operators. (Remember that an expression can be an operand in a larger expression, as in X*(Y Z).

When a class variable, analysis variable, or statistic is used as an operand, it may be followed by an equal sign and label:

classvariable = '*labeltext*'

analysisvariable = *'labeltext'*
statistic = *'labeltext'*

A statistic operand can be a statistic keyword, such as SUM or STD, or a percent expression with the form

PCTN <*denominatorcrossing...*>
PCTSUM <*denominatorcrossing...*>

where *denominatorcrossing* is of the form:

variable

or

*variable *variable ...*

A format specification operand is of the form:

F | FORMAT = *format*

A more elaborate TABLE statement for the last example may be

```
TABLE REPNAME * NUMBER, SUM * F=12. PCTSUM <REPNAME> * F=12.2;
```

where F=12. and F=12.2 are format specifications and <REPNAME> is a denominator crossing.

A TABLE statement can define only one table. Multiple TABLE statements can appear after the PROC TABULATE statement, each defining a separate table.

Table statement options The options that can appear in the TABLE statement are described below. If any options are specified, a slash (/) must precede the first option. The slash is not necessary if no options are used.

MISSTEXT=*'text'*
: supplies up to twenty characters of text to be printed in table cells containing missing values.

PRINTMISS
: requests that all possible rows and columns print even though a particular row or column interaction does not exist in the data. This situation arises, for example, when a data set has variables A and B and the following observations:

A	B
1	1
2	1
2	2

A TABLE statement

```
TABLE A * B, N;
```

requests rows for all interactions of values of A and B; however, one interaction does not exist in the data, namely, A=1 B=2. This row does not appear in the table unless you specify PRINTMISS. If the TABLE statement is

```
TABLE N, A * B;
```

the same analysis applies to the columns of the table.

FUZZ=*nnn*
: supplies a numeric value against which analysis variable values and table cell values are compared to eliminate trivial values (absolute

values less than FUZZ) from computation and printing. A number whose absolute value is less than FUZZ is treated as zero for computations and printing. The default FUZZ value is the smallest representable floating point number on the system on which you are running.

RTSPACE=*n*
RTS=*n*

supplies an integer value that specifies the number of print positions allotted to row titles. The print positions include those for the left and right boundaries of row titles. (The right row title boundary is also the left boundary of table cells.) The default value is one-fourth of the LINESIZE value.

BOX=_PAGE_
BOX=*variablename*
BOX=*'string'*

specifies the text to be placed in the empty box above the row titles. BOX=_PAGE_ causes the page dimension text to appear in the box. If page dimension text does not fit, it is placed in its normal position and the box left empty. BOX=*variablename* causes the name or label of a variable to appear in the box. BOX=*'string'* causes the quoted string to appear in the box. Any name, label, or quoted string that does not fit is truncated.

ROW=FLOAT
ROW=CONSTANT
ROW=CONST

specifies whether all title elements in a row crossing are allotted space whether blank or not. The default is CONSTANT. If ROW=FLOAT and a row title element is blank (for example, N=' ' in the row dimension) the row title space is divided equally among the nonblank title elements in the crossing.

CONDENSE

requests that multiple logical pages be printed on a single physical page. TABULATE continues to condense the output as long as one or more complete logical pages fits on a single printed page.

KEYLABEL Statement

KEYLABEL *keyword='text'*;

where

keyword is one of the valid statistic names discussed above or the universal class variable ALL.

text is up to 40 characters of labeling information. The value of *text* must be enclosed in quotes.

The replacement text is used in any label where the specified keyword is used, unless another label is specified in the TABLE statement. The KEYLABEL statement is useful for relabeling a keyword name once rather than for each occurrence in one or more TABLE statements. Only one keyword label can be specified for each keyword in a particular PROC TABULATE step; if multiple labels are requested for the same keyword, the last one specified is used. An example of a KEYLABEL statement is

```
KEYLABEL ALL='TOTAL $'
         MEAN='AVERAGE'
         PCTSUM='PERCENT OF SUM';
```

DETAILS

Input Data Set

Classification variables can have either alphabetic or numeric values. PROC FORMAT can be used to reduce many input values for a classification variable to a few class levels and to give more descriptive titles to raw level values. Analysis variables must be numeric.

Default Statistics

When an analysis variable but no statistic is specified, the default statistic is SUM. If neither an analysis variable nor a statistic is specified, the default statistic is N, the frequency of occurrence of an interaction of crossed class values.

Missing Values

Missing values may occur in class variables or in analysis variables. A missing value in a class variable causes the observation to be ignored unless MISSING is specified in the PROC statement. The MISSING option causes a missing value to be treated as another classification level; special missing values form other distinct levels.

A missing analysis variable increments the statistic NMISS, the number of observations in the subgroup having a missing value in the analysis variable. The missing value does not affect any other calculations.

Missing table cell values can result from interactions that do not appear in the data (even though individual class values do appear) or from analysis variables that have all missing values. Use the MISSTEXT TABLE statement option to replace missing table cell values with up to twenty characters of text.

Row Title Space

You can use the RTS TABLE statement option to control the space used for the width of row titles. If no RTS value is specified, TABULATE uses one fourth of the linesize. This amount of space is frequently much more than is needed.

The Universal Class Variable ALL

The universal class variable represents a special class that has only one value. When embedded in a crossing, ALL collapses the levels of class variables grouped with it to produce subtotals and totals. The following table illustrates the hierarchy discussed earlier:

1

B=1		B=2		B=3	
A=1	A=2	A=1	A=2	A=1	A=2

If B and A are CLASS variables you can summarize all values of A within each value of B with the expression B*(A ALL). The new table follows:

1

B=1			B=2			B=3		
A=1	A=2	ALL	A=1	A=2	ALL	A=1	A=2	ALL

The additional nodes represent the unions of all A values that share a common B value.

ALL may be specified more than once in an expression. For example, (ALL B)*(ALL A) produces the following table:

1

ALL			B=1			B=2			B=3		
ALL	A=1	A=2	ALL	A=1	A=2	ALL	A=1	A=2	ALL	A=1	A=2

Consider the marketing research example we have been developing. You can use ALL to produce sales summaries in several dimensions. There are two sets of columns, one for wholesale and one for retail sales. Specifying (SALETYPE ALL) *(QUANTITY AMOUNT) produces a third set of columns that summarize the previous two. There are also two sets of rows, one for REGION and one for CITYSIZE. Each of these sets individually accounts for all sales of a given product. If totaled, each set should yield the same total sales value for each product (unless one of the class variables has missing values). Specifying REGION ALL CITYSIZE ALL produces two summary rows, one for REGION and one for CITYSIZE. There is an individual logical page for each product code. The concatenation, ALL PRODUCT, in the page dimension produces a summary page that incorporates sales for all products. The complete TABLE statement is

```
TABLE ALL PRODUCT, REGION ALL CITYSIZE ALL,
    (SALETYPE ALL)*(QUANTITY*F=6. AMOUNT*F=10.2);
```

1

ALL

	SALETYPE					
	R		W		ALL	
	QUANT-ITY	AMOUNT	QUANT-ITY	AMOUNT	QUANT-ITY	AMOUNT
	SUM	SUM	SUM	SUM	SUM	SUM
REGION						
NC	3810	95200.00	3810	76200.00	7620	171400.00
NE	4869	121725.00	4869	97380.00	9738	219105.00
SO	5706	143450.00	5706	114120.00	11412	257570.00
WE	5576	139400.00	5576	111520.00	11152	250920.00
ALL	19961	499775.00	19961	399220.00	39922	898995.00
CITYSIZE						
L	9651	241275.00	9651	193020.00	19302	434295.00
M	7400	185950.00	7400	148000.00	14800	333950.00
S	2910	72550.00	2910	58200.00	5820	130750.00
ALL	19961	499775.00	19961	399220.00	39922	898995.00

2

PRODUCT A100

	SALETYPE					
	R		W		ALL	
	QUANT-ITY	AMOUNT	QUANT-ITY	AMOUNT	QUANT-ITY	AMOUNT
	SUM	SUM	SUM	SUM	SUM	SUM
REGION						
NC	1250	31250.00	1250	25000.00	2500	56250.00
NE	1600	40000.00	1600	32000.00	3200	72000.00
SO	1880	47000.00	1880	37600.00	3760	84600.00
WE	1840	46000.00	1840	36800.00	3680	82800.00
ALL	6570	164250.00	6570	131400.00	13140	295650.00
CITYSIZE						
L	3190	79750.00	3190	63800.00	6380	143550.00
M	2440	61000.00	2440	48800.00	4880	109800.00
S	940	23500.00	940	18800.00	1880	42300.00
ALL	6570	164250.00	6570	131400.00	13140	295650.00

3

PRODUCT A200

	SALETYPE					
	R		W		ALL	
	QUANT-ITY	AMOUNT	QUANT-ITY	AMOUNT	QUANT-ITY	AMOUNT
	SUM	SUM	SUM	SUM	SUM	SUM
REGION						
NC	1295	32375.00	1295	25900.00	2590	58275.00
NE	1645	41125.00	1645	32900.00	3290	74025.00
SO	1925	48925.00	1925	38500.00	3850	87425.00
WE	1885	47125.00	1885	37700.00	3770	84825.00
ALL	6750	169550.00	6750	135000.00	13500	304550.00
CITYSIZE						
L	3250	81250.00	3250	65000.00	6500	146250.00
M	2500	63500.00	2500	50000.00	5000	113500.00
S	1000	24800.00	1000	20000.00	2000	44800.00
ALL	6750	169550.00	6750	135000.00	13500	304550.00

4

PRODUCT A300

	SALETYPE					
	R		W		ALL	
	QUANT-ITY	AMOUNT	QUANT-ITY	AMOUNT	QUANT-ITY	AMOUNT
	SUM	SUM	SUM	SUM	SUM	SUM
REGION						
NC	1265	31575.00	1265	25300.00	2530	56875.00
NE	1624	40600.00	1624	32480.00	3248	73080.00
SO	1901	47525.00	1901	38020.00	3802	85545.00
WE	1851	46275.00	1851	37020.00	3702	83295.00
ALL	6641	165975.00	6641	132820.00	13282	298795.00
CITYSIZE						
L	3211	80275.00	3211	64220.00	6422	144495.00
M	2460	61450.00	2460	49200.00	4920	110650.00
S	970	24250.00	970	19400.00	1940	43650.00
ALL	6641	165975.00	6641	132820.00	13282	298795.00

Percentages: PCTN and PCTSUM

The general form of a percent specification is

(PCTN or PCTSUM) <*denominatordefinitions*> =*label*

PCTN is percentage of frequency (N); it may apply to the frequency of non-missing analysis variable values or to the frequency of an interaction of class variables. PCTSUM is percentage of SUM; it must apply to the SUM of analysis variable values. Obtain the desired percentages by constructing denominator definitions that collapse appropriate classification levels into totals for the specified analysis variables or interactions.

Denominator definitions The role of the denominator definition is to instruct TABULATE how to collapse classification levels in TABLE statement crossings and how to choose an analysis variable for the denominator. If you understand how ALL is used to summarize classification levels you will understand how denominator definitions work. When you concatenate ALL with a class variable, the result is two crossings. One crossing collects and presents statistics for each level of the class variable; the other crossing collapses the levels of the class variable into a summary or total statistic. When the statistic is N or SUM, ALL represents a total.

You frequently calculate percentages by summing values into a total and then dividing values by the total. TABULATE sums values for this total in the same way that ALL produces totals—by collapsing multiple class levels into a single class level. Denominator definitions tell TABULATE what class levels to collapse. Each denominator definition is a crossing of class variables and possibly a single analysis variable. Multiple definition crossings may appear within brackets. A denominator definition contains a subset of the variables from the TABLE statement crossing. TABULATE adds to the TABLE statement crossing a new crossing in which those class variables named in the denominator definition are replaced by ALL.

For example, **Output 26.8** presents a frequency for each level of B within A and a total frequency of all levels of B within each level of A. **Output 26.9** shows percentages for each level of B within A.

Output 26.8 Table A*(B ALL)

1

A					
1			2		
B		ALL	B		ALL
1	2		1	2	
N	N	N	N	N	N
10	30	40	20	40	60

Output 26.9 Table A*B*PCTN<B>

1

A			
1		2	
B		B	
1	2	1	2
PCTN	PCTN	PCTN	PCTN
25	75	33	67

The denominators are the sums of B level frequencies within each level of A; that is, the values presented by ALL in the first table. The denominator definition <B> instructs TABULATE to replace B in the TABLE crossing A*B with ALL. The new crossing is A*ALL or simply A. During the data reduction process the new crossing sums the appropriate values into denominator totals.

When there are analysis variables, the denominator totals are N or SUM values for one of them. You can choose any analysis variable by including it in a denominator crossing or you can use each analysis variable in turn by not including any of them in the definition.

The following example presents Y SUM values as percentages of X SUM values.

```
TABLE A*B,C*(X*SUM Y*(SUM PCTSUM<A*B*X>))/RTS=15;
```

There are three class variables. The denominator definition A*B*X instructs TABULATE to collapse the levels of A and B to form a total SUM value of X. The TABLE statement crossing that contains PCTSUM is A*B*C*Y*PCTSUM. A*B is from the row dimension; the rest of the crossing is from the column dimension. The new crossing, constructed as described above, is ALL*ALL*C*X or simply C*X. A and B have been replaced by ALL, and the selected analysis variable is X.

In the table shown in **Output 26.10**, the denominator value used when C=1 is 217 and when C=2 is 374. Obtain these values by collapsing all levels of A and B for X; that is, sum X over all levels of A and B. (217 is the total of 59 + 78 + 21 + 59 and 374 is the total of 59 + 14 + 140 + 161.) When A=1 and B=1, the SUM of Y is 123. 123 is 57 percent of 217.

Output 26.10 Using Y Sum Values as Percentages of X Sum Values

1

		C					
		1			2		
		X	Y		X	Y	
		SUM	SUM	PCTSUM	SUM	SUM	PCTSUM
A	B						
1	1	59	123	57	59	100	27
	2	78	49	23	14	28	7
2	B						
	1	21	71	33	140	106	28
	2	59	49	23	161	2	0

Selecting a definition Each TABLE statement crossing must have a denominator definition to use. It is possible that several definitions in the list apply to a crossing, but only one will yield the correct denominator values. In selecting a definition, TABULATE looks first for a definition that is completely contained in the TABLE statement crossing—both the CLASS variables and the analysis variable. If no such definition exists, TABULATE looks for a definition whose class variables are all contained in the TABLE statement crossing. A definition that contains only an analysis variable is such a definition—even if the analysis variable is not in the crossing. If no analysis variable is in the definition the analysis variable from the crossing is used.

Note that the order of denominator definitions may affect which definition is chosen. Note also that a definition may be contained in a crossing even if the definition class variables are not contiguous in the crossing, so long as the order of the variables is the same.

Percentages of row totals If all classes in the column dimension and only classes in the column dimension appear in the denominator definition, TABULATE collapses all levels in the column crossing into a denominator total but leaves the row levels uncollapsed. The denominator value is the total for each row. For example,

```
TABLE A,B*(N PCTN<B>);
```

produces the table in **Output 26.11**.

Output 26.11 Table Producing Percentages of Row Totals

1

	B			
	1		2	
	N	PCTN	N	PCTN
A				
1	10	25	30	75
2	20	33	40	67

The denominator value for PCTN in row 1 is 40, the total of N values in row 1. The denominator value for PCTN in row 2 is 60, the total of N values in row 2.

Percentages of column totals If all classes in the row dimension and only classes in the row dimension appear in the denominator definition, TABULATE calculates percentages of column totals for each row dimension crossing. For example,

```
TABLE A,B*(N PCTN<A>);
```

produces the table in **Output 26.12**.

Output 26.12 Table Producing Percentages of Column Totals

1

	B			
	1		2	
	N	PCTN	N	PCTN
A				
1	10	33	30	43
2	20	67	40	57

The denominator value for PCTN in column 2 is 30, the total of N values in column 1. The denominator value for PCTN in column 4 is 70, the total of N values in column 3.

Percentages of other totals If all classes in the page dimension and only classes in the page dimension appear in the denominator definition, TABULATE calculates percentages of row and column totals for each page dimension crossing.

Denominator definitions may contain class variables from more than one dimension. The percentages calculated are of sub-table totals. For example,

```
TABLE A,B*(N PCTN<A*B>);
```

produces the table in **Output 26.13**.

Output 26.13 Percentages of Row and Column Totals

1

	B			
	1		2	
	N	PCTN	N	PCTN
A				
1	10	10	30	30
2	20	20	40	40

The denominator value for all PCTN cells in this table is 100, the total of the N values in the sub-table of the denominator definition.

Percentages of other analysis variables (a multiple response example) Many applications require the percentage that N or SUM of one analysis variable is of the N or SUM statistic for another analysis variable in the same category. For example, a market research survey may ask for a number of responses to each of several questions. Each observation in this data set contains the following variables:

ID identification number of respondent

Q coded question number

V1-V5 five possible responses: a 1 value signifies that response was selected; a missing value indicates no response.

The following statement expresses the frequency of V1-V5 as percentages of the total number of respondents, the frequency of ID. The essential structure of the TABLE statement is

```
TABLE ID*N (V1 V2 V3 V4 V5) * (N PCTN<ID>),Q;
```

Formatting and TABLE statement options have been included below to produce a more attractive table, seen in **Output 26.14**.

```
PROC TABULATE F=7.2;
   TITLE 'PERCENTAGES OF VARIABLES';
   CLASS Q;
   VAR ID V1-V5;

   TABLE ID*N='RESPONSES'*F=7. (V1 V2 V3 V4 V5)*(N='COUNT'*F=7.
         PCTN<ID>='PERCENT'),
         Q / RTS=20

   LABEL ID='TOTAL'
         V1='RESPONSE 1'
         V2='RESPONSE 2'
         V3='RESPONSE 3'
         V4='RESPONSE 4'
         V5='RESPONSE 5'
         Q ='QUESTIONS';
```

Output 26.14 Using Formatting and Table Statement Options

```
                              PERCENTAGES OF VARIABLES                                  1
```

		QUESTIONS					
		1	2	3	4	5	6
TOTAL	RESPONSES	300	296	281	286	294	300
RESPONSE 1	COUNT	122	116	108	129	109	110
	PERCENT	40.67	39.19	38.43	45.10	37.07	36.67
RESPONSE 2	COUNT	114	123	111	101	112	113
	PERCENT	38.00	41.55	39.50	35.31	38.10	37.67
RESPONSE 3	COUNT	133	129	107	100	118	128
	PERCENT	44.33	43.58	38.08	34.97	40.14	42.67
RESPONSE 4	COUNT	121	122	127	114	131	114
	PERCENT	40.33	41.22	45.20	39.86	44.56	38.00
RESPONSE 5	COUNT	129	122	111	101	103	123
	PERCENT	43.00	41.22	39.50	35.31	35.03	41.00

Details If no denominator definition list follows the percent keyword, the percentages are calculated on data set totals (or BY-group totals if a BY statement is used).

You can include denominator values in the table by including crossings that collect the same totals. Construct these crossings by substituting ALL for each class variable in the expression crossing that is also in the denominator crossing. For row, column, and page percentages, concatenate ALL in the appropriate dimension, and include ALL as a denominator definition.

The following code and **Output 26.15** illustrate the use of ALL with column percentages. The denominator value is 460, the total of SUM values in column 1.

```
TABLE A*B ALL,X*(SUM PCTSUM<A*B ALL>)/RTS=16;
```

Output 26.15 Using ALL with Column Percentages

1

		X	
		SUM	PCTSUM
A	B		
1	1	160	35
	2	80	17
2	B		
	1	100	22
	2	120	26
ALL		460	100

TABLE statement crossings can be abbreviated if you group elements. For example, A*B*(C D) abbreviates the longer expression (A*B*C A*B*D). However, no grouping is allowed in denominator definitions. Nevertheless, all concatenations that contain a percent keyword must be represented among the denominator definitions for that keyword. In the above example, if the denominators are B*C and B*D, then both crossings must appear in the denominator list, as in

```
TABLE A*B,(C D)*(N PCTN<B*C B*D>);
```

If the denominator is A*B, the crossing needs to be specified only once since it is fully contained in both concatenations, as in this example:

```
TABLE A*B,(C D)*(N PCTN<A*B>);
```

Titling and Formatting

There are four sources of text for page, row, and column titles:

- formatted class values
- literals attached to variable or keyword names in the TABLE statement
- variable names or labels (for both class and analysis variables)
- keyword names or labels (for statistics and ALL).

Formatted class values can be supplied directly from the input data set, or variables can be associated with formats created by the FORMAT procedure. Variable names and keywords are used as titles unless some text has been designated for use in place of the name. Literals may be included in the TABLE statement following the name to which they apply (for example, ALL='REGIONAL TOTAL'). Literals attached to percent keywords must follow the bracketed denominator definition list. Multiple instances of the same name may be attached to different literals. (See ALL in the following example.)

If a LABEL or KEYLABEL statement has been used for a variable or keyword and no literal has been attached to the name in the TABLE statement, then the label text is used in the table titles. Some instances of a name may be attached to a literal in the TABLE statement while others are associated with a label. The appropriate text is used in each case. The syntax of the KEYLABEL statement is identical with that of the LABEL statement.

TABULATE automatically splits title text to fit the space allotted. If a blank or hyphen appears in the title, the split occurs at the blank or hyphen. If there is no blank or hyphen, TABULATE inserts a hyphen at the last position of the current line and continues the title on the next line. If a word in a title is known to be too long to fit in the allotted space, you can force a split by inserting a hyphen into the label or formatted value. For example, if SEPTEMBER is the title of a column 7 or 8 positions wide, you can force a break between M and B by formatting the value as 'SEPTEM-BER'.

Table cell values are formatted using SAS or user defined formats in format items: FORMAT=*formatname*. or F=*formatname*.. Format items appear in the TABLE statement as though they were class or variable names. Format items can appear in any dimension. If two or more format items become crossed with each other, the format with the least scope (that is, the format closer to the column dimension, or closer to the end of the statement) overrides the other formats.

Formats that appear in the page dimension apply to all rows and columns in the associated pages. Formats that appear in the row dimension apply to all columns in the associated rows. Formats that appear in the column dimension apply to all rows in the associated columns. More than one format may apply to rows on the same logical page. Each column width for the logical page is the width of the widest row element in that column. The default format is F=12.2. The following example reworks the marketing research tables used previously. **Output 26.16** shows the resulting tables.

```
PROC FORMAT;
    VALUE $REGFMT  NC='NORTH CENTRAL'
                   NE='NORTHEAST'
                   SO='SOUTH'
                   WE='WEST';
    VALUE $SIZEFMT  S='UNDER 50000'
                   M='50000 TO 500000'
                   L='OVER 500000';
    VALUE $SALEFMT  W='WHOLESALE'

PROC TABULATE;
    TITLE 'SALES FIGURES';
    CLASS PRODUCT REGION CITYSIZE SALETYPE;
    VAR QUANTITY AMOUNT;
    FORMAT REGION $REGFMT.;
    FORMAT CITYSIZE $SIZEFMT.;
    FORMAT SALETYPE $SALEFMT.;
    LABEL PRODUCT='PRODUCT CODE'
          REGION='REGION OF COUNTRY'
          CITYSIZE='CITY SIZE'
          SALETYPE='TYPE OF SALE'
          AMOUNT='$ AMOUNT';

    TABLE (ALL PRODUCT)*F=8., REGION ALL='REGIONAL TOTAL',
          (SALETYPE ALL)*(QUANTITY AMOUNT);
    KEYLABEL SUM = 'OF SALES'
             ALL = 'TOTAL';
```

Output 26.16 Tables Presenting Sales of a Product

SALES FIGURES 1

TOTAL

	TYPE OF SALE					
	RETAIL		WHOLESALE		TOTAL	
	QUANTITY OF SALES	$ AMOUNT OF SALES	QUANTITY OF SALES	$ AMOUNT OF SALES	QUANTITY OF SALES	$ AMOUNT OF SALES
REGION OF COUNTRY						
NORTH CENTRAL	3810	95200	3810	76200	7620	171400
NORTHEAST	4869	121725	4869	97380	9738	219105
SOUTH	5706	143450	5706	114120	11412	257570
WEST	5576	139400	5576	111520	11152	250920
REGIONAL TOTAL	19961	499775	19961	399220	39922	898995

SALES FIGURES 2

PRODUCT CODE A100

	TYPE OF SALE					
	RETAIL		WHOLESALE		TOTAL	
	QUANTITY OF SALES	$ AMOUNT OF SALES	QUANTITY OF SALES	$ AMOUNT OF SALES	QUANTITY OF SALES	$ AMOUNT OF SALES
REGION OF COUNTRY						
NORTH CENTRAL	1250	31250	1250	25000	2500	56250
NORTHEAST	1600	40000	1600	32000	3200	72000
SOUTH	1880	47000	1880	37600	3760	84600
WEST	1840	46000	1840	36800	3680	82800
REGIONAL TOTAL	6570	164250	6570	131400	13140	295650

SALES FIGURES 3

PRODUCT CODE A200

	TYPE OF SALE					
	RETAIL		WHOLESALE		TOTAL	
	QUANTITY OF SALES	$ AMOUNT OF SALES	QUANTITY OF SALES	$ AMOUNT OF SALES	QUANTITY OF SALES	$ AMOUNT OF SALES
REGION OF COUNTRY						
NORTH CENTRAL	1295	32375	1295	25900	2590	58275
NORTHEAST	1645	41125	1645	32900	3290	74025
SOUTH	1925	48925	1925	38500	3850	87425
WEST	1885	47125	1885	37700	3770	84825
REGIONAL TOTAL	6750	169550	6750	135000	13500	304550

SALES FIGURES 4

PRODUCT CODE A300

	TYPE OF SALE					
	RETAIL		WHOLESALE		TOTAL	
	QUANTITY OF SALES	$ AMOUNT OF SALES	QUANTITY OF SALES	$ AMOUNT OF SALES	QUANTITY OF SALES	$ AMOUNT OF SALES
REGION OF COUNTRY						
NORTH CENTRAL	1265	31575	1265	25300	2530	56875
NORTHEAST	1624	40600	1624	32480	3248	73080
SOUTH	1901	47525	1901	38020	3802	85545
WEST	1851	46275	1851	37020	3702	83295
REGIONAL TOTAL	6641	165975	6641	132820	13282	298795

A logical page can contain more rows and columns than can be printed on one physical page. If so, TABULATE automatically divides the logical page into subsets and prints all rows for a given set of columns before moving to the next set of columns. The single logical page depicted below would be divided as indicated:

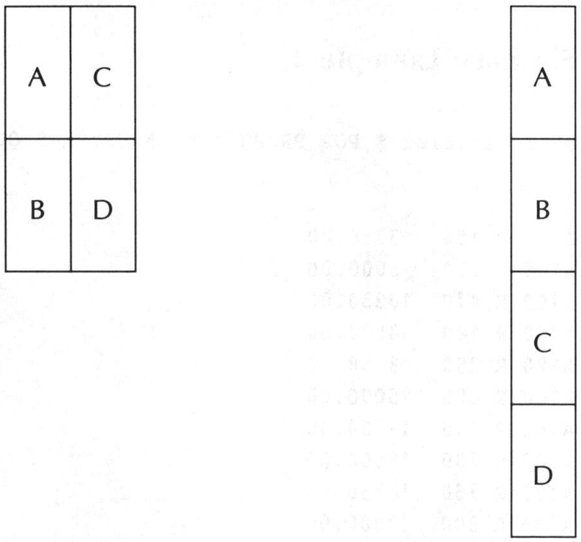

Figure 26.1 Logical Pages in PROC TABULATE Output

TABULATE never places multiple logical pages on one physical page. But if a logical page is small, you can force multiple logical pages onto a single physical page with the CONDENSE TABLE statement option.

Limitations

All cell values for a logical page must fit in memory at one time. Increasing the memory available to the SAS System will increase the number of table cells per logical page that can be handled.

Historical Note

TABULATE was inspired in part by the pioneer software package TPL (Table Producing Language) developed at the Bureau of Labor Statistics.

EXAMPLES

The following examples illustrate a number of features of TABULATE. **Example 1** uses several different kinds of formats. **Examples 2** and **3** demonstrate tables containing statistics on readings produced by two hypothetical laboratory machines in each of several labs. This data set contains one observation for each machine for each day of the year. **Example 2** contains the values organized into reports on individual machines. **Example 3** reorganizes the table to place statistics for each machine in the row dimension.

All examples use FORMAT, LABEL, and KEYLABEL statements to provide descriptive titles. Statistic keyword labels illustrate automatic title splitting at blanks. **Example 3** illustrates explicit title splitting using hyphens in the formatted month names. Table cells are formatted in the page dimension except for frequency (N) cells. In each case a format associated with N overrides the page dimension format. The examples produce summary rows using the universal classifier ALL.

Using Various Formats: Example 1

```
DATA SALES;
   INPUT REGION $ CITYSIZE $ POP PRODUCT $ SALETYPE $ QUANTITY AMOUNT
   ;
   CARDS;
NC S    25000 A100 R 150    3750.00
NE S    37000 A100 R 200    5000.00
SO S    48000 A100 R 410   10250.00
WE S    32000 A100 R 180    4500.00
NC M   125000 A100 R 350    8750.00
NE M   237000 A100 R 600   15000.00
SO M   348000 A100 R 710   17750.00
WE M   432000 A100 R 780   19500.00
NC L   625000 A100 R 750   18750.00
NE L   837000 A100 R 800   20000.00
.
.
.
;

PROC FORMAT;
   VALUE $REGFMT NC='NORTH CENTRAL'
                 NE='NORTHEAST'
                 SO='SOUTH'
                 WE='WEST';
   VALUE $SIZEFMT S='UNDER 50000'
                  M='50000 TO 500000'
                  L='OVER 500000';
   VALUE $SALEFMT R='RETAIL'
                  W='WHOLESALE';

PROC FORMAT;
   PICTURE PCT LOW - <0 =  '000.00%' (PREFIX='-')
               0 - HIGH = '0000.00%';

PROC TABULATE;
   TITLE 'USING FORMATS';
   CLASS REGION SALETYPE;
   VAR   AMOUNT;
   FORMAT REGION $REGFMT.;
   FORMAT CITYSIZE $SIZEFMT.;
   FORMAT SALETYPE $SALEFMT.;
```

```
TABLE ALL*F=DOLLAR11. REGION*F=COMMA11.,      /*ROW DIMENSION*/

   SALETYPE='REGIONAL SALES ANALYSIS'*     /*COLUMN DIMENSION*/
       AMOUNT=' '*
       (SUM    PCTSUM<REGION ALL>*F=PCT.
       N*F=6. PCTN  <REGION ALL>*F=PCT.)

   /RTSPACE=12;                               /*TABLE OPTIONS*/

KEYLABEL SUM     = 'REVENUE'
         N       = 'LOCA-TIONS'
         PCTSUM = 'PERCENT OF SALES'
         PCTN    = 'PERCENT OF LOCNS'
         ALL     = 'TOTAL';
```

Output 26.17 Using Various Formats

USING FORMATS 1

	REGIONAL SALES ANALYSIS							
	RETAIL				WHOLESALE			
	REVENUE	PERCENT OF SALES	LOCA- TIONS	PERCENT OF LOCNS	REVENUE	PERCENT OF SALES	LOCA- TIONS	PERCENT OF LOCNS
TOTAL	$499,775	100.00%	36	100.00%	$399,220	100.00%	36	100.00%
REGION								
NORTH CENTRAL	95,200	19.04%	9	25.00%	76,200	19.08%	9	25.00%
NORTHEAST	121,725	24.35%	9	25.00%	97,380	24.39%	9	25.00%
SOUTH	143,450	28.70%	9	25.00%	114,120	28.58%	9	25.00%
WEST	139,400	27.89%	9	25.00%	111,520	27.93%	9	25.00%

Individual Reports of Machine Readings: Example 2

```
PROC FORMAT;
   VALUE MONFMT  1='JANUARY'
                 2='FEBRUARY'
                 3='MARCH'
                 4='APRIL'
                 5='MAY'
                 6='JUNE'
                 7='JULY'
                 8='AUGUST'
                 9='SEPTEMBER'
                10='OCTOBER'
                11='NOVEMBER'
                12='DECEMBER';

   VALUE MFMT    1='MACHINE 1'
                 2='MACHINE 2';
```

```
PROC TABULATE;
   TITLE 'MACHINE REPORT FORMAT1';
   CLASS LAB_ID M_ID MONTHNUM;
   VAR   READING;
   FORMAT MONTHNUM MONFMT.;
   FORMAT M_ID MFMT.;
   LABEL LAB_ID=LABORATORY
         M_ID='MACHINE LAB REPORT'
         MONTHNUM='MONTH';
   KEYLABEL ALL='SUMMARY'
            N='FREQUENCY'
            STD='STANDARD DEVIATION';
   TABLE LAB_ID*F=9.3, MONTHNUM ALL, M_ID*READING*
   (N*F=9. MEAN RANGE STD) / RTS=12;
```

Output 26.18 Individual Reports of Machine Readings

MACHINE REPORT FORMAT 1 1

LABORATORY 1

	MACHINE LAB REPORT							
	MACHINE 1				MACHINE 2			
	READING				READING			
	FREQUENCY	MEAN	RANGE	STANDARD DEVIATION	FREQUENCY	MEAN	RANGE	STANDARD DEVIATION
MONTH								
JANUARY	31	0.578	2.616	0.643	31	0.588	2.132	0.493
FEBRUARY	28	0.479	2.460	0.574	28	0.483	1.891	0.427
MARCH	31	0.527	2.215	0.515	31	0.582	2.046	0.502
APRIL	30	0.479	2.677	0.575	30	0.554	2.182	0.518
MAY	31	0.428	1.858	0.414	31	0.458	2.210	0.586
JUNE	30	0.579	2.467	0.589	30	0.339	1.726	0.439
JULY	31	0.529	2.133	0.466	31	0.464	2.353	0.578
AUGUST	31	0.445	2.068	0.453	31	0.528	1.837	0.457
SEPTEMBER	30	0.602	1.933	0.459	30	0.492	1.965	0.464
OCTOBER	31	0.576	2.355	0.627	31	0.474	1.726	0.437
NOVEMBER	30	0.542	2.082	0.532	30	0.413	2.085	0.531
DECEMBER	31	0.610	2.256	0.523	31	0.625	2.052	0.482
SUMMARY	365	0.532	3.000	0.530	365	0.501	2.669	0.495

MACHINE REPORT FORMAT 1 2

LABORATORY 2

MACHINE LAB REPORT								
	MACHINE 1				MACHINE 2			
	READING				READING			
	FREQUENCY	MEAN	RANGE	STANDARD DEVIATION	FREQUENCY	MEAN	RANGE	STANDARD DEVIATION
MONTH								
JANUARY	31	0.532	1.971	0.518	31	0.596	1.550	0.442
FEBRUARY	28	0.467	1.932	0.495	28	0.463	1.819	0.474
MARCH	31	0.410	1.997	0.567	31	0.442	1.537	0.429
APRIL	30	0.487	1.831	0.433	30	0.479	2.352	0.600
MAY	31	0.630	2.042	0.506	31	0.493	1.685	0.432
JUNE	30	0.497	2.468	0.631	30	0.528	1.843	0.510
JULY	31	0.563	1.974	0.495	31	0.688	1.645	0.388
AUGUST	31	0.578	1.800	0.396	31	0.450	2.170	0.446
SEPTEMBER	30	0.367	1.632	0.415	30	0.346	2.154	0.504
OCTOBER	31	0.621	1.735	0.428	31	0.535	2.068	0.451
NOVEMBER	30	0.459	1.773	0.464	30	0.557	1.809	0.468
DECEMBER	31	0.452	2.051	0.546	31	0.420	1.971	0.496
SUMMARY	365	0.506	2.719	0.494	365	0.500	2.566	0.473

Comparative Reports of Machine Readings by Rows: Example 3

This example uses the same machine data as **Example 2** but organizes the report differently.

```
PROC FORMAT;
   VALUE MONFMT  1='JANU-ARY'
                 2='FEBRU-ARY'
                 3='MARCH'
                 4='APRIL'
                 5='MAY'
                 6='JUNE'
                 7='JULY'
                 8='AUGUST'
                 9='SEPTEMBER'
                10='OCTO-BER'
                11='NOVEM-BER'
                12='DECEM-BER';

   VALUE MFMT    1='1'
                 2='2';


PROC TABULATE;
   TITLE 'MACHINE REPORT FORMAT 2';
   CLASS LAB_ID M_ID MONTHNUM;
   VAR   READING;
```

```
FORMAT MONTHNUM MONFMT.;
FORMAT M_ID MFMT.;
LABEL LAB_ID  ='LABORATORY'
      M_ID    ='MACHINE'
      MONTHNUM='MONTH';
KEYLABEL ALL='SUMMARY'
         N  ='NUMBER OF READINGS'
         STD='STANDARD DEVIATION';
TABLE LAB_ID*F=6.3, (M_ID ALL)*(N*F=6. MEAN RANGE STD),
      READING*(MONTHNUM ALL) / RTS=22;
```

Output 26.19 Comparative Reports of Machine Readings by Rows

MACHINE REPORT FORMAT 2 1

LABORATORY 1

		READING												
		MONTH												SUMMARY
MACHINE		JANUARY	FEBRUARY	MARCH	APRIL	MAY	JUNE	JULY	AUGUST	SEPTEMBER	OCTOBER	NOVEMBER	DECEMBER	
1	NUMBER OF READINGS	31	28	31	30	31	30	31	31	30	31	30	31	365
	MEAN	0.355	0.407	0.484	0.635	0.560	0.465	0.630	0.464	0.504	0.532	0.518	0.511	0.506
	RANGE	2.445	2.010	2.072	1.988	2.257	1.586	1.776	2.495	1.232	1.398	2.786	2.485	3.210
	STANDARD DEVIATION	0.600	0.494	0.445	0.497	0.532	0.404	0.457	0.474	0.326	0.380	0.623	0.569	0.490
2	NUMBER OF READINGS	31	28	31	30	31	30	31	31	30	31	30	31	365
	MEAN	0.531	0.512	0.576	0.478	0.378	0.595	0.504	0.533	0.419	0.612	0.535	0.512	0.516
	RANGE	2.038	2.167	2.047	2.132	1.853	2.128	2.429	2.648	2.385	1.287	2.622	2.358	3.043
	STANDARD DEVIATION	0.539	0.481	0.485	0.518	0.459	0.499	0.570	0.591	0.544	0.334	0.624	0.578	0.520
SUMMARY	NUMBER OF READINGS	62	56	62	60	62	60	62	62	60	62	60	62	730
	MEAN	0.443	0.459	0.530	0.556	0.469	0.530	0.567	0.499	0.461	0.572	0.526	0.511	0.511
	RANGE	2.869	2.479	2.173	2.441	2.308	2.290	2.429	2.746	2.385	1.398	2.961	2.752	3.292
	STANDARD DEVIATION	0.573	0.486	0.464	0.510	0.501	0.455	0.517	0.533	0.447	0.357	0.618	0.568	0.505

MACHINE REPORT FORMAT 2 2

LABORATORY 2

		READING												
		MONTH												SUMMARY
		JANUARY	FEBRUARY	MARCH	APRIL	MAY	JUNE	JULY	AUGUST	SEPTEMBER	OCTOBER	NOVEMBER	DECEMBER	
MACHINE														
1	NUMBER OF READINGS	31	28	31	30	31	30	31	31	30	31	30	31	365
	MEAN	0.510	0.490	0.594	0.488	0.572	0.498	0.450	0.601	0.685	0.551	0.656	0.545	0.554
	RANGE	1.927	2.592	1.252	2.338	1.583	2.070	1.864	2.348	1.920	2.403	2.399	2.144	2.941
	STANDARD DEVIATION	0.445	0.535	0.334	0.517	0.377	0.468	0.433	0.523	0.518	0.506	0.590	0.490	0.480
2	NUMBER OF READINGS	31	28	31	30	31	30	31	31	30	31	30	31	365
	MEAN	0.472	0.566	0.519	0.679	0.361	0.616	0.560	0.505	0.335	0.507	0.582	0.415	0.509
	RANGE	2.519	1.990	1.755	2.103	1.961	1.718	2.338	2.252	2.197	2.529	1.861	1.873	2.916
	STANDARD DEVIATION	0.607	0.474	0.472	0.522	0.460	0.425	0.543	0.493	0.493	0.603	0.468	0.467	0.507
SUMMARY	NUMBER OF READINGS	62	56	62	60	62	60	62	62	60	62	60	62	730
	MEAN	0.491	0.528	0.557	0.584	0.466	0.557	0.505	0.553	0.510	0.529	0.619	0.480	0.531
	RANGE	2.519	2.592	1.768	2.368	1.961	2.070	2.393	2.470	2.210	2.714	2.399	2.224	3.101
	STANDARD DEVIATION	0.528	0.503	0.408	0.524	0.430	0.448	0.490	0.506	0.532	0.553	0.529	0.479	0.494

Demographic Data Application: Example 4

Data for the following table are selected characteristics of U.S. cities with populations over 50,000 according to *County and City Data Book, 1983*. The class variables are POPGRP with three levels and REGION with four levels. The TABLE statement requests a table of POPGRP by REGION containing the number of observations, means, and standard deviation for the variable INCOMES, which is specified in the VAR statement. See **Output 26.20** for the resulting table.

```
PROC TABULATE DATA=CITIES;
   TITLE'CENSUS DATA: OUTPUT FROM TABULATE PROCEDURE';
   FORMAT POPGRP PC.;
   VAR INCOME;
   CLASS POPGRP REGION;
   TABLE POPGRP*REGION, INCOME*(N*F=4.0 MEAN STD) / RTSPACE=22;
```

Output 26.20 Demographic Data Application

CENSUS DATA: OUTPUT FROM TABULATE PROCEDURE 1

1980 POPULATION ESTIMATE	REGION	PER CAPITA MONEY INCOME (1979) N	MEAN	STD
50,001-75,000	NORTH CENTRAL	46	8255.61	1863.10
	NORTHEAST	33	6903.67	1044.48
	SOUTH	40	7144.55	1263.73
	WEST	43	8527.63	2421.11
75,001-100,000	NORTH CENTRAL	27	7889.59	1520.11
	NORTHEAST	18	6652.89	1743.41
	SOUTH	13	6621.85	1548.09
	WEST	29	8006.28	1637.41
OVER 100,000	NORTH CENTRAL	39	7354.59	941.13
	NORTHEAST	23	6474.70	1197.22
	SOUTH	61	7170.39	1171.39
	WEST	46	8255.61	1180.18

A Marketing Research Application: Example 5

The following marketing research example analyzes advertisement recognition. Each observation contains the sex, income, and yes/no responses of a participant in the study. A yes response is coded as 1, a no response as 0. The DATA step sets the variable NORESP to 1 if all participant responses are missing; otherwise, it sets NORESP to missing. "No" responses are recoded as missing. The first table accumulates the count of nonmissing response values for each ad variable (AD1-AD7) and crosstabulates response frequencies with participant age, sex, and income. The second table crosstabulates income with ad recognition frequencies and calculates percentage of response for each level of income. See **Output 26.21** for the two tables.

Ideas for this example were contributed by The Guttman Group, Inc.

```
PROC FORMAT;
   VALUE AGEFMT 0-29 = 'UNDER 30'
                30-49= '30-49'
                50-70= '50-70'
                OTHER= 'OVER 70';
   VALUE INCFMT 0-9999 = 'UNDER 10,000'
                10000-15000 = '10,000-15,000'
                15001-50000 = 'OVER 15000'
                . = 'NO ANSWER';
   VALUE $SEXFMT 'M'=MALE
                 'F'=FEMALE;
```

```
OPTIONS LS=120;
PROC TABULATE F=10. MISSING FORMCHAR='
   TITLE 'AD RECOGNITION STUDY';
   CLASS SEX AGE INCOME;
   VAR   AD1 AD2 AD3 AD4 AD5 AD6 AD7 NORESP;

   FORMAT AGE AGEFMT.;
   FORMAT INCOME INCFMT.;
   FORMAT SEX $SEXFMT.;

   LABEL  AD1 = 'MAN IN CLOWN SUIT'
          AD2 = 'MAN IN ONE RED SHOE'
          AD3 = 'CLOCK FACE'
          AD4 = 'SILHOUETTE'
          AD5 = 'SAW SOMETHING IN MAGAZINE'
          AD6 = 'SAW SOMETHING ON TV'
          AD7 = 'SAW SOMETHING IN NEWSPAPER'
          NORESP = 'NO RESPONSE';

   TABLE ALL='----   TOTAL    ----'          /*ROW DIMENSION*/
         AD1 AD2 AD3 AD4 AD5 AD6 AD7 NORESP,

         (ALL                                 /*COLUMN DIMENSION*/
          SEX='+---S E X---+'
          AGE='+----------A G E----------+'
          INCOME='+-------I N C O M E-------+')
          *N='------'*F=6.
         / RTS=30
           BOX='NUMBER OF NON-MISSING RESPONSES FOR EACH AD';

   TABLE ALL*(N PCTN) INCOME*PCTN,
         ALL AD1 AD2 AD3 AD4 AD5 AD6 AD7
         / RTS=18 ROW=FLOAT
           BOX='RESPONSE PERCENTAGES FOR INCOME LEVELS';

   KEYLABEL N='COUNT'
            ALL='TOTAL'
            PCTN='PERCENT';
```

Output 26.21 A Marketing Research Application

```
                                           AD RECOGNITION STUDY                                              1

NUMBER OF NON-MISSING                                 +----------A G E----------+ +-------I N C O M E-------+
RESPONSES FOR EACH AD              +---S E X---+                                                              
                                                   UNDER                      OVER    NO   UNDER  10,000  OVER
                            TOTAL  FEMALE  MALE     30    30-49  50-70     70  ANSWER 10,000 15,000 15000
                           ------ ------ ------ ------ ------ ------ ------ ------ ------ ------ ------

----    TOTAL    ----         100     53     47     34     26     15     25     11     21     11     57
MAN IN CLOWN SUIT              34     18     16     18      5      5      6      3      7      4     20
```

(continued on next page)

(continued from previous page)

MAN IN ONE RED SHOE	62	25	37	21	16	10	15	6	15	6	35
CLOCK FACE	31	15	16	9	5	5	12	2	8	2	19
SILHOUETTE	27	11	16	7	6	5	9	3	5	3	16
SAW SOMETHING IN MAGAZINE	44	28	16	17	14	3	10	7	7	6	24
SAW SOMETHING ON TV	28	14	14	7	8	4	9	3	7	1	17
SAW SOMETHING IN NEWSPAPER	19	13	6	6	5	3	5	2	6	3	8
NO RESPONSE	2	2	0	2	0	0	0	0	1	1	0

AD RECOGNITION STUDY 2

RESPONSE PERCENTAGES FOR INCOME LEVELS		TOTAL	MAN IN CLOWN SUIT	MAN IN ONE RED SHOE	CLOCK FACE	SILHOUETTE	SAW SOMETHING IN MAGAZINE	SAW SOMETHING ON TV	SAW SOMETHING IN NEWSPAPER
TOTAL	COUNT	100	34	62	31	27	44	28	19
	PERCENT	100	100	100	100	100	100	100	100
INCOME									
NO ANSWER	PERCENT	11	9	10	6	11	16	11	11
UNDER 10,000	PERCENT	21	21	24	26	19	16	25	32
10,000- 15,000	PERCENT	11	12	10	6	11	14	4	16
OVER 15000	PERCENT	57	59	56	61	59	55	61	42

A Detailed Budget Summary: Example 6

This example uses a DATA step to calculate row totals and PROC TABULATE to display the report with column sub-totals and totals. See **Output 26.22**.

```
PROC FORMAT;
   VALUE DEPT 1='ACCOUNTING'
              2='HUMAN RESOURCES'
              3='SYSTEMS'
              4='PRODUCTION'
              5='MARKETING' ;

DATA TABULATE;
   INPUT DEPT ACCT JAN FEB MAR BUDGET;
   TOTAL=JAN + FEB + MAR;
   LEFT=BUDGET - TOTAL;
CARDS;
01  01345  12980  14009  17800  40000
01  01578   8000   7900   4500  40000
01  01674  11950  13534  17994  40000
02  02134  34520  26560  24399  80000
02  02403  10435  15494  10009  40000
03  04138  24850  22530  24399  70000
```

```
03  04279   9984  14209  13500  40000
03  04290  10948  14539  11459  40000
04  05139  12000  14532  12098  40000
04  05260  15893  14099   7304  40000
04  05370  11980  13900  11480  40000
04  05399  20435  19095  18053  60000
05  06120  23435  23543  19054  60000
05  06342  13049  15349  18943  50000
05  06401  20943  25943  19432  65000
;

PROC TABULATE;
   TITLE1 '  ';
   TITLE2 '  ';
   TITLE3 'FLEET FOOTWEAR, INC.';
   TITLE4 'DEPARTMENTAL BUDGETARY REPORT';
   TITLE5 'FOR THE FIRST QUARTER';
   TITLE6 '  ';
   CLASS DEPT ACCT;
   VAR JAN FEB MAR TOTAL LEFT BUDGET;
   FORMAT DEPT DEPT.;
   LABEL TOTAL='QUARTER TOTAL';
   LABEL BUDGET='ALLOCATED FUNDS';
   LABEL LEFT='REMAINING FUNDS';
   LABEL JAN='JANUARY EXPENDITURES';
   LABEL FEB='FEBRUARY EXPENDITURES';
   LABEL MAR='MARCH EXPENDITURES';

   TABLE /*---ROW DIMENSION---*/
        (DEPT=' '*(ACCT=' ' ALL='SUB-TOTAL') ALL='TOTAL')
        *F=COMMA12.2,

        /*---COLUMN DIMENSION---*/
        ((JAN FEB MAR)*SUM=' '
        TOTAL*SUM=' '
        (BUDGET LEFT)*SUM=' ') /

        /*---TABLE OPTIONS---*/
        BOX='DEPARTMENT      ACCOUNT';
```

Output 26.22 A Detailed Budget Summary

1

FLEET FOOTWEAR, INC.
DEPARTMENTAL BUDGETARY REPORT
FOR THE FIRST QUARTER

DEPARTMENT	ACCOUNT	JANUARY EXPENDITURES	FEBRUARY EXPENDITURES	MARCH EXPENDITURES	QUARTER TOTAL	ALLOCATED FUNDS	REMAINING FUNDS
ACCOUNTING	1345	12,980.00	14,009.00	17,800.00	44,789.00	40,000.00	-4,789.00
	1578	8,000.00	7,900.00	4,500.00	20,400.00	40,000.00	19,600.00
	1674	11,950.00	13,534.00	17,994.00	43,478.00	40,000.00	-3,478.00
	SUB-TOTAL	32,930.00	35,443.00	40,294.00	108,667.00	120,000.00	11,333.00
HUMAN RESOURCES	2134	34,520.00	26,560.00	24,399.00	85,479.00	80,000.00	-5,479.00
	2403	10,435.00	15,494.00	10,009.00	35,938.00	40,000.00	4,062.00
	SUB-TOTAL	44,955.00	42,054.00	34,408.00	121,417.00	120,000.00	-1,417.00
SYSTEMS	4138	24,850.00	22,530.00	24,399.00	71,779.00	70,000.00	-1,779.00
	4279	9,984.00	14,209.00	13,500.00	37,693.00	40,000.00	2,307.00
	4290	10,948.00	14,539.00	11,459.00	36,946.00	40,000.00	3,054.00
	SUB-TOTAL	45,782.00	51,278.00	49,358.00	146,418.00	150,000.00	3,582.00
PRODUCTION	5139	12,000.00	14,532.00	12,098.00	38,630.00	40,000.00	1,370.00
	5260	15,893.00	14,099.00	7,304.00	37,296.00	40,000.00	2,704.00
	5370	11,980.00	13,900.00	11,480.00	37,360.00	40,000.00	2,640.00
	5399	20,435.00	19,095.00	18,053.00	57,583.00	60,000.00	2,417.00
	SUB-TOTAL	60,308.00	61,626.00	48,935.00	170,869.00	180,000.00	9,131.00
MARKETING	6120	23,435.00	23,543.00	19,054.00	66,032.00	60,000.00	-6,032.00
	6342	13,049.00	15,349.00	18,943.00	47,341.00	50,000.00	2,659.00
	6401	20,943.00	25,943.00	19,432.00	66,318.00	65,000.00	-1,318.00
	SUB-TOTAL	57,427.00	64,835.00	57,429.00	179,691.00	175,000.00	-4,691.00
TOTAL		241,402.00	255,236.00	230,424.00	727,062.00	745,000.00	17,938.00

Medical Events by Age Group: Example 7

This example displays row, column, and data set percentages in the same table. Data are for a hypothetical survey of medical events in a study population. Each observation contains a numeric subject id, the age of the subject, and a medical event code. On the table, % OF THIS EVENT shows how each event is distributed across age groups, a row percent. % OF AGE GROUP shows how each age group is distributed across events, a column percent. % OF ALL EVENTS shows how the whole population is distributed across events and age groups, a data set percentage. See **Output 26.23** for the resulting table.

```
PROC FORMAT;
   VALUE AGEFMT 0  - 20 = '30 - 35'
                21 - 50 = '36 - 40'
                51 - 70 = '41 - 45'
                71 -100 = '46 - 50';
   VALUE CDFMT  0  - 50 = 'CHEST PAIN'
                51 - 75 = 'HOSPITAL VISIT'
                76 - 90 = 'HEART ATTACK'
                91 -100 = 'MORTALITY';

PROC TABULATE F=7.2;
   TITLE 'MEDICAL EVENTS';
   CLASS AGE CODE;
   VAR ID;

   TABLE
         /*---ROW DIMENSION---*/
         (ALL CODE=' ')*
            ( N*F=5.
             (PCTN<ID AGE>='% OF THIS EVENT'
              PCTN<CODE ALL>='% OF AGE GROUP'
              PCTN<ALL*AGE*ID ALL*ID CODE*AGE*ID CODE*ID>
                              ='% OF ALL EVENTS' )*F=7.2),

         /*---COLUMN DIMENSION---*/
         ID AGE

         /*---TABLE OPTIONS---*/
         / RTS=33 MISSTEXT='NONE'
           BOX='MEDICAL EVENTS BY AGE GROUP';

   LABEL ID = 'ALL AGE GROUPS'
         AGE = 'AGE GROUPS';

   FORMAT AGE AGEFMT.;
   FORMAT CODE CDFMT.;

   KEYLABEL ALL = 'ALL EVENTS'
              N = 'FREQUENCY';
```

Output 26.23 Row, Column, and Data Set Percents

MEDICAL EVENTS   1

MEDICAL EVENTS BY AGE GROUP		ALL AGE GROUPS	AGE GROUPS 30 - 35	36 - 40	41 - 45	46 - 50
ALL EVENTS	FREQUENCY	100	15	35	21	29
	% OF THIS EVENT	100.00	15.00	35.00	21.00	29.00
	% OF AGE GROUP	100.00	100.00	100.00	100.00	100.00
	% OF ALL EVENTS	100.00	15.00	35.00	21.00	29.00
CHEST PAIN	FREQUENCY	50	6	19	10	15
	% OF THIS EVENT	100.00	12.00	38.00	20.00	30.00
	% OF AGE GROUP	50.00	40.00	54.29	47.62	51.72
	% OF ALL EVENTS	50.00	6.00	19.00	10.00	15.00
HOSPITAL VISIT	FREQUENCY	20	3	5	6	6
	% OF THIS EVENT	100.00	15.00	25.00	30.00	30.00
	% OF AGE GROUP	20.00	20.00	14.29	28.57	20.69
	% OF ALL EVENTS	20.00	3.00	5.00	6.00	6.00
HEART ATTACK	FREQUENCY	24	4	8	5	7
	% OF THIS EVENT	100.00	16.67	33.33	20.83	29.17
	% OF AGE GROUP	24.00	26.67	22.86	23.81	24.14
	% OF ALL EVENTS	24.00	4.00	8.00	5.00	7.00
MORTALITY	FREQUENCY	6	2	3	NONE	1
	% OF THIS EVENT	100.00	33.33	50.00	NONE	16.67
	% OF AGE GROUP	6.00	13.33	8.57	NONE	3.45
	% OF ALL EVENTS	6.00	2.00	3.00	NONE	1.00

A Multiple Response Survey: Example 8

In many cases you can use TABULATE to analyze multiple response data. In this example the survey questions are

1. Which cereal do you buy?
2. Which of the following reasons made you choose this cereal? (Circle all that apply.)

   Flavor
   Texture
   Nutritional value
   Price
   Availability.

Each observation contains a respondent id, a cereal code, and five yes/no (1/missing) response values. Percentages in the table are percentages of respondents for each cereal. You can easily obtain percentages of total respondents as well. See the resulting table in **Output 26.24**.

```
PROC FORMAT;
   VALUE CFMT 1 = 'CRUNCHY NUGGETS'
              2 = 'BREAK-FAST FANTASY'
              3 = 'SUNRISE SERE-NADE'
              4 = 'SUGAR BOWL'
              5 = 'FULL-O-FIBER';

PROC TABULATE F=7.2;
   TITLE 'MULTIPLE RESPONSES';
   CLASS CEREAL;
   VAR ID R1-R5;
   TABLE ID*N='RESPONDENTS'*F=7.
         (R1 R2 R3 R4 R5)*(N='COUNT'*F=7. PCTN<ID>='PERCENT'),
         CEREAL=' ' ALL='ALL CEREALS'
         / RTS=27 BOX='CEREAL SURVEY';
   LABEL ID='TOTAL'
         R1='FLAVOR'
         R2='TEXTURE'
         R3='NUTRITIONAL VALUE'
         R4='PRICE'
         R5='AVAILABIL-ITY';
   FORMAT CEREAL CFMT.;
```

Output 26.24 Multiple Response Survey

MULTIPLE RESPONSES 1

CEREAL SURVEY		CRUNCHY NUGGETS	BREAK-FAST FANTASY	SUNRISE SERE-NADE	SUGAR BOWL	FULL-O-FIBER	ALL CEREALS
TOTAL	RESPONDENTS	270	322	312	267	329	1500
FLAVOR	COUNT	215	266	247	215	255	1198
	PERCENT	79.63	82.61	79.17	80.52	77.51	79.87
TEXTURE	COUNT	212	239	228	198	249	1126
	PERCENT	78.52	74.22	73.08	74.16	75.68	75.07
NUTRITIONAL VALUE	COUNT	173	206	204	161	224	968
	PERCENT	64.07	63.98	65.38	60.30	68.09	64.53
PRICE	COUNT	132	163	160	134	159	748
	PERCENT	48.89	50.62	51.28	50.19	48.33	49.87
AVAILABIL-ITY	COUNT	108	127	122	104	129	590
	PERCENT	40.00	39.44	39.10	38.95	39.21	39.33

REFERENCES

County and City Data Book, 1983 Files on Tape (machine-readable data file)/ prepared by the Bureau of the Census. Washington: The Bureau (producer and distributor), 1984.

County and City Data Book, 1983 Files on Tape Technical Documentation/ prepared by the Data User Services Division, Bureau of the Census. Washington: The Bureau, 1984.

Chapter 27

The TIMEPLOT Procedure

ABSTRACT

The TIMEPLOT procedure is used to plot one or more variables over time intervals.

INTRODUCTION

For each plot requested, PROC TIMEPLOT produces a plot and a listing of observations in the data set similar to that produced by PROC PLOT and PROC PRINT.

However, the TIMEPLOT procedure has several distinctive features:

- The vertical axis always represents the sequence of observations in the data set; thus, if the observations are arranged in date or time order, the vertical axis represents time.
- The horizontal axis contains values of the variable or variables you are examining.
- A plot produced by TIMEPLOT may occupy more than one page.
- Each observation appears sequentially on a separate line of the plot; no observations are "hidden", as may occur with the PLOT procedure.
- Each observation in the plot is accompanied by a printing of the values plotted.

PROC TIMEPLOT is especially useful for combining multiple observations into a single line in the plot. TIMEPLOT can also overlay multiple plots on a single set of axes, as PLOT does.

Output 27.1 illustrates one type of plot produced by TIMEPLOT. In this example, the plotting section contains the high, low, and closing values of the Dow Jones Index of prices on the New York Stock Exchange. The symbols for the variables are joined by a line. The minimum and maximum values label the horizontal axis; a vertical reference line appears at the mean low value. The listing on the left side of the output contains, for each observation, the date and volume of stocks traded; and the low, closing, and high prices for that day are printed for each observation. The statements that produced this example appear in the **Examples** section at the end of the chapter.

Output 27.1 High-Low-Close Stock Market Report: PROC TIMEPLOT

```
                                            HIGH-LOW-CLOSE STOCK MARKET DATA                                             1

   DATE     VOLUME IN         LOW      CLOSE       HIGH     MIN                                                        MAX
            THOUSANDS                                       883.66                                                  961.47
            OF SHARES                                       *------------------------------------------------------------*
03AUG81     3219.3         940.45     946.25     955.48     |                             |              L---C------H    |
04AUG81     2938.5         937.40     945.97     951.39     |                             |            L-----C---H       |
05AUG81     4177.8         942.16     953.58     958.81     |                             |               L--------C---H |
06AUG81     3975.7         947.30     952.91     961.47     |                             |                   L----C----H|
07AUG81     3884.3         938.45     942.54     954.15     |                             |             L--C-------H     |
10AUG81     2937.7         935.88     943.68     948.82     |                             |           L-----C--H         |
11AUG81     5262.9         939.50     949.30     955.48     |                             |             L-------C---H    |
12AUG81     4005.2         942.26     945.21     955.86     |                             |               L--C-------H   |
13AUG81     3680.8         938.55     944.35     952.91     |                             |             L---C------H     |
14AUG81     3714.1         933.79     936.93     947.77     |                             |         L-C--------H         |
17AUG81     3432.7         924.37     926.75     939.40     |                             | L-C--------H                 |
18AUG81     4396.7         916.38     924.37     932.74     |                         L---|-C-----H                      |
19AUG81     3517.3         918.38     926.46     932.08     |                          L--|--C----H                      |
20AUG81     3811.9         923.52     928.37     935.31     |                             |L---C----H                    |
21AUG81     2625.9         917.14     920.57     930.65     |                         L--C|------H                       |
24AUG81     4736.1         896.97     900.11     917.43     |          L-C-------------H  |                              |
25AUG81     4714.4         887.46     901.83     904.30     |   L----------C-H            |                              |
26AUG81     3279.6         893.65     899.26     908.39     |        L---C------H         |                              |
27AUG81     3676.1         883.66     889.08     900.49     |L---C--------H               |                              |
28AUG81     3024.2         884.80     892.22     898.78     | L----C----H                 |                              |
                                                            *------------------------------------------------------------*
```

SPECIFICATIONS

The following statements are used to control the TIMEPLOT procedure:

> **PROC TIMEPLOT** *options;*
> **PLOT** *requests / options;*
> **CLASS** *variables;*
> **BY** *variables;*
> **ID** *variables;*

No more than one CLASS, ID, and BY statement should appear. There is no restriction on the number of PLOT statements that can be given.

PROC TIMEPLOT Statement

PROC TIMEPLOT *options;*

The following options are used with the PROC TIMEPLOT statement:

UNIFORM indicates that the scale used for a given plot request is to be the same for all BY groups. If UNIFORM is omitted and a BY statement is used, the scale is determined for each BY group separately. In addition, UNIFORM indicates that a REF= specification (see below) of the form MEAN(*variables*) is to represent the mean over all observations for all BY groups.

MAXDEC=*n* indicates the maximum number of decimal positions printed for a number. A decimal specification in a format overrides a MAXDEC= specification. The default is MAXDEC=2.

PLOT Statement

PLOT *requests / options;*

The PLOT statement specifies the plots to be produced. One PROC TIMEPLOT statement can be followed by several PLOT statements, and each PLOT statement can request several plots.

Each plot specification consists of a variable with an optional symbol variable or value. Unless the OVERLAY option is used, each variable specified appears in a separate plot. A plot specification can be given as any of the following types:

variable1...variablen
variable1=symbol1...variablen=symboln
(variables)=symbol1...(variables)=symboln

Variable1...variablen indicates that each variable is to be plotted using the default symbol, the first character of the variable name. For example, the statement

```
PLOT GROSS NET;
```

causes the values of GROSS to be plotted with a G and the values of NET with an N.

Variable1=symbol1... variablen=symboln indicates that each variable is to be plotted using the symbol specified. The symbol can be a single character enclosed in quotes or a variable name. If a variable name is given, the first nonblank character of the formatted value of the variable is used as the plotting symbol. The symbol variable may be either character or numeric. In this example

```
PLOT GROSS='*' NET=PROFLOSS;
```

the values of GROSS are plotted using an asterisk (*) and the values of NET are plotted using the first nonblank character of the value of PROFLOSS for that observation.

(Variables)=symbol1...(variables)= symboln indicates that each variable within the parentheses is to be plotted using the symbol associated with that group. The symbol may be a single character enclosed in single quotes or a variable name. If a variable name is given, the first nonblank character of the formatted value of the variable is used as the plotting symbol. For example, the statement

```
PLOT (NC SC VA GL FL)='*'
     (AL AR MS LA TX)='+';
```

plots the values of the variables in the first group using an asterisk (*) and the values of variables in the second group using a cross (+). A single PLOT statement can contain requests in more than one of these forms.

The listing on the left side of the output contains different information depending on whether a CLASS statement is used. If no CLASS statement is used, each observation is printed (and plotted) on a separate line. If a CLASS statement is used without a symbol variable being specified, all observations for a given combination of class variable values are plotted on the same line; the last value of the plotting variable appears in the print column, thus omitting some values from printing and plotting. If a CLASS statement and a symbol variable are used, all observations for a given combination of CLASS variable values are plotted on the same line, using the first-character values of the symbol variable as plotting characters. In the print section, each value of the symbol variable has a different column, and the value of the plotting variable is printed in the column for its symbol value. If more than one observation within a class has the same value of a symbol variable, only the first occurrence of the value is plotted and printed, and a warning message appears in the log.

The following options are used with the PLOT statement:

OVERLAY
: indicates that all the plot specifications requested in the PLOT statement are to be printed in the same plot. Otherwise, each specification is printed separately.

HILOC
: indicates that the leftmost non-reference symbol is to be connected to the rightmost non-reference symbol by a line of hyphens (-). The HILOC option is ignored if the JOINREF option is also specified. This option is often used in HIGH-LOW-CLOSE applications.

JOINREF
: indicates that the leftmost symbol is to connect to the rightmost symbol, regardless of whether the symbols are reference symbols or plotting symbols. However, if a line contains only reference symbols, the symbols are not connected.

REVERSE
: indicates that the plot is to be printed with the values of the horizontal axis descending, so that the maximum value is plotted in the leftmost plot position and the minimum value is plotted in the rightmost position. This order of plotting is also used if the AXIS= values are in descending order. Therefore, if AXIS= is specified with descending values, the REVERSE option is ignored.

POS=*n*
: indicates the number of positions comprising the plotting section. If you specify POS=0 and also specify the AXIS= option, the plot is expanded to fill the page, with each axis value comprising several plot positions instead of just one. If POS= and AXIS= are both omitted, an initial POS= value of 20 is assumed, but it may be increased to fill the page width along with the value section. See the **Details** section for more information.

AXIS=*specification*
: indicates the tick marks for the horizontal axis. When you specify an AXIS= value, each tick mark of the axis range consists of one plot column unless the POS= option is also specified. (See the POS= option for more information.) Examples of axis specifications include the following:

Specification	Tick marks
AXIS=10 TO 100 BY 10	10, 20, 30...100
AXIS=10,30,40	10, 30, 40
AXIS=10,20,30 TO 40 BY 2	10, 20, 30, 32...40
AXIS='01JAN85'D TO	01JAN85 01FEB85...
'01JAN86'D BY MONTH	01JAN86
'01JAN86'D BY QTR	01JAN85 01APR85...
	01JAN86

In the last two examples, the FROM and TO values can be any of the valid SAS date, time, or datetime values described for the SAS functions INTCK and INTNX. The BY value can be any of the valid values listed for the *interval* argument in the SAS functions INTCK and INTNX. You must use a FORMAT statement to print the tick mark values in an understandable form.

If an AXIS= list is given, the scale of the plot is not modified to encompass all values of plotting variables or reference lines. Any plotting value outside the range specified by AXIS= is indicated by a < or > on the left or right border of the plot, respectively. A REF= value outside the AXIS= range is ignored.

REF=*values*

indicates the position of one or more vertical reference lines in the plotting section. Constant values may be given, as well as values in the form

MEAN(*variables*)

If values of this form are given, the mean is evaluated for each variable in parentheses, and a reference line is drawn for each.

If UNIFORM is specified in the TIMEPLOT statement, the MEAN values are the calculated mean for the variables over all observations for all BY groups.

If any REF= value is less than the minimum value of any plotting variable, or if any REF= value is greater than the maximum of any plotting variable, the scale of the plot is adjusted to allow the reference line to be printed (unless the AXIS= option is used). Reference lines are printed using the character specified in the REFCHAR= option (or |, if none is specified). If a plotting variable value is to be plotted in the column where a REF= value goes, the plotting symbol is printed instead of the REFCHAR= value.

REFCHAR=*charactervalue*

indicates the character to print for reference lines. If no REFCHAR= option is given, the vertical bar (|) is used. If you are using the JOINREF or HILOC option, you should not use a REFCHAR that is the same as any plotting symbol since TIMEPLOT does not connect REFCHAR symbols to each other.

OVPCHAR=*charactervalue*

indicates the character to be printed if two plotting symbols are to be plotted in the same column. If no OVPCHAR= option is given, @ is used. Note that if a plotting symbol is to be plotted on the same column as a REFCHAR value, the plotting symbol is printed, not the OVPCHAR value. TIMEPLOT never actually overprints two symbols.

NOSYMNAME

controls whether symbol variable names are printed in the column headings for symbol values when a CLASS statement is used. If the NOSYMNAME option is used, only the value of the symbol variable appears in the column heading, as in

VALUE
PLOTTING VARIABLE

If NOSYMNAME is omitted, headings have the form

SYMBOLNAME: VALUE
PLOTTING VARIABLE

If a CLASS statement is not used, this option is ignored.

CLASS Statement

CLASS *variables;*

If a CLASS statement is used, only one line is printed for each combination of class variable values. It is not necessary that the data be sorted by the class variables, but the output may be more meaningful if the data are grouped according to values of the class variables. (The grouping of data is similar to applications of other procedures that use the NOTSORTED option in a BY statement.) Class variables can be numeric or character. The CLASS statement is normally used only in conjunction with a symbol variable. Class variable values are printed, but not plotted. Only one CLASS statement can be used.

BY Statement

BY *variables;*

A BY statement can be used with PROC TIMEPLOT to obtain separate plots for observations in groups defined by the BY variables. When a BY statement appears, the procedure expects the input data set to be sorted in order of the BY variables. If your input data set is not sorted in ascending order, use the SORT procedure with a similar BY statement to sort the data, or, if appropriate, use the BY statement options NOTSORTED or DESCENDING. For more information, see the discussion of the BY statement in *SAS Language Guide for Personal Computers*. The BY statement should appear only once.

ID Statement

ID *variables;*

The ID statement is used to print variables in the printed value section without plotting them. ID variables can be numeric or character. Only one ID statement can be used.

DETAILS

Missing Values

A missing value of a plotting variable appears as a missing value (. or one of the special missing values A-Z and underscore) in the listing, and it is not plotted.

If a CLASS statement and a symbol value are used, the observations in a given class may not contain all values of the symbol variable. For example, if the values of the symbol variable are 'PREDICTED' and 'ACTUAL', classes representing future dates may not have a value for 'ACTUAL'. In this case the value of ACTUAL is represented in the print section by a blank and is not plotted.

A missing value of a CLASS variable is treated as a valid level of the variable and defines a class of observations. The missing value appears as a missing value in the print section. A missing value of an ID variable is printed as a missing value. A missing value of a symbol variable is treated like any other value of that variable. A print column is established for that value and the value is plotted. However, even if the missing value is a blank (as occurs when the symbol variable is a character variable), the column heading and the plot represent the value as a period (.) .

Input Data Set

The input data set usually contains a date variable to be used as either a CLASS or an ID variable. Although the data set does not have to be sorted by date, the output is usually more meaningful if the data are in chronological order. In addition, if a CLASS statement is used, the output is more meaningful if observations are grouped according to combinations of CLASS variable values. CLASS, ID, BY, and symbol variables can be numeric or character; plotting variables must be numeric.

Printed Output

The procedure prints one or more pages of printed values and plots for each plot request. The page is divided into two sections: the listing and the plot.

The listing contains printed values for

1. CLASS variables.
2. ID variables (the value printed for each ID variable is the first value in that class group).
3. plotting variables.
4. column headings for CLASS and ID variables. These consist of either variable labels (if they are present and if space permits) or variable names. To suppress variable labels in column headings, use the NOLABEL system option. (See the OPTIONS statement in *SAS Language Guide for Personal Computers* for a description of the NOLABEL option.)
5. column headings for plotting variables. These consist of two parts: the variable label or name, and the name (unless NOSYMNAME is used) and value of the symbol variable (if a CLASS statement and a symbol variable are both used). If a format is associated with a variable, the value is printed using that format.

The plot contains

6. plotted values of variables.
7. tick marks.
8. reference lines. The maximum and minimum values of the horizontal axis are the maximum and minimum values of the data. The plot is

labeled with the minimum and maximum values being plotted, if space permits.

9. if a POS= value is given, a page arrangement as follows: (1) the size of the plot is determined from the POS= values; (2) the space for the listing is determined from the width of the columns of printed values, equally spaced and with a maximum of five positions between columns; (3) the output is centered on the page. If a POS= value is not given, the width of the listing is determined, and the plot is expanded to fill the rest of the page.
10. if there is not sufficient room for all values to be printed along with a plot, an error message in the log. That plot is not printed; however, other plots are not affected.

EXAMPLES

How Well a Model Fits the Data: Example 1

This example uses TIMEPLOT to demonstrate how well a model fits actual data. The REG procedure is used to produce the data. First, TIMEPLOT overlays the plot of a predicted and an actual value. The mean of the actual values is given as a reference line. Next, TIMEPLOT shows how residuals digress from the origin by using the REF=0 option to produce a reference line at the origin and the JOINREF option to connect the residuals with the origin. See **Output 27.2.**

```
DATA GRUNFELD;
   INPUT YEAR I F C @@;
   LABEL I='GROSS INVESTMENT GE'
         C='CAPITAL STOCK LAGGED GE'
         F='VALUE OF SHARES GE LAGGED';
   CARDS;
1935  33.1  1170.6  97.8   1936  45.0  2015.8 104.4
1937  77.2  2803.3 118.0   1938  44.6  2039.7 156.2
1939  48.1  2256.2 172.6   1940  74.4  2132.2 186.6
1941 113.0  1834.1 220.9   1942  91.9  1588.0 287.8
1943  61.3  1749.4 319.9   1944  56.8  1687.2 321.3
1945  93.6  2007.7 319.6   1946 159.9  2208.3 346.0
1947 147.2  1656.7 456.4   1948 146.3  1604.4 543.4
1949  98.3  1431.8 618.3   1950  93.5  1610.5 647.4
1951 135.2  1819.4 671.3   1952 157.3  2079.7 726.1
1953 179.5  2371.6 800.3   1954 189.6  2759.9 888.9
;
PROC REG;
   MODEL I = F C ;
   OUTPUT OUT=C R=RESID P=PRED;
   TITLE 'GRUNFELD''S INVESTMENT MODEL';
PROC TIMEPLOT DATA=C;
   PLOT PRED='P' I='A'/OVERLAY REF=MEAN(I);
   PLOT RESID/JOINREF REF=0;
```

Output 27.2 Fitting a Model to Actual Data: PROC TIMEPLOT

```
                              GRUNFELD'S INVESTMENT MODEL                                        1

DEP VARIABLE: I        GROSS INVESTMENT GE
                                        ANALYSIS OF VARIANCE

                                     SUM OF          MEAN
              SOURCE     DF         SQUARES        SQUARE      F VALUE       PROB>F

              MODEL       2     31632.03023   15816.01511       20.344       0.0001
              ERROR      17     13216.58777     777.44634
              C TOTAL    19     44848.61800

                 ROOT MSE        27.88272     R-SQUARE        0.7053
                 DEP MEAN          102.29     ADJ R-SQ        0.6706
                 C.V.             27.2585

                                        PARAMETER ESTIMATES

                            PARAMETER        STANDARD      T FOR H0:                       VARIABLE
     VARIABLE  DF            ESTIMATE           ERROR    PARAMETER=0     PROB > |T|          LABEL

     INTERCEP   1         -9.95630645     31.37424914         -0.317         0.7548     INTERCEPT
     F          1          0.02655119      0.01556610          1.706         0.1063     VALUE OF SHARES GE LAGGED
     C          1          0.15169387      0.02570408          5.902         0.0001     CAPITAL STOCK LAGGED GE
```

GRUNFELD'S INVESTMENT MODEL 2

❸ PREDICTED VALUE	❹ GROSS INVESTMENT ❸ GE
35.96	33.10
59.40	45.00
82.37	77.20
67.89	44.60
76.13	48.10
74.96	74.40
72.25	113.00
75.86	91.90
85.02	61.30
83.58	56.80
91.83	93.60
101.16	159.90
103.26	147.20
115.07	146.30
121.85	98.30
131.01	93.50
140.18	135.20
155.41	157.30
174.41	179.50
198.16	189.60

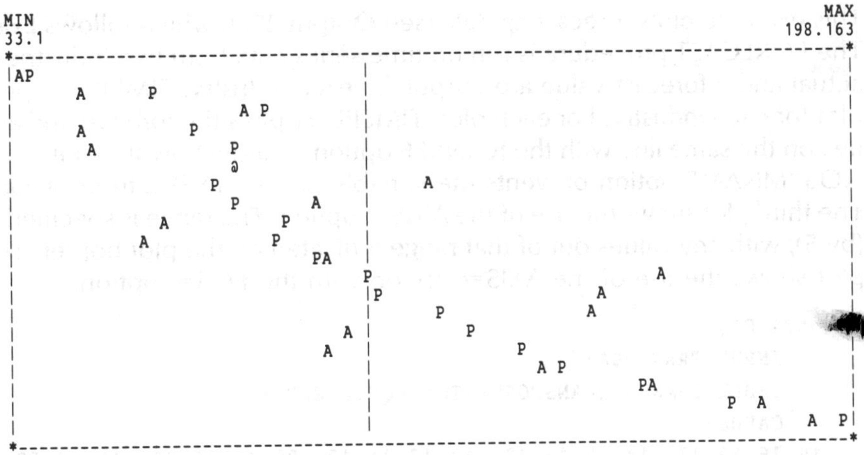

```
                                        GRUNFELD'S INVESTMENT MODEL                                          3

RESIDUALS   MIN                                                                                            MAX
            -37.511                                                                                   58.73724
            *--------------------------------------------------------------------------------------------------------*
   -2.86    |                                     R---|                                                              |
  -14.40    |                         R---------------|                                                              |
   -5.17    |                                   R-----|                                                              |
  -23.29    |               R-------------------------|                                                              |
  -28.03    |          R------------------------------|                                                              |
   -0.56    |                                        R|                                                              |
   40.75    |                                         |------------------------------------------R                   |
   16.04    |                                         |----------------R                                             |
  -23.72    |               R-------------------------|                                                              |
  -26.78    |            R----------------------------|                                                              |
    1.77    |                                         |R                                                             |
   58.74    |                                         |-------------------------------------------------------------R|
   43.94    |                                         |---------------------------------------------R                |
   31.23    |                                         |-------------------------------R                              |
  -23.55    |               R-------------------------|                                                              |
  -37.51    |R----------------------------------------|                                                              |
   -4.98    |                                   R-----|                                                              |
    1.89    |                                         |-R                                                            |
    5.09    |                                         |----R                                                         |
   -8.56    |                               R---------|                                                              |
            *--------------------------------------------------------------------------------------------------------*
```

Interrelationship of Forecast and Actual Values: Example 2

This example plots forecasting data (see **Output 27.3**, which follows **Example 3**). The FORECAST procedure is run on time series data from two industries, and an actual and a forecast value are output for each industry. TIMEPLOT produces a plot for each industry. For each plot, TIMEPLOT plots the forecast and actual values on the same line with the JOINREF option to show how they interrelate. The NOSYMNAME option prevents the variable name _TYPE_ from being printed. The third plot shows the use of the AXIS= option. The range is specified as 12-77 (by 5), with any values out of that range indicated on the plot border. The fourth plot shows the use of the AXIS= option with the POS= option.

```
DATA D1;
   INPUT TRANS @@;
   LABEL TRANS='TRANSPORTATION EQUIPMENT';
   CARDS;
14 16 13 17  14 14 13 17  10 12 11 12  08 13 16 20  18 26 28 28
23 25 24 26  21 23 25 36  28 36 34 34  24 29 33 40  37 47 52 53
38 42 34 31  22 22 21 20  18 22 27 28  25 32 34 34  22 28 26 34
26 33 36 38  31 40 41 46  37 49 52 61  52 64 69 70
;
DATA D2;
   INPUT STONE @@;
   LABEL STONE='STONE CLAY GLASS';
   CARDS;
06 09 09 08  06 07 06 08  04 04 03 05  04 07 08 11  08 12 12 14
10 09 09 10  09 10 10 11  09 11 10 15  11 13 16 24  17 22 23 26
18 20 18 19  17 15 11 12  13 17 21 18  18 20 18 19  14 16 18 22
14 19 17 20  16 17 17 20  17 18 17 22  19 23 23 27
;
DATA C;
   MERGE D1 D2;
   QTR=MOD(_N_-1,4)+1;
   YEAR=INT((_N_-1)/4)+1947;
   DATE=YYQ(YEAR,QTR);
   FORMAT DATE YYQ4.;
```

```
PROC FORECAST DATA=C OUT=O1 OUTEST=OE AR=5
   OUTDATA OUT1STEP OUTLIMIT
   INTERVAL=QTR;
   ID DATE;
   VAR TRANS STONE;
PROC TIMEPLOT DATA=O1 UNIFORM;
   PLOT (TRANS STONE)=_TYPE_/JOINREF NOSYMNAME;
   CLASS DATE;
   TITLE 'FORECASTING EXAMPLE';
DATA TRANS;
   SET O1;
   IF _TYPE_='ACTUAL' AND TRANS~=.;
PROC TIMEPLOT;
   PLOT TRANS/AXIS=12 TO 77 BY 5;
   PLOT TRANS/AXIS=12 TO 77 BY 5 POS=0;
```

High-Low-Close Stock Market Reports: Example 3

The statements below produced the stock market example at the beginning of the chapter (see **Output 27.1**). This example overlays three plots on the same axes. The HILOC option causes the leftmost non-reference symbol (representing the low value of the Dow Jones Index) to be joined to the rightmost non-reference symbol (representing the high value). The reference line at MEAN (LOW) allows each day's values to be compared with the average low value of the index. The ID statement causes the values of DATE and VOLUME to be printed without being plotted.

```
DATA DOW;
   INPUT DATE DATE7. VOLUME HIGH LOW CLOSE;
   LABEL VOLUME='VOLUME IN THOUSANDS OF SHARES';
   FORMAT DATE DATE7.;
   CARDS;
03AUG81 3219.3 955.48 940.45 946.25
04AUG81 2938.5 951.39 937.40 945.97
05AUG81 4177.8 958.81 942.16 953.58
06AUG81 3975.7 961.47 947.30 952.91
07AUG81 3884.3 954.15 938.45 942.54
10AUG81 2937.7 948.82 935.88 943.68
11AUG81 5262.9 955.48 939.50 949.30
12AUG81 4005.2 955.86 942.26 945.21
13AUG81 3680.8 952.91 938.55 944.35
14AUG81 3714.1 947.77 933.79 936.93
17AUG81 3432.7 939.40 924.37 926.75
18AUG81 4396.7 932.74 916.38 924.37
19AUG81 3517.3 932.08 918.38 926.46
20AUG81 3811.9 935.31 923.52 928.37
21AUG81 2625.9 930.65 917.14 920.57
24AUG81 4736.1 917.43 896.97 900.11
25AUG81 4714.4 904.30 887.46 901.83
26AUG81 3279.6 908.39 893.65 899.26
27AUG81 3676.1 900.49 883.66 889.08
28AUG81 3024.2 898.78 884.80 892.22
;
PROC TIMEPLOT;
   PLOT LOW CLOSE HIGH/OVERLAY HILOC REF=MEAN(LOW);
   ID DATE VOLUME;
```

```
FORMAT VOLUME 6.1 HIGH LOW CLOSE 6.2;
TITLE 'HIGH-LOW-CLOSE STOCK MARKET DATA';
```

Output 27.3 Plotting Actual and Forecast Data: PROC TIMEPLOT

```
                                                 FORECASTING EXAMPLE                                                  1
 ❶               ❷                     ❹
                    ACTUAL              FORECAST                 L95                 U95
DATE      TRANSPORTATION        TRANSPORTATION        TRANSPORTATION      TRANSPORTATION   MIN                              MAX
               EQUIPMENT             EQUIPMENT             EQUIPMENT           EQUIPMENT   8                          73.65622
                                                                                           *--------------------------------*
47Q1               14.00                 12.50                                             | FA                             |
47Q2               16.00                 14.28                                             |  FA                            |
47Q3               13.00                 16.09                                             | A-F                            |
47Q4               17.00                 13.18                                             | F-A                            |
48Q1               14.00                 17.41                                             |  AF                            |
48Q2               14.00                 15.79                                             |  AF                            |
48Q3               13.00                 11.77                                             | @                              |
48Q4               17.00                 16.20                                             |   @                            |
49Q1               10.00                 15.42                                             |A--F                            |
49Q2               12.00                 11.41                                             | @                              |
49Q3               11.00                 11.69                                             |AF                              |
49Q4               12.00                 15.84                                             | A-F                            |
50Q1                8.00                  9.26                                             AF                               |
50Q2               13.00                 11.59                                             | @                              |
50Q3               16.00                 14.01                                             |  FA                            |
50Q4               20.00                 18.94                                             |    FA                          |
51Q1               18.00                 18.11                                             |    @                           |
51Q2               26.00                 21.56                                             |     F-A                        |
51Q3               28.00                 26.88                                             |        @                       |
51Q4               28.00                 30.16                                             |        AF                      |
52Q1               23.00                 24.73                                             |      AF                        |
52Q2               25.00                 26.64                                             |       AF                       |
52Q3               24.00                 25.16                                             |       @                        |
52Q4               26.00                 24.37                                             |       @                        |
53Q1               21.00                 22.38                                             |     AF                         |
53Q2               23.00                 22.66                                             |      @                         |
53Q3               25.00                 22.21                                             |      FA                        |
53Q4               36.00                 27.18                                             |        F---A                   |
54Q1               28.00                 31.90                                             |        A-F                     |
54Q2               36.00                 28.87                                             |         F--A                   |
54Q3               34.00                 33.67                                             |           @                    |
54Q4               34.00                 40.18                                             |           A--F                 |
55Q1               24.00                 26.54                                             |       AF                       |
55Q2               29.00                 28.52                                             |         @                      |
55Q3               33.00                 26.94                                             |        F--A                    |
55Q4               40.00                 34.03                                             |           F--A                 |
56Q1               37.00                 32.33                                             |          F--A                  |
56Q2               47.00                 38.22                                             |             F---A              |
56Q3               52.00                 45.28                                             |                 F--A           |
56Q4               53.00                 52.88                                             |                    @           |
57Q1               38.00                 45.42                                             |             A---F              |
57Q2               42.00                 39.83                                             |              FA                |
57Q3               34.00                 40.74                                             |           A--F                 |
57Q4               31.00                 35.00                                             |          A-F                   |
58Q1               22.00                 20.77                                             |     FA                         |
58Q2               22.00                 26.40                                             |      A-F                       |
58Q3               21.00                 19.40                                             |    FA                          |
58Q4               20.00                 23.38                                             |     AF                         |
59Q1               18.00                 18.26                                             |    @                           |
59Q2               22.00                 22.17                                             |      @                         |
59Q3               27.00                 25.34                                             |      FA                        |
59Q4               28.00                 30.21                                             |       AF                       |
60Q1               25.00                 29.52                                             |      A-F                       |
60Q2               32.00                 29.78                                             |        FA                      |
```

```
                                                  FORECASTING EXAMPLE                                                         2

                    ACTUAL            FORECAST                 L95                 U95
DATE        TRANSPORTATION      TRANSPORTATION      TRANSPORTATION      TRANSPORTATION    MIN                           MAX
                 EQUIPMENT           EQUIPMENT           EQUIPMENT           EQUIPMENT    8                        73.65622
                                                                                          *-------------------------------*
60Q3                 34.00               36.85                                            |            A-F                |
60Q4                 34.00               37.14                                            |            A-F                |
61Q1                 22.00               33.03                                            |       A----F                  |
61Q2                 28.00               28.72                                            |         AF                    |
61Q3                 26.00               31.33                                            |        A--F                   |
61Q4                 34.00               31.26                                            |           FA                  |
62Q1                 26.00               28.85                                            |        A-F                    |
62Q2                 33.00               33.58                                            |            @                  |
62Q3                 36.00               33.11                                            |            FA                 |
62Q4                 38.00               44.31                                            |              A--F             |
63Q1                 31.00               34.42                                            |           AF                  |
63Q2                 40.00               37.21                                            |              FA               |
63Q3                 41.00               42.68                                            |                @              |
63Q4                 46.00               44.86                                            |                 FA            |
64Q1                 37.00               41.37                                            |              A-F              |
64Q2                 49.00               43.63                                            |                 F-A           |
64Q3                 52.00               48.50                                            |                   F-A         |
64Q4                 61.00               56.12                                            |                       F-A     |
65Q1                 52.00               52.31                                            |                     @         |
65Q2                 64.00               57.34                                            |                       F--A    |
65Q3                 69.00               60.89                                            |                         F---A |
65Q4                 70.00               71.81                                            |                             AF|
66Q1                                     58.63               49.30               67.96    |                   L----F---U  |
66Q2                                     61.12               48.85               73.40    |                   L-----F----U|
66Q3                                     59.53               45.40               73.66    |                  L-----F-----U|
66Q4                                     58.58               43.87               73.28    |                 L------F-----U|
67Q1                                     48.96               32.25               65.67    |           L-------F-------U   |
67Q2                                     49.43               31.86               66.99    |           L--------F-------U  |
67Q3                                     47.61               29.62               65.61    |          L--------F-------U   |
67Q4                                     48.63               30.63               66.63    |           L-------F--------U  |
68Q1                                     43.55               25.44               61.67    |        L--------F-------U     |
68Q2                                     45.63               27.51               63.75    |         L--------F-------U    |
68Q3                                     45.82               27.68               63.97    |         L--------F-------U    |
68Q4                                     49.04               30.61               67.47    |           L-------F--------U  |
                                                                                          *-------------------------------*
```

❷

```
                                                  FORECASTING EXAMPLE                                                    3
                 ACTUAL             FORECAST             L95              U95
DATE              STONE                STONE           STONE            STONE     MIN                                  MAX
                   CLAY                 CLAY            CLAY             CLAY     3                               32.11593
                  GLASS                GLASS           GLASS            GLASS     *--------------------------------------*
47Q1               6.00                 6.16                                      |    @
47Q2               9.00                 6.27                                      |    F---A
47Q3               9.00                 8.28                                      |       FA
47Q4               8.00                 8.35                                      |      AF
48Q1               6.00                 7.70                                      |    A-F
48Q2               7.00                 8.00                                      |     AF
48Q3               6.00                 7.16                                      |    AF
48Q4               8.00                 6.09                                      |    F-A
49Q1               4.00                 6.95                                      | A---F
49Q2               4.00                 6.00                                      | A--F
49Q3               3.00                 5.05                                      |A--F
49Q4               5.00                 6.03                                      |   AF
50Q1               4.00                 4.30                                      | AF
50Q2               7.00                 5.82                                      |    FA
50Q3               8.00                 7.31                                      |     FA
50Q4              11.00                 9.58                                      |        F-A
51Q1               8.00                10.03                                      |      A--F
51Q2              12.00                10.24                                      |         F-A
51Q3              12.00                11.84                                      |           @
51Q4              14.00                12.94                                      |             FA
52Q1              10.00                11.20                                      |         AF
52Q2               9.00                12.32                                      |        A---F
52Q3               9.00                 9.67                                      |        @
52Q4              10.00                10.77                                      |         AF
53Q1               9.00                 8.40                                      |       FA
53Q2              10.00                 9.41                                      |        FA
53Q3              10.00                10.65                                      |         AF
53Q4              11.00                11.24                                      |          @
54Q1               9.00                10.93                                      |        A-F
54Q2              11.00                10.75                                      |          @
54Q3              10.00                11.60                                      |         A-F
54Q4              15.00                11.54                                      |           F---A
55Q1              11.00                13.29                                      |          A--F
55Q2              13.00                12.86                                      |             @
55Q3              16.00                12.67                                      |            F----A
55Q4              24.00                17.76                                      |                   F-------A
56Q1              17.00                18.34                                      |                  AF
56Q2              22.00                17.02                                      |                  F-----A
56Q3              23.00                20.81                                      |                       F-A
56Q4              26.00                24.07                                      |                           F-A
57Q1              18.00                18.33                                      |                   @
57Q2              20.00                19.46                                      |                     FA
57Q3              18.00                18.74                                      |                   AF
57Q4              19.00                18.54                                      |                    @
58Q1              17.00                13.61                                      |             F----A
58Q2              15.00                17.58                                      |               A---F
58Q3              11.00                14.31                                      |          A---F
58Q4              12.00                13.37                                      |           A-F
59Q1              13.00                12.54                                      |            FA
59Q2              17.00                13.28                                      |             F----A
59Q3              21.00                14.92                                      |               F-------A
59Q4              18.00                20.17                                      |                   A--F
60Q1              18.00                18.31                                      |                   @
60Q2              20.00                19.91                                      |                     FA
```

```
                                                 FORECASTING EXAMPLE                                                 4
                 ACTUAL            FORECAST             L95             U95
DATE              STONE               STONE           STONE           STONE     MIN                                MAX
                   CLAY                CLAY            CLAY            CLAY     3                             32.11593
                  GLASS               GLASS           GLASS           GLASS     *------------------------------------*
60Q3              18.00               21.25                                     |                  A---F             |
60Q4              19.00               16.42                                     |                F--A                |
61Q1              14.00               18.70                                     |             A-----F                |
61Q2              16.00               16.59                                     |                @                   |
61Q3              18.00               15.88                                     |               F--A                 |
61Q4              22.00               18.80                                     |                   F---A            |
62Q1              14.00               18.37                                     |             A-----F                |
62Q2              19.00               16.93                                     |                 F-A                |
62Q3              17.00               20.21                                     |                 A---F              |
62Q4              20.00               20.01                                     |                     @              |
63Q1              16.00               15.83                                     |               FA                   |
63Q2              17.00               20.06                                     |                 A---F              |
63Q3              17.00               17.16                                     |                 @                  |
63Q4              20.00               19.81                                     |                    FA              |
64Q1              17.00               18.21                                     |                 AF                 |
64Q2              18.00               18.95                                     |                  AF                |
64Q3              17.00               19.15                                     |                 A--F               |
64Q4              22.00               20.12                                     |                     F-A            |
65Q1              19.00               20.32                                     |                   A-F              |
65Q2              23.00               20.54                                     |                     F--A           |
65Q3              23.00               22.16                                     |                       FA           |
65Q4              27.00               25.32                                     |                           F-A      |
66Q1                                  23.83           19.09           28.57     |                   L-----F-----U    |
66Q2                                  25.48           19.89           31.08     |                    L-------F------U|
66Q3                                  24.54           18.62           30.46     |                   L------F-------U |
66Q4                                  26.07           20.02           32.12     |                     L------F------U|
67Q1                                  23.42           16.59           30.25     |                L--------F--------U |
67Q2                                  24.29           17.36           31.22     |                 L--------F--------U|
67Q3                                  23.58           16.65           30.52     |                L--------F--------U |
67Q4                                  24.48           17.53           31.42     |                 L--------F--------U|
68Q1                                  22.98           15.99           29.97     |                L-------F--------U  |
68Q2                                  23.92           16.90           30.94     |                 L--------F--------U|
68Q3                                  23.79           16.71           30.86     |                L--------F--------U |
68Q4                                  24.60           17.48           31.72     |                 L--------F--------U|
                                                                                *------------------------------------*
```

```
         FORECASTING EXAMPLE                                                  5

TRANSPORTATION          MIN         MAX
     EQUIPMENT          12           77
                       *--------------*
            14         |T             |
            16         |T             |
            13         |T             |
            17         | T            |
            14         |T             |
            14         |T             |
            13         |T             |
            17         | T            |
            10         <              |
            12         |T             |
            11         <              |
            12         |T             |
             8         <              |
            13         |T             |
            16         |T             |
            20         | T            |
            18         | T            |
            26         |  T           |
            28         |   T          |
            28         |   T          |
            23         |  T           |
            25         |  T           |
            24         |  T           |
            26         |  T           |
            21         | T            |
            23         |  T           |
            25         |  T           |
            36         |    T         |
            28         |   T          |
            36         |    T         |
            34         |    T         |
            34         |    T         |
            24         |  T           |
            29         |   T          |
            33         |    T         |
            40         |     T        |
            37         |     T        |
            47         |       T      |
            52         |        T     |
            53         |        T     |
            38         |     T        |
            42         |      T       |
            34         |    T         |
            31         |   T          |
            22         |  T           |
            22         |  T           |
            21         | T            |
            20         | T            |
            18         | T            |
            22         |  T           |
            27         |   T          |
            28         |   T          |
            25         |  T           |
            32         |    T         |
```

```
                    FORECASTING EXAMPLE                                           6

             TRANSPORTATION          MIN             MAX
                  EQUIPMENT          12               77
                                     *---------------*
                         34          |    T          |
                         34          |    T          |
                         22          |  T            |
                         28          |   T           |
                         26          |  T            |
                         34          |    T          |
                         26          |  T            |
                         33          |    T          |
                         36          |    T          |
                         38          |     T         |
                         31          |   T           |
                         40          |     T         |
                         41          |     T         |
                         46          |      T        |
                         37          |     T         |
                         49          |       T       |
                         52          |        T      |
                         61          |         T     |
                         52          |        T      |
                         64          |          T    |
                         69          |           T   |
                         70          |           T   |
                                     *---------------*
```

```
                                             ❾ FORECASTING EXAMPLE                                                7

TRANSPORTATION     MIN                                                                                              MAX
     EQUIPMENT     12                                                                                                77
                   *----------------------------------------------------------------------------------------------------*
            14     |      T
            16     |      T
            13     |      T
            17     |             T
            14     |      T
            14     |      T
            13     |      T
            17     |             T
            10     <
            12     |      T
            11     <
            12     |      T
             8     <
            13     |      T
            16     |      T
            20     |             T
            18     |             T
            26     |                    T
            28     |                           T
            28     |                           T
            23     |                    T
            25     |                    T
            24     |                    T
            26     |                    T
            21     |             T
            23     |                    T
            25     |                    T
            36     |                                  T
            28     |                           T
            36     |                                  T
            34     |                                  T
            34     |                                  T
            24     |                    T
            29     |                           T
            33     |                                  T
            40     |                                         T
            37     |                                         T
            47     |                                                       T
            52     |                                                              T
            53     |                                                              T
            38     |                                         T
            42     |                                                T
            34     |                                  T
            31     |                           T
            22     |                    T
            22     |                    T
            21     |             T
            20     |             T
            18     |             T
            22     |                    T
            27     |                           T
            28     |                           T
            25     |                    T
            32     |                                  T
```

```
                                                  FORECASTING EXAMPLE                                                 8

TRANSPORTATION     MIN                                                                                              MAX
     EQUIPMENT     12                                                                                                77
                   *----------------------------------------------------------------------------------------------------*
            34     |                                  T                                                               |
            34     |                                  T                                                               |
            22     |                    T                                                                             |
            28     |                           T                                                                      |
            26     |                    T                                                                             |
            34     |                                  T                                                               |
            26     |                    T                                                                             |
            33     |                                  T                                                               |
            36     |                                  T                                                               |
            38     |                                         T                                                        |
            31     |                           T                                                                      |
            40     |                                         T                                                        |
            41     |                                         T                                                        |
            46     |                                                T                                                 |
            37     |                                         T                                                        |
            49     |                                                       T                                          |
            52     |                                                              T                                   |
            61     |                                                                     T                            |
            52     |                                                              T                                   |
            64     |                                                                            T                     |
            69     |                                                                                   T              |
            70     |                                                                                   T              |
                   *----------------------------------------------------------------------------------------------------*
```

Chapter 28

The TRANSPOSE Procedure

ABSTRACT

The TRANSPOSE procedure transposes a SAS data set, changing observations into variables and vice versa.

INTRODUCTION

The TRANSPOSE procedure reads a SAS data set and creates a new data set as its only output. The rows of the original data matrix become columns, and columns become rows. Variables in the new data set correspond to observations in the old data set, and observations in the new data set correspond to variables in the old data set. TRANSPOSE also creates a variable in the new data set that contains the names of the variables from the old data set that were transposed.

For example, these statements produce **Output 28.1**.

```
DATA A;
   INPUT A B C;
   CARDS;
1 2 3
4 5 6
;
```

```
PROC TRANSPOSE;
PROC PRINT;
   TITLE 'SIMPLE TRANSPOSE EXAMPLE';
```

Output 28.1 A Transposed Data Set

```
                         SIMPLE TRANSPOSE EXAMPLE                                    1

                        OBS    _NAME_    COL1    COL2

                         1       A         1       4
                         2       B         2       5
                         3       C         3       6
```

PROC TRANSPOSE can be used with a BY statement to rearrange complex data sets in a variety of ways. In the following example, you have collected length and weight measurements for a sample of two species of fish, Mugil Curema (White Mullet) and Brevoortia Tyrannus (Atlantic Menhaden). During data collection it was convenient to enter the date and species once and string the measurements along the same line. Each line, therefore, represents a particular sample group and date.

What you need, however, are two data sets: one containing a separate observation for each length value, and one containing a separate observation for each weight value. Each data set must also indicate the group, species, and date corresponding to each length or weight measurement. These statements produce the output shown in **Output 28.2**.

```
DATA FISHDATA;
   INPUT GROUP DATE DATE7. SPECIES $
         L1 W1 L2 W2 L3 W3 L4 W4;
   FORMAT DATE DATE7.;
   CARDS;
1  2JUN84 CUR 31 .25 32 .3  32 .25 33 .3
2  2JUN84 CUR 30 .20 36 .45 33 .25 36 .35
3  2JUN84 CUR 32 .35 32 .25 33 .30  .  .
1 11JUL84 MEN 72 4.0 82 5.5 70 4.0 79 4.3
1 14JUL84 MEN 79 4.1 78 3.8 80 3.8 74 3.6
1 13AUG84 MEN 86 70  83 54  89 76  80 49
;
PROC SORT;
   BY SPECIES DATE GROUP;
PROC PRINT;
   TITLE 'FISHDATA';

PROC TRANSPOSE DATA=FISHDATA OUT=LENGTH;
   BY SPECIES DATE GROUP;
   VAR L1-L4;
PROC PRINT;
   TITLE 'NEW DATA SET WITH LENGTH MEASUREMENTS';

PROC TRANSPOSE DATA=FISHDATA OUT=WEIGHT;
   BY SPECIES DATE GROUP;
```

```
   VAR W1-W4;
PROC PRINT;
   TITLE 'NEW DATA SET WITH WEIGHT MEASUREMENTS';
```

Output 28.2 PROC TRANSPOSE Converts the Data into a More Usable Form

FISHDATA 1

OBS	GROUP	DATE	SPECIES	L1	W1	L2	W2	L3	W3	L4	W4
1	1	02JUN84	CUR	31	0.25	32	0.30	32	0.25	33	0.30
2	2	02JUN84	CUR	30	0.20	36	0.45	33	0.25	36	0.35
3	3	02JUN84	CUR	32	0.35	32	0.25	33	0.30	.	.
4	1	11JUL84	MEN	72	4.00	82	5.50	70	4.00	79	4.30
5	1	14JUL84	MEN	79	4.10	78	3.80	80	3.80	74	3.60
6	1	13AUG84	MEN	86	70.00	83	54.00	89	76.00	80	49.00

NEW DATA SET WITH LENGTH MEASUREMENTS 2

OBS	SPECIES	DATE	GROUP	_NAME_	COL1
1	CUR	02JUN84	1	L1	31
2	CUR	02JUN84	1	L2	32
3	CUR	02JUN84	1	L3	32
4	CUR	02JUN84	1	L4	33
5	CUR	02JUN84	2	L1	30
6	CUR	02JUN84	2	L2	36
7	CUR	02JUN84	2	L3	33
8	CUR	02JUN84	2	L4	36
9	CUR	02JUN84	3	L1	32
10	CUR	02JUN84	3	L2	32
11	CUR	02JUN84	3	L3	33
12	CUR	02JUN84	3	L4	.
13	MEN	11JUL84	1	L1	72
14	MEN	11JUL84	1	L2	82
15	MEN	11JUL84	1	L3	70
16	MEN	11JUL84	1	L4	79
17	MEN	14JUL84	1	L1	79
18	MEN	14JUL84	1	L2	78
19	MEN	14JUL84	1	L3	80
20	MEN	14JUL84	1	L4	74
21	MEN	13AUG84	1	L1	86
22	MEN	13AUG84	1	L2	83
23	MEN	13AUG84	1	L3	89
24	MEN	13AUG84	1	L4	80

NEW DATA SET WITH WEIGHT MEASUREMENTS 3

OBS	SPECIES	DATE	GROUP	_NAME_	COL1
1	CUR	02JUN84	1	W1	0.25
2	CUR	02JUN84	1	W2	0.30
3	CUR	02JUN84	1	W3	0.25
4	CUR	02JUN84	1	W4	0.30
5	CUR	02JUN84	2	W1	0.20
6	CUR	02JUN84	2	W2	0.45
7	CUR	02JUN84	2	W3	0.25
8	CUR	02JUN84	2	W4	0.35
9	CUR	02JUN84	3	W1	0.35
10	CUR	02JUN84	3	W2	0.25
11	CUR	02JUN84	3	W3	0.30
12	CUR	02JUN84	3	W4	.
13	MEN	11JUL84	1	W1	4.00
14	MEN	11JUL84	1	W2	5.50
15	MEN	11JUL84	1	W3	4.00
16	MEN	11JUL84	1	W4	4.30
17	MEN	14JUL84	1	W1	4.10
18	MEN	14JUL84	1	W2	3.80
19	MEN	14JUL84	1	W3	3.80
20	MEN	14JUL84	1	W4	3.60
21	MEN	13AUG84	1	W1	70.00
22	MEN	13AUG84	1	W2	54.00
23	MEN	13AUG84	1	W3	76.00
24	MEN	13AUG84	1	W4	49.00

SPECIFICATIONS

The statements used with PROC TRANSPOSE are

PROC TRANSPOSE *options;*
VAR *variables;*
ID *variable;*
IDLABEL *variable;*
COPY *variables;*
BY *variables;*

PROC TRANSPOSE Statement

PROC TRANSPOSE *options;*

These options can appear in the PROC TRANSPOSE statement:

DATA=*SASdataset*
: names the SAS data set to be transposed. If DATA= is omitted, the most recently created SAS data set is used.

PREFIX=*name*
: specifies a prefix to be used in constructing new variable names. For example, if PREFIX=VAR, the new variable names will be VAR1, VAR2,...,VAR*n*.

OUT=*SASdataset*
: specifies the name of the SAS data set that is created. If you want to create a permanent SAS data set, you must specify a two-level name. (See *SAS Language Guide for Personal Computers* for more information on permanent SAS data sets.) If OUT= is omitted, the SAS System still creates an output data set and automatically names it according to the DATA*n* convention, just as if you omitted a data set name in a DATA statement.

NAME=*name*
: provides a name for the variable in the output data set that contains the names of the transposed variables in the input data set. If NAME= is not specified, a variable is created automatically with the name _NAME_.

LABEL=*name*
: provides a name for the variable in the output data set that contains the labels of the transposed variables in the input data set. If LABEL= is not specified and at least one variable being transposed has a label, then a variable is created automatically with the name _LABEL_.

LET
: allows duplicate values of an ID variable within the data set or, if a BY statement is used, within a BY group. The observation containing the last occurrence of a particular ID value is transposed.

VAR Statement

VAR *variables;*

The VAR statement lists the variables to be transposed. Both numeric and character variables can be included.

If no VAR statement is used, all numeric variables in the old data set that are not listed in another statement are transposed. Character variables must be listed in a VAR statement if they are to be transposed. Variables that are not transposed are omitted from the new data set unless listed in the COPY or BY statements.

For example, these statements produce **Output 28.3** .

```
DATA B;
   INPUT A 1 B 3 X $5;
   CARDS;
1 2 X
3 4 Y
5 6 Z
;
PROC TRANSPOSE DATA=B;
PROC PRINT;
   TITLE 'NUMERIC VARIABLES TRANSPOSED BY DEFAULT';

PROC TRANSPOSE DATA=B;
   VAR X;
PROC PRINT;
   TITLE 'CHARACTER VARIABLE TRANSPOSED USING VAR STATEMENT';
```

Output 28.3 Using the VAR Statement

```
          NUMERIC VARIABLES TRANSPOSED BY DEFAULT                                    1
          OBS    _NAME_    COL1    COL2    COL3

           1       A        .       .       .
           2       B        .       .       .
```

```
      CHARACTER VARIABLE TRANSPOSED USING VAR STATEMENT                              2

           OBS    _NAME_    COL1    COL2    COL3

            1       X
```

ID Statement

ID *variable;*

An ID statement causes the formatted values of the ID variable to be used as the names of the transposed variables in the new data set. Each formatted ID value should occur only once in the old data set, or, if a BY statement is used, only once within a BY group. Duplicate values cause PROC TRANSPOSE to issue an error message and stop unless the LET option is specified.

TRANSPOSE will change a formatted ID value into a valid SAS name whenever necessary. If the formatted value looks like a numeric constant, TRANSPOSE changes the characters "+", "−", and "." to "P","N", and "D", respectively. If the first character is numeric, an underscore is prefixed to the value, truncating the last character of an 8-character value. Any remaining invalid characters are replaced by underscores.

If an ID statement is used, observations with missing ID values are omitted from the new data set. For example, the statements below produce **Output 28.4**.

```
DATA C;
   INPUT A 1 B 3 X $5;
   CARDS;
1 2 X
```

```
3 4 Y
5 6 Z
7 8
;
PROC TRANSPOSE;
   ID X;
PROC PRINT;
   TITLE 'TRANSPOSING WITH AN ID STATEMENT';
```

Output 28.4 Using the ID Statement

```
                    TRANSPOSING WITH AN ID STATEMENT                    1

                           OBS    _NAME_

                            1       A
                            2       B
```

IDLABEL Statement

IDLABEL *variable;*
IDL *variable;*

If an ID statement is present, the IDLABEL statement can also be used to specify a character or numeric variable to provide labels for the transposed variables in the new data set.

COPY Statement

COPY *variables;*

All variables in the COPY statement are copied directly from the input data set to the output data set without being transposed. The output data set is padded with missing values if necessary. For example, these statements produce **Output 28.5**.

```
DATA D;
   INPUT A B C;
   CARDS;
 1  2  3
 4  5  6
 7  8  9
 11 22 33
;
PROC TRANSPOSE;
   COPY C;
PROC PRINT;
   TITLE 'TRANSPOSING WITH A COPY STATEMENT';
```

Output 28.5 Using the COPY Statement

```
                    TRANSPOSING WITH A COPY STATEMENT                          1

        OBS     C    _NAME_     COL1    COL2    COL3    COL4

         1      3      A         1       4       7       11
         2      6      B         2       5       8       22
         3      9               .       .       .        .
         4     33               .       .       .        .
```

BY Statement

BY *variables;*

When a BY statement is used, PROC TRANSPOSE transposes each BY group. The BY variables are included in the output data set but are not transposed. The statements below produce **Output 28.6** .

```
DATA E;
   INPUT B X $ Y $;
   CARDS;
1 X1 Y1
2 X2 Y2
3 X3 Y3
;
PROC TRANSPOSE;
   VAR X Y;
   BY B;
PROC PRINT;
   TITLE 'TRANSPOSING WITH A BY STATEMENT';
```

Output 28.6 Using the BY Statement

```
                    TRANSPOSING WITH A BY STATEMENT                            1

                     OBS     B    _NAME_    COL1

                      1      1      X        X1
                      2      1      Y        Y1
                      3      2      X        X2
                      4      2      Y        Y2
                      5      3      X        X3
                      6      3      Y        Y3
```

When a BY statement appears, the procedure expects the input data set to be sorted in order of the BY variables. If your input data set is not sorted in ascending order, use the SORT procedure with a similar BY statement to sort the data, or, if appropriate, use the BY statement options NOTSORTED or DESCENDING.

For more information, see the discussion of the BY statement in *SAS Language Guide for Personal Computers*, and in **Using a BY Statement**, below.

DETAILS

Output Data Set

Contents The new data set has a character variable that contains the variable names from the old data set. The name of the variable is specified by the NAME= option. If NAME= is not specified, a variable is created automatically and named _NAME_. If the old data set has variable labels for the transposed variables, the labels are placed in a character variable in the new data set. The name of the variable is specified by the LABEL= option. If LABEL= is not specified, a variable is created automatically and named _LABEL_. However, if the variables referenced by the NAME= or LABEL= options (or, if these options are omitted, variables called _NAME_ or _LABEL_), are listed in the COPY or BY statements, then PROC TRANSPOSE does not create variables with duplicate names containing the names or labels of the transposed input variables.

All transposed output variables are the same type and length. If all input variables to be transposed are numeric, then the transposed output variables are numeric. If **any** such input variable is character, then **all** transposed output variables are character. The character values of transposed numeric variables in the output data set are the formatted values of the input numeric variables. The length of the transposed output variables is equal to the length of the longest transposed input variable.

All variables listed in the COPY statement are copied to the new data set.

Variable names There are four ways that the transposed variables in the new data set can be named:

1. by an ID statement specifying the name of a variable in the old data set. The formatted values of this variable are used as names for the output variables.
2. by the PREFIX= option in the PROC TRANSPOSE statement. For example, if you request PREFIX=VAR, the new variable names will be VAR1, VAR2,...,VAR*n*.
3. by an input variable _NAME_. If you use neither the ID statement nor the PREFIX= option, PROC TRANSPOSE looks for an input variable called _NAME_ from which to get the output variable names. The variable _NAME_ can be the result of a previous execution of PROC TRANSPOSE. If so, the variable names are identical to the variable names in the original (untransposed) data set.
4. by default. If you do not use an ID statement or the PREFIX= option, and there is no input variable called _NAME_, PROC TRANSPOSE assigns the names COL1, COL2,..., COL*n* to the variables in the output data set.

Using a BY Statement

If a BY statement is used with PROC TRANSPOSE, there is one observation corresponding to each transposed variable of the old data set in each BY group in the new data set. The method of naming the output variables determines what output variables appear in the new data set.

If the output variables are named by the PREFIX= option or by the default prefix COL, the number of transposed output variables is the maximum number of observations in any BY group of the old data set. If a BY group in the old data set has fewer than the maximum number of observations, then the BY group in the new data set has missing values for the variables with no corresponding input observations. The following example shows the use of a BY statement and the

PREFIX= option with the data set FISHDATA. These statements produce the output shown in **Output 28.7**.

```
PROC SORT DATA=FISHDATA;
   BY GROUP;
PROC PRINT DATA=FISHDATA;
   TITLE 'FISHDATA: ORIGINAL DATA SET';

PROC TRANSPOSE DATA=FISHDATA OUT=TRAN PREFIX=VAR;
   VAR L1-L4 W1-W4;
   BY GROUP;
PROC PRINT DATA=TRAN;
   TITLE 'FISHDATA TRANSPOSED WITH BY GROUPS USING THE
      PREFIX=VAR OPTION';
```

Output 28.7 FISHDATA is Transposed and the Output Data Set is Called TRAN

FISHDATA: ORIGINAL DATA SET 1

OBS	GROUP	DATE	SPECIES	L1	W1	L2	W2	L3	W3	L4	W4
1	1	02JUN84	CUR	31	0.25	32	0.30	32	0.25	33	0.30
2	1	11JUL84	MEN	72	4.00	82	5.50	70	4.00	79	4.30
3	1	14JUL84	MEN	79	4.10	78	3.80	80	3.80	74	3.60
4	1	13AUG84	MEN	86	70.00	83	54.00	89	76.00	80	49.00
5	2	02JUN84	CUR	30	0.20	36	0.45	33	0.25	36	0.35
6	3	02JUN84	CUR	32	0.35	32	0.25	33	0.30	.	.

FISHDATA TRANSPOSED WITH BY GROUPS USING THE PREFIX=VAR OPTION 2

OBS	GROUP	_NAME_	VAR1	VAR2	VAR3	VAR4
1	1	L1	31.00	72.0	79.0	86
2	1	L2	32.00	82.0	78.0	83
3	1	L3	32.00	70.0	80.0	89
4	1	L4	33.00	79.0	74.0	80
5	1	W1	0.25	4.0	4.1	70
6	1	W2	0.30	5.5	3.8	54
7	1	W3	0.25	4.0	3.8	76
8	1	W4	0.30	4.3	3.6	49
9	2	L1	30.00	.	.	.
10	2	L2	36.00	.	.	.
11	2	L3	33.00	.	.	.
12	2	L4	36.00	.	.	.
13	2	W1	0.20	.	.	.
14	2	W2	0.45	.	.	.
15	2	W3	0.25	.	.	.
16	2	W4	0.35	.	.	.
17	3	L1	32.00	.	.	.
18	3	L2	32.00	.	.	.
19	3	L3	33.00	.	.	.
20	3	L4	.	.	.	.
21	3	W1	0.35	.	.	.
22	3	W2	0.25	.	.	.
23	3	W3	0.30	.	.	.
24	3	W4	.	.	.	.

If an ID statement is used so that the output names are taken from an input variable, there is one output variable for each distinct value of the ID variable. The output variables are ordered according to the first appearance of their names in the old data set. If a value for the ID variable does not appear in a BY group, the corresponding output variable has missing values in that BY group. For example, when the FISHDATA data set is transposed with an ID statement in the program

```
PROC TRANSPOSE DATA=FISHDATA OUT=TRAN2;
   ID DATE;
   BY GROUP;
PROC PRINT;
   TITLE 'FISHDATA TRANSPOSED WITH BY GROUPS USING AN ID STATEMENT';
```

the output data set looks like that shown in **Output 28.8.**

Output 28.8 FISHDATA is Transposed and the Output Data Set is Called TRAN2

```
              FISHDATA TRANSPOSED WITH BY GROUPS USING AN ID STATEMENT                         1

OBS    GROUP    _NAME_    _02JUN84      _11JUL84      _14JUL84      _13AUG84

  1      1        L1        31.00         72.0          79.0           86
  2      1        W1         0.25          4.0           4.1           70
  3      1        L2        32.00         82.0          78.0           83
  4      1        W2         0.30          5.5           3.8           54
  5      1        L3        32.00         70.0          80.0           89
  6      1        W3         0.25          4.0           3.8           76
  7      1        L4        33.00         79.0          74.0           80
  8      1        W4         0.30          4.3           3.6           49
  9      2        L1        30.00           .             .             .
 10      2        W1         0.20           .             .             .
 11      2        L2        36.00           .             .             .
 12      2        W2         0.45           .             .             .
 13      2        L3        33.00           .             .             .
 14      2        W3         0.25           .             .             .
 15      2        L4        36.00           .             .             .
 16      2        W4         0.35           .             .             .
 17      3        L1        32.00           .             .             .
 18      3        W1         0.35           .             .             .
 19      3        L2        32.00           .             .             .
 20      3        W2         0.25           .             .             .
 21      3        L3        33.00           .             .             .
 22      3        W3         0.30           .             .             .
 23      3        L4          .             .             .             .
 24      3        W4          .             .             .             .
```

EXAMPLES

Transposing a Data Set Twice: Example 1

This example shows that transposing a data set twice can produce a data set similar to the original data set, except for the new variable _NAME_. See **Output 28.9**.

```
DATA A;
   INPUT A B C;
   CARDS;
1 2 3
4 5 6
7 8 9
10 11 12
;
PROC PRINT;
   TITLE 'BEFORE TRANSPOSING';
```

```
PROC TRANSPOSE;
PROC PRINT;
   TITLE 'AFTER TRANSPOSING ONCE';

PROC TRANSPOSE;
PROC PRINT;
   TITLE 'AFTER TRANSPOSING TWICE';
```

Output 28.9 Transposing a Data Set Twice

```
                         BEFORE TRANSPOSING                                  1

                        OBS    A     B     C

                         1     1     2     3
                         2     4     5     6
                         3     7     8     9
                         4    10    11    12
```

```
                         AFTER TRANSPOSING ONCE                              2

             OBS    _NAME_    COL1    COL2    COL3    COL4

              1       A         1       4       7      10
              2       B         2       5       8      11
              3       C         3       6       9      12
```

```
                        AFTER TRANSPOSING TWICE                              3

                    OBS    _NAME_     A     B     C

                     1     COL1       1     2     3
                     2     COL2       4     5     6
                     3     COL3       7     8     9
                     4     COL4      10    11    12
```

Converting a List to a Table: Example 2

The data below are a list of cities with temperatures in January, July, or August. The desired output is a table with cities as rows and two columns showing minimum winter and maximum summer temperatures. The cities should be ordered from coldest to hottest mean temperature. See **Output 28.10**.

```
DATA LIST;
   INPUT CITY $15. MONTH $15. TEMP;
   CARDS;
RALEIGH        JULY           77.5
RALEIGH        JANUARY        40.5
MIAMI          AUGUST         82.9
MIAMI          JANUARY        67.2
LOS_ANGELES    AUGUST         69.5
LOS_ANGELES    JANUARY        54.5
JUNEAU         JULY           55.7
JUNEAU         JANUARY        23.5
PHOENIX        JULY           91.2
PHOENIX        JANUARY        51.2
BISMARCK       JANUARY         8.2
BISMARCK       JULY           70.8
```

```
CHICAGO         AUGUST         71.1
CHICAGO         JANUARY        22.9
WICHITA         JULY           80.7
WICHITA         JANUARY        31.3
HONOLULU        AUGUST         80.7
HONOLULU        JANUARY        72.3
BOSTON          JULY           73.3
BOSTON          JANUARY        29.2
DULUTH          JULY           65.6
DULUTH          JANUARY         8.5
;

PROC SORT;
   BY CITY;
PROC PRINT;
   TITLE 'ORIGINAL DATA IN LIST FORM';

PROC TRANSPOSE;
   BY CITY;
   ID MONTH;
DATA; SET;
   WINTER=JANUARY;
   SUMMER=MAX(JULY,AUGUST);
   MEAN=MEAN(JANUARY,JULY,AUGUST);
PROC SORT;
   BY MEAN;
PROC PRINT;
   TITLE 'TABULAR DATA';
   ID CITY;
   VAR WINTER SUMMER;
```

Output 28.10 Converting Data in List Form to Tabular Form

```
                    ORIGINAL DATA IN LIST FORM                    1

            OBS    CITY           MONTH      TEMP

              1    BISMARCK       JANUARY     8.2
              2    BISMARCK       JULY       70.8
              3    BOSTON         JULY       73.3
              4    BOSTON         JANUARY    29.2
              5    CHICAGO        AUGUST     71.1
              6    CHICAGO        JANUARY    22.9
              7    DULUTH         JULY       65.6
              8    DULUTH         JANUARY     8.5
              9    HONOLULU       AUGUST     80.7
             10    HONOLULU       JANUARY    72.3
             11    JUNEAU         JULY       55.7
             12    JUNEAU         JANUARY    23.5
             13    LOS_ANGELES    AUGUST     69.5
             14    LOS_ANGELES    JANUARY    54.5
             15    MIAMI          AUGUST     82.9
             16    MIAMI          JANUARY    67.2
             17    PHOENIX        JULY       91.2
             18    PHOENIX        JANUARY    51.2
             19    RALEIGH        JULY       77.5
             20    RALEIGH        JANUARY    40.5
             21    WICHITA        JULY       80.7
             22    WICHITA        JANUARY    31.3
```

```
                         TABULAR DATA                                         2

                CITY          WINTER    SUMMER

                DULUTH          8.5      65.6
                BISMARCK        8.2      70.8
                JUNEAU         23.5      55.7
                CHICAGO        22.9      71.1
                BOSTON         29.2      73.3
                WICHITA        31.3      80.7
                RALEIGH        40.5      77.5
                LOS_ANGELES    54.5      69.5
                PHOENIX        51.2      91.2
                MIAMI          67.2      82.9
                HONOLULU       72.3      80.7
```

Rearranging Data from a Factorial Design: Example 3

The data below are from a subject-by-drug-by-exercise factorial design. This example shows how PROC TRANSPOSE can rearrange a more complicated data set using BY groups and ID variables. See **Output 28.11**.

```
DATA A1;
   INPUT SUBJECT $ DRUG $ EXERCISE $ RESPONSE;
   CARDS;
SMITH     ASPIRIN    LIGHT      5
SMITH     ASPIRIN    MEDIUM     8
SMITH     ASPIRIN    HEAVY      9
SMITH     PLACEBO    LIGHT      4
SMITH     PLACEBO    HEAVY      7
JONES     ASPIRIN    LIGHT      6
JONES     ASPIRIN    MEDIUM     7
JONES     ASPIRIN    HEAVY      9
JONES     PLACEBO    LIGHT      3
JONES     PLACEBO    MEDIUM     4
JONES     PLACEBO    HEAVY      6
;
PROC SORT;
   BY SUBJECT DRUG;
PROC PRINT;
   BY SUBJECT;
   TITLE 'DATA SET A1';

PROC TRANSPOSE OUT=A2 NAME=RESPNAME;
   BY SUBJECT DRUG;
   ID EXERCISE;
   VAR RESPONSE;
PROC PRINT;
   BY SUBJECT;
   TITLE 'DATA SET A2';

PROC TRANSPOSE OUT=A3 NAME=EXERCISE;
   BY SUBJECT RESPNAME;
   ID DRUG;
   VAR LIGHT MEDIUM HEAVY;
PROC PRINT;
   BY SUBJECT;
   TITLE 'DATA SET A3';

PROC TRANSPOSE OUT=A4 NAME=DRUG;
```

```
      BY SUBJECT EXERCISE NOTSORTED;
      ID RESPNAME;
   PROC PRINT;
      BY SUBJECT;
      TITLE 'DATA SET A4';
```

Output 28.11 Data from a Subject-by-Drug-by-Exercise Factorial Design

```
                                        DATA SET A1                                          1
---------------------------------------------------SUBJECT=JONES----------------------------------------------------

                            OBS     DRUG       EXERCISE     RESPONSE

                             1     ASPIRIN     LIGHT          6
                             2     ASPIRIN     MEDIUM         7
                             3     ASPIRIN     HEAVY          9
                             4     PLACEBO     LIGHT          3
                             5     PLACEBO     MEDIUM         4
                             6     PLACEBO     HEAVY          6

---------------------------------------------------SUBJECT=SMITH----------------------------------------------------

                            OBS     DRUG       EXERCISE     RESPONSE

                             7     ASPIRIN     LIGHT          5
                             8     ASPIRIN     MEDIUM         8
                             9     ASPIRIN     HEAVY          9
                            10     PLACEBO     LIGHT          4
                            11     PLACEBO     HEAVY          7
```

```
                                        DATA SET A2                                          2
---------------------------------------------------SUBJECT=JONES----------------------------------------------------

                 OBS     DRUG       RESPNAME     LIGHT     MEDIUM     HEAVY

                  1     ASPIRIN     RESPONSE       6          7          9
                  2     PLACEBO     RESPONSE       3          4          6

---------------------------------------------------SUBJECT=SMITH----------------------------------------------------

                 OBS     DRUG       RESPNAME     LIGHT     MEDIUM     HEAVY

                  3     ASPIRIN     RESPONSE       5          8          9
                  4     PLACEBO     RESPONSE       4          .          7
```

```
                                        DATA SET A3                                          3
---------------------------------------------------SUBJECT=JONES----------------------------------------------------

                     OBS     RESPNAME     EXERCISE     ASPIRIN     PLACEBO

                      1     RESPONSE      LIGHT           6            3
                      2     RESPONSE      MEDIUM          7            4
                      3     RESPONSE      HEAVY           9            6

---------------------------------------------------SUBJECT=SMITH----------------------------------------------------

                     OBS     RESPNAME     EXERCISE     ASPIRIN     PLACEBO

                      4     RESPONSE      LIGHT           5            4
                      5     RESPONSE      MEDIUM          8            .
                      6     RESPONSE      HEAVY           9            7
```

```
                                DATA SET A4                                        4

-----------------------------------------------------SUBJECT=JONES-----------------------------------------------------

                         OBS    EXERCISE     DRUG      RESPONSE

                          1     LIGHT       ASPIRIN       6
                          2     LIGHT       PLACEBO       3
                          3     MEDIUM      ASPIRIN       7
                          4     MEDIUM      PLACEBO       4
                          5     HEAVY       ASPIRIN       9
                          6     HEAVY       PLACEBO       6

-----------------------------------------------------SUBJECT=SMITH-----------------------------------------------------

                         OBS    EXERCISE     DRUG      RESPONSE

                           7    LIGHT       ASPIRIN       5
                           8    LIGHT       PLACEBO       4
                           9    MEDIUM      ASPIRIN       8
                          10    MEDIUM      PLACEBO       .
                          11    HEAVY       ASPIRIN       9
                          12    HEAVY       PLACEBO       7
```

Chapter 29

The UNIVARIATE Procedure

ABSTRACT

The UNIVARIATE procedure produces simple descriptive statistics (including quantiles) for numeric variables.

INTRODUCTION

The UNIVARIATE procedure differs from other SAS procedures that produce descriptive statistics because it provides greater detail on the distribution of a variable. Features in PROC UNIVARIATE include:

- detail on the extreme values of a variable
- quantiles, such as the median
- several plots to picture the distribution
- frequency tables
- a test to determine that the data are normally distributed.

If a BY statement is used with PROC UNIVARIATE, descriptive statistics are calculated separately for groups of observations. PROC UNIVARIATE can also create one or more data sets containing calculated statistics.

SPECIFICATIONS

The following statements control the UNIVARIATE procedure:

PROC UNIVARIATE *options;*
VAR *variables;*
BY *variables;*
FREQ *variable;*
WEIGHT *variable;*
ID *variables;*
OUTPUT OUT=*SASdataset keyword=names...;*

Several OUTPUT statements are permitted, but only one each of the other statements. The statements after the PROC statement can be listed in any order.

PROC UNIVARIATE Statement

PROC UNIVARIATE *options;*

The options that can appear in the PROC UNIVARIATE statement are listed below:

DATA=*SASdataset*
: names the SAS data set to be used by PROC UNIVARIATE. If DATA= is omitted, the most recently created SAS data set is used.

NOPRINT
: suppresses all printed output. NOPRINT can be used when the only purpose for executing the procedure is to create new data sets.

PLOT
: causes PROC UNIVARIATE to produce a stem-and-leaf plot (or a horizontal bar chart), a box plot, and a normal probability plot. If a BY statement is used, box plots for groups defined by the BY variables also appear side-by-side.

FREQ
: requests a frequency table consisting of the variable values, frequencies, percentages, and cumulative percentages.

NORMAL
: causes PROC UNIVARIATE to compute a test statistic for the hypothesis that the input data come from a normal distribution. The probability of a more extreme value of the test statistic is also printed.

PCTLDEF=*value*
: specifies which of the four definitions presented in **Computational Methods** is to be used to calculate percentiles. The PCTLDEF= value can be 1, 2, 3, 4, or 5. If PCTLDEF= is omitted, definition 5 is used.

VARDEF=DF
VARDEF=WEIGHT | WGT
VARDEF=N
VARDEF=WDF

specifies the divisor to be used in the calculation of the variances. VARDEF=DF requests that the degrees of freedom (N−1) be used as the divisor. VARDEF=WEIGHT requests that the sum of the weights be used. VARDEF=N requests that the number of observations (N) be used. VARDEF=WDF requests that the sum of the weights minus one be used. The default is VARDEF=DF.

VAR Statement

VAR *variables;*

Univariate descriptive measures are calculated for all numeric variables listed in the VAR statement. If no VAR statement appears, all numeric variables in the data set are analyzed. A VAR statement must be included when an OUTPUT statement is used.

BY Statement

BY *variables;*

A BY statement can be used with PROC UNIVARIATE to obtain separate analyses on observations in groups defined by the BY variables. When a BY statement appears, the procedure expects the input data set to be sorted in order of the BY variables. If your input data set is not sorted in ascending order, use the SORT procedure with a similar BY statement to sort the data, or, if appropriate, use the BY statement options NOTSORTED or DESCENDING. For more information, see the discussion of the BY statement in *SAS Language Guide for Personal Computers.*

FREQ Statement

FREQ *variable;*

When a FREQ statement appears, each observation in the data set being analyzed is assumed to represent *n* observations, where *n* is the value of the FREQ variable. If the FREQ variable has a value that is less than one, the observation is not used in the analysis. If the value is not an integer, only the integer portion is used.

The statistics calculated using a FREQ statement are identical to an analysis produced using a data set that contains *n* observations in place of each observation in the input data set.

WEIGHT Statement

WEIGHT *variable;*

When a WEIGHT statement is specified, PROC UNIVARIATE uses the value of the WEIGHT variable, w_i, to calculate a weighted mean $\bar{x}_w$ and a weighted variance s_w^2 as

$$\bar{x}_w = \Sigma_i w_i x_i \, / \Sigma_i \, w_i$$

and

$$s_w^2 = \Sigma_i w_i (x_i - \bar{x}_w)^2 / d$$

where the x_i are the variable values and the divisor d is controlled by the VARDEF= option. The divisor can be $n-1$ (VARDEF=DF), Σw_i (VARDEF=WEIGHT | WGT), n (VARDEF=N) or Σw_i-1 (VARDEF=WDF) where n is the number of values.

If the value of the WEIGHT variable is less than zero, then a value of zero for the weight is assumed.

The value of the WEIGHT variable is used only to calculate the first two sample moments and related statistics. Hence, if a WEIGHT statement is used, measures of skewness and kurtosis are not calculated and are reported as missing values. The WEIGHT variable has no effect on the calculation of quantiles or extremes.

ID Statement

ID *variables;*

When an ID statement is used, up to eight characters of the first variable specified are used to identify observations in the printed listing of the five largest and five smallest values. However, the *values* of these ID variables are written to any OUTPUT data set specified in their entirety. In addition, if one or more OUTPUT statements are used, the values of the ID variables are placed in each output data set. The values of the ID variables used in the output data set are taken either from the first observation in the data set analyzed by PROC UNIVARIATE or from the first observation in the current BY group, if a BY statement is used.

OUTPUT Statement

OUTPUT OUT=*SASdataset keyword=names...;*

The OUTPUT statement requests that PROC UNIVARIATE output statistics to a new SAS data set. The options name the new data set and specify the variables to be included.

OUT=*SASdataset*

names the output data set. If you want to create a permanent SAS data set, you must specify a two-level name (see *SAS Language Guide for Personal Computers* for more information on permanent data sets).

keyword=names

specifies the statistics you want in the new data set and names the new variables that contain the statistics. Write the keyword for the desired statistic, an equal sign, and the variable or variables to contain the statistic.

In the output data set, the first variable listed after a keyword in the OUTPUT statement contains that statistic for the first variable listed in the VAR statement; the second variable contains the statistic for the second variable in the VAR statement, and so on.

The list of variables following the equal sign can be shorter than the list of variables in the VAR statement.

The valid keywords and the statistics they represent are as follows:

N	the number of observations on which the calculations are based
NMISS	the number of missing values
NOBS	the number of observations
MEAN	the mean

SUM	the sum
STD	the standard deviation
VAR	the variance
SKEWNESS	skewness
KURTOSIS	kurtosis
SUMWGT	the sum of the weights
MAX	the largest value
MIN	the smallest value
RANGE	the range
Q3	the upper quartile or the seventy-fifth percentile
MEDIAN	the median or the fiftieth percentile
Q1	the lower quartile or the twenty-fifth percentile
QRANGE	the difference between the upper and lower quartiles, that is, Q3-Q1
P1	the first percentile
P5	the fifth percentile
P10	the tenth percentile
P90	the ninetieth percentile
P95	the ninety-fifth percentile
P99	the ninety-ninth percentile
MODE	the most frequent value. If there is more than one mode, the smallest mode is used.
SIGNRANK	the signed rank statistic
NORMAL	the test statistic for normality. If the sample size is less than or equal to 2000 this is the Shapiro-Wilk statistic. Otherwise, it is the Kolmogorov statistic.

The following options are used in the OUTPUT statement to produce additional percentiles (that is, in addition to P1, P5, P10, P90, P95, and P99).

PCTLNAME=*percentile name* ...

specifies names for the additional percentiles you request. List the percentile names in the same order that the percentiles are specified with the PCTLPTS= option (see below). For example, if you specify

```
OUTPUT PCTLPTS=33 66 PCTLNAME=P33 P66;
```

the new percentiles are P33 (for the thirty-third percentile) and P66 (for the sixty-sixth percentile).

If you do not use this option when generating new percentiles, the new percentiles are assigned default names. If the percentile is an integer value, as in the example above, the name is simply the value (for example, 33). Otherwise, an underscore replaces the decimal point in the name. For example, if you specify

```
OUTPUT PCTLPTS=33.3 66.7;
```

then the new percentiles are named 33_3 and 66_7. (Decimal values are truncated to one decimal place.) The same naming conventions apply if you specify fewer names with PCTLNAME= than the number of percentiles requested by PCTLPTS=.

PCTLPTS=*percentile value* ...

specifies the values for which you want additional percentiles. For example, if you want the twentieth, fortieth, sixtieth, and eightieth percentiles, specify PCTLPTS=20 40 60 80. This option must be specified to generate additional percentiles.

PCTLPRE=*variable prefix* ...

specifies prefixes used to create names for the output variables containing the new percentiles. The designated prefix is combined with the percentile name (either a default or the name specified with PCTLNAME=) to create the output variable name. If you are requesting percentiles for more than one variable in the input data set, then specify prefixes in the same order that the variables appear in the VAR statement. This option must be specified if you are creating new percentiles.

For example:

```
VAR TESTA TESTB TESTC;
OUTPUT PCTLPTS=33.3 66.7 PCTLPRE=A B C
       PCTLNAME=P33_3 P66_7;
```

When these statements are used, the output variables containing the new percentiles are called AP33_3, AP66_7, BP33_3, BP66_7, CP33_3, and CP66_7.

If combining the prefix and percentile name results in a name longer than eight characters, the prefix is truncated to the necessary length. For example, COUNTYP75 becomes COUNTP75.

The number of observations in the new data set corresponds to the number of groups for which statistics are calculated. The variables in the BY statement and the ID statement, as well as the computed statistics, are included in the new data set.

For example, consider these statements:

```
PROC UNIVARIATE;
     VAR GRADE1 GRADE2;
     BY SEX;
     OUTPUT OUT=NEW MEAN=AVE1 AVE2 VAR=VAR1
            PCTLPRE=ONE TWO PCTLPTS=33.3 66.7;
```

If the BY variable SEX has two values, F and M, the data set NEW contains two observations. Each of these observations contains the variables SEX, AVE1, AVE2, VAR1, ONE33_3, ONE66_7, TWO33_3, and TWO66_7.

Any number of OUTPUT statements can be used with each execution of PROC UNIVARIATE.

DETAILS

Missing Values

If a variable for which statistics are to be calculated has a missing value, that value is ignored in the calculation of statistics and the missing values are tabulated separately. A missing value for one such variable does not affect the treatment of other variables in the same observation.

If the WEIGHT variable has a missing value, the weight is taken to be zero. However, the observation is still used to calculate quantiles and extremes. If the FREQ variable has a missing value, the observation is not used at all.

If a variable in a BY or ID statement has a missing value, the procedure treats it as it would treat any other value of a BY or ID variable.

Output Data Set

If an OUTPUT statement is used, the corresponding output data set contains an observation for each unique set of values of the variables in the BY statement or a single observation if there is no BY statement. The variables in each observation consist of the variables in the BY statement, the variables in the ID statement, and a selection of the statistics from the list above as selected in the OUTPUT statement.

The values of the variables listed in the BY statement are taken as those of the corresponding BY group, the values of the ID variables are taken from the first observation of each BY group, and the values of the statistics are computed from the values of the variables within each BY group or across all the data if there is no BY statement.

Computational Methods

The sample mean, the sample standard deviation, the minimum, and the maximum are computed using the original data. All other statistics are computed after the data have been truncated to single precision (approximately seven significant digits).

Standard algorithms (Fisher 1973) are used to compute the moment statistics. Using the PCTLDEF= option, you can specify one of five methods for computing quantile statistics.

Let n be the number of nonmissing values for a variable and let $x_1, x_2, \ldots, x_n$ represent the ordered values of the variable. For the tth percentile, where $p=t/100$, let

$$np = j + g$$

where j is the integer part and g is the fractional part of np.

The tth percentile, y, for example, is defined as:

DEFINITION 1: weighted average at x_{np}

$$y = (1-g)x_j + gx_{j+1}$$

where x_o is taken to be x_1

DEFINITION 2: observation numbered closest to np

$$y = x_i$$

where i is the integer part of $np + 1/2$

DEFINITION 3: empirical distribution function

$$y = x_j \quad \text{if } g = 0$$
$$y = x_{j+1} \text{ if } g > 0$$

DEFINITION 4: weighted average aimed at $x_{p(n+1)}$

$$y = (1-g)x_j + gx_{j+1}$$

where $(n+1)p = j + g$, and

x_{n+1} is taken to be x_n

DEFINITION 5: empirical distribution function with averaging

$$y = (x_j + x_{j+1})/2 \text{ if } g=0$$
$$y = x_{j+1} \quad \text{if } g>0$$

where $np=j+g$.

The signed rank statistic S is computed as

$$S = \Sigma r_i^+ - n(n+1)/4$$

where r_i^+ is the rank of $|x_i|$, n is the number of nonzero x_i values, and the sum is over those x_i greater than zero. Average ranks are used for tied values. The significance of the S is computed by treating

$$(|S|-.5)/\sqrt{V}$$

as a standard normal deviate where V is computed as

$$V = (n(n+1)(2n+1) - .5\Sigma t_i(t_i+1)(t_i-1))/24$$

where the sum is over groups tied in absolute value and t_i is the number of values in the ith group (Lehmann 1975).

Test of Normality

When the NORMAL option is specified in the PROC UNIVARIATE statement, the procedure produces a test statistic for the null hypothesis that the input data values are a random sample from a normal distribution.

If the sample size is less than or equal to 2000, the Shapiro-Wilk statistic, W, is computed. The W statistic is the ratio of the best estimator of the variance (based on the square of a linear combination of the order statistics) to the usual corrected sum of squares estimator of the variance. W must be greater than zero and less than or equal to one, with small values of W leading to rejection of the null hypothesis. When the sample size is greater than six, the coefficients for calculating the linear combination of the order statistics are approximated by the method of Shapiro and Wilk (1965).

With a sample size of three, the probability distribution of W is known and is used to determine the significance level. When the sample size is greater than three, simulation results are used to determine the significance levels. For sample size, n, between four and six, the W statistic, W_n, is transformed to an equivalent W statistic of sample size three, W_3, where the significance levels can be evaluated (Royston 1982). For sample size, n, greater than six, the significance level of W is obtained by Royston's approximate normalizing transformation

$$Z_n = ((1-W_n)^\gamma - \mu) / \sigma$$

where

Z_n is a standard normal variate, and
γ, μ, and σ are functions of *n*, obtained from simulation results.

Large values of Z_n indicate departure from normality.

If the sample size is greater than 2000, the data are tested against a normal distribution with mean and variance equal to the sample mean and variance. The usual Kolomogorov D statistic is computed and printed. The probability of a larger test statistic is obtained by forming the value

$$(\sqrt{n} - .01 + .85 / \sqrt{n})D$$

where *n* is the number of nonmissing values. This value is used to interpolate linearly within the range of simulated critical values given in Stephens (1974).

Plots

When the PLOT option is specified in the PROC UNIVARIATE statement, the procedure generates three data plots.

The first plot is a stem-and-leaf plot (Tukey 1977) if no more than forty-eight observations fall into a single interval. Otherwise, the procedure plots a horizontal bar chart.

The second plot is a box plot or schematic plot. The bottom and top edges of the box are located at the sample 25th and 75th percentiles. The center horizontal line is drawn at the sample median and the central plus sign (+) is at the sample mean. It is possible for all of these statistics to fall on the same printer line. The central vertical lines, called "whiskers," extend from the box as far as the data extend, to a distance of at most 1.5 interquartile ranges. (An interquartile range is the distance between the 25th and the 75th sample percentiles.) Any value more extreme than this is marked with a zero if it is within three interquartile ranges of the box, or with an asterisk (*) if it is still more extreme. For more explanation about this plot, see Tukey (1977). When a BY statement also appears, PROC UNIVARIATE produces side-by-side box plots in order of the BY variables after the separate analyses of each BY group.

The third plot, a normal probability plot, is a quantile-quantile plot of the data. The empirical quantiles are plotted against the quantiles of a standard normal distribution. Asterisks (*) mark the data values. The vertical coordinate is the data value, and the horizontal coordinate is

$$\Phi^{-1}((r_i - 3/8)/(n + 1/4))$$

where

r_i is the rank of the data value,
Φ^{-1} is the inverse of the standard normal distribution function,
n is the number of nonmissing data values. The plus signs (+) provide a reference straight line that is drawn using the sample mean and standard deviation. If the data are from a normal distribution, they should tend to fall along the reference line.

Computer Resources

The data are stored internally in single precision. For most time-efficient processing, the amount of memory for temporary storage in bytes is

$$M = 20 * \Sigma_i\ U_i + 252 * V + 112$$

where

V is the number of variables in the VAR list (or the number of numeric variables if the VAR list is omitted)

U_i is the number of unique values for the *i*th variable.

If M bytes are not available, UNIVARIATE must pass through the data several times to collect all the statistics. If this happens, the minimum amount of temporary storage required in bytes is

$$20 * MAX_i (U_i) + 252 * V + 112$$

When the option NORMAL is specified, the temporary storage must be increased by $4 * MAX_i\ [n_i / 2\ ]$ bytes, where

n_i is the number of nonmissing values for the *i*th variable

$[n_i/2]$ is the largest integer less than or equal to $n_i/2$.

Additional storage is also required for the PLOT option and for each output data set.

Printed Output

For each variable, PROC UNIVARIATE prints:

1. VARIABLE=, the name of the variable
2. the variable label
3. N, the number of observations on which the calculations are based
4. SUM WGTS, the sum of the weights of these observations
5. the MEAN
6. the SUM
7. STD DEV, the standard deviation
8. the VARIANCE
9. the measure of SKEWNESS
10. the measure of KURTOSIS
11. USS, the uncorrected sum of squares
12. CSS, the corrected sum of squares
13. CV, the coefficient of variation
14. STD MEAN, the standard error of the mean
15. T: MEAN=0, the Student's *t* value for testing the hypothesis that the population mean is 0
16. PROB>|T|, the probability of a greater absolute value for this *t* value
17. SGN RANK, the centered signed rank statistic for testing the hypothesis that the population mean is 0
18. PROB>|S|, an approximation of the probability of a greater absolute value for this statistic under the hypothesis that the population mean is 0
19. NUM ˆ =0, the number of nonzero observations
20. MAX, the largest value
21. Q3, Q1, and MED, the upper and lower quartiles, and the median
22. MIN, the smallest value
23. the RANGE
24. Q3-Q1, the difference between the upper and lower quartiles
25. the MODE
26. the 1st, 5th, 10th, 90th, 95th, and 99th percentiles
27. the five largest, HIGHEST, and five smallest, LOWEST, values.

If missing values occur for a variable, the following are printed:

28. the MISSING VALUE
29. COUNT, the number of occurrences
30. %COUNT/NOBS, the count as a percentage of the total number of observations
31. %COUNT/NMISS, the count as a percentage of the total number of missing values (not shown).

UNIVARIATE can also print:

32. W:NORMAL...D:NORMAL, test statistics
33. associated probabilities, PROB<W or PROB>D, for testing the hypothesis that the data come from a normal distribution
34. STEM LEAF, a stem-and-leaf plot (if any value's count is greater than forty-eight, a horizontal bar chart is printed instead)
35. BOXPLOT, a box plot
36. a NORMAL PROBABILITY PLOT
37. VALUE, a frequency table of variable values
38. COUNT, frequencies
39. CELL, percentages
40. CUM, cumulative percentages
41. SCHEMATIC PLOTS, side-by-side box plots for groups defined by the BY variables.

EXAMPLE

Census Data Analysis Using PROC UNIVARIATE

In the following example, descriptive statistics are produced for the 1970 and 1980 census populations by sex for the fifty states (plus two fictional states to illustrate missing values). Several OUTPUT statements are used in the DATA step to create the necessary BY groups for schematic plots. **Output 29.1** contains the descriptive statistics for one of the BY groups, DECADE=70 SEX=FEMALE (others are omitted for brevity). **Output 29.2** contains schematic plots for all groups defined by the BY variables. An output data set from PROC UNIVARIATE containing percentile values is illustrated in **Output 29.3**.

```
DATA PF70 PM70 PF80 PM80;
   INPUT STATE $ POP_F70 POP_M70 POP_F80 POP_M80 @@;
   DROP POP_M70 POP_F70 POP_M80 POP_F80;
   DECADE= 70;
   SEX= 'FEMALE';
   POP= POP_F70;  OUTPUT PF70;
   SEX= 'MALE';
   POP= POP_M70;  OUTPUT PM70;
   DECADE= 80;
   POP= POP_M80;  OUTPUT PM80;
   SEX= 'FEMALE';
   POP= POP_F80;  OUTPUT PF80;
   CARDS;
ALA    1.78  1.66  2.02  1.87   ALASKA 0.14  0.16  0.19  0.21
ARIZ   0.90  0.87  1.38  1.34   ARK    0.99  0.93  1.18  1.10
```

```
CALIF 10.14  9.82 12.00 11.67   COLO   1.12  1.09  1.46  1.43
CONN   1.56  1.47  1.61  1.50   DEL    0.28  0.27  0.31  0.29
FLA    3.51  3.28  5.07  4.68   GA     2.36  2.23  2.82  2.64
HAW    0.37  0.40  0.47  0.49   IDAHO  0.36  0.36  0.47  0.47
ILL    5.72  5.39  5.89  5.54   IND    2.66  2.53  2.82  2.67
IOWA   1.45  1.37  1.50  1.41   KAN    1.15  1.02  1.21  1.16
KY     1.64  1.58  1.87  1.79   LA     1.87  1.77  2.17  2.04
ME     0.51  0.48  0.58  0.55   MD     2.01  1.92  2.17  2.04
MASS   2.97  2.72  3.01  2.73   MICH   4.53  4.39  4.75  4.52
MINN   1.94  1.86  2.08  2.00   MISS   1.14  1.07  1.31  1.21
MO     2.42  2.26  2.55  2.37   MONT   0.35  0.35  0.39  0.39
NEB    0.76  0.72  0.80  0.77   NEV    0.24  0.25  0.40  0.41
NH     0.38  0.36  0.47  0.45   NJ     3.70  3.47  3.83  3.53
NM     0.52  0.50  0.66  0.64   NY     9.52  8.72  9.22  8.34
NC     2.59  2.49  3.03  2.86   ND     0.31  0.31  0.32  0.33
OHIO   5.49  5.16  5.58  5.22   OKLA   1.31  1.25  1.55  1.48
ORE    1.07  1.02  1.34  1.30   PA     6.13  5.67  6.18  5.68
RI     0.48  0.46  0.50  0.45   SC     1.32  1.27  1.60  1.52
SD     0.34  0.33  0.35  0.34   TENN   2.03  1.90  2.37  2.22
TEXAS  5.72  5.48  7.23  7.00   UTAH   0.54  0.52  0.74  0.72
VT     0.23  0.22  0.26  0.25   VA     2.35  2.30  2.73  2.62
WASH   1.72  1.69  2.08  2.05   W.VA   0.90  0.84  1.00  0.95
WIS    2.25  2.17  2.40  2.31   WYO    0.16  0.17  0.23  0.24
XX     .     .     .     .      YY     .     .     .     .
;
DATA POPSTATE;
  SET PF70 PM70 PF80 PM80;
  LABEL POP= 'CENSUS POPULATION IN MILLIONS';

PROC UNIVARIATE DATA=POPSTATE FREQ PLOT NORMAL;
   VAR POP;
   ID STATE;
   BY DECADE SEX;
   OUTPUT OUT= UNIVOUT MEAN= POPNMEAN MEDIAN= POPN50
      PCTLPRE= POP_  PCTLPTS= 50, 95 TO 100 BY 2.5;

PROC PRINT DATA= UNIVOUT;
   TITLE 'OUTPUT DATASET FROM PROC UNIVARIATE';
   FORMAT POPN50 POP_50 POP_95 POP_97_5 POP_100 BEST8.;
```

Ouptut 29.1 Descriptive Statistics for State Census Population Date: PROC UNIVARIATE

```
---------------------------------------------- DECADE=70 SEX=FEMALE ------------------------------------------------      1

                                                 UNIVARIATE
   (1)                    (2)
VARIABLE=POP            CENSUS POPULATION IN MILLIONS

             MOMENTS                                                                      QUANTILES(DEF=5) (26)

(3)N               50  SUM WGTS(4)        50                          (20)100% MAX      10.14       99%        10.14
(5)MEAN        2.0786  SUM(6)         103.93                               75% Q3        2.42       95%         6.13
 STD DEV(7)  2.232345  VARIANCE(8)  4.983363                          (21) 50% MED      1.385       90%        5.605
(9)SKEWNESS(11) 2.0465 KURTOSIS(10) 4.466265                               25% Q1         .51       10%         .295
 USS         460.2137  CSS(12)      244.1848                                0% MIN(22)    .14        5%          .23
(13)CV       107.3966  STD MEAN(14) .3157012                                                          1%          .14
 T:MEAN=0(15) 6.584073 PROB>|T|(16)    .0001                          (23) RANGE           10
(17)SGN RANK    637.5  PROB>|S|(18)    .0001                               Q3-Q1(24)     1.91
 NUM ^= 0(19)      50                                                 (25) MODE            .9
(32)W:NORMAL .7619694  PROB<W(33)       .001

                                               (27) EXTREMES

                                     LOWEST    ID         HIGHEST    ID
                                       .14(ALASKA  )        5.72(ILL      )
                                       .16(WYO     )        5.72(TEXAS    )
                                       .23(VT      )        6.13(PA       )
                                       .24(NEV     )        9.52(NY       )
                                       .28(DEL     )       10.14(CALIF    )

                                          MISSING VALUE          .   (28)
                                                  COUNT (29)     2
                                          % COUNT/NOBS        3.85   (30)
 (34)                                         (35)                                                (36)
STEM LEAF                      #           BOXPLOT                                 NORMAL PROBABILITY PLOT
  10 1                         1              *                10.25+                                                *
   9 5                         1              *                     |                                            *
   9                                                           9.25+
   8                                                                |
   8                                                            8.25+
   7                                                                |                                                   +
   7                                                            7.25+                                                ++
   6                                                                |                                             +++
   6 1                         1              0                 6.25+                                          * ++
   5 577                       3              0                     |                                      ***++
   5                                          0                 5.25+                                      * ++
   4 5                         1              |                     |                                    *++
   4                                          |                 4.25+                                  ++
   3 57                        2              |                     |                                ++**
   3 0                         1              |                 3.25+                              ++
   2 67                        2              |                     |                            +++ ***
   2 003444                    6           +--+--+              2.25+                          ++ ****
   1 5667899                   7           |     |                  |                       ++ ***
   1 0111233                   7           *-----*              1.25+                     +****
   0 5555899                   7           +-----+                  |                  *****
   0 12223334444              11              |                  .25+   *   * ** *******
     ----+----+----+----+                                            +----+----+----+----+----+----+----+----+----+----+
                                                                         -2        -1          0       +1        +2
```

```
------------------------------------------------- DECADE=70 SEX=FEMALE -------------------------------------------------
                                                                                                                        2
                                                       UNIVARIATE

VARIABLE=POP              CENSUS POPULATION IN MILLIONS

                                                     FREQUENCY TABLE
```

❸❼ VALUE	❸❽ COUNT	❸❾ PERCENTS CELL	❹⓿ PERCENTS CUM	VALUE	COUNT	PERCENTS CELL	PERCENTS CUM	VALUE	COUNT	PERCENTS CELL	PERCENTS CUM
.14	1	2.0	2.0	.9	2	4.0	36.0	2.03	1	2.0	68.0
.16	1	2.0	4.0	.99	1	2.0	38.0	2.25	1	2.0	70.0
.23	1	2.0	6.0	1.07	1	2.0	40.0	2.35	1	2.0	72.0
.24	1	2.0	8.0	1.12	1	2.0	42.0	2.36	1	2.0	74.0
.28	1	2.0	10.0	1.14	1	2.0	44.0	2.42	1	2.0	76.0
.31	1	2.0	12.0	1.15	1	2.0	46.0	2.59	1	2.0	78.0
.34	1	2.0	14.0	1.31	1	2.0	48.0	2.66	1	2.0	80.0
.35	1	2.0	16.0	1.32	1	2.0	50.0	2.97	1	2.0	82.0
.36	1	2.0	18.0	1.45	1	2.0	52.0	3.51	1	2.0	84.0
.37	1	2.0	20.0	1.56	1	2.0	54.0	3.7	1	2.0	86.0
.38	1	2.0	22.0	1.64	1	2.0	56.0	4.53	1	2.0	88.0
.48	1	2.0	24.0	1.72	1	2.0	58.0	5.49	1	2.0	90.0
.51	1	2.0	26.0	1.78	1	2.0	60.0	5.72	2	4.0	94.0
.52	1	2.0	28.0	1.87	1	2.0	62.0	6.13	1	2.0	96.0
.54	1	2.0	30.0	1.94	1	2.0	64.0	9.52	1	2.0	98.0
.76	1	2.0	32.0	2.01	1	2.0	66.0	10.14	1	2.0	100.0

Output 29.2 Producing Schematic Plots

```
                                                                                                        3

                                              UNIVARIATE
                                        ❹❶ SCHEMATIC PLOTS

VARIABLE=POP              CENSUS POPULATION IN MILLIONS

       |
    15 +
       |
       |
       |                              *         *
       |
    10 +          *         *
       |                    *         0
       |                                        0
       |                              0         0
       |          0         0         |         |
     5 +          0         0         |         |
       |          |         |         |         |
       |          |         |      +-----+   +-----+
       |       +--+--+   +--+--+   *--+--*   |  +  |
       |       *-----*   *-----*   +-----+   *-----*
     0 +          |      +-----+      |         |
        ----------+---------+---------+---------+------------
   SEX          FEMALE      MALE     FEMALE      MALE
DECADE              70        70         80        80
```

Ouptut 29.3 Producing an Output Data Set

OUTPUT DATASET FROM PROC UNIVARIATE 4

OBS	DECADE	SEX	STATE	POPNMEAN	POPN50	POP_50	POP_95	POP_97_5	POP_100
1	70	FEMALE	ALA	2.0786	1.385	1.385	6.13	9.52	10.14
2	70	MALE	ALA	1.9704	1.32	1.32	5.67	8.72	9.82
3	80	FEMALE	ALA	2.323	1.575	1.575	7.23	9.22	12
4	80	MALE	ALA	2.1958	1.49	1.49	7	8.34	11.67

REFERENCES

County and City Data Book, 1983 Files on Tape (machine-readable data file)/ prepared by the Bureau of the Census. Washington: The Bureau (producer and distributor), 1984.

County and City Data Book, 1983 Files on Tape Technical Documentation/ prepared by the Data User Services Division, Bureau of the Census. Washington: The Bureau, 1984.

Fisher, R.A. (1973), *Statistical Methods for Research Workers*, 14th Edition, New York: Hafner Publishing Company.

Lehmann, E.L. (1975), *Nonparametrics: Statistical Methods Based on Ranks*, San Francisco: Holden-Day, Inc.

Royston, J.P. (1982), "An Extension of Shapiro and Wilk's W Test for Normality to Large Samples," *Applied Statistics*, 31, 115-124.

Shapiro, S.S. and Wilk, M.B. (1965), "An Analysis of Variance Test for Normality (complete samples)," *Biometrika*, 52, 591-611.

Stephens, M.A. (1974), "EDF Statistics for Goodness of Fit and Some Comparisons," *Journal of the American Statistical Association*, 69, 730-737.

Tukey, J.W. (1977), *Exploratory Data Analysis*, Reading, Massachusetts: Addison-Wesley.

U.S. Bureau of the Census (1977), *County and City Data Book, 1977* (Machine-readable data file) Washington, D.C.: U.S. Government Printing Office.

Chapter 30

The UPLOAD Procedure

ABSTRACT

The micro-to-mainframe link allows you to use mainframe capabilities when you need them under PC DOS. You can use your PC as a development system and choose either local (on the PC) or remote (on the mainframe) processing for your SAS programs. In addition, you can easily transfer SAS data sets between systems with utilities that the micro-to-mainframe link provides.

This chapter documents one part of the link, the UPLOAD procedure. (See also "The DOWNLOAD Procedure.")

INTRODUCTION

You should be familiar with the SAS System for PC DOS before using PROC UPLOAD. If you need more information about the SAS System for PC DOS, see *SAS Introductory Guide for Personal Computers*.

The UPLOAD procedure copies a SAS data set stored on the local PC system to the remote mainframe system.

PROC UPLOAD executes only under SAS Display Manager. There are two Display Manager commands you need to know about in order to use the UPLOAD procedure:

SIGNON
: If you have not already established the micro-to-mainframe link, issue the SIGNON command. The SIGNON command establishes the link between your PC and the remote mainframe system. See *SAS Language Guide for Personal Computers* for details on the SIGNON command.

RSUBMIT
RSUB
: The RSUBMIT, or RSUB, command (for remote submit) sends the program statements in the Program Edit window to the remote mainframe system for execution. See *SAS Language Guide for Personal Computers* for details on the RSUBMIT command.

: Even though the program executes in the remote mainframe environment, the information that displays on your PC is the same as if you had executed the program locally on the PC.

SPECIFICATIONS

The only statement used with the UPLOAD procedure is

PROC UPLOAD [*options*];

PROC UPLOAD Statement

PROC UPLOAD [*options*];

The following options can be used in the PROC UPLOAD statement:

DATA=*input SASdataset*
: names the SAS data set that you want to upload, or copy, from the PC to the mainframe. When you do not specify the DATA= option, the SAS System copies the last data set created on the PC in your SAS program.

OUT=*output SASdataset*
: names the SAS data set to which you want the copied data set written. When you do not specify the OUT= option, the SAS System creates a temporary WORK data set.

EXAMPLE

Suppose you have previously created a data set on the PC by entering the following program and then issuing the SUBMIT command.

```
DATA FROGS;
   INPUT NAME $ SIZE;
   CARDS;
FRED  3
FATS  8
CLYDE 2
;
RUN;
```

After you have issued the SUBMIT command to create the data set on the PC, you can then invoke PROC UPLOAD to copy the FROG data set from the PC to the remote mainframe.

```
PROC UPLOAD DATA=FROGS OUT=MAINFROG;
RUN;
```

Remember that you must use the RSUBMIT command for PROC UPLOAD because the program executes in the remote mainframe environment.

Appendix

Version 6 Changes and Enhancements to Base SAS® Software: Procedures

The Version 6 base SAS Software product features four new procedures and contains a subset of procedures from Version 5. This appendix summarizes how those procedures that are available in Version 5 have been changed or enhanced for Version 6. The four new procedures are also listed and briefly described.

NEW PROCEDURES

The DBF Procedure

This new procedure converts dBASE II or dBASE III files to SAS data sets and vice versa.

The DIF Procedure

This new procedure converts files in the Data Interchange Format (DIF) to SAS data sets and vice versa. VisiCalc files and Lotus 1-2-3 files use the DIF format.

The DOWNLOAD Procedure

PROC DOWNLOAD copies a SAS data set stored on a mainframe computer to a personal computer.

The UPLOAD Procedure

PROC UPLOAD copies a SAS data set stored on a personal computer to a mainframe computer.

CHANGES AND ENHANCEMENTS TO EXISTING PROCEDURES

The CHART Procedure

Overprinting is not available with the CHART procedure in Version 6.

The CONTENTS Procedure

The default value for the MEMTYPE= option is now ALL, instead of DATA. Therefore, if you do not specify MEMTYPE=, PROC CONTENTS describes all types of SAS files within the specified library, not just SAS data sets (members of type DATA).

Valid values for the MEMTYPE= option are now:

ALL (the default)	all of the following types
CAT	full-screen catalogs
DATA	SAS data sets
FORMAT	formats catalog

The following options are not available with PROC CONTENTS in Version 6:

HISTORY
NOSOURCE

The COPY Procedure

Valid values for the MEMTYPE= option are now:

ALL (the default)	all of the following types
CAT	full-screen catalogs
DATA	SAS data sets
FORMAT	formats catalog

The following options are not available with PROC COPY in Version 6:

EXPORT
IMPORT
NOHISTORY
PROTECT=

The CORR Procedure

You must now use the new OUT= option to create a SAS data set. OUT= replaces all of the following output data set options:

OUTH=
OUTK=
OUTP=
OUTS=

The following statistical options have also been deleted:

HOEFFDING
KENDALL
PEARSON
SPEARMAN

The WITH statement is no longer available.

The DATASETS Procedure

Full-screen processing is not available; thus, the NOFS option (used to request processing without the full-screen feature) has been removed.

If you do not specify MEMTYPE= in the PROC statement and in an associated statement, the default value of the MEMTYPE= option is now ALL (instead of DATA).

Valid values for the MEMTYPE= option are now:

ALL (the default)	all of the following types
CAT	full-screen catalogs
DATA	SAS data sets
FORMAT	formats catalog

Three new associated statements have been added:

APPEND Statement
: appends observations from one SAS data set to the end of another SAS data set; thus, the utility function of PROC APPEND is now available within the PROC DATASETS step.

CONTENTS Statement
: describes the contents of one or more SAS files in the SAS data library referenced by the LIBRARY= option in the PROC statement. This statement provides a utility function similar to that provided by PROC CONTENTS.

COPY Statement
: copies one or more SAS files from one SAS library into another library. You can also use the SELECT and EXCLUDE statements in conjunction with the COPY statement; thus, utility functions similar to those provided by PROC COPY are available within the PROC DATASETS step.

The FORMAT Procedure

User-written formats created using PROC FORMAT are now written into a special SAS file called a *formats catalog*. A formats catalog can contain one or more user-written formats. The formats catalog is named FORMATS and is stored with the PC file type SFL. FORMATS.SFL is temporary if created in the WORK library or permanent if you specify the LIBRARY= option in the PROC statement.

To access permanent user-written formats, you must use the LIBNAME statement to associate the special libref LIBRARY with the directory containing the permanent formats catalog FORMATS.SFL.

The DECK option is not available with PROC FORMAT in Version 6.

The FORMS Procedure

FILE= is an additional option name that can be used instead of DDNAME= or DD= to refer to the external file into which PROC FORMS writes its printed output.

The default value for the WIDTH= option is now the width of the widest forms unit, instead of 40.

The MEANS Procedure

The CLASS statement is now available. You use it to name variables to be used for subgroups.

You cannot request SKEWNESS and KURTOSIS statistics for printed output.

The PLOT Procedure

The PLOT procedure can now be used interactively.

To plot all unique combinations of a list of variables, you can now specify a variable list, for example,

```
PLOT (A B C);
```

plots the following combinations: A*B, A*C, B*C.

The following options are new:

BOX	draws a box around the plot.
HPERCENT= VPERCENT=	produces multiple plots on a single page or one plot that spans several pages.
FORMCHAR=	allows you to specify characters to be used for constructing the plot.
HEXPAND	expands horizontal axis to eliminate excessive white space.
HREVERSE	reverses the order of the values on the horizontal axis.
NOMISS	requests that observations be excluded from the axes calculation if either variable is missing.
SLIST=	offers an alternative way of specifying symbols for each contour value in ascending order. In previous versions, the S options provided the only way to override default symbols.
VTOH=	specifies the aspect ratio (vertical to horizontal) of the characters on the output device.
VEXPAND	expands vertical axis to eliminate excessive white space.

The SORT Procedure

The NODUPKEY option is new for the PROC SORT statement. This option checks for and eliminates records with duplicate keys.

The following options are no longer supported:

EQUALS | NOEQUALS
NODUPLICATES | NODUP
NATIONAL
REVERSE
DANISH | NORWEGIAN
FINNISH | SWEDISH
MESSAGE | M
LIST | L
LEAVE=*n*
TECHNIQUE=*xxxx* | T=*xxxx*
SORTWKNO=*number*
DIAG
SORTSIZE=*parameter* | SIZE=*parameter*

The STANDARD Procedure

PROC STANDARD now produces printed output, which includes the input frequency, mean, and standard deviation for each variable standardized.

The SUMMARY Procedure

PROC SUMMARY now produces printed output. The following options have been added:

PRINT=	prints descriptive statistics.
MAXDEC=	specifies the maximum number of decimal places.
FW=	specifies the field width to use in printing each statistic.

The TABULATE Procedure

The NOSEPS option has been added. Use it in the PROC TABULATE statement to request that no horizontal separator lines appear in the body of the table.

The TABLE statement has a new option, PRINTMISS. PRINTMISS requests that all possible rows and columns print.

The UNIVARIATE Procedure

The OUTPUT statement has the following new percentile options:

PCTLRPRE=	prefix names in order of the variables in the VAR statement.
PCTLPTS=	specifies that percentile values can range from 0 to 100.
PCTLNAME=	specifies that percentile names are to be in the same order as PCTLPTS.

Index

M

N

O

P

Q

R

S

Your Turn

If you have comments about SAS software or the *SAS Procedures Guide for Personal Computers, Version 6 Edition*, please send us your ideas on a photocopy of this page. If you include your name and address, we will reply to you.

Please return to the Publications Division, SAS Institute Inc., SAS Circle, Box 8000, Cary, NC 27511-8000.